MARKETS ON TRIAL: THE ECONOMIC SOCIOLOGY OF THE U.S. FINANCIAL CRISIS: PART B

RESEARCH IN THE SOCIOLOGY OF ORGANIZATIONS

Series Editor: Michael Lounsbury

Recent Volumes

RESEARCH IN THE SOCIOLOGY OF ORGANIZATIONS
VOLUME 30B

MARKETS ON TRIAL: THE ECONOMIC SOCIOLOGY OF THE U.S. FINANCIAL CRISIS: PART B

EDITED BY

MICHAEL LOUNSBURY

*University of Alberta School of Business and
National Institute for Nanotechnology,
Edmonton, Alberta, Canada*

PAUL M. HIRSCH

*Kellogg School of Management,
Northwestern University, Evanston, IL, USA*

United Kingdom – North America – Japan
India – Malaysia – China

Emerald Group Publishing Limited
Howard House, Wagon Lane, Bingley BD16 1WA, UK

First edition 2010

Copyright © 2010 Emerald Group Publishing Limited

Reprints and permission service
Contact: booksandseries@emeraldinsight.com

British Library Cataloguing in Publication Data
A catalogue record for this book is available from the British Library

ISBN: 978-0-85724-207-5
ISSN: 0733-558X (Series)

Awarded in recognition of
Emerald's production
department's adherence to
quality systems and processes
when preparing scholarly
journals for print

INVESTOR IN PEOPLE

CONTENTS

LIST OF CONTRIBUTORS

Mitchel Y. Abolafia	Rockefeller College of Public Affairs and Policy, State University of New York at Albany, Albany, NY, USA
Tim Bartley	Department of Sociology, Indiana University, Bloomington, IN, USA
Thomas D. Beamish	Department of Sociology, University of California at Davis, Davis, CA, USA
Nicole Woolsey Biggart	Graduate School of Management, University of California, Davis, CA, USA
Fred Block	Department of Sociology, University of California, Davis, CA, USA
John L. Campbell	Department of Sociology, Dartmouth College, Hanover, NH, USA and International Center for Business and Politics, Copenhagen Business School, Copenhagen, Denmark
Bruce G. Carruthers	Department of Sociology, Northwestern University, Chicago, IL, USA
Gerald F. Davis	Ross School of Business, University of Michigan, Ann Arbor, MI, USA
Rich DeJordy	College of Business Administration, Northeastern University, Boston, MA, USA
Frank Dobbin	Department of Sociology, Harvard University, Cambridge, MA, USA
Neil Fligstein	Department of Sociology, University of California, Berkeley, CA, USA

Mary Ann Glynn   Winston Center for Leadership and Ethics,
                         Carroll School of Management, Boston
                         College, Chestnut Hill, MA, USA

Adam Goldstein   Department of Sociology, University of
                         California, Berkeley, CA, USA

Mauro F. Guillén   The Wharton School, University of
                         Pennsylvania, Philadelphia, PA, USA

Doug Guthrie   Stern School of Business, New York
                         University, New York, NY, USA

Paul M. Hirsch   Kellogg School of Management,
                         Northwestern University, Evanston,
                         IL, USA

Stefanie Hiss   Institute of Sociology, Friedrich Schiller
                         University of Jena, Jena, Germany

Jiwook Jung   Department of Sociology, Harvard
                         University, Cambridge, MA, USA

Greta R. Krippner   Department of Sociology, University of
                         Michigan, Ann Arbor, MI, USA

Michael Lounsbury   Alberta School of Business, University of
                         Alberta, Edmonton, Alberta, Canada

Michael Maher   Graduate School of Management,
                         University of California, Davis,
                         CA, USA

Gerald A. McDermott   Sonoco International Business
                         Department, Moore School of Business,
                         University of South Carolina, Columbia,
                         SC, USA

Mark S. Mizruchi   Department of Sociology, University of
                         Michigan, Ann Arbor, MI, USA

Donald Palmer   Graduate School of Management,
                         University of California, Davis,
                         CA, USA

Charles Perrow	Department of Sociology, Yale University, New Haven, CT, USA
Jo-Ellen Pozner	Haas School of Business, University of California, Berkeley, CA, USA
Akos Rona-Tas	University of California, La Jolla, CA, USA
Anna Rubtsova	Department of Sociology, Emory University, Atlanta, GA, USA
Marc Schneiberg	Department of Sociology, Reed College, Portland, OR, USA
David Slocum	Berlin School of Creative Leadership, Franklinstraße, Berlin, Germany
Mary Kate Stimmler	Haas School of Business, University of California, Berkeley, CA, USA
Sandra L. Suárez	Department of Political Science, Temple University, Philadelphia, PA, USA
Richard Swedberg	Department of Sociology, Cornell University, Ithaca, NY, USA
Mayer Zald	Department of Sociology, University of Michigan, Ann Arbor, MI, USA
Ezra W. Zuckerman	Sloan School of Management, Cambridge, MA, USA

ADVISORY BOARD

SERIES EDITOR

Michael Lounsbury
Alex Hamilton Professor of Business,
University of Alberta School of Business, and
National Institute for Nanotechnology, Edmonton, Alberta, Canada

ADVISORY BOARD

ACKNOWLEDGMENTS

We would like to congratulate and thank all of the contributors to the volume for their spirited engagement and excellent work despite time duress. In addition, we wish to thank non-volume contributors Lis Clemens, Martin Greller, Brayden King, David Lubin, Chris Marquis, Monica Prasad, and Klaus Weber for assisting as discussants and chairs, and Paola Sapienza for her provocative keynote talk at our *Markets on Trial* workshop organized by the University of Alberta School of Business and Kellogg School of Management in October 2009. We would also like to express special thanks to Richard Swedberg for his astute suggestions and support throughout the project. This volume is a collective achievement, and what we hope is a sign of the ongoing collective mobilization of economic sociologists to address important issues of the day.

PART B

INTRODUCTION TO THE
SPECIAL TWO-VOLUME SET

MARKETS ON TRIAL: TOWARD A POLICY-ORIENTED ECONOMIC SOCIOLOGY

Michael Lounsbury and Paul M. Hirsch

Market failures often have devastating societal effects, and the more dramatic and widespread they are, the more ideologies and policies underlying them require critical scrutiny (Polanyi, 1944). Similar to the 1929 stock market crash and Great Depression, events in the early 21st century have created heightened uncertainty and ambiguity, as well as efforts to reevaluate received wisdom. Over the past three decades, neoclassical models of the Chicago and Austrian Schools of free market economics infused and guided U.S. government policy and enforcement, leading to severe cut backs in regulation of the banking and investment industries. Although these ideas and practices also spread around the world, the United States provided the beacon. Wall Street became the *wild west* with repeated market bubbles and collapses, culminating in the so-called *Great Recession*, ushered in by the subprime meltdown in 2008 and concomitant global financial collapse. During the aftermath of the most recent debacle, Federal Reserve Chairman Alan Greenspan admitted, "Those of us who have looked to the self-interest of lending institutions to protect shareholders' equity, myself included, are in a state of shocked disbelief" (*New York Times*, October 24, 2008). After the housing bubble burst in 2008, Greenspan acknowledged a "flaw in the model that

Markets on Trial: The Economic Sociology of the U.S. Financial Crisis: Part B
Research in the Sociology of Organizations, Volume 30B, 5–26
Copyright © 2010 by Emerald Group Publishing Limited
All rights of reproduction in any form reserved
ISSN: 0733-558X/doi:10.1108/S0733-558X(2010)000030B029

I perceived is the critical functioning structure that defines how the world works" (*PBS News Hour*, October 23, 2008).

Such remarkable confessions should give pause to those continuing to promulgate the neoliberal agenda. For social scientists, the *Great Recession* has invited and opened up the possibility for a wider array of conceptualizations and approaches to financial markets. And given that free market approaches rooted in neoclassical microeconomics have garnered increased scrutiny in recent years, the current global calamity provides even greater impetus for the flowering of alternative perspectives on the economy from both within and outside of the economics discipline. The development of paradigmatic variants from within economics has included the expansion of institutional economics (North, 1990; Williamson, 2000), the embrace of richer approaches to the psychology of individuals via behavioral economics (e.g., Akerlof & Shiller, 2009), as well as the revitalization of macroeconomics, which includes a revival of (albeit modified) Keynesianism (e.g., Hayes, 2008). In contradistinction to these *heretical* movements from within, this volume focuses attention on the contributions of a powerful, ascendant paradigm that has emerged outside of the economics discipline – economic sociology. Our aims are to demonstrate the fruitfulness of economic sociology as a lens to explore the financial crisis and address key architectural and policy issues regarding the financial system, as well as advocate for the development of a more policy-oriented economic sociology.

Economic sociology is an international field that is diverse and rapidly growing. It differs from free market and other variants of economic theory in several fundamental ways (e.g., Block, 1990). A key difference is that most economic models rely on an assumption of human rationality that is very narrowly conceived. Economic sociologists challenge this by highlighting how rationality is socially constructed and culturally contingent (e.g., Fligstein, 1990; Dobbin, 1994; Hamilton & Biggart, 1988). In addition, instead of employing a taken-for-granted understanding of markets as sites for calculating economic actors, economic sociologists have questioned universalistic notions of markets and their inherent efficiency, taking a more critical and empirically grounded approach to assessment of their broader architecture and dynamics (see especially Fligstein, 2001).

Economic sociologists point to the importance of taking better account of such critical factors as power, national context, the state, regulators, culture, and social networks. Economists tend to ignore how economic action is fundamentally interpenetrated with such wider concerns (Swedberg, 1994; Granovetter, 1985). Although the intellectual roots of economic sociology are found in the classical writings of scholars such as Max Weber, Karl Marx, and Emile Durkheim (e.g., see Granovetter & Swedberg, 1992), the development of economic sociology as a formal subfield in sociology is relatively recent. Sociologist Amitai Etzioni contributed by founding the Society for the Advancement of Socio-Economics (SASE) in 1989. SASE is an international organization that through its annual meetings and journal, *Socio-Economic Review*, supports interdisciplinary approaches to the analysis of the economy. A host of economic sociology textbooks and volumes have been published over the past two decades (e.g., Carruthers & Babb, 1999; Dobbin, 2004; Granovetter & Swedberg, 1992; Guillén, Collins, England, & Meyer, 2002; Swedberg, 1990) as well as two editions of a *Handbook of Economic Sociology* (Smelser & Swedberg, 1994, 2005). In 2001, U.S.-based economic sociologists created a formal section in the American Sociological Association.

As contemporary economic sociology has developed over the past four decades, increasing attention has been directed toward understanding financial markets and their role in the wider economy. However, the tremendous body of work that has accumulated has dedicated little attention to economic and financial policy concerns (but see, e.g., Block, 1990; Dobbin, 1993; Krippner, 2007), hindering the impact of this intellectual movement. Even though scholarship in the discipline of sociology, including some work in economic sociology, has contributed a great deal to our understanding and the development of social policy more generally (e.g., Coleman et al., 1966; Jencks, 1992; Dobbin, 2009), this volume represents the first systematic effort to cultivate a more socio-logically informed approach to financial market and economic policy. Fortunately, economic sociology has a rich base of empirical findings and conceptual developments that give it a distinctive edge, and should be useful in guiding the development of unique policy insights and recommendations.

In an important early study, Baker (1984) showed how network relationships among traders on the floor of a stock option exchange shaped the direction and magnitude of option price volatility, contradicting ideal-typical economic models of market behavior based on hyper-rationality. Abolafia (1996) extended these basic insights in the context of the New York Stock Exchange, highlighting how the behavior of traders was shaped by social, cultural, and political dynamics (see also Abolafia & Kilduff, 1988). A key insight in this work is that the pursuit of narrow self-interest, a key assumption behind economic models of markets, is culturally conditioned and variably expressed even in financial market trading where we would be most likely to find the idealized neoclassical economic approach to markets to have descriptive validity.

These foundational economic sociology insights have been reinforced by comparative work that highlights considerable cross-national variation in economic behavior (e.g., Biggart & Guillén, 1999; Dobbin, 1993, 1994; Hamilton & Biggart, 1988; Hollingsworth & Boyer, 1997) as well as economic and managerial ideas (Fourcade, 2009; Guillén, 1994). However, given their seductive simplicity and prevailing use in policy circles, the allure of American-based economic ideas, and the power of their promulgators in the United States and major international institutions such as the International Monetary Fund, have threatened to reduce such variation around the world (Babb, 2001; Campbell & Pedersen, 2001; Fourcade-Gourinchas & Babb, 2002; Prasad, 2006). This was vividly exhibited in the great neoliberal market experimentations in Russia, Eastern Europe, and elsewhere after the fall of the Berlin Wall in 1989 (e.g., Sachs, 1992, 1993). To wit, economic sociologists have shown how the reformulation of financial and corporate practices to fit fashionable Chicago School free market economic ideas in the latter part of the 20th century was not limited to the United States – core economic and financial institutions such as central banks (Polillo & Guillén, 2005) and stock exchanges (Weber, Davis, & Lounsbury, 2009) spread dramatically across nation-states, and new global configurations of financial markets emerged (e.g., Knorr Cetina & Bruegger, 2002). Although these trends have not been without their detractors (e.g., World Trade Organization and International Monetary Fund protests), more scholarly attention to the role of contentious politics in and around market institutions is required (King & Pearce, in press).

The widespread cultural diffusion and broad application of American financial economic ideas and tools has been referred to as "financialization" (e.g., Krippner, 2005, 2010a). Financialization is considered "a pattern of accumulation in which profit-making occurs increasingly through financial channels rather than through trade and commodity production" (Krippner, 2005). Many economic sociologists argue that trends related to financialization were crucial to the over-leveraging that underpinned the recent bubble and collapse. Going even further, in *Managed by Markets: How Finance Reshaped America*, Davis (2009) catalogs how the historical development of financial markets has also profoundly reshaped American society. He argues that the emergence of the financialization era entailed many changes including a shift from a Puritan ethic of frugality to an investment-based logic that has affected all aspects of social life from how we think about home ownership to how we value social relations. Since policies and practices rooted in neoclassical economic models of the economy have been shown to have considerable potency in subversively (as well as overtly) reconfiguring how we think and act (e.g., Beunza & Stark, 2004; Ferraro, Pfeffer, & Sutton, 2005; Knorr Cetina & Preda, 2004; MacKenzie, 2008; MacKenzie & Millo, 2003; Preda & Knorr Cetina, in press; Whitley, 1986), one of the key promises of economic sociology lies in its ability to offer a useful broadening of our intellectual imagination and reflexive capacity to more critically assesses the role of ideas in constituting the economy, as well as to contribute to richer policy debate and more informed policy design.

In addition to tracking broad ideational developments and trends in practice, economic sociologists have also cultivated a rich body of scholarship on specific segments of the field of finance. Building on fundamental insights of Harrison White (1981, 2002), many studies have highlighted how social networks shape the behavior of key financial actors. Podolny (1993) highlighted how status structures shape the behavior of investment banks. Others have examined how concrete relational networks have shaped the investments of venture capital firms (Sorenson & Stuart, 2001) and firm financing (Uzzi, 1999).

Many scholars have also emphasized the role of cultural and institutional processes. Zelizer (1979) showed how the development of life insurance relied on a shift in societal-level cultural beliefs that legitimized the valuation of human life. In subsequent work, Zelizer (1995) highlighted how the meaning of money is socially and culturally conditioned (see also Carruthers & Babb, 1996, and Carruthers, 2005, for a review of the sociology of money and credit). Zuckerman (1999) has demonstrated how the categorization of a firm's portfolio of businesses influences the way securities analysts rate corporate securities. Lounsbury (2002, 2007) showed how the rise of market logics reshaped activity in the field of finance and the mutual fund industry as conservative approaches to wealth management (e.g., trusteeship) were eschewed in favor of professional experts such as money managers that became valorized as highly skilled actors who could effectively manage risk and "beat the market". Marquis and colleagues have looked at how institutional logics and public policy have contingent effects on the growth and structure of commercial banking (e.g., Marquis & Lounsbury, 2007; Marquis & Huang, 2009). Schneiberg and colleagues have highlighted how the structure and regulation of the American insurance industry is bound up in broader cultural–political processes (e.g., Schneiberg & Bartley, 2001; Schneiberg, King, & Smith, 2008).

A great deal of attention has also been paid to the relationship between finance and corporate governance. For example, building on 20th century

Marxist financial capital theory, bank control theorists posited that banks and insurance companies were able to influence corporate strategy in a way that served their own interests (Glasberg & Schwartz, 1983; but see Davis & Mizruchi, 1999, on the decline of direct bank influence on corporate boards). In the 1980s and into the 1990s, this conversation facilitated the creation of a cottage industry in studying director interlocks between financial and nonfinancial organizations and an assessment of how corporations are controlled (e.g., Fligstein & Brantley, 1992; Mintz & Schwartz, 1985; Mizruchi, 1982; Mizruchi & Stearns, 1994; Palmer, 1983; for reviews see Mizruchi, 1996; Stearns & Mizruchi, 2005). There also emerged a stream of corporate governance focused research that examined the role of institutional investors (e.g., Davis & Thompson, 1994; Useem, 1996) and tracked the rise of hostile takeovers (e.g., Hirsch, 1986; Davis, 1991), deconglomeration (Davis, Diekmann, & Tinsley, 1994), and merger waves (e.g., Davis & Stout, 1992; Palmer, Barber, Zhou, & Soysal, 1995; Palmer & Barber, 2001). And in a seminal book, Fligstein (1990) tracked how the financial thinking increasingly reshaped the corporation in the second half of the 20th century as firms hired CEOs with financial backgrounds (as opposed to operations or marketing) and began managing business units as elements of a financial portfolio (see also Perrow, 2002; Roy, 1997, for important historical treatments).

Although this brief overview of economic sociology approaches to financial markets only scratches the surface of the body of knowledge that has accumulated, it highlights the considerable depth of insight that careful empirical research on the interpenetrated dynamics of society and economy can reveal. And given the remarkable failure of the economics profession to predict and forestall the recent global financial crisis, the inspiration for the development of this volume was to gather some of the top scholars in economic sociology to provide an alternative collective voice through analyses of various aspects of the crisis and the development of policy recommendations based on their analyses. As a whole, the contributions to this volume contemplate and make initial efforts to detail the implications of cultural and relational approaches to markets in economic sociology for financial policy and reform.

The contributors to this volume propose and agree on a number of interesting policy recommendations, some of which have been addressed by Congress since the mortgage meltdown and economic collapse of 2008. The major conceptual emphasis that runs through many of the contributions to this volume is that the design of financial policy needs to be informed by an approach that understands and analyzes financial products, organizations, regulators, and infrastructure organizations (e.g., rating agencies), and other experts as elements of an interconnected system. In addition, such a systemic approach to policy must appreciate the rich cultural and relational embeddedness of actors and practices, as well as how the stratified nature of different systems create power relations that may threaten the integrity of policy, the independence of regulators, and the utility of different forms of expertise and kinds of experts (see also Zald & Lounsbury, in press). To wit, many articles in the volume demonstrate the crucial role played by regulators and other government officials in creating and supporting market practices and orientations that ultimately went awry; the implication is that any policy approach that takes the separation of markets and the state as its starting point is doomed to failure. Although we do not detail all the policy implications discussed in the volume here, our contributors as a whole make many specific policy recommendations to address issues related to lending practices, the transparency and accountability of rating agencies, the capital ratios of banks, the role of the Federal Reserve, derivative products, and the creation of an independent system regulator.

In the following text, we catalog contributions to the volume. Each of them sheds light on some aspects of the current financial crisis, and also paves a theoretically oriented research agenda for economic sociology that highlights the fruitfulness of addressing questions that have important policy implications. Given that the aftermath of the initial financial crisis shock will continue to roll on, our volume only addresses one small part of what will unfortunately be a great and long drama. Nonetheless, we believe that this volume demonstrates the power of economic sociology as a unique lens to address core capitalistic institutions and processes – especially those related to the financial system. In addition, it provides a foundation for future work that can shed light on the interpenetration of society and economy, and how social concerns are fundamentally intertwined with economic and financial practices.

OVERVIEW OF SCHOLARLY TERRAIN AND ARGUMENTS

Our volume is comprised of six sections: (1) the crisis; (2) its similarities to, and differences from being a "normal accident;" (3) sociological and historical explanations for the meltdown; (4) analyses of comparable speculative bubbles and business cycles; (5) international parallels and consequences; (6) analysis of how we might approach the future development of society and economy; and also a section of postscripts for looking ahead to future policy and prevention. Each contribution addresses its main topic, and concludes with practical policy recommendations for a better future.

Articles in the first section offer perspectives on the *financial crisis and its unfolding*, tracking problems related to mortgage securitization, especially subprime lending and failures of rating agencies. The first article by *Fligstein and Goldstein, The Anatomy of the Mortgage Securitization Crisis* builds on Fligstein's (2001) architecture of markets perspective to show how narrow economic rationality did not guide the behavior of mortgage-backed securities (MBS) actors; instead, to understand the dramatic rise and fall of the MBS market, they demonstrate the importance of situating it amidst the broader field of relationships between regulators, mortgage originators, mortgage packagers (both commercial and investment banks), rating agencies, and the holders of such bonds. They show that from 1993 until 2003, a rapid expansion in the residential real estate and MBS markets led mega banks to enter the market, and ultimately turn to riskier subprime mortgages when the supply of prime and conventional mortgages dried up. Fligstein and Goldstein highlight the key role government played in creating the MBS market and, for a time, coaxing the banks into the MBS business. Suggesting a form of regulatory capture, they argue that Democratic and Republican presidents and Congresses enacted financial reforms that expanded the MBS market and allowed the largest banks to operate virtually without any controls. In short, regulators actively relinquished their duties.

In developing their sociological account of the crisis, Fligstein and Goldstein dispel several claims that underpin conventional economic accounts of the crisis. They challenge the notion that MBS products such as collateralized debt obligations were more opaque and difficult to understand relative to other complex securities. They also highlight how the MBS market was not as fragmented as typically thought, but that five firms controlled at least 40% of the overall market. Overall, Fligstein and Goldstein provide a compelling account of the crisis, offer useful policy recommendations, and forcefully argue for the utility of a sociologically informed field analysis of markets.

That trouble was brewing was apparent by Spring 2008, when Bear Stearns failed, but the panic stage of the crisis was not reached until Lehman Brothers' failure in the fall of 2008. *Swedberg's* article, on *The Structure of Confidence and the Collapse of Lehman Brothers*, vividly traces and explains these developments. Drawing on Walter Bagehot's classic, *Lombard Street* [(1873) 1992], he proposes financial panics are typically catalyzed by hidden losses and declines in the confidence of markets. A focus on such mechanisms provides useful leverage for understanding the ultimate bankruptcy of Lehman and the global financial panic that followed in late 2008 and early 2009. Noting that scant attention has been paid to the role of confidence in financial markets, Swedberg argues for a sociological conceptualization of confidence as a belief that action can be based on proxy signs, rather than on direct information about the economic situation itself. He argues that such a sociological approach to confidence is needed to counter more impoverished psychologically focused efforts by behavioral economists that emphasize "irrationality" as a mechanism and suggest that confidence belongs to our "animal spirits" (e.g., Akerlof & Shiller, 2009). Swedberg aptly notes how "references to human nature fall pretty flat when confronted with the task of analyzing sophisticated social institutions of the type that make up the modern financial system."

The articles by Rona-Tas and Hiss, and Carruthers probe the role of rating agencies in the crisis. In *The Role of Ratings in the Subprime Mortgage Crisis: The Art of Corporate and the Science of Consumer Credit Rating, Rona-Tas and Hiss* provocatively compare consumer and corporate rating agencies, and highlight how faulty decision-making approaches by rating agencies hindered effective judgment about the quality of securities and contributed to the crisis. For instance, they highlight how the formalization of consumer credit scoring contributed to the meltdown as the past provided an increasingly worse predictor of the future for estimating the likelihood of defaults. In addition, they identify many problems related to issues such as performativity, endogeneity, reactivity, and conflict of interest, and suggest that the ratings of corporate securities might be best provided by a public institution whose business model does not rely on the resources of individual issuers. It is important to note that their article engages with an important literature in the social studies of finance (e.g., Beunza & Stark, 2004; Knorr Cetina & Preda, 2004; MacKenzie, 2008; MacKenzie & Millo, 2003; Preda & Knorr Cetina, in press) that extends the science and technology studies tradition into the world of finance. Rona-Tas and Hiss highlight the fruitfulness of further engagement between economic sociologists and this more ethnographic tradition.

Carruthers' Knowledge and Liquidity: Institutional and Cognitive Foundations of the SubPrime Crisis expands on this theme by focusing on how credit rating agencies stimulated the bubble by continuing to provide favorable ratings for MBS that warranted much greater scrutiny.

The information (i.e., ratings) they provided underpins liquidity in financial markets. When the ratings were revealed to be misleading, liquidity dried up – investors stopped investing and banks ceased lending (see Carruthers & Stinchcombe, 1999, on the social structure of liquidity). Carruthers suggests that the recommendations provided by rating agencies were influenced not only by their analysis, but also by the financial community in which they were embedded. He notes that the financial community is "a distinctive audience that is tightly-integrated, self-aware, and prone to various kinds of herding and emulative behavior," and that it was the interaction between this audience and rating agencies that produced knowledge that helped create the bubble.

Pozner, Stimmler, and *Hirsch* conclude the first section with *Terminal Isomorphism and the Self-Destructive Potential of Success: Lessons from Sub-Prime Mortgage Origination and Securitization.* This provocative article focuses on cognitive processes and micro-mechanisms, which underlay the dysfunctional decision-making at financial firms that nearly destroyed the financial markets. Their article documents how practices that appeared rational at the organizational level (i.e., subprime lending) could fuel the crisis and collective irrationality that occurred at the system level. They highlight possibilities for future inquiry at the interface of organizational institutionalism and more micro and meso theories of organization learning and cognition.

Articles in the second section build on and develop Perrow's *normal accident perspective* (see Perrow, 1984), investigating its utility in conceptualizing the global financial crisis. They also raise and assess the issue of agency – could the severity of the meltdown have been reduced, and when was it seen to be coming? *Palmer* and *Maher's A Normal Accident Analysis of the Mortgage Meltdown* lays out Perrow's theory of normal accidents and applies it to the mortgage meltdown. To qualify as a "normal accident," the conditions of high complexity, tight coupling, and interdependence must be present. They show how the financial sector met these conditions. In their view, once these conditions were in place, the meltdown was hard to prevent and became an accident waiting to happen. Palmer and Maher also raise and review the question of wrongdoing. They note "normal accident" theory has generally assumed good faith on the part of the actors involved, and raise the issue of how much that was missing in the case of the meltdown. Although all the articles in this section address and debate these agentic questions, their authors agree that for policies to avert such disasters in the future, the financial system must be made less complex, less tightly coupled, and become more decentralized.

In *The Global Crisis of 2007–2009: Markets, Politics, and Organizations,* *Guillén* and *Suárez* emphasize the organizational and agentic precursors, which led up to and enabled the normal accident in which financial systems collapsed, in not only the United States but worldwide also. They show how the scaffolding, of greater complexity and tighter coupling, was largely built through forceful lobbying by the same organizations and industries that were among those most impacted by the consequences of the deregulation they pushed for. The lack of oversight and transparency they helped create, enabled the international sale of "toxic" financial instruments and credit swaps to banks and governments in Iceland, Ireland, Greece, and other nations. Guillén and Suárez counsel looser coupling among financial players in the United States, and reforms in other nations in keeping with their political and economic circumstances.

Schneiberg and *Bartley's Regulating and Redesigning Finance: Market Architectures, Normal Accidents and Dilemmas of Regulatory Reform* expands on policy options available to deter financial meltdowns, focusing on two types of economic reforms. The first takes financial architectures as given and suggests a range of reforms for trying to regulate complex and tightly coupled systems that are prone to normal accidents. These include increasing the order of magnitude in the administrative capacities of rating agencies, and developing regulation as learning systems to deal with the uncertainties produced by interconnectedness, innovation, and a steady stream of financial innovation. The second set of reforms suggests using regulation to redesign existing market architectures, reducing complexity, and loosening coupling, by decentralizing the financial services industry and creating redundancies. For example, they suggest curtailing the influence of investment banks over the rating agencies that assess the quality of investment products and provide bond ratings, and promoting more alternative, locally based community banks and credit unions. Schneiberg and Bartley also highlight many provocative avenues for research, and compellingly argue for the importance of directing scholarly attention to the dynamics of market regulation in a more sustained and systematic way. In a prepublication review, Goldstein (2010, p. 4) refers to this article as "perhaps the most trenchant and bold" in the volume for its emphasis on how the architecture of financial markets is fundamentally imprinted and shaped by regulatory institutions.

In *The Meltdown Was Not An Accident, Charles Perrow* considers analyses of the Great Recession and explains where he sees them conforming to his model of the normal accident, to the cultural emphasis of new institutional theory, and to the roles played by agency and what he calls "executive failure." Although elements of the normal accident framework are indeed present here, Perrow notes that it also portrays those engaged in it as working hard to prevent their systems from unfolding. But in this case, he notes many involved did quite the opposite: Here, "they were well warned and knowingly did damage to their organizations and their clients, as well as to the society as a whole." Although Perrow makes clear that the mortgage meltdown meets the tightly coupled, interdependent, and highly complex criteria for a normal accident, he urges its analysts to not stop there, but attend more to the contribution of the agents involved and their "executive failure."

The third section provides a set of provocative sociological and historical analyses of the crisis. Why did it occur and how might it have been prevented? How many saw it coming? Economic perspectives that argued for stronger incentives to generate greater risk-taking, and increased profits and higher stock prices, are seen by the authors in this section to have produced results that counter what they had envisioned. Instead, the radical shift from managerialism to financialization, advocated by agency theory and neoliberalism, is found to have set the stage for the crisis that followed.

In their critique, *The Misapplication of Mr. Michael Jensen: How Agency Theory Brought Down the Economy and Why it Might Again*, Dobbin and *Jung* trace how the shift to executive compensation based on the provision of stock options, with bonuses tied to a rise in share price, resulted in a greater focus on short-term gains, a greater reliance on debt financing, and a reconstitution of boards that engaged in less oversight. Agency theory's dismissal of stakeholder rights in favor of (only) shareholders' reduced corporations' concerns for their employees and communities. Finally, the movement to de-diversify, while producing huge returns for investment banks, made companies more vulnerable to business cycles because directing their focus to a single "core competence" removed the hedges against bad times provided by a presence in more than one line of business.

Campbell's article, on *Neoliberalism in Crisis: Regulatory Roots of the U.S. Financial Meltdown*, critiques the economic and political tenets of neoliberalism, which advocates smaller government and less regulation of the financial sector. He traces how the "hands off" policies that neoliberalism advocates contributed to the subprime mortgage crisis. Campbell notes that markets are licensed by the state, which sets the rules and parameters in which they operate. Following neoliberal logic, these rules and parameters were relaxed by the state, whereas the licenses remained unchallenged. When the financial sector's unregulated run-up of risk got out of hand, there was no objection from deregulation's neoliberal advocates regarding the government's enormous bailout of these organizations (see also Guthrie & Slocum, 2010). Like Dobbin and Jung, Campbell warns that unless there is a change in the current policy – of banks keeping gains while the state underwrites their losses – there is nothing to discourage more unregulated risk taking, with few adverse consequences for those taking them when they fail.

In *The American Corporate Elite and the Historical Roots of the Financial Crisis of 2008*, *Mizruchi* takes note of an interesting change in the composition and actions of America's business elite – from a relatively cohesive and pragmatic "inner circle," to what became a more fragmented collection of CEO's. Although the earlier elite was conservative, it took part in a business–government partnership, which included the formation of broad social policy. In contrast, their counterparts today are more likely to avoid such engagement, instead sending lobbyists to represent them on a much narrower set of issues that may affect their firms' interests. The change Mizruchi notes is consistent with the broader shift in our cultural thought and social policy, toward what Krippner (2005, 2010b) calls "financialization," and Davis (2009, 2010) sees as the new mindset of the "ownership society."

In *The Political Economy of Financial Exuberance*, *Krippner* sheds impressive light on the political costs and benefits of inflation. Much as a rising tide raises all ships, Krippner notes rising values for housing and other assets enriched and empowered their owners. Although economic inequalities increased and overall affluence fell between 1970 and 2007, the acknowledgement and treatment of these problems was left unattended. It was deterred by inflation, with increasing home prices enabling doubtful collateral to be accepted for billions of dollars in loans issued to build, purchase, or refinance houses. Inflation thus deferred acknowledgement and response to the distributional problems we see now, which Krippner notes represent tradeoffs between scarce resources and social priorities that were masked for over a generation, until this bubble burst.

The fourth section looks specifically at crisis production, examining different approaches to *speculative bubbles and business cycles*. In *Abolafia's* article, *The Institutional Embeddedness of Market Failure: Why Speculative Bubbles Still Occur*, market crises are conceptualized as driven by problems related to broader trends in and the pathos of academic, political, and regulatory institutions. Abolafia argues that although asset bubbles are not always disastrous for society, they can be when they are more tightly connected to the core of the economic system and exacerbate systemic risk. In addition, even though we have the tools at our disposal to prevent the formation of crippling speculative bubbles, such man-made disasters are unlikely to be averted due to our limited understanding of how the economy is institutionally embedded. Abolafia is particularly critical of ideologies that support the notion that financial markets are self-regulating and require minimal state intervention (i.e., market fundamentalism). Theoretically, he critiques conventional approaches to bubbles that either conceptualize bubbles as triggered by exogenous shocks (Kindleberger & Aliber, 2005) or rely on psychological reductionism to explain the behavior of actors such as in a *Minsky moment* (Minsky, 1986). Instead, Abolafia promotes a social constructionist approach (see also Abolafia, 1996; Abolafia & Kilduff, 1988) that understands behavior in economic life, such as speculation, as enacted in the context of social relationships, cultural idioms, and political and economic institutions.

In *The Social Construction of Causality: The Effects of Institutional Myths on Financial Regulation*, Rubtsova, DeJordy, Glynn, and Zald echo Abolafia's emphasis on the role of broader ideas in constituting markets and market crises. Focusing on the historical development of stock markets in the United States up to the collapse of 1929 and ensuing Great Depression, Rubtsova and colleagues highlight how historically situated assumptions, values, and beliefs related to appropriate market practices shape the socially constructed theories of causality for market crises and subsequent regulatory action taken by the government. They demonstrate not only that the state creates markets, but also how it is affected by the historical development of markets and their dominant logics as embodied in institutional myths and professional norms. By endogenizing the state, they are able to show how the development, form, and content of governmental regulation is institutionally embedded and shaped (see also Davis, 2009). In agreement with Abolofia's conclusions, the implication of their analysis is that serious market reform must grapple with the reform of a broader array of institutions and beliefs within which markets operate.

Like Abolafia and Rubtsova et al., *Beamish* and *Biggart* are critical of standard, equilibrium-oriented economic approaches to understanding crises, and argue that economic sociology can better contribute to understanding such situations by offering a kind of middle-range meso-economic approach. In their article, *Mesoeconomics: Business Cycles, Entrepreneurship, and Economic Crisis in Commercial Building Markets*, they focus attention on how *market orders* can become destabilized and break down as a result of both macro-level shifts in business cycles and more micro-level entrepreneurial activity. Drawing on the case of commercial building, a hard-hit industry during the recent financial crisis, they emphasize the primacy of understanding how markets are embedded in a social and institutional context that constitutes actors and appropriate conduct in markets.

The fifth section offers a couple of articles that aim to situate the U.S. crisis more globally by exploring comparative institutional dynamics. In *Through the Looking Glass: Inefficient Deregulation in the United States and Efficient State Ownership in China, Guthrie* and *Slocum* compare developments in the United States and China to highlight how recent bailouts of major economic firms is contradictory to deregulation and makes laissez-fair approaches to markets inefficient. They challenge conventional conceptualizations of private and state-owned enterprises, highlighting how private firms like General Motors can be woefully inefficient, whereas state-owned firms like PetroChina can be extremely efficient. They argue that a more nuanced understanding of private–public partnerships is required to assess how such mixed structures can enable innovation and economic growth.

The state-market tension is further elaborated by *McDermott* in his article, *Precedence for the Unprecedented: A Comparative Institutionalist View of the Financial Crisis.* McDermott argues that contrary to conventional wisdom, the modern capitalist economy is not characterized by a "market preserving state" that merely enforces minimalist rules of property rights (Weingast, 1995), but rather by an "experimental regulatory state," where public and private actors construct complex institutions where active engagement, learning, and experimentation are central (Bruszt, 2002; Sabel, 1994; see also Schneiberg & Bartley, 2010). McDermott argues for developing a comparative institutionalist agenda to assess what alternative policy approaches exist and are being pursued, and to facilitate learning across nation-states (see also McDermott, 2007). Such an approach foreshadows the importance of how markets are institutionally configured, highlighting the limits of falling back on overly simplistic market-based policy approaches that valorize narrow technocratic expertise. It is clear that a more systematic comparative agenda is absolutely essential to the development of a more impactful policy-oriented economic sociology (Campbell, 2004; McDermott, 2002; Sabel & Zeitlin, 1997; see also Guillén & Suárez, 2010).

Sixth section features an article by *Gerald F. Davis* entitled, *After the ownership society: Another world is possible.* Building on his landmark (2009) book, *Managed by Markets: How Finance Re-shaped America,* Davis catalogs the death of a corporate-centered society, the brief rise and fall of an ownership society, and the prospects for innovation in a postindustrial, postcorporate society where large corporations employ an increasingly small percentage of employees relative to historical norms (Davis & Cobb, in press). Davis claims that the 2008 financial crisis pounds the nails into the coffin of the George Bush era experimentation with an ownership society model built around financial markets – individual retirement accounts and health savings accounts invested in the stock market, and broadened home ownership enabled by mortgage securitization. The implosion of this financial market approach to society and economy coupled with the reduced role of corporate employment necessitates more intense policy focus on employment. This is echoed by the recent book by Reinhart and Rogoff (2010) where they show that bank-centered crises, including the most recent one, have all led to major unemployment problems, not to mention the bailout costs and loss of tax revenue. Davis suggests that state- and local-level policy development will be especially crucial to create a context for organizational innovation in which employment is an explicit goal. In particular, through policy and legislation, local governments can facilitate experimentation in organizational forms that privilege employees over shareholder value, and create a foundation for a more progressive and sustainable society and economy.

The postscript features an overview and commentaries from two expert contributors to the field of economic sociology, on the issues addressed and essays in Markets on Trial. In *What If We Had Been in Charge? The Sociologist as Builder of Rational Institutions*, Zuckerman focuses on the "realist" versus "constructionist" underpinnings of the policies followed, and actions taken by all the players in the Great Recession (some of whom he suggests may be missed in the preceding essays). He notes the collapse of the housing bubble was both predicted and widely anticipated, and argues that whereas sociologists are right to be skeptical about naïve claims of rational pricing, it must remain a central goal for our regulatory prescriptions. To attain this, an understanding of the institutional mechanisms that promote or undermine market efficiency is required. Zuckerman's analysis provides support for some of the regulatory reforms endorsed by many contributors (e.g., greater market transparency).

Block's concluding postscript, *Markets on Trial: The Economic Sociology of the U.S. Financial Crisis*, sees economics as a discipline having lost touch with its history of working with other social science disciplines to fill out and better test its models. The economic sociology-based essays in *Markets on Trial* constitute a step toward greater dialogue, in which we invite more colleagues in economics to engage. Block also prescribes more attention to earlier crashes, noting how the Federal Reserve and Securities and Exchange Commission were established in response to crises. From a policy standpoint, it appears the Great Recession has not been followed by analogous reforms. Finally, Block rightly points to a next step for economic sociology – devoting more attention not only to what should be stopped, but also toward creating better conditions for investment in upgrading neglected infrastructures. Such "prosocial" actions, to generate better living conditions and needed jobs, would enable placing a better verdict on the actions surveyed by the authors in *Markets on Trial*.

REFERENCES

Abolafia, M. Y. (1996). *Making markets.* Cambridge, MA: Harvard University Press.
Abolafia, M. Y., & Kilduff, M. (1988). Enacting market crisis: The social construction of a speculative bubble. *Administrative Science Quarterly, 33,* 177–193.
Akerlof, G., & Shiller, R. (2009). *Animal spirits: How human psychology drives the economy, and why it matters for global capitalism.* Princeton, NJ: Princeton University Press.
Babb, S. (2001). *Managing Mexico: Economists from nationalism to neoliberalism.* Princeton, NJ: Princeton University Press.
Bagehot, W. ([1873] 1922). *Lombard street: A description of the money market.* London: John Murray.
Baker, W. E. (1984). The social structure of a national securities market. *American Journal of Sociology, 89,* 775–811.
Beunza, D., & Stark, D. (2004). Tools of the trade: The socio-technology of arbitrage in a wall street trading room. *Industrial and Corporate Change, 13,* 369–400.
Biggart, N. C., & Guillén, M. F. (1999). The automobile industry in four countries. *American Sociological Review, 64,* 722–747.
Block, F. L. (1990). *Postindustrial possibilities: A critique of economic discourse.* Berkeley, CA: University of California Press.
Bruszt, L. (2002). Market making as state making: Constitutions and economic development in post-communist Eastern Europe. *Constitutional Political Economy, 13,* 53–72.
Campbell, J. L. (2004). *Institutional change and globalization.* Princeton, NJ: Princeton University Press.
Campbell, J. L., & Pedersen, O. K. (Eds). (2001). *The rise of neoliberalism and institutional analysis.* Princeton, NJ: Princeton University Press.
Carruthers, B. G. (2005). The sociology of money and credit. In: N. Smelser & R. Swedberg (Eds), *The handbook of economic sociology* (2nd ed., pp. 355–378). Princeton, NJ: Princeton University Press.
Carruthers, B. G., & Babb, S. L. (1996). The color of money and the nature of value: Greenbacks and gold in postbellum America. *American Journal of Sociology, 101,* 1556–1591.
Carruthers, B. G., & Babb, S. L. (1999). *Economy/society: Markets, meaning and social structure.* Thousand Oaks, CA: Pine Forge Press.
Carruthers, B. G., & Stinchcombe, A. L. (1999). The social structure of liquidity: Flexibility in markets and states. *Theory and Society, 28,* 353–382.

Coleman, J. S., Campbell, E. Q., Hobson, C. J., McPartland, J., Mood, A. M., Weinfeld, F. D., & York, R. L. (1966). *Equality of educational opportunity*. Washington, DC: Government Printing Office.

Davis, G. F. (1991). Agents without principles? The spread of the poison pill through the intercorporate network. *Administrative Science Quarterly, 36*, 583–613.

Davis, G. F. (2009). *Managed by markets: How finance re-shaped America*. New York: Oxford University Press.

Davis, G. F., & Cobb, J. A. (in press). Corporations and economic inequality around the world: The paradox of hierarchy. *Research in Organizational Behavior*.

Davis, G. F., Diekmann, K. A., & Tinsley, C. H. (1994). The decline and fall of the conglomerate firm in the 1980s: The deinstitutionalization of an organizational form. *American Sociological Review, 59*, 547–570.

Davis, G. F., & Mizruchi, M. S. (1999). The money center cannot hold: Commercial banks in the U.S. system of governance. *Administrative Science Quarterly, 44*, 215–239.

Davis, G. F., & Stout, S. K. (1992). Organization theory and the market for corporate control: A dynamic analysis of the characteristics of large takeover targets, 1980–1990. *Administrative Science Quarterly, 37*, 605–633.

Davis, G. F., & Thompson, T. A. (1994). A social movement perspective on corporate control. *Administrative Science Quarterly, 39*, 141–173.

Davis, J. (2010). After the ownership society: Another world is possible. In: M. Lounsbury & P. M. Hirsch (Eds), *Markets on trial: The economic sociology of the U.S. financial crisis: Part B*. Research in the Sociology of Organizations. Bingley, UK: Emerald.

Dobbin, F. (1993). The social construction of the great depression: Industrial policy during the 1930s in the United States, Britain, and France. *Theory and Society, 22*, 1–56.

Dobbin, F. (1994). *Forging industrial policy: The United States, Britain, and France in the railway age*. Cambridge, UK: Cambridge University Press.

Dobbin, F. (Ed.) (2004). *The new economic sociology: A reader*. Princeton, NJ: Princeton University Press.

Dobbin, F. (2009). *Inventing equal opportunity*. Princeton, NJ: Princeton University Press.

Ferraro, F., Pfeffer, J., & Sutton, R. I. (2005). Economics language and assumptions: How theories can become self-fulfilling. *Academy of Management Review, 30*, 8–24.

Fligstein, N. (1990). *The transformation of corporate control*. Cambridge, MA: Harvard University Press.

Fligstein, N. (2001). *The architecture of markets: An economic sociology of twenty-first-century capitalist societies*. Princeton, NJ: Princeton University Press.

Fligstein, N., & Brantley, P. (1992). Bank control, owner control, or organizational dynamics: Who controls the large modern corporation? *American Journal of Sociology, 98*, 280–307.

Fourcade, M. (2009). *Economists and societies: Discipline and profession in the United States, Britain, and France, 1890s to 1990s*. Princeton, NJ: Princeton University Press.

Fourcade-Gourinchas, M., & Babb, S. (2002). The rebirth of the liberal creed: Paths to neoliberalism in four countries. *American Journal of Sociology, 108*, 533–579.

Glasberg, D. S., & Schwartz, M. (1983). Ownership and control of corporations. *Annual Review of Sociology, 9*, 311–332.

Goldstein, A. (2010). Markets on trial: Progress and prognosis for economic sociology's response to the financial crisis. *Accounts (American Sociological Association Economic Sociology Newsletter), 9*, 2–6.

Granovetter, M. (1985). Economic action and social structure: The problem of embeddedness. *American Journal of Sociology, 91*, 3–11.

Granovetter, M., & Swedberg, R. (Eds). (1992). *The sociology of economic life.* Boulder, CO: Westview Press.

Guillén, M. F. (1994). *Models of management: Work, authority, and organization in a comparative perspective.* Chicago, IL: The University of Chicago Press.

Guillén, M. F., & Suárez, S. L. (2010). The global crisis of 2007–2009: Markets, politics, and organizations. In: M. Lounsbury & P. M. Hirsch (Eds), *Markets on trial: The economic sociology of the U.S. financial crisis: Part A.* Research in the Sociology of Organizations. Bingley, UK: Emerald.

Guillén, M. F., Collins, R., England, P., & Meyer, M. (Eds). (2002). *The new economic sociology: Developments in an emerging field.* New York: Russell Sage Foundation.

Guthrie, D., & Slocum, D. (2010). Through the looking glass: Inefficient deregulation in the United States and efficient state ownership in China. In: M. Lounsbury & P. M. Hirsch (Eds), *Markets on trial: The economic sociology of the U.S. financial crisis: Part B.* Research in the Sociology of Organizations. Bingley, UK: Emerald.

Hamilton, G. G., & Biggart, N. W. (1988). Market, culture, and authority: A comparative analysis of management and organization in the far east. *American Journal of Sociology, 94*, S52–S94.

Hayes, M. G. (2008). *The economics of Keynes: A new guide to the general theory.* New York: Edward Elgar Publishing.

Hirsch, P. M. (1986). From ambushes to golden parachutes: Corporate takeovers as an instance of cultural framing and institutional integration. *American Journal of Sociology, 91*, 800–837.

Hollingsworth, J. R., & Boyer, R. (Eds). (1997). *Contemporary capitalism: The embeddedness of institutions.* New York: Cambridge University Press.

Jencks, C. (1992). *Rethinking social policy: Race, poverty, and the underclass.* Cambridge, MA: Harvard University Press.

Kindleberger, C., & Aliber, R. (2005). *Manias, panics, and crashes: A history of financial crisis.* Hoboken, NJ: Wiley.

King, B. G., & Pearce, N. A. (in press). Markets, contentious politics, and institutional change. *Annual Review of Sociology.*

Knorr Cetina, K., & Bruegger, U. (2002). Global microstructures: The virtual societies of financial markets. *American Journal of Sociology, 107*, 905–950.

Knorr Cetina, K., & Preda, A. (Eds). (2004). *The sociology of financial markets.* Oxford, UK: Oxford University Press.

Krippner, G. R. (2005). The financialization of the American economy. *Socio-Economic Review, 3*, 173–208.

Krippner, G. R. (2007). The making of US monetary policy: Central bank transparency and the neoliberal dilemma. *Theory and Society, 36*, 477–513.

Krippner, G. R. (2010a). *Capitalizing on crisis: The political origins of the rise of finance in the U.S. economy.* Cambridge, MA: Harvard University Press.

Krippner, G. (2010b). The political economy of financial exuberance. In: M. Lounsbury & P. M. Hirsch (Eds), *Markets on trial: The economic sociology of the U.S. financial crisis: Part B.* Research in the Sociology of Organizations. Bingley, UK: Emerald.

Lounsbury, M. (2002). Institutional transformation and status mobility: The professionalization of the field of finance. *Academy of Management Journal, 45*, 255–266.

Lounsbury, M. (2007). A tale of two cities: Competing logics and practice variation in the professionalizing of mutual funds. *Academy of Management Journal, 50*, 289–307.

MacKenzie, D. (2008). *An engine, not a camera: How financial models shape markets.* Cambridge, MA: MIT Press.

MacKenzie, D., & Millo, Y. (2003). Constructing a market, performing theory: The historical sociology of a financial derivatives exchange. *American Journal of Sociology, 109*, 107–145.

Marquis, C., & Huang, Z. (2009). The contingent nature of public policy and the growth of U.S. commercial banking. *Academy of Management Journal, 52*, 1222–1246.

Marquis, C., & Lounsbury, M. (2007). Vive la Résistance: Competing logics in the consolidation of community banking. *Academy of Management Journal, 50*, 799–820.

McDermott, G. A. (2002). *Embedded politics: Industrial networks and institutional change in postcommunism.* Ann Arbor, MI: The University of Michigan Press.

McDermott, G. A. (2007). Politics, power, and institution building: Bank crises and supervision in East Central Europe. *Review of International Political Economy, 14*, 220–250.

Minsky, H. (1986). *Stabilizing an unstable economy.* New Haven, CT: Yale University Press.

Mintz, B., & Schwartz, M. (1985). *The power structure of American business.* Chicago, IL: University of Chicago Press.

Mizruchi, M. S. (1982). *The American corporate network: 1904–1974.* Beverly Hills, CA: Sage.

Mizruchi, M. S. (1996). What do interlocks do? An analysis, critique, and assessment of research on interlocking directorates. *Annual Review of Sociology, 22*, 271–298.

Mizruchi, M. S., & Stearns, L. B. (1994). A longitudinal study of borrowing by large American corporations. *Administrative Science Quarterly, 39*, 118–140.

New York Times. (2008). Greenspan concedes error on regulation. *New York Times,* October 24, p. B1 of New York edition.

North, D. (1990). *Institutions, institutional change and economic performance.* Cambridge, UK: Cambridge University Press.

Palmer, D. (1983). Broken ties: Interlocking directorates and intercorporate coordination. *Administrative Science Quarterly, 28*, 40–55.

Palmer, D., Barber, B. M., Zhou, X., & Soysal, Y. (1995). The friendly and predatory acquisition of large U.S. corporations in the 1960s: The other contested terrain. *American Sociological Review, 60*, 469–500.

Palmer, D. A., & Barber, B. M. (2001). Challengers, elites, and owning families: A social class theory of corporate acquisitions in the 1960s. *Administrative Science Quarterly, 46*, 87–120.

PBS News Hour. (2008). Greenspan admits 'flaw' to congress, predicts more economic problems. *PBS News Hour,* October 23. Available at www.pbs.org/newshour/bb/business/july-dec08/crisishearing_10-23.html. Retrieved on March 2010.

Perrow, C. (1984). *Normal accidents: Living with high risk technologies.* Princeton, NJ: Princeton University Press.

Perrow, C. (2002). *Organizing America: Wealth, power, and the origins of corporate capitalism.* Princeton, NJ: Princeton University Press.

Podolny, J. M. (1993). A status-based model of market competition. *American Journal of Sociology, 98*, 829–872.

Polanyi, K. (1944). *The great transformation.* New York: Farrar & Rinehart.

Polillo, S., & Guillén, M. F. (2005). Globalization pressures and the state: The global spread of central bank independence. *American Journal of Sociology, 110*, 1764–1802.

Prasad, M. (2006). *The politics of free markets: The rise of neoliberal economic policies in Britain, France, Germany, and the United States.* Chicago, IL: University of Chicago Press.

Preda, A., & Knorr Cetina, K. (Eds.), (in press). *Handbook of the sociology of finance.* Oxford: Oxford University Press.

Reinhart, C., & Rogoff, K. (2010). *This time is different: Eight centuries of financial folly.* Princeton, NJ: Princeton University Press.

Roy, W. G. (1997). *Socializing capital: The rise of the large industrial corporation in America.* Princeton, NJ: Princeton University Press.

Sabel, C. (1994). Learning by monitoring: The institutions of economic development. In: N. J. Smelser & R. Swedberg (Eds), *The handbook of economic sociology* (pp. 137–165). Princeton and New York: Princeton University Press and Russell Sage Foundation.

Sabel, C., & Zeitlin, J. (Eds). (1997). *World of possibilities: Flexibility and mass production in western industrialization.* Cambridge, UK: Cambridge University Press.

Sachs, J. D. (1992). Privatization in Russia: Some lessons from Eastern Europe. *American Economic Review, 80,* 43–48.

Sachs, J. D. (1993). *Poland's jump to the market economy.* Cambridge, USA: MIT Press.

Schneiberg, M., & Bartley, T. (2001). Regulating American industries: Markets, politics, and the institutional determinants of fire insurance regulation. *American Journal of Sociology, 107,* 101–146.

Schneiberg, M., & Bartley, T. (2010). Regulating and redesigning finance: Market architectures, normal accidents and dilemmas of regulatory reform. In: M. Lounsbury & P. M. Hirsch (Eds), *Markets on trial: The economic sociology of the U.S. financial crisis: Part A.* Research in the Sociology of Organizations. Bingley, UK: Emerald.

Schneiberg, M., King, M., & Smith, T. (2008). Social movements and organizational form: Cooperative alternatives to corporations in the American insurance, dairy and grain industries. *American Sociological Review, 73,* 635–667.

Smelser, N. J., & Swedberg, R. (Eds). (1994). *The handbook of economic sociology.* Princeton, NJ: Princeton University Press.

Smelser, N. J., & Swedberg, R. (Eds). (2005). *The handbook of economic sociology* (2nd ed.). Princeton, NJ: Princeton University Press.

Sorenson, O., & Stuart, T. E. (2001). Syndication networks and the spatial distribution of venture capital investments. *American Journal of Sociology, 106,* 1546–1588.

Stearns, L. B., & Mizruchi, M. S. (2005). Banking and financial markets. In: N. J. Smelser & R. Swedberg (Eds), *Handbook of economic sociology* (2nd ed., pp. 284–306). Princeton, NJ: Princeton University Press.

Swedberg, R. (1990). *Economics and sociology: Redefining their boundaries: Conversations with economists and sociologists.* Princeton, NJ: Princeton University Press.

Swedberg, R. (1994). Markets as social structures. In: N. Smelser & R. Swedberg (Eds), *The handbook of economic sociology* (pp. 255–282). Princeton, NJ: Princeton University Press.

Useem, M. (1996). *Investor capitalism.* New York: Basic Books.

Uzzi, B. (1999). Embeddedness in the making of financial capital: How social relations and networks benefit firms seeking financing. *American Sociological Review, 64,* 481–505.

Weber, K., Davis, G. F., & Lounsbury, M. (2009). Policy as myth and ceremony? The spread of stock exchanges, 1980–2005. *Academy of Management Journal, 52,* 1319–1347.

Weingast, B. (1995). The economic role of political institutions: Market preserving federalism and economic development. *The Journal of Law, Economics and Organization, 11,* 1–31.

White, H. C. (1981). Where do markets come from? *American Journal of Sociology, 87*, 517–547.
White, H. C. (2002). *Markets from networks: Socioeconomic models of production.* Princeton, NJ: Princeton University Press.
Whitley, R. (1986). The transformation of business finance into financial economics: The roles of academic expansion and changes in U.S. capital markets. *Accounting, Organizations and Society, 11*, 171–192.
Williamson, O. E. (2000). The new institutional economics: Taking stock, looking ahead. *Journal of Economic Literature, 38*, 595–613.
Zald, M. N., & Lounsbury, M. (in press). The wizards of OZ: Towards an institutional approach to elites, expertise and command posts. *Organization Studies.*
Zelizer, V. A. (1979). *Morals and markets: The development of life insurance in the United States.* New York: Columbia University Press.
Zelizer, V. A. (1995). *The social meaning of money.* New York: Basic Books.
Zuckerman, E. W. (1999). The categorical imperative: Securities analysts and the illegitimacy discount. *American Journal of Sociology, 104*, 1398–1438.

SECTION III
HISTORICAL ORIGINS OF
THE U.S. FINANCIAL CRISIS

THE MISAPPLICATION OF MR. MICHAEL JENSEN: HOW AGENCY THEORY BROUGHT DOWN THE ECONOMY AND WHY IT MIGHT AGAIN

Frank Dobbin and Jiwook Jung

ABSTRACT

Agency theorists diagnosed the economic malaise of the 1970s as the result of executive obsession with corporate stability over profitability. Management swallowed many of the pills agency theorists prescribed to increase entrepreneurialism and risk-taking; stock options, dediversification, debt financing, and outsider board members. Management did not swallow the pills prescribed to moderate risk: executive equity holding and independent boards. Thus, in practice, the remedy heightened corporate risk-taking without imposing constraints. Both recessions of the new millennium can be traced directly to these changes in strategy. To date, regulators have proposed nothing to undo the perverse incentives of the new "shareholder value" system.

Markets on Trial: The Economic Sociology of the U.S. Financial Crisis: Part B
Research in the Sociology of Organizations, Volume 30B, 29–64
Copyright © 2010 by Emerald Group Publishing Limited
All rights of reproduction in any form reserved
ISSN: 0733-558X/doi:10.1108/S0733-558X(2010)000030B006

The stagflation of the 1970s, a decade of lackluster stock market performance, and the specter of Japanese domination of auto and high technology manufacturing had sent America's Fortune 500 companies on a spiritual quest by 1980. What was wrong with the model of management? Answers came from all quarters, pointing to everything from human resources policies (Ouchi, 1981) to rigid Fordist production techniques (Piore & Sabel, 1984). When it came to corporate governance and business strategy, agency theory offered a diagnosis of the problem and a ready remedy. Spelled out in an article by Michael Jensen and William Meckling in the *Journal of Financial Economics* in 1976, the theory challenged the way that firms were being run, suggesting that the interests of principals (shareholders) and their agents (executives) were out of synch (Whitley, 1986; Hirsch, 1986; Useem, 1984). Executives were serving their own interests rather than those of owners. They had been building large diversified empires that could shield them from downturns in any particular industry, but which maximized corporate size rather than profitability. Profits went to buy new businesses to expand the pyramids executives sat atop. Meanwhile they rebuffed monitoring efforts that might bring their behavior into line with principals' goal, of maximizing profits, by dominating the boards that were charged with overseeing them (Jensen & Meckling, 1976; Fama, 1980; Fama & Jensen, 1983, 1985). The result was that Fortune 500 companies became unmanageable multi-industry behemoths that did not live up to their potential. So went the diagnosis.

Agency theorists prescribed revolutionary changes in corporate governance and strategy. Three changes were designed to increase corporate profitability by changing incentives to managers, reinforcing industrial focus, and altering financing of new endeavors. First was the prescription to alter incentives to executives, using stock options to guarantee they would focus on increasing the value of the firm, and designing compensation to ensure they held equity in the firms they ran. Second was the prescription to focus the firm on the management team's industry of expertise and leave portfolio diversification to investors. Third was the prescription to use debt financing for new endeavors, leveraging equity, and putting an end to the executive practice of spending profits to buy new businesses just to expand their empires. These three changes would focus management on excelling in a single sector and improving the bottom line. They would encourage entrepreneurial, risk-taking strategies that promised great reward. A fourth prescription was designed to discipline executives and monitor risk. Firms should expand board oversight by making boards more independent of top management teams – through outside directors, smaller and more accountable boards, and appointment of an independent board chair. Independent, agile boards could end executive feathering-the-nest and prevent undue risk-taking. Executive equity stakes would also dampen risk, by ensuring that the CEO had skin in the long-term game.

After some prodding from institutional investors, in the 1980s America's biggest firms embraced agency theory prescriptions enthusiastically, if selectively. They pursued pay for performance with stock options and bonuses that tied executive compensation to shareholder returns, but did not require executives to hold equity. They deliberately dediversified, spinning off business units in disparate industries (Davis, Diekmann, & Tinsley, 1994; Fligstein & Markowitz, 1993). They used debt to finance new activities, and returned profits to shareholders through share buybacks. They restructured boards, making them smaller and appointing more outsiders, but did not actually make boards more independent; instead they gave more CEOs the title of chairman.

The parts of the formula that firms embraced heightened risk. Stock options were structured to reward executives for short-term share price gains without punishing them for losses, so executives placed bets on business strategies with strong upside and downside possibilities. Dediversification left companies susceptible to the vicissitudes of the market for a single product, and those in cyclical industries susceptible to failure in the trough of the business cycle. Debt made companies vulnerable when the economy soured and income dropped, and when the economy soared and interest rates rose. These risks might have been moderated had firms swallowed the pills designed to moderate risk and increase monitoring, but those are the pills they spit out. On the one hand, new compensation schemes did not force executives to increase their equity stakes, which could have caused them to self-monitor and be wary of high-risk endeavors. On the other hand, boards gained symbolic independence, with more outside members, and became more responsive, with smaller rosters, but they did not begin to monitor or discipline management because they remained under the thumb of the CEO. The result of the changes promoted by agency theory was that by the late 1990s America's corporate leaders were drag racing without brakes. We argue that neither the Sarbanes–Oxley Act nor the post-sub-prime-crisis regulatory proposals address these failures in implementation of agency theory. Chalk one up for Hegel; a theory brought down the economy.

By increasing risk without increasing monitoring, these changes set the stage for both the corporate failures behind the 2001 recession and the bank failures behind the Great Recession at the end of the decade. While managerialism and mindless diversification may have contributed to the poor financial results of America's leading firms in the 1970s, the strategy was predicated on executive efforts to minimize risk to their firms. Every firm tried to become too big to fail; too large and diversified to go down even if a major business unit crashed. Thus firms in industries at risk (the R.J. Reynolds tobacco empire) went to the altar with firms that could weather any storm (the Nabisco packaged foods Empire). Perhaps CEOs just created industrial cornucopias to secure their own sinecures, and perhaps that strategy undermined profits, but the strategy surely dampened corporate risk.

In the pages that follow, we discuss each of the four main agency theory prescriptions for corporate behavior. We examine longitudinal data on large U.S. firms to show which prescriptions firms have taken up, and which they have left on the table. We chronicle how pay-for-performance, dediversification, and debt-financing exposed firms to risk, while board governance reforms failed to improve monitoring.

A word about methodology before we turn to the story. In the following text, we present evidence from a representative sample of 783 major American firms to track the move toward agency theory prescriptions between 1980 and 2005. We chose a representative group of firms from Fortune lists of industry leaders, selecting equal numbers of firms from aerospace, apparel, building materials, chemicals, communications, computers, electrical machinery, entertainment, food, health care, machinery, metals, oil, paper, pharmaceuticals, publishing, retail, textiles, transportation, transportation equipment, utilities, and wholesale. We sampled from Fortune lists every year between 1965 and 2005 so as to achieve a sample that represents both rising and declining firms. In the following text, we use these data to show that American business did buy certain agency theory prescriptions, and to show which elements they failed to implement or misapplied.

THE MISAPPLICATION OF AGENCY THEORY

The story of the popularization and partial institutionalization of agency theory principles in the corporate world offers lessons for theories of corporate evolution and change. Agency theory has been wildly influential, considering that it was cooked up by a couple of business school professors at the University of Rochester and not by a titan of industry. There are two prevailing approaches to understanding the kind of broad change in business strategy that agency theory brought about. On the one hand, the evolutionary model favored by business historians suggests that corporate dilemmas posed by technological innovation and industrial expansion are solved by management pioneers, and the best solutions spread across industry and dominate inferior solutions (Chandler, 1977). On the other hand, the institutional model favored by organizational sociologists suggests that perceived economic crises offer innovators with new management prescriptions the chance to compete for a hold over the inter-organizational field. The models that win are not necessarily the best, and they are not necessarily better than those they replace. But a crisis offers the chance for entrepreneurs of management theories to try to win over the corporate world. While we cannot fully test these models in the allotted space, we suggest that as time goes on, the broadly functionalist stories favored by business historians have become more difficult to support, largely because so many lousy approaches have won wide followings and because innovations that do not improve upon the status quo frequently succeed.

Organizational institutionalists have long argued that new management practices diffuse through networks of firms like fads spread through high schools (Meyer & Rowan, 1977; DiMaggio & Powell, 1983). In their models, new paradigms are socially constructed as appropriate solutions to perceived problems or crises. Economic crises often punctuate the equilibrium of existing institutional arrangements (Krasner, 1984), leading to a search for new strategies. Expert groups that stand to gain from having their preferred strategies adopted by firms then enter the void, competing to have their own models adopted (Fligstein, 1990). As we noted at the outset, the economic crisis of the 1970s, fueled by the oil crisis early in the decade and then by economic stagnation coupled with inflation, palpably disrupted the management equilibrium of the 1950s and 1960s. Some called for us to follow Japan. Others called for us to mimic Italian small-firm networks. Others still pointed to France's industrial coordination. Professional theorization of new management models is key to their success (Strang & Meyer, 1994), and Jensen and Meckling faced a number of competing experts with their own theories of the malaise, but they clearly won out in the corporate world. William Ouchi's (1981) Japanese-inspired prescription had a short shelf life, but agency theory has colored the air we breathe. Organizations that conform to emerging management norms are thought to win access to both legitimacy and resources (Meyer & Rowan, 1977), and firms that followed agency theory certainly won out.

Institutionalists argue that different groups of experts and professionals, inside and outside of firms, typically develop and promote new management models in response to equilibrium-challenging crises. Professional groups push models they have construed as compatible with their own interests, either because they can gain position and prestige by being the proponents of the leading model of management, or because the new model advances the interests of the group. In the case of agency theory, finance-trained executives within firms became vocal proponents of the model, but only after institutional investors and securities analysts promoted elements of the model from outside of the firm (Zuckerman, 2000; Davis et al., 1994; Dobbin & Zorn, 2005). CEOs, money managers, and securities analysts succeeded in institutionalizing the components of the model that were in their own interests. Short-term pay-for-performance systems advantaged CEOs, by increasing their income, and they aligned CEO interests with fund manager interests, for fund manager bonuses were based on short-term increases in stock value, and mutual funds increasingly followed the New York performance logic of maximizing shareholder value over the Boston trustee logic (Lounsbury, 2007). Dediversification was favored by fund managers, who preferred to diversify portfolios themselves, and was promoted by securities analysts, who preferred to analyze single-industry firms that could be compared in horse races with their competitors. Debt financing was preferred by institutional investors and executives because it could leverage corporate equity. Moreover, by borrowing to finance new endeavors and using profits to buy back stock, companies could raise stock price and boost CEO and fund manager compensation. Companies did not follow the agency theory prescriptions that were not in the perceived interest of any of these constituencies. They did not institutionalize long-term equity holding by CEOs, for CEOs preferred to diversify their personal risk. They did not institutionalize independent board monitoring of CEOs, for independent boards could depose CEOs. What got institutionalized were the agency–theory components that had proponents. In the following pages we focus on components of the agency theory model that won out and why these components also raised corporate risk-taking without increasing pressures for restraint. While we do not focus on why these particular components were chosen, we sketch that story in the process.

Agency Theory

In the 1950s and 1960s, America's leading companies were run by, and for, managers according to agency theorists. Jensen and Meckling (1976) proposed that the managers of firms should rightly be working for shareholders. From the perspective of the early nineteenth century, this view was radical. When governments chartered banks, canals, and railroads as public corporations early in the 1800s, charters stipulated that the benefits of incorporation (limited liability, the right to issue stock) were granted in return for the performance of a public duty (Roy, 1997). The earliest corporations, and their managers, worked for the public good as well as for the private purposes of their shareholders. Later in the nineteenth century, general laws of incorporation permitted firms with purely private purposes (or the sole public purpose of fueling economic growth) to incorporate. This changed the view of what incorporation meant, and of who the corporation was working for, but publicly chartered firms retained a duty to customers and employees as well as to investors, in the public mind. By the 1970s, management thinkers treated the customer, the workforce, and the shareholder as stakeholders in private purpose corporations, and still debated their relative primacy.

The shareholder primacy norm advocated by agency theorists challenged that view, suggesting that corporations could only rightly be run for the benefit of owners (Whitley, 1986; Fligstein & Markowitz, 1993; Hirsch, 1991; Useem, 1996). According to that norm, the job of the board was to promote the interests of shareholders. Agency theorists proposed that firms should compensate executives based on stock performance, disassemble bloated conglomerates so that investors could make their own diversification decisions, finance new acquisitions with debt to rein in wayward executives on buying binges, and improve executive monitoring and discipline by giving corporate boards more independence.

Michael Jensen, a finance professor at the University of Rochester who took an appointment at Harvard Business School in 1985 and became partner at The Monitor Group consultancy in 2000, preached not only in finance journals, but in practitioner outlets such as Harvard Business Review (Jensen, 1984). The popular business press was full of advice about how to implement agency theory prescriptions for pursuit of the shareholder primacy norm (Baker & Smith, 1998; Hammer & Champy, 1993; Walther, 1997; Pralahad & Hamel, 1990). Finance had already become the lead specialization in many MBA programs (Fligstein, 1990), and now financial economics and agency theory came to dominate the curriculum (Fourcade & Khurana, 2008). The theory succeeded largely because it was promoted directly by institutional fund managers, as we argue below, and less directly by securities analysts. Executives mostly opposed agency theory at first, for it blamed poor corporate performance on CEOs, and on their propensity to serve themselves. But with time CEOs joined the bandwagon. They saw that the new compensation formulas could work to their advantage.

Agency theory moved quickly beyond the ivory tower in the context of the economic crisis of the 1970s, which had called into question the conglomerate approach to management. Agency theory had a more rapid, and more thorough, effect on corporate managers than any other theory hatched in academia (Guillén, 1994). Next we take the four main precepts of agency theory that were picked up by managers and discuss how they went wrong in practice.

ALIGNING CEO AND SHAREHOLDER INTERESTS

Part of the agency theory diagnosis of America's malaise was that CEOs were busy fortifying their empires against collapse rather that making money for shareholders. The prescription was to stop paying managers on the basis of the size of the firms they managed, and start paying them on the basis of how much they increased share price. If the old system rewarded expansive acquisitions, the new system was to reward money making (Jensen & Meckling, 1976; Jensen & Murphy, 1990). Agency theorists called for CEOs to hold equity and to be paid for performance through stock options and bonuses. Stock options enabled executives to buy a certain number of shares at a certain future date, typically three years hence, but at the market price of the stock on a the date of issue or thereabouts. Executives would thus benefit from increases in stock price between the date of pricing and the date of vesting. Stock options had been around for decades and had won favorable tax treatment, which allowed option recipients to defer taxes and firms to keep options off their expense sheets (although expensing was required as of 2006) (Karmel, 2004).

From the early 1980s, stock options were championed by leading institutional investors such as the California Public Employees' Retirement System (CalPERS) (Useem, 1996; Proffitt, 2001; Gourevitch & Shinn, 2005). Organizations representing institutional investors, such as the Council of Institutional Investors (CII), soon got into the act. Institutional fund managers repeated the mantra that stock options would align executive and shareholder interests, but options even more closely aligned executive and fund manager interests, because fund managers earned bonuses based on increases in the value of the portfolios they managed just as CEOs now made money based on increases in the value of the firms they managed. Executives and fund managers alike were paid when stock price rose, but did not have to pay when it fell. Fund manager bonuses, like stock option rewards, did not have to be returned in bad years. Clawbacks would have been compatible with agency theory, but perhaps institutional investors did not demand clawbacks because the same principle might have been applied to their own bonuses.

The spread of stock options increased executive compensation sharply after 1980, and caused total compensation to be much more closely aligned with firm performance (Hall & Liebman, 1998). Now executives who could make the stock price rise took home boatloads of cash. Fig. 1 shows that that median CEO compensation in our sample of big American firms rose sevenfold from 1984 to 2004, to over $3,500,000. Much of the rise came in the form of stock option grants and bonuses.

The new compensation system encouraged executives to take risk, but because the system was implemented to reward executives for increasing stock price in the near term, but not to punish them for declines, it encouraged reckless risk-taking. Because they could only win, executives could afford to do deals that offered huge potential for profits and losses

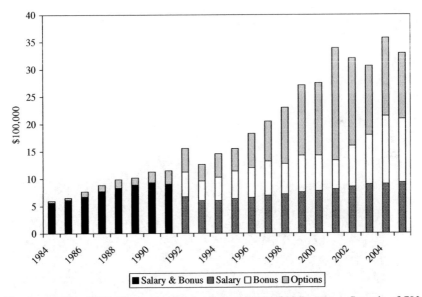

Fig. 1. Median CEO Compensation by Source (1984–2005). *Notes:* Sample of 783 large U.S. Corporations. Salary and bonus are not reported separately until 1992. The spike in 1992 results from a smaller sample (of larger firms) for that one year. Data on CEO compensation from 1984 to 1991 were provided by David Yermack. CEO compensation data after 1992 are from Standard and Poor's ExecuComp database, available through Compustat.

alike, knowing that for them, there was only an upside. After a few good years, CEOs could walk away if the risk they took soured.

The Failure to Induce Executives to Hold Equity

While boards compensated executives for increasing share price, they did not follow the agency theory dictum of requiring executives to hold more equity, perhaps because institutional investors did not push that point as their own bonuses were based on short-term results. Fund managers controlled over 60% of the shares in the average firm in our sample by 2005, up from 20% in 1970, and so they increasingly determined stock price. Executive interests were thus not aligned with the long-term interests of shareholders so much as with the short-term interests of institutional fund managers. Fig. 2 shows equity ownership by executives in our sample of 783 firms between 1992 and 2005, excluding unexercised options. Data on earlier years are not available. We can see from Fig. 1 that executives had much greater resources to invest after 1992, because their compensation

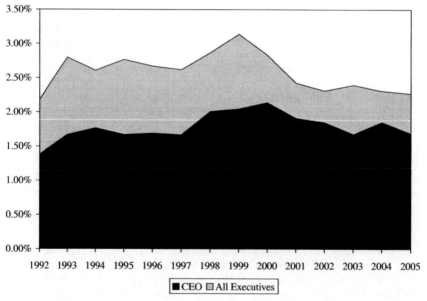

Fig. 2. Average Executive Equity Holdings. *Notes:* Sample of 783 large U.S. Companies. Unexercised options excluded. Data on executive equity holding are from the ExecuComp database.

skyrocketed. But equity ownership by CEOs, and by all executives, scarcely changes over the period. While investors favored long-term incentive plans for executives, such as plans that required equity ownership, they did not hold boards' feet to the fire. Westphal and Zajac (1998) find that investors bid up the price of firms that announce such plans, particularly when they use agency language. But they do not punish firms that fail to follow through on implementing those plans. Perhaps, again, because their bonuses depend on short-term rises in stock price. Moreover, Westphal and Zajac find, announcing a long-term incentive plan can forestall the implementation of board governance oversight mechanisms.

It is clear that agency theory was misapplied, to the extent that boards did not tie executive rewards to the long-term interests of shareholders. Would requiring executives to increase their equity holdings improve stock performance, as agency theory suggests it should? Hundreds of studies say no. In a meta-analysis of evidence from more than 200 studies, Dalton and colleagues (2003) found that firms whose executives held substantial equity performed no better than firms whose CEOs held little equity. If stock options infused executives with avarice, equity unfortunately did not make them better managers.

Short-Termism and Earnings Management

A new dynamic emerged among market makers in the 1980s. Fund managers looked to quarterly profit reports to value firms, and came to rely heavily on securities analysts to assess which firms were good values. Profits alone had become a poor metric of corporate value in new sectors of the economy, for Amazon could lose money every quarter on its way to dominating Internet commerce. Fund managers came to base their valuations of firms on whether they met analysts' quarterly profit projections. They did this in part because the efficient markets hypothesis, which had been taken up by the finance community, suggested that the present stock value of a firm represents all public knowledge of the firm. When a firm reports earnings lower than analysts project, it signals that experts had overvalued the firm. So a poor earnings report that was expected by securities analysts often has no effect on stock price, on the theory that the poor performance is already built in to the stock's price. But a poor earnings report that is unexpected often leads to a decline in stock price.

This produced a form of short-termism much more acute than one might expect, given the typical three-year period of option vesting. CEOs focused on quarterly profit projections, and seeking to meet or beat analysts' expectations every three months so as to be able to sustain stock price. As Justin Fox wrote in *Fortune* in 1997:

> This is what chief executives and chief financial officers dream of: quarter after quarter after blessed quarter of not disappointing Wall Street. Sure, they dream about other things too—megamergers, blockbuster new products, global domination. But the simplest, most visible, most merciless measure of corporate success in the 1990s has become this one: Did you make your earnings last quarter? (Fox, 1997).

To make the numbers, CEOs and CFOs held conference calls with analysts and updated sales and cost figures regularly, trying to ensure accurate analyst forecasts. They also began to issue earnings preannouncements, to bring analysts' forecasts into line with their own forecasts. Among the firms we studied, the first did this in the early 1990s, and by 2002, 42% were doing it. The quarterly profit report, and its relationship to analyst projections, became the focus of CEO attention. Michael Jensen (Jensen & Murphy, 1990) himself argued that his theory had been misapplied, and that stock option grants were encouraging short-termism.

Options created an incentive for executives to "manage" earnings statements, inflating earnings when they were depressed and deflating when they were above expectations, so as to have something for a rainy day. Firms increasingly used aggressive accounting techniques that allowed them to report sales in advance, move profits forward in time, manipulate the bottom line in other ways so as to be able to meet analyst expectations. Some of these techniques amounted to little more than fraud. Some studies showed that earnings restatements among Fortune 500 companies increased significantly over time, and were driven by stock option grants (Burns & Kedia, 2006; Efendi, Srivastava, & Swanson, 2007). One study suggested that the sharp rise in restatements over three decades was driven by highly leveraged firms in pursuit of favorable loan terms (Richardson, Tuna, & Wu, 2002). Earnings management can also be seen in the increasing likelihood a firm will meet, or beat, analyst estimates (Dobbin & Zorn, 2005).

INDUSTRIAL FOCUS TO HARNESS MANAGERIAL COMPETENCE

The portfolio theory of investment offered a logic to back up the corporate diversification fad of the 1950s through the 1970s. According to that theory, the modern firm should run an internal capital market, investing in promising sectors and spreading risk across different sorts of industries.

The idea was promoted by finance-trained executives at the top of firms and by business educators (Fligstein, 1990). The institutional economist Oliver Williamson (1975) argued that conglomerates could acquire poorly performing firms and improve their profitability by managing them under financial accounting methods. The major consulting firms – McKinsey, Arthur D. Little, the Boston Consulting Group – had developed accounting technologies to facilitate management of diversified conglomerates, which they proffered in the process of promoting diversification. By the end of the 1970s, 45% of the Fortune 500 had adopted these portfolio management techniques (Davis et al., 1994, p. 554).

In the midst of the stagflation of the 1970s, agency theorists argued that managers had pursued diversification as a hedge against the collapse of a particular enterprise or industry and that diversification was not in the interest of shareholders. Managers alone stood to gain by acquiring businesses of questionable value that would stay corporate collapse (Jensen & Meckling, 1976). Financial economists argued that shareholders should shy away from ponderous conglomerates that held poorly performing enterprises in industries little understood by their executives (Shleifer & Vishny, 1989, 1997). They suggested that the investor, not the firm, should assemble portfolios to spread risk (Amihud & Lev, 1981; Teece, 1982; Bettis, 1983).

Others echoed the sentiment that conglomerates were too unwieldy to manage, and that they had been managed to suit executives rather than shareholders. Jack Welch at General Electric argued for hands-on management and corporate focus. Management consultants turned against conglomerates en masse in the wake of publication of the first blockbuster management bible, *In Search of Excellence* (Peters & Waterman, 1982), which admonished executives to "stick to the knitting," focusing on the core business of the firm. In 1990, the reengineering gurus C.K. Pralahad and Gary Hamel published "The Core Competencies of the Firm" in *Harvard Business Review* arguing that a management team can excel at one or two things, but cannot be good at everything. As Michael Useem (1996, p. 153) argues, "While diversification had been a hallmark of good management during the 1960s, shedding unrelated business had become the measure during the 1980s and 1990s."

Takeover firms, institutional investors, and securities analysts encouraged the corporate focus trend in their own ways. The threat of hostile takeover fueled dediversification early in the game. In the 1970s and 1980s, hostile takeover firms targeted diversified conglomerates that they could break into pieces to be resold at a profit (Fligstein & Markowitz, 1993; Davis et al.,

1994; Liebeskind, Opler, & Hatfield, 1996; Matsusaka, 1993). While diversification had not depressed stock price in the early 1970s, it did so by the late 1970s and so takeover firms could make money simply by selling business units. Beginning in 1976, Kohlberg Kravis & Roberts (KKR) bought over 40 companies and broke up most, including such behemoths as Beatrice Companies and RJR Nabisco (Useem, 1993, p. 35). KKR often played the role of "white knight," saving the management team from other takeover firms, but the end result was the sell-off of business units just the same.

Michael Jensen (1984, p. 10) argued that the possibility of hostile takeover disciplined executives, serving a "fundamental economic function" by helping to create an efficient market for corporate control.

> In the corporate takeover market, managers compete for the right to control – that is, to manage – corporate resources. Viewed in this way, the market for corporate control is an important part of the managerial labor market ... After all, potential chief executive officers do not simply leave their applications with personnel officers. Their on-the-job performance is subject not only to the normal internal control mechanisms of their organizations but also to the scrutiny of the external market for control.

Jensen described the hostile takeover not as a form of disruptive speculation, but as a restraint on managerial malfeasance (Jacoby, 2006; Securities Regulations and Law Report, 1985). Between 1985 and 1988, more than 6% of Fortune 500 companies received tender offers each year, and in the course of a decade, one-third received hostile takeover bids (Davis & Stout, 1992, p. 622). These activities put the fear of God into executives, for executives typically lost their jobs in takeovers (Davis et al., 1994). Two-thirds of the Fortune 500 instituted takeover defenses such as poison pills and golden parachutes, and so by the 1990s takeover attempts were rare (Useem, 1996, p. 2; Davis, 1991).

Institutional investors had come to favor focused firms because they preferred to choose diversification strategies themselves and to invest in firms with clear profiles (Dobbin & Zorn, 2005). By the 1980s they were pushing firms to dediversify under the flag of agency theory. Where institutional investors held the sway, firms were fast to dediversify. From the 1980s, Fortune-500 companies with concentrated ownership were most likely to spin off unrelated businesses (Useem, 1996, p. 153).

Securities analysts encouraged dediversification through word and deed alike. They argued that focused firms were better performers, and they focused their professional attention on them. Analysts specialized by industry and conglomerates that did not fall into a neat category usually failed to win coverage. Because coverage was overwhelmingly positive, executives coveted coverage. This led them to dediversify in order to win coverage and boost institutional investor interest (Zuckerman, 1999, 2000).

The preferences of fund managers and analysts for single-industry firms translated into changes in business strategy. Thus diversification continued to decline even after the hostile takeover wave subsided, as executives voluntarily spun off units unrelated to their core businesses. In Fig. 3, we chart the level of diversification among our sample of large American firms. The entropy index, which measures diversification based on the contribution of each industry to the firm's sales, shows a consistent decline between 1980 and 1998, and then a leveling off. As firms dediversified, they began to hire executives with industry backgrounds and training rather than with backgrounds in general finance and the intricacies of financial management of conglomerates (Ocasio & Kim, 1999). Finance experts fought back by promoting agency theory principles from economics, and not industry expertise, as the key to good management.

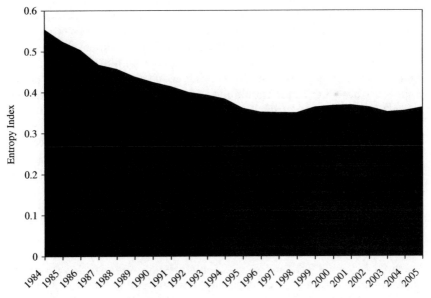

Fig. 3. Average Level of Diversification. *Notes:* Sample of 783 large U.S. Companies. The trend is adjusted for accounting rule changes in 1997 that caused firms to report operations in more industries. The entropy index of diversification is calculated using data from the Compustat Industry Segment database.

Mixed Evidence on the Efficiency of Dediversification

While it is clear that firms dediversified with the aim of improving profitability and stock returns (Zuckerman, 1999; Campa & Kedia, 2002), the evidence of a link between diversification and performance is weak at best. Some studies find a "conglomeration discount" in stock price in the 1960s and after the mid-1970s, but not in between (Servaes, 1996; Matsusaka, 1993), and others find no discount (Campa & Kedia, 2002; Villalonga, 2004). Alfred Chandler (1977) argued that the conglomerate's components, the multidivisional form pioneered at General Motors by Alfred P. Sloan (1963) and modern financial accounting systems, helped the conglomerate to outcompete the single-industry firm. Glenn Hubbard and Darius Palia (1998) find that investors themselves recognized this source of efficiency in the 1960s. Investors rewarded companies that announced diversifying takeovers in the 1960s, though by the 1990s, by which time agency theory had tarnished diversification, investors were rewarding companies that announced spin-offs. Studies of profitability show inconsistent effects of diversification, and this tends to suggest that the post-1975 conglomerate stock price discount may have been a product of the self-fulfilling prophesy of agency theory (Wernerfelt & Montgomery, 1988; LeBaron & Speidell, 1987). Another chink in the armor of the focused-firm paradigm is that the within-industry mergers that became the alternative to diversifying acquisitions in the 1980s do not appear to have increased profitability, despite the fact that they quelled competition (Jensen & Ruback, 1983). Some suggest that diversification is efficient in some markets but not in others. George Baker and colleagues argue that when capital and management talent are scarce, a large firm can acquire a poorly managed, capital-starved company and manage it efficiently as a subsidiary. When capital and talent markets are strong, these advantages disappear (Baker, 1992; Baker & Smith, 1998; Baker, Gibbons, & Murphy, 2001).

Corporate focus may also have failed to improve performance for another reason. One critique financial economists aimed at the portfolio theory of the firm was that the cost of selling a business can be prohibitive, and potential buyers scarce, and so conglomerates are often stuck with poorly performing acquisitions. Yet when large institutional investors hold blocks of stock, they often face similar constraints, finding it difficult to sell a large block without depressing share price. Thus large institutional investors may face constraints in unloading struggling enterprises similar to those faced by executives at conglomerates.

The evidence that single-industry firms perform better than conglomerates is mixed at best. Evidence that single-industry firms had higher stock prices after 1975 may simply be proof of the growing hegemony of agency theory. When market makers came to believe that focused firms are more valuable than conglomerates, so they were.

Dediversification and Increased Risk

Financial economists have long argued that investors, not companies, should make portfolio diversification decisions, choosing companies to invest in based on their own preferences for risk versus stability, long-term versus short-term gains, etc. The critique of managerialism was that executives diversified to moderate risk to their own firms and in the process, denied investors the potential for large gains (Amihud & Lev, 1981; Fligstein, 1990). While diversifying mergers tend to water down the profits of the best performers in the conglomerate portfolio, they also tend to moderate risk to individual business units. The internal capital market of the conglomerate can be used to prop up firms that are going through rough spots. Even the utter collapse of one business unit does not usually doom the corporation. Just as diversification reduces the risk of firm failure for managers, it reduces systemic risk across the economy in economic downturns, for each conglomerate is buoyed by its stronger business units. Hence while it is not clear that nondiversified firms earn superior profits, and while it is not clear that they improve stock performance except through the self-fulfilling prophesy of agency theory, it does seem clear that dediversification increases corporate risk.

DEBT FINANCING

Jensen and Meckling (1976) based some of their core arguments about the agency costs associated with equity versus debt financing on the arguments of financial economists (Modigliani & Miller, 1958; Miller & Modigliani, 1961). The agency costs associated with turning over management to nonowners stem from the propensity of management to, first, sacrifice profitability so as to minimize the risk of firm failure; second, over-reward themselves and drain profits; and third, pursue short-term strategies that will benefit management rather than long-term strategies that will benefit shareholders. One way of reducing agency costs is to have managers hold equity. If they hold 100% of equity, agency costs drop to zero. Another way is to force managers to pay dividends, which will lead them to issue additional stock to fund new endeavors and thereby open themselves up to additional shareholder monitoring. A third way of reducing agency costs, according to Jensen and Meckling (1976) is to take on debt. By reducing total equity financing, debt moderates the conflict of interest between shareholders and managers. According to the theory, managers will take on debt only when they are convinced that they can achieve rates of return, on new endeavors, that exceed the cost of debt. As a CEO, you wouldn't borrow money at 6% for an endeavor that would return 4%, but you might choose to invest profits in the same endeavor.

Under the theory, shareholders came to favor firms that used debt financing, taking debt financing as a signal of management's conviction that a new endeavor will pay off. Debt financing also permitted firms to leverage equity, multiplying the returns to investors. Shareholders should prefer debt financing to the issuance of new stock for that reason, and they should prefer to see profits returned to shareholders through dividends or share buybacks that boost share value (Westphal & Zajac, 1998; Zajac & Westphal, 2004).

In Fig. 4 we see that the firms in our sample of 783 large U.S. corporations indeed took on more debt in the years following the popularization of

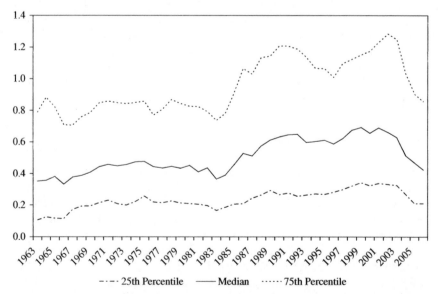

Fig. 4. Debt-to-Equity Ratio. *Notes:* Sample of 783 large U.S. Companies. Debt-to-equity ratio is calculated as total long-term debt divided by common equity. Data on both items are from Compustat.

agency theory. We report the debt equity ratios by quartiles from 1963 to 2005. Before the mid-1980s, the median firm had about 40 cents of debt for every dollar of equity. This rose to about 60 cents after the mid-1980s. The rise of junk bonds, spearheaded by Michael Milken and Drexel Burnham Lambert, coincided with the new theory and made debt available even to struggling firms.

Debt and Risk

Modigliani and Miller (1958) recognized that relying on debt can increase corporate vulnerability. Recent studies show that firms with heavy debt burdens are especially vulnerable during economic downturns (Campello, 2003, 2006). If returns from a new investment do not exceed interest on the bonds used to finance it, a firm may find itself with debt it cannot pay off. Moreover, debt may encourage managers to undertake high-risk investments to pay bondholders when their initial investments do not pay off (Crutchley & Hansen, 1989, p. 37). Many accounts of the crisis point to excess leverage by mortgage lenders, which put them at risk when mortgage-backed securities and mortgages themselves failed, and encouraged them to try even riskier moves to save themselves (Johnson, 2008; Sorkin, 2009; Posner, 2009). Firms also took on debt to prevent takeover, but we see from Fig. 4 that high debt levels continued after the 1980s, when hostile takeovers subsided.

BOARD INDEPENDENCE TO MONITOR RISK

Agency theorists argued that independent corporate boards could address the more general problem of agency costs – of executives behaving in their own interests (Fama, 1980, p. 293). The thinking was that outside directors, small focused boards, and independent chairmen could help to monitor executive behavior, ensuring that it conformed to investor interests. First, outside directors are better monitors. Insiders (company executives) rarely challenge the CEO either because they depend on him, or because it is in their interest, as in the executive's, to favor strategies that maximize corporate stability over profitability (Byrd & Hickman, 1992; Hermalin & Weisbach, 1988). Insiders are particularly unlikely to vote for CEO ouster and they oppose takeovers that might increase share value, for fear of losing their jobs, and so they back costly takeover shields such as poison pills and golden parachutes (Weisbach, 1988). Recall that Jensen (1984) argued against such antitakeover measures, defining the takeover as an effective means of replacing ineffective management teams. Second, small boards are more accountable and less unwieldy, and thus more likely to monitor CEO behavior. Third, boards with independent chairmen should better monitor the CEO than those on which the CEO is also chair (Daily, Dalton, & Cannella, 2003; Beatty & Zajac, 1994). Boards chaired by the company CEO are particularly unlikely to call for CEO ouster.

Institutional investors promoted board monitoring under agency theory principles just as they had promoted pay for performance and dediversification. CalPERS was one of the first to advocate board independence (Schwab & Thomas, 1998). CalPERS sponsored more shareholder resolutions to update governance after 1984, when California lifted a restriction limiting its stock holdings to 25% of portfolio value (Blair, 1995). CalPERS officials were instrumental in the creation of the CII in 1985, which brought together 30 funds (29 of them public) controlling assets of $132 billion, and which now includes a wide range of funds with assets in excess of $3 trillion (http://www.cii.org/about). CII's "Shareholder bill of rights" called for independent oversight of executive compensation and auditing, equal treatment for different categories of shareholders (to prevent a minority of, for instance, shareholders from the founder's lineage dominating a board), and shareholder approval of key strategic decisions (Jacoby, 2006). CalPERS and CII sponsored proposals that boards be composed of a majority of outsiders, and that compensation committees be composed exclusively of outsiders. In many companies they opposed antitakeover strategies, such as the poison pill, designed to keep incumbent executives in place at all costs (Davis & Stout, 1992; Jacoby, 2006).

Executives and boards followed the dictates of agency theorists when it came to outside directors and board size. Fig. 5 reports the average percentage of outside directors among sampled firms between 1980 and 2005. In the average firm, outside directors held 66% of seats in 1980, and 83% in 2005. Analysts have often questioned whether independent directors are truly independent, and we can see that they had cause for concern. From 1996, when data on outside directors' ties to the firm were first available, the figure shows the percent of directors with no familial ties or employment history with the firm (*independent* directors). In 1996, in the average firm, nearly 80% of directors were outsiders, but less than 60% were independent. Thus while board members were more likely to be outsiders, many of those

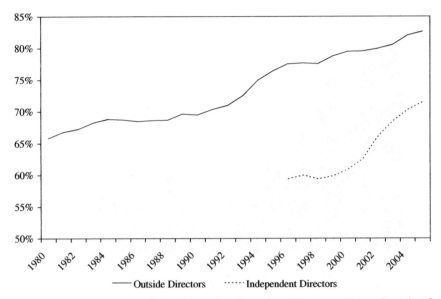

Fig. 5. Average Percent of Outside and Independent Directors. *Notes:* Sample of 783 large U.S. Companies. Data on outside directors who are *independent* are available only from 1996. Outside directors are defined as any directors not employed by the firm. For this, we referred to *Standard & Poor's Register.* After 1996, we use data from the Investor Responsibility Research Center (IRRC) Directors database to further classify outside directors into affiliated and independent directors.

outsiders had links to management. Moreover, because candidates for board positions are nominated by the board's own nominating committee, boards are often made up of friends of the chair, and friends-of-friends. In theory they represent shareholders, but in fact, they are appointed by a committee that operates under the CEO/Chairman.

Companies reduced the size of their boards on the advice of agency theorists, so they did not achieve a greater proportion of outsiders by adding new members. Fig. 6 shows that the average number of directors declined from 11.7 to 10.2 between 1980 and 2005. A 15% decrease over 25 years may seem meager, but it proved difficult to reduce board size because directors typically hold lifetime appointments, and tend to hang on because the compensation is attractive and the duties are not particularly onerous, although they have expanded since passage of the Sarbanes–Oxley Act.

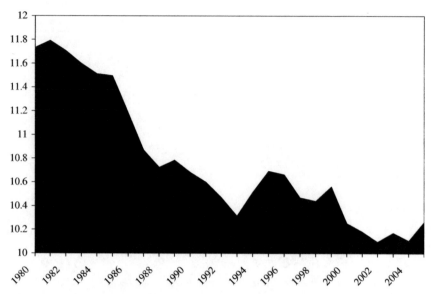

Fig. 6. Average Number of Directors. *Notes:* Sample of 783 large U.S. Companies. We calculated the average number of directors on the board using information from *Standard & Poor's Register.*

The Failed Mandate of Chair Independence

Boards did not, however, take up the advice to appoint independent chairmen (see Daily et al., 2003). The call for separating the CEO and Chair positions was challenged by a countertrend: firms sought to appoint celebrity CEOs to fuel stock price growth through positive media attention. Boards responded to poor stock performance by hiring well-known CEOs so as to send the message that the firm was now in competent hands (Khurana, 2002). Celebrity CEOs often held the upper hand in negotiations, and agreed to serve only if they were offered the title of chairman. After all, now that agency theory directed boards to oust CEOs who did not return strong results, incoming CEOs had good reason to keep the position of chair out of the hands of a potential critic. Between 1980 and 2000, CEOs in our sample who held the title of chairman of the board rose from 57 to 75%, dropping back to 67% by 2005 (see Fig. 7). Even firms that appointed someone other than the CEO to chair the board often appointed the former CEO, or a chum of the current CEO, and so even non-CEO chairs were often closely allied with management.

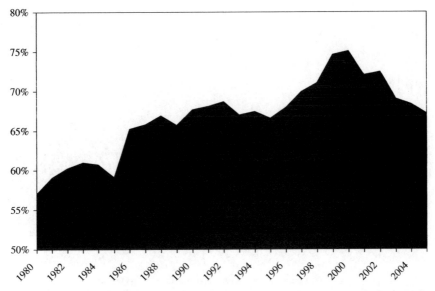

Fig. 7. Percent of Firms in which CEO is Chair. *Notes:* Sample of 783 large U.S. Companies. To identify CEOs who held the title of chairman of the board, we referred to *Standard & Poor's Register.*

Failure of Board Monitoring: The Difficulty of Ousting CEOs

Agency theorists charged boards with ousting CEOs for poor performance, the ultimate stick to complement the carrot of stock options. CEO turnover did increase across the period, from 9.7% per annum in the 1980s to 11.5% in the 1990s and 12.6% between 2000 and 2006 (see Fig. 8). It is difficult to judge how much of the increase was the result of board ouster, because CEOs who see the writing on the wall often leave quietly to "pursue other interests" or to "spend more time with the family," but even if all of the change over time was a consequence of board ouster, the change accounted for less than a quarter of all CEO turnover in the new millennium. There was hardly an upswell in board ouster of poor performers. There was an increase in the appointment of outside CEOs over this period. Rakesh Khurana (2002) ties this to board efforts to signal a change of course, and bolster lagging stock price.

Limits to the Effectiveness of Board Monitoring

Press reports and academic research suggest that boards have not played the monitoring and disciplining role that agency theory suggests they should

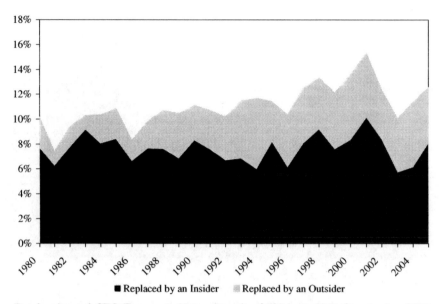

Fig. 8. Annual CEO Turnover. *Notes:* Sample of 783 large U.S. Companies. CEO replacement events were identified in two steps. First, we noted any changes in the names of CEOs in consecutive volumes of *Standard & Poor's Register of Corporations, Directors, and Executives.* Then, we confirmed that these changes in the names reflected actual CEO succession events, using the *Wall Street Journal Index*, the *New York Times Index*, and the Lexis-Nexis service.

play. One comparative study found that Japanese firms with lackluster performance were much more likely to appoint outside directors than American firms with the same problem, suggesting that in Japan alone boards respond to challenges by seeking outside input. Moreover, outsider appointments in Japan alone presage CEO turnover, suggesting that outsiders there actually monitor executives and encourage replacement of poor performers (Kaplan, 1994; Kaplan & Minton, 1994).

Notwithstanding the leadership of CII in encouraging board activism and monitoring, institutional investors have proven reluctant to hold boards to account and to dictate to top management teams. Shareholder proposals do increase in number over time, but they are disproportionately initiated by public pension funds. One reason for this may be that mutual funds have conflicting interests. They invest in companies with one hand and with the other, market retirement instruments to them. This creates a disincentive to fund managers to fall out of favor with top managers, through challenges to management decisions or calls for the ouster of top management team members (Gourevitch & Shinn, 2005; Davis & Kim, 2007).

The increase in outside board members has also produced something of a conundrum for monitoring. Directors should ideally know the industry well, to be able to assess the company's business strategy and prospects for growth and profitability. But antitrust provisions, and concerns about trade and strategic secrecy, prevent firms from appointing outside directors who are industry insiders. In consequence, outside directors frequently know little or nothing about the industry in question. Insiders then typically have a significant knowledge advantage over outsiders, and are better positioned to judge corporate strategy. Those on the board who are best able to assess strategy are thus least likely, by dint of their insider status, to challenge the CEO.

To the extent that the corporations wrought by agency theory are more oriented to increasing share value, more lean and industry focused, and more disciplined by the use of debt, they will behave more entrepreneurially, and take more risks that promise great rewards. More risk for more reward is the new mantra of managers. But the failure of corporate board reform has left firms without the discipline and restraint that, according to agency theory, should have had the effect of putting the brakes on risk. Independent boards should be the ones to implement some components of agency theory, such as stock options, and indeed their compensation committees have done that. But they have not generally exercised greater oversight over business strategy or disciplined executives who took undue risks or failed to increase share value. One reason for this pattern, of boards whose compensation committees embrace the generic prescription of stock options but do not monitor fine-grained corporate strategic decisions, may be that board energy is limited and the industry knowledge of outsiders is finite (information asymmetry plays an obvious role). Boards may be better equipped to implement an out-of-the-box compensation system than to roll up their sleeves and question the minutiae of strategy.

CONCLUSION

Since the early 1980s, large American corporations have transformed themselves to conform to the new "shareholder value" model of the firm. That model can be traced to the conflicts agency theorists depicted between interests of managers and shareholders, and the prescriptions they set out for minimizing those conflicts. First, they suggested that firms should align the interests of these two groups by paying managers for increasing stock price (through stock options) and making sure they hold equity in the firm. Second, firms should focus on one core business, leaving the job of portfolio diversification to investors, because the huge diversified conglomerate did not produce an efficient market for capital. Third, corporations should finance new endeavors and expansion with debt, leveraging the investment of shareholders and at the same time disciplining executives tempted to use profits to expand into low-return ventures. These three changes should make the firm more entrepreneurial and focused, and give managers incentives to take risks that promise strong returns. Fourth, corporate boards should be more independent of management, to increase monitoring of executives and guarantee discipline when management strays off course. Outside directors, small and agile boards, and independent board chairmen were what the doctor ordered. If the first three innovations lead to greater risk-taking, the fourth should restrain executives and help to protect shareholder investment. In fact, both the compensation and governance prescriptions serve the dual functions of encouraging entrepreneurialism and restraining recklessness. In compensation, the executive–equity formula restrains risk-taking and short-termism, while the stock-option formula promotes initiative. In governance, autonomous boards should encourage executive entrepreneurialism yet discourage ill-advised risk.

The data we present on the compensation systems, business strategies, and governance structures of 783 large American corporations suggest that firms have indeed followed certain agency theory prescriptions (see also Zuckerman, 1999; Davis et al., 1994; Fligstein & Markowitz, 1993). They have revolutionized executive compensation, dediversified, financed new endeavors with debt, appointed outside board directors, and reduced board size. Companies followed these strategies largely at the behest of fund managers, who themselves benefitted from the steady increases in stock price that these strategies promised, for fund manager bonuses were tied to improvements in the value of the portfolios they managed. CEOs at first resisted these innovations, but soon realized that they stood to win big by taking stock options and by focusing on increases in stock value rather than on growth for its own sake. They embraced some of the innovations simply to keep fund managers happy.

We argue that while the average firm has assiduously applied the agency theory principles that increase corporate entrepreneurialism and risk, it has not applied the principles that bolster monitoring and foster executive self-restraint. Executives have not been required to hold more equity, and boards have not truly gained independence. These changes encouraged corporations to invest in riskier ventures and to deceive shareholders in the early years of the first decade of the twenty-first century, producing high-profile failures at Enron, WorldCom, and Tyco and contributing to the recession of 2001. These changes then encouraged banks, insurance companies, and industries to assume speculative risk at the end of that decade, contributing to the Great Recession. There was nothing to prevent firms from pursuing excessive risk, and little to prevent them from committing outright fraud, and there still is little to restrain either pattern of behavior.

First, the CEOs of GM, GE, and IBM were paid salaries of a million dollars or so in 1970. By 2000, the chiefs of these companies were paid with stock options, and those who could raise share value could expect ten, twenty, or a hundred times the old salaries. Tying CEO earnings to stock price seemed like a good idea, but agency theory was misapplied, for firms did not simultaneously require executives to hold more equity. CEOs now gained from short-term increases in stock price but had little invested in the long run. They even benefitted from volatility. CEOs made out when the stock price plummeted in the window of option pricing and then spiked when it was time to exercise options. Because CEOs didn't expand their equity holdings, and didn't have to return money earned through options when stock prices plunged, the new compensation system encouraged CEOs to gamble on short-run endeavors that would increase firm value rather than to look after the long-term vitality of the firm. Not only was the theory misapplied, empirical evidence suggests that it may have been wrong in the first place. Econometric studies raise questions about whether stock options and equity holdings improve corporate performance. Moreover, the literature in behavioral economics and psychology suggests that "extrinsic" systems of motivation such as pay-for-performance may not improve managerial performance (Benabou & Tirole, 2003).

Second, dediversification certainly made America's firms more focused over the period we study. Yet empirical studies question whether focused firms are more efficient than conglomerates. The profits of single-industry firms and conglomerates do not show clear patterns of difference, and single-industry firms show superior *stock* performance only in the heyday of agency theory. We suggested that this pattern may indicate a self-fulfilling prophesy – if investors believe single-industry firms to be better values, their values will indeed rise. Moreover, in the same period, securities analysts preferred to rate focused firms, and institutional investors preferred to create portfolios out of focused firms. Those preferences may well be fleeting, and thus they may not continue to affect value. While it is uncertain whether focused firms earn higher profits, or attain higher market valuations, than conglomerates, it seems likely that they face greater risk. As we have argued, focused firms do not have the cushion that conglomerates enjoy from operating in industries with different business cycle profiles and at different life-course stages. A cyclical enterprise can be buffered by countercyclical enterprises in a diversified conglomerate, but does not have that buffer if it is on its own. A youthful enterprise in need of capital can be fueled by a sunset enterprise, but not when it is on its own. The dediversified firm almost certainly faced greater risk of failure, and may not have made up for that risk with improved performance.

Third, the idea that by requiring management to finance expansion with debt, shareholders could discipline CEOs and prevent them from buying low-yield enterprises just to expand their empires, seemed sound. It also made sense that debt could leverage the investment of shareholders, who came to see executive decisions to take on debt as evidence of their confidence in the firm's prospects. But debt clearly increased corporate risk. Meanwhile the rise of junk bonds allowed even struggling firms to take on debt to solve short term problems. But the business cycle could undermine debt-financing strategies, for good times brought higher interest rates that increased the cost of debt and bad times brought reduced demand and lower profits with which to pay off debt. There was a downside to debt, then, but executives came to understand that debt could improve their own compensation. CEOs could use profits for share buybacks, raising the value of their options, and then turn around and leverage option value through debt-financed expansion. Because corporations did not claw back money previously earned from options when stock price sank, executives did not lose their previous winnings when debt-financed expansion did not pay off. This dynamic certainly contributed to the bank defaults of the Great Recession. Shareholders discovered that investment banks were highly leveraged in 2008, and wildly optimistic about their holdings of opaque and volatile investment vehicles such as collateralized debt obligations. Banks failed, but their executives did very well.

If these first three proposals were to encourage managers to behave entrepreneurially, and to make the firm more tractable, the fourth proposal was to exert restraint and monitoring by the delegates of shareholders. Corporate boards should look out for shareholder interests, and to do this they need to be independent of management. If managers were running the firm for their own benefit, boards could discipline them or throw them out. Agency theorists prescribed boards small enough to actually oversee strategy, filled with outsiders rather than inside managers, and headed by independent chairs. It was a good theory, but firms put it into practice very selectively. They did make their board smaller. They did appoint more outsiders, although many had ties to the chief executives or employment histories with the firm. "Outsiders" weren't exactly shareholder representatives. Where boards did nominate true outsiders, they chose people from outside of the industry to comply with antitrust laws, which often meant that the outsiders were least able to assess firm strategy. Most importantly, CEOs became more, not less, likely to simultaneously hold the position of chairman of the board, and this undermined the core precept of true board independence, for when CEOs chaired boards, boards did not challenge corporate strategy and they rarely ousted the chief.

We have shown that the average company embraced agency theory dictums that served fund managers and CEOs, and that incidentally increased corporate exposure to risk, without embracing the dictums that imposed restraints on corporate behavior. But agency theory had much broader effects on the American economy, for its short-term pay-for-performance prescription won favor in other sectors, and it exposed those sectors as well to new forms of risk-taking.

The Wider Misapplication of Agency Theory's Compensation Formula

The misapplication of agency theory, in the form of short-term incentives for fluctuations in the market value of firms, came to affect pay systems well beyond the world of industrial firms. Investment banks had been organized as partnerships, but now they listed themselves on the stock market, making their partners wealthy through initial public offerings and ensuring that executives no longer faced the downside risk they had faced as partners. Institutional investors too were compensated based on annual performance, earning a proportion of the paper gains in their portfolios. Hedge fund managers and private equity fund managers were likewise paid based on the performance of their portfolios. In short order, key decision makers across the economy were being paid for moving the market value of corporations up, and all of these compensation systems suffered from the same focus on short-term gains and lack of a disincentive for taking risks that caused medium-term share price collapse. In this period as well the focus of the American economy was moving toward finance, and finance workers gained both prestige and income (Lounsbury, 2002; Davis, 2009).

This common approach to compensation encouraged all participants to overvalue firms, since private equity managers, hedge fund managers, institutional investors, and captains of the industry were paid for increases in value, but not sanctioned for subsequent losses. All benefitted from short-term increases in the book value of firms. Hedge funds, for instance, typically charged investors a flat fee of 2% of funds under management and 20% of gains. They did not pay back 20% of losses. University endowment managers were compensated with bonuses for portfolio gains, and it led them as well to favor high values, especially for illiquid assets where value could be a matter of dispute. As an investment bank reported on Harvard's paper loss on private equity investments in 2008, the cause was "unrealistic pricing levels at which funds continued to hold their investments" and "fantasy valuations." The system encouraged CEOs and fund managers to promote paper gains in value, as a self-appointed oversight committee from Harvard's class of 1969 argued of the Harvard Management Corporation's 2008 losses; "The events of the last year show that the whole procedure of rewarding people so handsomely based on increases on paper value of the endowment was deeply flawed" (Condon & Vardi, 2009).

The partnership offered the ideal compensation system, if you listened to agency theorists, because executives were the shareholders. But partners in investment banks recognized the benefits of public ownership and stock options. Partners in the leading investment banks took their banks public, and became executives paid through stock options and bonuses rather than partners sharing in the profits. Now the heads of investment banks like the heads of industrial firms shared in the gains of their firms, but did not share in the losses. More generally, agency theory did not move industrial firms toward the logic of partnership by increasing equity holding. It moved all of these sectors toward a logic of gambling in increases in equity value. Risk-taking became contagious. Once your competitors, in industrial management, investment banking, institutional investment, hedge funds, or private equity begin engaging in high-risk, high-reward activities, it is difficult to resist. To keep the best talent at your investment bank, the logic goes, you have to offer compensation opportunities that equal those of your competitors. The system encouraged risk at Enron, WorldCom, and Tyco but also at the commercial banks that were issuing subprime mortgages, at the investment banks that were putting those mortgages into collateralized debt obligations and selling the tranches to institutional investors, at mutual funds that bought CDOs, and at insurers such as AIG that insured them. There was no downside risk to anyone in this chain of financial executives. None of these executives stood to lose from the failure of individual enterprises, even of their own enterprises.

Missteps in Regulatory Response

Will regulation remedy these problems? Efforts to regulate corporate malfeasance driven by the perverse incentives stock options created for executives have been meager. The Sarbanes–Oxley Act of July 30, 2002 defined the failures of Enron and WorldCom and Tyco as resulting from accounting fraud. The Senate title of the bill says it all; "'Public Company Accounting Reform and Investor Protection Act." The bill made it marginally more difficult for CEOs and CFOs to file fictitious earnings reports and thereby boost stock price. Yet the Act did nothing to alter the stock option compensation system that had encouraged CEOs to delude the public. If Sarbanes–Oxley had outlawed compensation tied to short-term changes in stock price, it might have removed the incentive to "manage" earnings. As it stands, we have seen corporate restatements of earnings, which amount to admissions of earnings management, *increase* after the passage of Sarbanes–Oxley. Some argue that the increase is a good sign, indicating that companies are confessing their transgressions. But transgressions they are.

Regulatory responses to the crisis of 2008 are still in process, but to date, no one has proposed regulations that would rewind corporate strategy and governance to 1970. Aside from policies designed to prevent the failure of mortgage issuers, insurers, automakers, and banks, the main policy responses have been classical Keynesian countercyclical spending and moderate regulatory reform. We have proposals for a consumer finance safety commission that would apprise investors of high-risk investment instruments. We have proposals to limit the size of financial institutions so as to limit the exposure of the economy to the failure of individual institutions. None of these changes will fundamentally alter the incentives to executives.

Globally it looks like agency theory is winning more converts, not facing the sort of challenge one might expect for a theory that contributed importantly to two major recessions within a decade. Japanese firms are increasingly appointing outside directors, reducing board size to make boards more accountable, and expanding investor relations services to boost investor confidence (Kaplan, 1994; Kaplan & Minton, 1994; Dore, 2000; Jacoby, 2005, 2006). The "shareholder value" model of the firm promoted by agency theory appears to be alive and well, and to have been checked very little by the Enron, WorldCom, and Tyco scandals that led to the Sarbanes–Oxley Act, and not at all by the Great Recession that followed.

ACKNOWLEDGMENT

We thank Mitch Abolafia and Andrew Hill for insightful comments on the first draft.

REFERENCES

Amihud, Y., & Lev, B. (1981). Risk reduction as a managerial motive for conglomerate mergers. *Bell Journal of Economics, 12*, 605–617.

Baker, G. P. (1992). Beatrice: A study in the creation and destruction of value. *Journal of Finance, 47*, 1081–1119.

Baker, G. P., Gibbons, R. S., & Murphy, K. J. (2001). Bringing the market inside the firm? *The American Economic Review, 91*, 212–218.

Baker, G. P., & Smith, G. D. (1998). *The new financial capitalists: Kohlberg Kravis Roberts and the creation of corporate value.* New York: Cambridge University Press.

Beatty, R. P., & Zajac, E. J. (1994). Managerial incentives, monitoring, and risk bearing: A study of executive compensation, ownership, and board structure in initial public offerings. *Administrative Science Quarterly, 39*, 313–335.

Benabou, R., & Tirole, J. (2003). Intrinsic and extrinisic motivation. *Review of Economic Studies, 70*, 489–520.

Bettis, R. A. (1983). Modern financial theory, corporate strategy and public policy: Three conundrums. *Academy of Management Review, 8*, 406–415.

Blair, M. M. (1995). *Ownership and control: Re-thinking corporate governance for the first century.* Washington, DC: Brookings Institution.

Burns, N., & Kedia, S. (2006). *The impact of performance-based compensation on misreporting.* San Antonio, TX: University of Texas.

Byrd, J. W., & Hickman, K. A. (1992). Do outside directors monitor managers? *Journal of Financial Economics, 32*, 195–221.

Campa, J. M., & Kedia, S. (2002). Explaining the diversification discount. *The Journal of Finance, 57*, 1731–1762.

Campello, M. (2003). Capital structure and product markets interactions: Evidence from business cycles. *Journal of Financial Economics, 68*, 353–378.

Campello, M. (2006). Debt financing: Does it hurt or boost firm performance in product markets? *Journal of Financial Economics, 82*, 135–172.

Chandler, A. D., Jr. (1977). *The visible hand: The managerial revolution in American business.* Cambridge, MA: Belknap.

Condon, B., & Vardi, N. (2009). How Harvard's investing superstars crashed. *Forbes*, February 20, 2009. Available at Forbes.com

Crutchley, C. E., & Hansen, R. S. (1989). A test of the agency theory of managerial ownership, corporate leverage, and corporate dividends. *Financial Management, 18*, 36–46.

Daily, C. M., Dalton, D. R., & Cannella, A. A., Jr. (2003). Introduction to special topic forum corporate governance: Decades of dialogue and data. *Academy of Management Review, 28*, 371–382.

Dalton, D. R., Daily, C. M., Certo, S. T., & Roengpitya, R. (2003). Meta-analyses of financial performance and equity: Fusion or confusion? *The Academy of Management Journal, 46,* 13–26.

Davis, G. F. (1991). Agents without principles: The spread of the poison pill through the intercorporate network. *Administrative Science Quarterly, 36,* 583–613.

Davis, G. F. (2009). *Managed by the markets: How finance re-shaped America.* New York: Oxford University Press.

Davis, G. F., Diekmann, K. A., & Tinsley, C. H. (1994). The decline and fall of the conglomerate firm in the 1980s: The deinstitutionalization of an organizational form. *American Sociological Review, 59,* 547–570.

Davis, G. F., & Kim, H. E. (2007). Business ties and proxy voting by mutual funds. *Journal of Financial Economics, 85,* 552–570.

Davis, G. F., & Stout, S. K. (1992). Organization theory and the market for corporate control: A dynamic analysis of the characteristics of large takeover targets. *Administrative Science Quarterly, 37,* 605–633.

Dimaggio, P. J., & Powell, W. W. (1983). The iron cage revisited-institutional isomorphism and collective rationality in organizational fields. *American Sociological Review, 48,* 147–160.

Dobbin, F., & Zorn, D. (2005). Corporate malfeasance and the myth of shareholder value. *Political Power and Social Theory, 17,* 179–198.

Dore, R. (2000). *Stock market capitalism: Welfare capitalism – Japan and Germany versus the Anglo-Saxons.* New York: Oxford University Press.

Efendi, J., Srivastava, A., & Swanson, E. P. (2007). Why do corporate managers misstate financial statements? The role of option compensation and other factors. *Journal of Financial Economics, 85,* 667–708.

Fama, E. F. (1980). Agency problems and the theory of the firm. *The Journal of Political Economy, 88,* 288–307.

Fama, E. F., & Jensen, M. C. (1983). Separation of ownership and control. *Journal of Law and Economics, 26,* 301–326.

Fama, E. F., & Jensen, M. C. (1985). Organizational forms and investment decisions. *Journal of Financial Economics, 14,* 101–119.

Fligstein, N. (1990). *The transformation of corporate control.* Cambridge, MA: Harvard University Press.

Fligstein, N., & Markowitz, L. (1993). Financial reorganization of American corporations in the 1980s. In: W. J. Wilson (Ed.), *Sociology and the public agenda.* Beverly Hills, CA: Sage Publications.

Fourcade, M., & Khurana, R. (2008). From social control to financial economics: The linked ecologies of economics and business in twentieth-century America. In: C. Camic, N. Gross & M. Lamont (Eds), *Making, evaluating, and using social science knowledge: The underground practice.* Chicago: University of Chicago Press.

Fox, J. (1997). Learn to play the earnings game (and Wall Street Will Love You). *Fortune, 6,* 76–80.

Gourevitch, P., & Shinn, J. (2005). *Political power and corporate control: The new global politics of corporate governance.* Princeton, NJ: Princeton University Press.

Guillén, M. F. (1994). *Models of management: Work authority and organization in a comparative perspective.* Chicago: University of Chicago Press.

Hall, B. J., & Liebman, J. B. (1998). Are CEOs really paid like bureaucrats? *The Quarterly Journal of Economics, 113,* 653–691.

Hammer, M., & Champy, J. (1993). *Reengineering the corporation: A manifesto for business.* New York: Harper Business.

Hermalin, B. E., & Weisbach, M. S. (1988). The determinants of board composition. *The Rand Journal of Economics, 19,* 589–606.

Hirsch, P. M. (1986). From ambushes to parachutes: Corporate takeovers as an instance of cultural framing and institutional integration. *American Journal of Sociology, 91,* 800–837.

Hirsch, P. M. (1991). Undoing the managerial revolution? Needed research on the decline of middle management and internal labor markets. *Annual meeting of the American Sociological Association,* Cincinnati, OH.

Hubbard, R. G. & Palia, D. (1998). *A re-examination of the conglomerate merger wave in the 1960s: An internal markets view.* NBER Working Paper no. 6539. National Bureau of Economic Research.

Jacoby, S. M. (2005). *The embedded corporation: Corporate governance and employment relations in Japan and the United States.* Princeton, NJ: Princeton University Press.

Jacoby, S. M. (2006). *Principles and agents: CalPERS and corporate governance change in Japan.* Los Angeles: Anderson School of Business, UCLA.

Jensen, M. C. (1984). Takeovers: Folklore and science. *Harvard Business Review,* November–December, pp. 109–121.

Jensen, M. C., & Meckling, W. H. (1976). Theory of the firm: Managerial behavior, agency costs and ownership structure. *Journal of Financial Economics, 3,* 305–360.

Jensen, M. C., & Murphy, K. J. (1990). Performance pay and top management incentives. *Journal of Political Economy, 98,* 225–264.

Jensen, M. C., & Ruback, R. (1983). The market for corporate control: The scientific evidence. *Journal of Financial Economics, 11,* 5–50.

Johnson, S. (2008). Hearing on faltering economic growth and the need for economic stimulus. Joint Economic Committee of Congress, October 30, 2008, Room 106 of the Dirksen Senate Office Building. Available at jec.senate.gov/index.cfm

Kaplan, S., & Minton, B. (1994). Appointments of outsiders to Japanese boards. *Journal of Financial Economics, 36,* 225–258.

Kaplan, S. N. (1994). Top executive rewards and firm performance: A comparison of Japan and the United States. *Journal of Political Economy, 102,* 510–546.

Karmel, R. S. (2004). Should a duty to the corporation be imposed on institutional shareholders. *Business Law, 60,* 1–17.

Khurana, R. (2002). *Searching for a corporate savior: The irrational quest for charismatic CEOs.* Princeton, NJ: Princeton University Press.

Krasner, S. D. (1984). Approaches to the state: Alternative conceptions and historical dynamics. *Comparative Politics, 17,* 223–246.

Lebaron, D., & Speidell, L. S. (1987). Why are the parts worth more than the sum? 'Chop Shop', a corporate valuation model. In: L. E. Browne & E. S. Rosengren (Eds), *The merger boom.* Boston, MA: Federal Reserve Bank of Boston.

Liebeskind, J., Opler, T., & Hatfield, D. (1996). Corporate restructuring and the consolidation of US industry. *Journal of Industrial Economics, 47,* 53–68.

Lounsbury, M. (2002). Institutional transformation and status mobility: The professionalization of the field of finance. *The Academy of Management Journal, 45,* 255–266.

Lounsbury, M. (2007). A tale of two cities: Competing logics and practice variation in the professionalizing of mutual funds. *Academy of Management Journal, 50,* 289–307.

Matsusaka, J. (1993). Takeover motives during the conglomerate merger wave. *Rand Journal of Economics, 24,* 357–379.

Meyer, J. W., & Rowan, B. (1977). Institutionalized organizations: Formal structure as myth and ceremony. *American Journal of Sociology, 83,* 340–363.

Miller, M. H., & Modigliani, F. (1961). Dividend policy, growth and the valuation of shares. *Journal of Business, 34,* 411–433.

Modigliani, F., & Miller, M. H. (1958). The cost of capital, corporation finance and the theory of investment. *American Economic Review* (June), 261–297.

Ocasio, W., & Kim, H. K. (1999). The circulation of corporate control: Selection of functional backgrounds of new CEOs in large U.S. manufacturing firms, 1981–1992. *Administrative Science Quarterly, 44,* 532–562.

Ouchi, W. G. (1981). *Theory Z: How American business can meet the Japanese challenge.* Reading, MA: Addison-Wesley.

Peters, T. J., & Waterman, R. H. (1982). *In search of excellence.* New York: Harper & Row.

Piore, M., & Sabel, C. (1984). *The second industrial divide-possibilities for prosperity.* New York: Basic Books.

Posner, R. A. (2009). *A failure of capitalism: The crisis of '08 and the descent into depression.* Cambridge, MA: Harvard University Press.

Pralahad, C. K., & Hamel, G. (1990). The core competencies of the corporation. *Harvard Business Review, 68,* 79–91.

Proffitt, W. T. (2001). *The evolution of institutional investor identity: Social movement mobilization in the shareholder activism field.* Evanston, IL: Northwestern University Press.

Richardson, S. A., Tuna, A. I., & Wu, M. (2002). Predicting earnings management: The case of earnings restatements. *Social Science Research Network Working Paper Series.*

Roy, W. (1997). *Socializing capital: The rise of the large industrial corporation in America.* Princeton, NJ: Princeton University Press.

Schwab, S. J., & Thomas, R. S. (1998). Realigning corporate governance: Shareholder activism by labor unions. *Michigan Law Review, 96,* 1018–1094.

Securities Regulations and Law Report. (1985). *Economists urge SEC to resist pleas for curbs on hostile takeovers.* Securities Regulations and Law Report. February 22, pp. 329–332.

Servaes, H. (1996). The value of diversification during the conglomerate merger wave. *Journal of Finance, 51,* 1201–1225.

Shleifer, A., & Vishny, R. W. (1989). Management entrenchment. *Journal of Financial Economics, 25,* 123–139.

Shleifer, A., & Vishny, R. W. (1997). A survey of corporate governance. *The Journal of Finance, 52,* 737–783.

Sloan, A. P. (1963). *My years with general motors.* Garden City, NJ: Doubleday.

Sorkin, A. R. (2009). *Too big to fail: The inside story of how Wall Street and Washington fought to save the financial system – and themselves.* New York: Viking.

Strang, D., & Meyer, J. W. (1994). Institutional conditions for diffusion. In: W. R. Scott & J. W. Meyer (Eds), *Institutional environments and organization: Structural complexity and individualism.* Thousand Oaks, CA: Sage.

Teece, D. J. (1982). Towards an economic theory of the multi-product firm. *Journal of Economic Behavior and Organization, 3,* 39–63.

Useem, M. (1984). *The inner circle: Large corporations and the rise of business political activity in the U.S. and U.K.* New York: Oxford University Press.

Useem, M. (1993). *Executive defense: Shareholder power and corporate reorganization.*
    Cambridge, MA: Harvard University Press.
Useem, M. (1996). *Investor capitalism: How money managers are changing the face of corporate
    America.* New York: Basic.
Villalonga, B. (2004). Does diversification cause the "Diversification discount? *Financial
    Management, 33,* 5–27.
Walther, T. (1997). *Reinventing the CFO: Moving from financial management to strategic
    management.* New York: McGraw Hill.
Weisbach, M. S. (1988). Outside directors and CEO turnover. *Journal of Financial Economics,
    20,* 431–460.
Wernerfelt, B., & Montgomery, C. A. (1988). Tobin's Q and the importance of focus in firm
    performance. *American Economic Review, 78,* 246–250.
Westphal, J. D., & Zajac, E. J. (1998). The symbolic management of stockholders: Corporate
    governance reforms and shareholder reactions. *Administrative Science Quarterly, 43,*
    127–153.
Whitley, R. (1986). The transformation of business finance into financial economics: The roles
    of academic expansion and changes in U.S. capital markets. *Accounting, Organizations
    and Society, 11,* 171–192.
Williamson, O. E. (1975). *Markets and hierarchies, analysis and antitrust implications: A study in
    the economics of internal organization.* New York: Free Press.
Zajac, E. J., & Westphal, J. D. (2004). The social construction of market value:
    Institutionalization and learning perspective on stock market reactions. *American
    Sociological Review, 69,* 433–457.
Zuckerman, E. W. (1999). The categorical imperative: Securities analysts and the illegitimacy
    discount. *American Journal of Sociology, 104,* 1398–1438.
Zuckerman, E. W. (2000). Focusing the corporate product: Securities analysts and
    de-diversification. *Administrative Science Quarterly, 45,* 591–619.

NEOLIBERALISM IN CRISIS:
REGULATORY ROOTS OF
THE U.S. FINANCIAL MELTDOWN

John L. Campbell

ABSTRACT

Social scientists have long been interested in how political institutions affect economic performance. Nowhere are these effects more apparent today than in the current U.S. financial meltdown. This article offers an analysis of the meltdown by showing how government regulation among other things helped cause it. Specifically, the article shows how regulatory reforms closely associated with neoliberalism created perverse incentives that contributed significantly to the increased lending in the mortgage market and increased speculation in other financial markets even as such behavior was becoming increasingly risky. The result was the failure of mortgage firms, banks, a major insurance company, and eventually the market for short-term business loans, which triggered a general liquidity crisis thereby thrusting the entire economy into a severe recession. Implications for future research are explored. The article also offers a few policy prescriptions and an assessment of their political viability going forward.

Markets on Trial: The Economic Sociology of the U.S. Financial Crisis: Part B
Research in the Sociology of Organizations, Volume 30B, 65–101
Copyright © 2010 by Emerald Group Publishing Limited
All rights of reproduction in any form reserved
ISSN: 0733-558X/doi:10.1108/S0733-558X(2010)000030B007

Social scientists have long been interested in how political institutions affect economic performance. Nowhere is the importance of these effects more apparent than in the meltdown that occurred in the U.S. housing market and quickly spread to the financial services sector in 2008 thereby precipitating the worst economic catastrophe in America since the Great Depression. I explain how the meltdown stemmed from a variety of regulatory policies stretching back to the 1970s – policies associated to a significant degree with the rise of neoliberalism, a loose bundle of conservative ideas and policy prescriptions including less government regulation, lower taxes and more. In other words, the financial meltdown is the manifestation of a broader crisis of neoliberalism.

The theoretical and political stakes here are high. Since the late 1970s national politics in the United States has been dominated increasingly by neoliberals who have argued that less government regulation is better for the economy. They have also argued that markets in the United States – one of the most lightly regulated economies in the OECD to begin with – are too tightly regulated and ought to be freed to a large extent from the state's grip. This, of course, is a view that is rooted in the classical writings of Friedrich Hayek (1944) and Milton Friedman (1962) who argued for free markets and against any form of state planning or state intervention into the economy other than for purposes of rectifying the most serious market failures or negative externalities. The largely unbridled pursuit of self-interest, they believed, facilitated the most efficient market behavior and, in turn, the most effective route to economic development and prosperity. This view came to political fruition in the United States with the election of Ronald Reagan as President in 1980 and has been pursued since then in varying degree by all presidents through George W. Bush.

Economic sociologists and historians disagree with this view. They have argued that market activity is always embedded in and constituted by political rules and regulations – that is, formal and informal political institutions including property rights (Campbell & Lindberg, 1990; Carruthers & Ariovich, 2004; Fligstein, 2001; North, 1990; Schneiberg, 1999). Indeed, these institutions are the essential fabric on which markets depend (Campbell, 2004; North, 2005). Without such regulatory institutions, they argue, markets are eventually doomed to failure and even collapse (Abolafia, 1996; Polanyi, 1944). Financial markets in particular require the state to deploy regulations in order to check excessive risk taking that could lead to speculative booms.[1] They also require the state to serve as the lender of last resort in order to contain collateral damage when speculative booms turn into busts (Kindleberger, 1978; Minsky, 1986). In the end there is no such thing as a truly free market. Following this line of reasoning I will show that the financial meltdown in 2008 stemmed not from too much regulation but too little. The inadequacy of regulation in the financial services industry encouraged the development of an ever more abundant supply of credit in the housing market in ways that sowed the seeds of the financial meltdown.

Some readers might wonder why I want to make this argument against neoliberalism now. After all, Barack Obama won the presidency in large part because he presented a clear alternative to neoliberalism. And since the financial meltdown occurred many have called for Washington to beef up its regulatory oversight of the financial services industry – including such previously staunch neoliberal advocates as Alan Greenspan, former chairman of the Federal Reserve Board, and Arthur Levitt, former chairman of the Securities and Exchange Commission (SEC). Yet, as I will explain, there are still powerful forces arguing and lobbying hard against regulatory reform in this industry and who want to preserve the neoliberal status quo. In my view, if they win, then the chances for another crisis will not have diminished significantly. That is why my argument needs to be made.

This is a story about what some might call deregulation – a shift toward a lighter regulatory burden. There is much debate about whether neoliberal reform involved deregulation. Some argue instead that it entailed only a reconfiguration and not a reduction in the overall regulatory burden on business (Braithwaite, 2009; Schneiberg & Bartley, 2008; Vogel, 1996). In the financial services industry, as we shall see, regulatory reform involved three things since the late 1970s. In a few cases state oversight and responsibility for financial markets was dramatically reduced although not eliminated entirely in a manner akin to deregulation in the conventional sense. More often, however, regulations were revised or reconfigured – not reduced. And on rare occasions as new markets were developing in the first place regulations were not imposed on them at all. But even then it turned out that the state was prepared to move swiftly into these as well as other financial markets as the lender of last resort when they began to collapse and threaten the rest of the economy.

Market regulation is a highly contested political process. The regulatory and other institutions in which market activity is embedded are political settlements born from power struggles, negotiation and compromise. They reflect the balance of political power. When that balance shifts, so too may the rules and regulations that govern markets (Campbell, 2004; Campbell, Hollingsworth, & Lindberg, 1991; Fligstein, 2001; Knight, 2001; Schneiberg, 1999). I will not discuss the politics involved in the many regulatory and other reforms described in this article. My intent is to focus on the effects – not the causes – of these reforms. But as several articles in this volume make clear neoliberal reform was always a politically contested process that involved powerful actors inside and outside the state – including members of the financial services industry and their political allies whose influence was especially pronounced on several very important occasions that contributed to the financial meltdown (e.g., Krippner, 2010; Mizruchi, 2010).

The causes of the meltdown are complicated. Some regulatory factors were more proximate to the meltdown than others. Moreover, the meltdown was not entirely due to regulatory policies (Jickling, 2009). For instance, technological advances in securities trading and risk assessment contributed to the story. I am not, however, arguing for some sort of regulatory or political determinism. The regulatory policies discussed here created incentives and constrained behavior such that the probability of a financial meltdown occurring was significant. But it was not inevitable. People may choose to do things other than what these regulatory incentives would encourage. In the end, however, these incentives and constraints were strong enough to contribute in important ways to the meltdown.

The causes of the meltdown are complicated for another reason too. Beginning in the late 1970s a variety of regulatory reforms occurred that contributed to the ultimate crash. Some were more important than others. And their effects accumulated slowly over time. Not all of them spelled disaster immediately because it was only after they were combined with particularly risky lending practices in the housing market that their collective effects began to emerge. In other words, it is impossible to point to a single cause of the meltdown. There were a considerable number of regulatory and other institutional reforms involved. This was a crisis that was long and complex in the making (see also Fligstein & Goldstein, 2010).

I begin by briefly reviewing the events of 2008 that constituted the financial meltdown. This story is well-known but is only the tip of a much more complicated regulatory iceberg that requires explanation. To provide that explanation I turn next to the regulatory underpinnings of the events of 2008. These include a variety of government policy decisions – some longstanding, others more recent. They also include a few decisions in the private sector but decisions that were still facilitated by or otherwise connected indirectly with regulatory policies of various sorts. Among the myriad regulatory reforms and practices in question, three stand out as being especially central to the financial meltdown: banking reforms that facilitated the development of a tightly coupled shadow banking system through which financial problems reverberated with alarming speed and damage in 2008; the absence of regulation of over-the-counter markets for asset-backed securities, which enabled firms to create and sell high-risk investment products at will; and lackadaisical oversight of the credit rating agencies whose extremely rosy assessments of these asset-backed securities convinced investors that these products were much safer than they turned out to be. Finally, I discuss the story's implications for future research and public policy going forward. I call for new regulations to separate commercial and investment banking; to regulate over-the-counter securities trading; and to establish new forms of payment and new rating practices in the credit rating industry.

THE FINANCIAL MELTDOWN IN BRIEF

As is now well-known, the catalyst for financial meltdown in late 2008 was the collapse of a bubble in the U.S. housing market and a rapid decline of housing prices beginning in late 2006. Driving the growth of this bubble in the first place was the increased availability of inexpensive mortgage credit, thanks in part to the Federal Reserve Board's low interest rates. But it was also due to the increased availability of subprime mortgages.[2] When the housing bubble burst people began to default on their loans in record numbers. This was especially true for those with subprime mortgages (Gwinner & Sanders, 2008; Standard and Poor's, 2009).

In turn, rising delinquencies set off a chain of events that reverberated through the mortgage, banking and insurance industries and eventually brought the entire financial system to the verge of collapse. First, mortgage companies failed including the New Century Financial, Countrywide, the Federal National Mortgage Association (Fannie Mae) and the Federal Home Mortgage Corporation (Freddie Mac). The latter two are government-sponsored entities with access to a credit line from the U.S. Treasury and an exemption from SEC oversight. Countrywide was bought by Bank of America in a deal orchestrated by the federal government. Fannie and Freddie were put into conservatorships by the federal government, which took over nearly 80% of their stock.

Second, banks failed. Because many of these risky subprime mortgages were frequently bundled with other types of loans as structured asset-backed securities and sold to banks and other investors, the collateral damage was unprecedented.[3] In March 2008, Bear Stearns was taken over by the Federal Deposit Insurance Corporation (FDIC) and sold to J.P. Morgan Chase. A similar fate awaited Washington Mutual a few months later. That fall several other large banks failed, including Merrill Lynch and Wachovia, and were bought by other banks. Finally, Lehman Brothers went bankrupt after the federal government decided not to bail it out for fear of creating perverse moral hazard incentives for other banks in the future. As a result, the markets for mortgages and bundled mortgage-backed securities began to seize up as concerns about the risky nature of these financial instruments started coming to light. In turn, mortgage firms and banks began to tighten their lending practices. Credit markets began to contract (Bank for International Settlements, 2008).

Third, the American International Group (AIG) faced collapse. Just prior to the meltdown it was the world's largest insurer. Many banks had purchased insurance called credit default swaps from AIG just in case the mortgage backed securities they held turned sour as a result of mortgage defaults.[4] So when the housing bubble burst and mortgage defaults mounted, AIG was faced with the calamitous possibility of an unprecedented number of payment claims being filed all at once against the swaps that it had sold. As a result, AIG's credit rating was downgraded and it found itself unable to raise enough new capital to cover its potential losses. Its stock value plunged. Concerned that AIG's failure would bring down other banks and investment firms, in September 2008 the federal government provided an initial $85 billion bailout loan in exchange for a 79.9% equity stake in the company. As AIG's situation continued to deteriorate the government put up more money bringing the total to $182 billion by March 2009.

Fourth, the crisis spread and the general credit market failed. AIG's problems sent shock waves through the financial community. Because many subprime mortgages had been bundled with other forms of debt and sold to investors many times over, nobody really knew where all of the subprime mortgages were, who owned them, or how many of them were in danger of default. And now nobody could be sure that the insurance (i.e., credit default swaps) that they had purchased in the event of default would cover the losses that they might incur. Without complete knowledge about how many of these potentially toxic assets they were holding or whether their swaps would actually cover the losses they might suffer, banks and other lenders further tightened their lending practices trying to keep as much capital on hand as possible.

The demise of Lehman Brothers amplified all of this. Lehman's bankruptcy undermined confidence in some of the safest investments – money market funds – and, in turn, the commercial paper market. Money market funds invest mainly in commercial paper, which are very short-term loans that businesses frequently take out to finance things like inventories and payrolls while waiting for payment from customers. The commercial paper market greases the day-to-day operation of the economy. One of these very large money market funds, the Reserve Primary Fund, had invested about $785 million of its investors' money in Lehman Brothers debt. So after Lehman collapsed people's investments with Reserve Primary began to lose value and they started pulling their money out of Reserve Primary and then similar mutual funds (Bruno, 2008). Concerned that such a run on the money markets could imperil the commercial paper market and bring the entire economy to its knees, the Fed intervened by providing liquidity to money market investors thereby ensuring existing money market deposits much like the FDIC guarantees bank deposits. Nevertheless, money market fund managers had been spooked and grew exceedingly cautious in lending. As a result, businesses began to see their lines of credit dry up as a general liquidity crisis suddenly gripped the entire economy. The economy had already been in recession since late 2007 but now it began to deteriorate rapidly.

The federal government moved swiftly to contain the damage. In October 2008, Congress passed the Troubled Asset Relief Program (TARP), which was intended to ease the credit markets by injecting them with $700 billion. In December, the Fed lowered its benchmark interest rate to nearly zero. In February 2009, Congress passed a $787 billion package of tax cuts and spending designed to stimulate the economy. A few days later the president announced another plan, which, if passed by Congress, would provide up to $275 billion more in direct spending to homeowners as well as additional financing to Freddie and Fannie to stabilize the mortgage market. The Treasury also announced in February a plan to muster as much as $2.5 trillion from the Fed and private investors to remove the toxic assets currently owned by the banks and to inject additional money into the financial system. All of this was designed to ease the credit crisis and get capital flowing again.

It is important not to lose sight of the key theoretical point in all of this detail. In the sense that the state was poised to intervene as the lender of last resort when the financial markets got into serious trouble these markets were never free markets at all. Federal agencies moved into the mortgage and banking markets rescuing several lenders including Bear Stearns, Washington Mutual, Fannie Mae, and Freddie Mac. They moved into the insurance market rescuing AIG and thereby protecting all of the investors in the asset-backed securities market who had purchased AIG swaps. They moved into the commercial paper market rescuing the money market funds by guaranteeing investors that their money market deposits were safe.

And they provided hundreds of billions of dollars to the banks through TARP to ease the liquidity crisis in the credit markets overall – an effort that was supplemented by the Fed dropping interest rates to an historic low. This was matched eventually by Congress, which provided several hundred billion dollars more in economic stimulus to pull the economy out of recession. Finally, the government planned additional moves to bail out troubled homeowners in the mortgage markets and help banks clear toxic assets off of their books. It is an open question whether the financial markets faith in the state's capacity and willingness to serve as the lender of last resort created moral hazards that contributed to the meltdown. But the fact is that when the chips were down, the state moved swiftly as the lender of last resort.

There is, however, a second sense in which the financial markets were not free markets. A variety of regulatory moves by the state affected how they were organized and how they performed in the first place. Much of this had the effect of aligning incentives among market actors so as to reinforce what we now know to have been excessive risk taking. These moves helped facilitate the disastrous chain reaction discussed above. To understand how this happened, we need to look closer at these regulatory moves.

REGULATORY ROOTS OF THE MELTDOWN

As noted above, the financial meltdown was triggered by a collapse of the housing market and its follow-on effects. The long-term economic roots of precarious mortgage debt – and consumer debt more generally – stretch back to the mid-1970s. As is well-known, wage stagnation since the 1970s pervaded the middle class and lower classes (Mishel, Bernstein, & Allegretto, 2005, p. 42). This made it increasingly difficult for families to maintain the standard of living that their parents' generation had enjoyed (Levy, 1998, Chapter 2; Mishel et al., 2005, p. 102). One way for them to do this was by borrowing money. Household debt rose from just under 80% of disposable income in 1986 to 140% by 2007. Much of this increase was due to rising mortgage debt (*The Economist*, 2008, p. 12; Leicht & Fitzgerald, 2007, Chapter 3).

But why were American families able to borrow so much money when, given their increasingly more tenuous earnings stream, their ability to repay that debt would seem to have become ever more questionable? The answer is twofold. First, the supply of consumer credit increased. And, second, the reason for this was that the financial services industry was engaging in increasingly risky investment behavior. Both were influenced by regulatory reform.

Supply of Mortgage Credit Grows

To be sure, an important factor contributing to rising consumer debt had little to do with regulatory change. This was monetary policy. During much of the 1990s until 1999 the Federal Reserve Board maintained low interest rates. It also did so in the aftermath of the 2000 dot-com stock market crash and subsequent recession during which time it cut the federal funds rate to 1%, leaving it there for a year and then raising it only timidly after that. So as consumers were turning increasingly to the credit markets to help maintain their standards of living, the price of credit was kept especially low. Nowhere was this more evident than in the housing market where mortgage rates were very low. When combined with unconventional mortgages, such as subprimes, the government in effect enticed families to incur more debt. Beyond monetary policy, however, several regulatory changes were also involved.

To begin with, the market for subprime mortgages soared in part after 2004 because the two government-backed mortgage giants, Fannie Mae and Freddie Mac, began buying up huge swaths of subprime mortgages. They did so in response to political pressure from Washington where politicians wanted to expand the financing for housing for the middle class. Fannie and Freddie's move to buy up subprime mortgages institutionalized the congressional will to help people buy homes. And it created additional incentives for mortgage lenders to make subprime loans because they knew that they could turn around and sell the mortgages to Fannie and Freddie. In effect, then, Fannie and Freddie began to regulate albeit informally how much money was available in the mortgage market. This in combination with the Fed's low interest rates and speculative building contributed to a booming housing market, rising property values and a housing bubble that finally burst in 2006. Sales fell off, housing prices dropped, and the housing industry began to experience a recession. This was compounded by the fact that in 2004 the Fed began raising interest rates to check inflation. This move increased adjustable subprime mortgage interest rates to a point where many homeowners could no longer afford to pay them and faced foreclosure (*The Economist*, 2008, pp. 10–20). And the decline in housing prices dashed many homeowners' hopes of refinancing these mortgages at lower rates.

A second factor contributing to the booming subprime market were regulatory reforms that helped encourage the development of a market for so-called nonconforming mortgages outside the model specified by Fannie, Freddie, and other government-sponsored enterprises (GSEs). Following problems with accounting and governance at these organizations, the GSE's capacity to expand lending was capped by new regulatory limits from the George W. Bush administration. This was also due to the administration's desire to reduce the dominance of GSEs in the mortgage market and foster more competition among private companies – a clear move in a neoliberal direction. The reform created an opportunity for private lenders to go into the mortgage markets in greater numbers, which they did. New entrants included large investment banks operating through recently acquired mortgage lending subsidiaries. At the same time, however, mortgage lending was becoming less profitable due to a wave of refinancing at low interest rates during the early 2000s. In other words, more private lenders were moving into a market whose profitability was declining. In order to compensate for declining profits these lenders began relaxing requirements in order to qualify more borrowers and sell more mortgages. These included new but riskier types of mortgages such as subprimes. For instance, second mortgages became easier to obtain and were often hidden from the originator of the first mortgage. In 1999, less than 1% of all subprime first mortgage loans had a so-called "silent second" attached to them but by 2006 more than 25% did (Ellis, 2008; Gramlich, 2007).

A third policy change – the 1986 Tax Reform Act – was complicit in this. The federal tax code has long permitted homeowners to deduct from their income taxes the interest paid on their mortgages. This was done in order to stimulate private home ownership after the Second World War. The tax code also let them deduct interest for other forms of consumer debt. However, the 1986 Act eliminated the latter interest deduction but allowed an unlimited interest deduction for mortgages on both first and second homes (Conlan, Wrightson, & Beam, 1990, p. 265). This created additional incentives for people to take out second mortgages on their homes. Why? Second mortgages provided a way to finance their spending and still benefit from an interest deduction.

A fourth part of the story involved the incentives institutionalized within mortgage companies that encouraged loan officers to lend to risky borrowers in order to boost profits and salaries. For example, at Washington Mutual, a bank deeply engaged in subprime mortgage lending, underwriters, who approved loan applications brought to them by brokers, faced intense pressure from management and brokers to approve mortgages despite concerns about the quality of the loans. According to one senior underwriter, volume was paramount and risky loans were pushed through because they were profitable to the company. As discussed in the next section, this was because even the riskiest mortgages could be easily packaged as asset-backed securities and sold to investors leaving the company free of losses if there was a default. And brokers pushed the mortgages hard because they could make hefty commissions. If underwriters resisted pressure to approve risky mortgages, they were punished and in some cases fired (MacKenzie, 2008; Morgenson, 2008).

Fifth, although these lending practices were devised by actors in the private sector they were embedded in a wider set of regulatory policies that facilitated shoddy mortgage lending practices. To begin with, thanks to regulatory reform independent lenders – that is, nondepository entities – were under much less regulatory authority than traditional mortgage lenders, such as commercial banks. For instance, in 1982 the Alternative Mortgage Transactions Parity Act became law allowing nonfederally chartered mortgage companies to write adjustable mortgages, such as those with interest-only payment and balloon payment schemes that were sold to subprime customers. These riskier mortgages eventually replaced many conventional fixed rate mortgages that had long been the norm in the conventional banking industry. Furthermore, in 2004 the Office of the Comptroller of the Currency (OCC) passed rules by which federally regulated lenders were exempted from state regulations, which were often stricter than federal regulations. Some of the practices banned under some state laws but that were now legal under the OCC ruling included mortgage prepayment penalties and balloon payments that tend to increase the risk associated with such loans and raise default rates (Ellis, 2008). In hindsight, the Obama administration recognized that at the root of shoddy lending practices had been a breakdown in mortgage underwriting standards enabled by lax or nonexistent regulation and a broad relaxation of discipline in the mortgage market (*The New York Times*, 2009, p. 41).[5]

In sum, several factors conspired to provide a greater supply of credit to consumers in the housing market. Almost all of them involved state regulation demonstrating again that the organization and functioning of markets is heavily affected by the state even in liberal market economies like the United States. These factors included Fannie and Freddie's move to buy up more subprime mortgages; regulatory limits to the activities of GSEs that created an opportunity for more private lenders to enter and compete in the mortgage market; changes in the tax treatment of interest on consumer loans; insufficient oversight of mortgage lending practices; regulatory permission to write riskier adjustable-rate mortgages; and regulatory exemption of some lenders from more rigorous state-level regulations.

In other words, the state helped create a set of institutional conditions that aligned incentives toward riskier and more competitive market behavior. However, this story of reckless mortgage lending was facilitated by another set of very widespread innovations in the broader financial services industry that put increasing sums of money at the disposal of mortgage lenders in the first place. These changes also encouraged riskier behavior, particularly among large investment banks and insurance companies that stood behind mortgage lenders. Among the most important were banking reform, a decision not to regulate derivatives markets, and lackadaisical oversight of credit rating and risk assessment.

Risky Behavior Grows in the Financial Services Industry

Banking Regulation
One of the most important sets of regulatory reforms that laid the foundation for the financial meltdown involved the banking sector. To begin with, interstate banking had long been effectively prohibited by state law. But Maine passed legislation in 1978 that permitted out-of-state banks to operate in the state. Other states eventually followed suit. In 1994, the federal government passed the Interstate Banking and Branching Efficiency Act, which mandated interstate banking by 1997 unless a state explicitly chose to opt out, which only two did. Banks based in one state could now operate branches in other states without explicit permission from these state regulatory authorities. This allowed banks to move to states that permitted higher interest rates on loans of various sorts. In turn, this triggered competition among state governments to relax their usury laws or risk losing banking business as banks moved to states with higher interest rate ceilings. Additionally, the U.S. Supreme court ruled in its "Marquette" decision of 1978 that banks and other lenders could charge interest rates whose ceilings would be limited only by the usury laws in their home state regardless of which other states they might be operating in even if the usury laws in these other states were more restrictive than in the home state (Ellis, 1998). Two years later Jimmy Carter signed the Depository Institutions Deregulation and Monetary Control Act, which phased out interest rate ceilings altogether and effectively eliminated state usury ceilings for residential mortgages and other bank loans (Federal Reserve Bank of Boston, 1980). Thus, thanks to regulatory reform lending became more profitable and so banks began offering more and more credit – often in new and riskier ways like giving credit cards to college students and selling subprime mortgages

(Leicht & Fitzgerald, 2007, Chapter 4; Strahan, 2002). The turn toward riskier lending practices was reflected not just in rising consumer debt, but also in a quadrupling of bankruptcies between 1978 and 1996 (Ellis, 1998).

More important still, the Glass-Steagall Act, which had separated most insurance, commercial and investment banking services since 1933, was repealed in 1999 by the Gramm–Leach–Bliley Financial Services Modernization Act – legislation that was driven politically by a desire to let banks diversify and grow in order to compete effectively in international markets. The banking and insurance industries strongly supported the new law. Its chief sponsor, Senator Phil Gramm (R-Texas), was an avid neoliberal and long-time advocate of banking deregulation. But Democrats supported it too like Robert Rubin, former cochair of Goldman Sachs, who actively supported the repeal when he was Treasury Secretary in the Clinton administration (Stiglitz, 2003, p. 160). Following its passage several huge mergers occurred (e.g., Bank of America's merger with Fleet Bank of Boston) or were solidified after having received temporary waivers to Glass-Steagall before it was repealed (e.g., the Citigroup conglomerate formed through the combination of Citibank, Smith Barney, Shearson, Primerica, and Travelers Insurance).

One important ramification of the growth of these huge financial institutions was an increase in their access to capital through means other than traditional bank deposits, such as borrowing. This raised the possibility for them to develop a wide range of elaborate, complex, and potentially risky financial instruments for investment purposes. The fact that this risk might be significantly greater than investors initially anticipated was reflected in the costs to investors of insurance against such risk – credit default swaps – which skyrocketed beginning in early 2006 (Bank for International Settlements, 2008).

In short, the Gramm–Leach–Bliley legislation facilitated the rapid growth of the so-called "shadow banking system," which was populated by increasingly large nonbank financial companies that channeled funds from investors to corporations through new securities, such as asset-backed securities and credit default swaps. Examples of organizations in the shadow banking system include investment banks (e.g., Goldman Sachs, Morgan Stanley, Lehman Brothers, Bear Stearns, Merrill Lynch), hedge funds (e.g., Long-Term Capital Management), money funds (e.g., Primary Reserve Fund), and other nonbank financial companies. Arguably, the development of the shadow banking system was one of the root causes of the financial meltdown because it was responsible for creating and selling asset-backed securities in the first place. The sums involved in the shadow banking system by 2007 were staggering. The five largest investment banks, for example, had combined assets worth about $4 trillion and U.S. hedge funds had assets worth about $1.8 trillion. The shadow banking system did not accept deposits like a commercial bank and, therefore, was not subject to the same safety and soundness regulations as traditional banks, such as capitalization requirements. During the 2000s the assets held by the U.S. shadow banking system grew to *exceed* the $10 trillion held by the traditional banking system (*The Economist*, 2009a, p. 18; Geithner, 2008; Wolf, 2009b).[6]

Securities Regulation
Several changes in securities regulation helped open up new and riskier credit markets for the shadow banking system. First, the SEC issued regulations that fostered the development in the 1990s of booming markets for asset-backed securities. About 70% of this market, which was comprised of $6.6 trillion of tradable securities in 2002, involved mortgage-backed securities issued primarily by government-backed lenders, notably Fannie Mae and Freddie Mac. A substantial portion of the rest involved credit card debt. The securitization of credit card debt through asset-backed securities was introduced in the mid-1980s by Banc One Corporation and laid the foundation for what is now a $400 billion asset-backed securities market in credit card debt alone. The development of the asset-backed securities market contributed directly to the explosion in consumer debt in the United States. Issuing mortgages and other loans became more attractive as traders could buy and sell bundles of these securities in ways that could be very profitable. In turn, this created incentives for lenders to make more credit available to those who wanted to borrow – even if the borrowers were willing to shoulder more debt than may have been financially prudent for them. In some cases, lenders bent over backwards to extend credit, such as by offering extremely low interest rates for the first year or two of the loan. And, as we have seen, consumers took the bait in order to borrow as a way to compensate for their faltering earnings and savings (Leicht & Fitzgerald, 2007, Chapter 5).

Second, and of paramount importance, once the asset-backed securities market began to flourish, the government decided in classic neoliberal fashion not to regulate it. As discussed above, asset-backed securities are financial derivatives – that is, financial instruments whose value is derived from the value of something else. The value of the derivative, such as a bundle of mortgages, is derived from the presumed value of the group of securities that constitute it. As the complexity of these instruments grew concerns mounted that they involved substantial risk, but risk that was exceedingly difficult to evaluate given their complexity. This is why in 2003 multibillionaire financier Warren Buffett described them as financial weapons of mass destruction. Why they were not regulated requires some explanation because the unbridled operation of the derivatives markets was another root cause of the financial meltdown.

In 1982, Congress banned trading stock-futures because the SEC, which regulates stock trading, and the Commodity Futures Trading Commission (CFTC), which regulates commodities futures trading, could not agree who should have regulatory jurisdiction over them. However, political pressure to permit their trading mounted because there was demand for these instruments and they were being traded profitably in Europe. Eventually, legislation was passed by Congress and signed by Clinton in 2000. The Commodity Futures Modernization Act, as it was called, was again cosponsored by Phil Gramm and other neoliberals among others. It removed the trading ban on stock-futures. But it also did something else particularly germane to the financial meltdown.

In 1998, Brooksley Born, Chair of the CFTC, proposed that asset-backed securities and other over-the-counter derivatives, particularly credit default swaps, should be regulated. Over-the-counter trades are privately conducted between two parties rather than on an exchange, where they would be subject to regulation and much greater transparency. During the booming stock market of the 1990s, these and other new but unregulated financial instruments were emerging and proving to be extremely lucrative.[7] The sort of regulation Born proposed would have dampened the ability of lenders to make so much credit available to consumers in the first place because it would have required holders of asset-backed securities to increase the capitalization of their firms in order to cover the risks associated with these investments, which would have reduced the amount of money they had to lend. However, the idea went nowhere as it ran into strong opposition from Federal Reserve Board chairman Alan Greenspan, SEC Chairman Arthur Levitt, and Treasury Secretary Robert Rubin, who all warned that regulation would undermine the efficiency with which they believed these new, exciting and profitable markets were operating (Wade, 2008, p. 14). The Commodity Futures Modernization Act officially preempted deriva- tives like these from government oversight. It also excluded from regulatory oversight credit default swaps for which by late 2008, there was a $60 trillion market (Cox, 2008). This was extremely important. It is reasonable to assume that without such swap insurance, prospective buyers would have been much less likely to have purchased asset-backed securities. So the decision not to regulate swaps made it even easier for companies to issue them and therefore contributed further to the growth of the asset-backed securities market. All of this meant that credit continued to flow more and more easily and especially to the housing market.

The importance of credit default swaps cannot be underestimated. As discussed previously, banks, securities firms, hedge funds, and others bought swaps from insurers like AIG in order to absolve themselves of responsibility for the financial risks associated with asset-backed securities investments. Insofar as banks were concerned, which were regulated and faced capitalization requirements, buying swaps also saved them from having to put capital aside to cover such risks as the regulations required. Hence, what would have been lower-rated securities were converted into higher-rated securities because they were covered by credit default swaps. This, of course, gave further impetus to the drive to invest in these complicated and, as it turned out, quite risky investments (*The Economist*, 2009a, p. 20). As Mitchell Abolafia (2010) argues at length, poor regulation of this sort created opportunities and incentives for extreme opportunism in the financial services markets.

Capitalization Requirements

SEC regulatory reforms contributed further to the availability of consumer and mortgage credit as well as riskier investments by securities firms and investment banks by easing in 2004 the capitalization requirements of these organizations.[8] The rule allowed these firms to shift capital from safer to riskier and potentially more profitable investments. Under the old rules, securities firms had to reserve a set percentage of every dollar of capital at risk to ensure solvency in the event of a market collapse or failure of a major client. Under the new rules, reserves are determined according to a more complex and nuanced calculation of risks including things like adverse market movements or changes in legislation. More important for our purposes, the new rules also let firms use noncash assets, such as derivative contracts, to offset risk. This freed up more capital to use as collateral in order to borrow money for leveraging investments. All of this was done to keep Wall Street firms competitive with their European counterparts by allowing these firms to shift capital from traditionally safe investments to riskier ones. The large investment banks lobbied hard for the ruling. Prior to the change the leverage ratio for these firms was typically about 12 to 1 but afterwards it shot up to about 33 to 1 for the industry. The five biggest Wall Street firms increased their leverage to nearly 27 to 1 by the end of 2005 as they began adjusting to the new rules (Blinder, 2009b; Onaran, 2007).

Additionally, the 2004 SEC ruling established a program whereby investment bank conglomerates (e.g., Goldman Sachs, Morgan Stanley, Merrill Lynch, Lehman Brothers, and Bear Stearns) need only agree *voluntarily* to SEC oversight of their capitalization, liquidity, and leverage positions. In order to avoid having their European operations regulated by the European Union they needed to be regulated in the United States, which is one reason why they pressed for the ruling. It turned out that voluntary regulation did not work because investment banks could opt in or out of supervision voluntarily and because they were not subject to specific legal authority of any other government agency. Hence, the SEC eventually shut down the program in September 2008 after it became clear that its lack of oversight was a contributing factor to the financial meltdown (Cox, 2008). But by then it was too late.

Risk Assessment
Underlying much of the shift toward riskier and more highly leveraged investments was a problem with evaluating the risk involved in the new and more complicated financial instruments like asset-backed securities and other forms of derivatives, which were exceedingly complicated to value. This was a major problem that government regulators left almost entirely to the private sector much to their explicit regret later. Had it not been for lackadaisical and highly misleading risk assessment investors would likely have been much less eager to purchase the risky asset-backed securities being offered in the derivatives markets by the shadow banking system.

Investment firms have risk managers who are responsible for evaluating the risks associated with their firm's various investments. At most firms risk managers were not viewed as profit centers. Although some of them began warning about the risky nature of the investments being made, they were largely ignored. They lacked the clout of the traders who were making fortunes for their firms (and for themselves) by dealing in these complicated securities. Trader's livelihoods depended on finding new ways to make money as did the competitive advantage of their financial firms. So as incentives to engage in these new and extremely lucrative financial instruments mounted the warnings of risk managers were often ignored (Dash & Crewsell, 2008; Nocera, 2009b).

Moreover, it became easy to ignore these warnings because firms that had created these financial instruments developed complicated mathematical models to assess the risk involved. The most widely used model was Value at Risk (VaR), developed by J.P. Morgan in the early 1990s and then distributed to anyone who wanted to use it. Eventually, the SEC began to worry about the amount of risk that derivatives posed and mandated that financial firms disclose the amount of such risk to investors. But the SEC left it up to the private sector to figure out how to do this. Hence, VaR became the de facto standard that almost everyone used for doing this. It turned out, however, that there were several problems with the model. Its projections were based on short two-year data histories. It ignored the slim possibility of giant losses, which could only occur through a catastrophic event, such as a 20% fall in house prices. It did not account for falling mortgage underwriting standards or certain kinds of leverage that might be involved with derivatives. Hence, unbeknownst to most people who used the model, it underestimated some of the low probability/high cost risks involved. Because it did so most corporate managers and regulators remained sanguine about the perils of derivatives, asset-backed securities, credit default swaps, and the like. In turn, because regulators used VaR to determine how much capital banks needed to put aside, it also contributed to the under capitalization problem (*The Economist*, 2009a, p. 13; Nocera, 2009b).

As Bruce Carruthers (2010) has detailed, independent credit rating agencies like Moody's, Standard and Poor's, and Fitch exacerbated these problems in very important ways. They assessed the credit worthiness of various financial instruments and the firms issuing them. They encouraged the proliferation of asset-backed securities like mortgage-backed securities by publishing what turned out to be overly optimistic assessments of their quality. In hindsight, this may not be surprising. For one thing, they struggled to keep up with the proliferation and increasing complexity of asset-backed securities and similar instruments during the 2000s. Few rating agencies had specific, comprehensive, written procedures for evaluating them (Casey, 2009). They also used extremely complicated albeit flawed risk assessment models to determine credit worthiness (Tett, 2009). These models typically failed to account for the effects of the U.S. housing bubble, the growth of mechanisms for transferring credit risk like asset-backed securities, and the increased appetite for risky debt in the U.S. housing market. Furthermore, these agencies faced a conflict of interest because they were paid by the issuers of the securities that they were rating. These conflicts were not always managed properly in part because there was no government oversight. This is one reason why in late 2006 Congress passed the Credit Rating Agency Reform Act, which ended a century of self-regulation by the credit rating agencies and gave the SEC jurisdiction over them (Casey, 2009).[9] Prior to that, however, most investor's knowledge of the properties of asset-backed securities and similar products was extremely superficial. It was based chiefly on the ratings, which were assumed to be trustworthy, rather than on a real understanding of the intricacies of the instruments themselves or their risks (MacKenzie, 2008, p. 6). Indeed, these financial instruments were so complicated that they were beyond the comprehension of most bankers, investors, and regulators (Tett, 2009). Hence, markets, regulators, and even the managers of many of the financial firms that were issuing these securities put increasing blind faith in the high credit ratings that these agencies issued (Dash & Crewsell, 2008; MacKenzie, 2008; *The Economist*, 2008).

Investment Bank Public Listing
Of course, the financial meltdown cannot be blamed just on regulatory decisions. For instance, another factor contributing to the propensity for risky behavior among investment banks was repeal by the New York Stock Exchange in 1970 of a rule preventing investment banks from going public – that is, to sell shares of the company on the exchange. Prior to that investment banks were private firms structured as partnerships that relied on the capital provided by the partners to finance operations. In those days investment banks were smaller and their business was more straightforward. Partners were liable for each other's mistakes and the resulting losses. Hence, partners were strongly motivated to monitor each other's behavior and they were more risk averse. But by the end of the 1980s virtually every large Wall Street firm was incorporated and publicly owned – the notable exception being Goldman Sachs, which went public in 1999. Incorporation and public listing lifted the burden of responsibility from the partners' shoulders and enabled them to take advantage of soaring stock prices. In other words, they could now begin to play with other people's money.

Going public also created an opportunity for their executives and top-level managers to be paid in stock options, although traders were still paid overwhelmingly in cash. The turn toward stock options as a key form of executive compensation and the need to keep shareholders happy by boosting daily share-price movements, total shareholder returns and quarterly results created strong incentives for bank executives and the traders and analysts who worked for them to maximize short-term profit even if this entailed taking risks that could have serious downside repercussions in the long term (*The Economist*, 2009a, p. 16; Guerrera, 2009). This too exacerbated the incentives for riskier but potentially very lucrative investment decisions (Stiglitz, 2003, Chapter 3; Surowiecki, 2008). Some of these investments were in new types of securities like the asset-backed securities that were being invented and that were subject to only modest, if any, regulation. Moreover, the amount of money these firms could borrow to leverage their investments increased now that they could increase their capitalization by selling company stock on the exchange. As a result, the aggregate debt of the U.S. financial sector jumped from 22 to 117% of GDP between 1981 and late 2008. Financial sector debt was the fastest growing component of private sector debt since the late 1990s (*The Economist*, 2009b; Wolf, 2009b).

To be sure, going public was a private decision. Yet the Obama administration acknowledges the problems that stemmed from the short-term incentive structure that it created and admits that there should have been more regulation by the state. It has recommended new regulations to align the compensation incentives of brokers and others involved in the securitization process with the long-term performance of the securities they issue, such as by changing accounting practices to better reflect the long-term performance of these securities. The government also wants to peg the fees firms charge to the long-term performance of these securities and reduce them if underwriting or asset quality problems emerge over time (*The New York Times*, 2009, p. 42).

To review briefly, whereas the actual meltdown of the financial services industry illustrates how important the state is for financial markets as the lender of last resort when things turn sour, the factors contributing to the crisis described in this section illustrate how important the state is as a regulator of these markets and how significant its role is in preventing – or causing – the booms that can initially create serious problems. On the one hand, regulatory decisions affected how much risk originators of various securities and the investors who bought them were able to take. For example, exempting over-the-counter derivatives from regulation helped allay concerns about trading asset-backed securities like bundles of subprime mortgages. The SEC's decision to ease capitalization requirements allowed firms to make a larger number of riskier investments. The absence of regulation of the credit rating agencies contributed to inadequate risk assessment of the new derivative securities, which is why Congress eventually imposed SEC oversight on them. On the other hand, regulatory decisions also encouraged the formation and development of some of these markets in the first place. Notably, regulatory reforms in banking facilitated the development of the shadow banking system, which invented many of the risky investment instruments central to the story. SEC securities regulation reform also helped spawn these markets. So did the Commodity Futures Modernization Act, which gave rise to a lucrative market for credit default swaps. Put differently, the state created a number of incentives that fostered ever-riskier market behavior. Not all of the factors contributing to the meltdown involved the state, but many did, especially as they stemmed from deep-seated beliefs in the virtue of relatively free and unfettered markets as the best way to organize an economy. And this brings us to the role of neoliberalism.

THE ROLE OF NEOLIBERALISM

If we stopped the story here it would appear perhaps that the crisis was simply the result of a number of isolated regulatory decisions and reforms and lacked any kind of overarching explanation. I do not believe that this is the case. Instead, many of these reforms were rooted in the rising prominence of neoliberalism as the guiding light for U.S. regulatory policy. The rise of neoliberalism was driven in large part by the financial services industry, especially those on Wall Street, and their powerful allies in Washington (Krippner, 2010). A full-blown and systematic discussion of how each of these regulatory moves stemmed from neoliberalism is well beyond the scope of this article. Nevertheless, some discussion is in order.

According to the National Bureau of Economic Research, the overall level of financial regulation in the United States dropped sharply between 1980 and 2009 (Wolf, 2009a). Nowhere was this more obvious than in the regulatory reform of the banking industry where the Carter administration phased out interest rate ceilings for residential mortgages and various other bank loans and where the Clinton administration supported repeal of the 1933 Glass-Steagall Act – a move that was pushed hard by neoliberals in Congress. Neoliberalism was also evident in the Clinton administration's decision not to regulate over-the-counter derivatives and credit default swaps because various influential members of the administration believed that doing so would stifle the efficiency of emergent markets for these things. Neoliberalism also influenced the Bush administration's SEC decision in 2004 to allow self-regulation of the investment bank conglomerates capitalization, liquidity and leverage positions. And neoliberalism was at the heart of the Bush administration's decision to reduce the dominance of GSEs, like Freddie and Fannie, in the mortgage market by capping their ability to expand lending thus creating new opportunities for private mortgage companies to compete in the market.

But neoliberalism is often about reforming the tax code as well as regulatory structures per se. In this regard, the 1986 Tax Reform Act, which eliminated the interest deduction for consumer debt other than mortgages, is important. This legislation was designed to do two things. First, it was intended to reduce tax rates in accordance with neoliberal ideals about limiting the role of government in the economy by limiting the resources available to it in the first place. Second, it sought to simplify the tax code by eliminating many of the so-called tax expenditures (i.e., loopholes) that had been inserted into the code over the years. This is why the interest deduction for consumer debt was removed. This too was inspired by neoliberalism to the extent that another of its tenets is the simplification of government – including its tax code – in order to make government more efficient. Neoliberalism was also at work insofar as broadening the tax base through loophole reduction was intended to avoid budget deficits that might otherwise result from reduced tax rates. Deficits, of course, are anathema in principle, if not always in practice, to neoliberals.

The fact that the government permitted much self-regulation in the financial services industry is another example of neoliberal ideas. Of course, neoliberalism does not advocate the complete elimination of all regulatory oversight in markets. Enforcement of property rights, for instance, is something neoliberals believe the state must do. But the preference is often for some form of self-regulation by market actors whenever possible, presumably because they would recognize that it is in their collective self-interest to police themselves rather than have the state do it for them. This assumption was put to the test by the financial meltdown. For instance, Washington reined in aggressive regulation by the SEC as part the neoliberal reform movement. This took pressure off self-regulatory associations on Wall Street, such as the National Association of Securities Dealers, which became so passive that traders in some markets were either ignorant or indifferent to its activities. A culture of tolerance resulted, which observers believe was inadequate for inhibiting the sort of opportunism in the markets that we now know caused such havoc (Abolafia, 1996, p. 34–35).

Neoliberal tendencies toward self-regulation also appeared in the area of risk assessment. For example, the troublesome effects of regulatory reform were compounded by the creation of and blind faith in fancy statistical models for estimating risk, credit assessment algorithms, and other cognitive devices that enabled mortgage lenders, financial services companies, investors, borrowers and others to ignore the mounting risks associated with the development of increasingly complicated financial instruments. The adoption of the VaR model as the de facto standard for estimating the risks associated with asset-backed securities and credit default swaps mystified not only the private sector but also government regulators. Here again the state assumed in classic neoliberal fashion that firms would behave responsibly – in this case by developing accurate risk assessment models and heeding the warnings of their own risk assessors when serious risks were detected. Neither of these things happened. Furthermore, the state permitted the credit rating agencies to police themselves even as they faced a conflict of interest in rating securities issued by the same firms that paid them, and even as they struggled to keep pace with the rapid evolution of increasingly complex and hard to understand investment products.

Recognizing that the credit rating agencies had failed to police themselves adequately, the Obama administration called for the SEC to tighten its regulatory oversight over them by requiring tougher standards of disclosing and managing conflicts of interest, explaining the methodologies involved in rating different types of securities, and informing investors of additional risks that might not be evident from the ratings. The administration also noted that regulators themselves had relied too heavily on the credit ratings of these agencies in their own regulatory and supervisory practices and should now refrain from doing so (*The New York Times*, 2009, pp. 42–44). In short, the administration called for an end to neoliberal self-regulation.

To adequately defend the argument that neoliberalism was behind all of the regulatory reforms that I have identified as contributing to the crisis one would have to develop case studies of all the reforms in question, identify the key supporters of these reforms and demonstrate that their neoliberal beliefs motivated their actions. This would require a book-length treatment of the events in question. Yet there is enough prima facie evidence here that I bet that such an exercise would support my claim.

CONCLUSION

I have argued that many roots of the financial meltdown stemmed from a number of regulatory decisions taken over the years that facilitated the creation of a large and ever riskier supply of credit into the housing market. Many of these decisions echoed the neoliberal prescriptions that policy-makers in Washington embraced increasingly since the 1970s. The result was a massive market failure that sent the financial services industry and eventually the entire economy into a tailspin as economic sociologists and historians would have predicted.

Implications for Future Research

The most obvious implication of my argument for future research, as suggested earlier, is that more attention needs to be paid to how the emergence of a neoliberal paradigm of policymaking influenced the events in question in the financial crisis. Scholars have spent much time trying to explain the rise of neoliberalism (e.g., Campbell & Pedersen, 2001; Hall, 1993; Prasad, 2006). They have also attempted to show how neoliberal ideas pushed by powerful actors from the political and business communities affected various isolated episodes of macroeconomic, monetary, fiscal, and regulatory policy (e.g., Blyth, 2002; Schmidt, 2002; Vogel, 1996). But to my knowledge nobody has examined how neoliberalism affected such a wide range of policy decisions over such an extended period of time in one sector of the economy like financial services. If this could be done, then we would have a comparatively exhaustive analysis of how time and again neoliberalism turned out not to be a blessing but a curse.

Another important avenue of research would be to take the sort of analysis I have developed here and push it in a cross-national direction. To date, virtually all of the work that has been published in the United States on the financial crisis has focused only on this country, such as how the Fed failed to handle the emerging housing bubble, how Lehman Brothers slid into bankruptcy, how hubris on Wall Street led to the collapse, and so on (e.g., Lanchester, 2009; Madrick, 2009). To my knowledge no comparative cross-national research has been published on the subject. I would be curious to know, for instance, why the United States and Britain experienced a more severe crisis than Canada. Was this because the regulatory infrastructures of the United States and Britain were more similar to each other than to Canada? Was this because neoliberalism held political sway to a much greater extent in the United States and Britain than it did in Canada? Or what? Research along these lines can better pinpoint exactly what sorts of regulatory infrastructures financial markets ought to have in order to avoid such crises in the future. There is certainly precedent for this sort of work in comparative historical and institutional analysis but it focuses on crises long past, such as the Great Depression (e.g., Gourevitch, 1986).

Several articles in this volume argue that the crisis stemmed from the tightly coupled nature of interorganizational relationships in the financial services industries (Guillén & Suárez, 2010; Palmer & Maher, 2010) – couplings that were facilitated in part by the small clique-like interpersonal networks of actors in these industries (Pozner, Stimmler, & Hirsch, 2010).

From my perspective, the question that needs further investigation is how state regulatory reforms contributed to the development of such tight coupling. Repeal of the Glass-Steagall Act is the most obvious example of how a regulatory reform can tighten the relationships among organizations. In this case, the firewall separating commercial and investment banking was torn down thereby enabling the intermingling and merging of various formerly independent firms such that some became too big to fail and received massive government bailouts. In other words, one wonders whether most of this tight coupling was solely the work of private actors on Wall Street or whether it also involved much cooperation from Washington. Economic and organizational sociologists have often argued that politics and policymaking affect interorganizational relationships in corporate America (Fligstein, 1990; Perrow, 2002). The financial meltdown provides an opportunity to expand on this line of research.

I also find it interesting that on some occasions leading up to the financial crisis courageous individuals stood up and warned that too much risk was being taken and was likely to be disastrous. Brooksley Born was one who confronted some of the most powerful politicians in Washington and argued for regulation of the derivatives markets only to be shouted down by them. Risk managers inside investment banks were another group of individuals who sounded alarms only to be told to be quiet. As is well-known, Max Weber was among the first economic sociologists to pay attention to the sometimes conflicted relationships that organizational leaders have with the staff that work for them and occasionally challenge their authority. Such theoretically diverse scholars as Talcott Parsons, Alvin Gouldner, Peter Blau and Richard Scott, and William Kornhauser among others extended this line of research (e.g., Campbell, 1987, p. 151). The financial crisis seems to present a wonderful set of cases by which researchers could compare such challenges in both public and private organizations in order to better understand their dynamics and why they succeed or fail.

Policy Implications

So far the Obama administration has proposed several regulatory reforms. These include, among other things, increasing the capitalization require-ments of banks; mandating that any firm issuing derivatives be obliged to purchase at least 5% of them itself; establishing a Financial Services Oversight Council to assess emerging risks in the industry; setting guidelines to better align the interests of corporate managers with long-term shareholder interests; setting up a consumer finance protection agency; and regulating all over-the-counter derivatives markets. All of this is intended to mitigate excessive risk taking and avoid new crises in the future.

While all of these make sense, given the preceding analysis it seems to me that there are three sets of reforms that are especially urgent. The first is to *separate commercial and investment banking* by reinstating a regulatory firewall between the two. Among others, Paul Volker, former chairman of the Fed, has urged the Obama administration to do this. As I have shown, repealing the Glass-Steagall Act permitted these two types of banking to be combined in ways that created a shadow banking system, which contributed significantly to the financial meltdown. Separating commercial and investment banking again would also help to reduce the tight interorganizational coupling that others have pointed to as another cause of the meltdown.

Another especially important reform is *regulating over-the-counter derivative markets.* The ability of firms to create and sell asset-backed securities over and over again with no government oversight was one of the most important causes of the financial meltdown. Indeed, former President Bill Clinton has acknowledged that signing the Commodity Futures Modernization Act was a serious mistake and that he should not have let himself be swayed by Greenspan, Rubin, Levitt, and others who pushed the legislation. He especially regretted that his administration did not put derivatives under the jurisdiction of the SEC and require more transparency in their trading. But he also believed that the Republicans in Congress would have overridden a veto anyway (Baker, 2009, p. 80). We will return later to the issue of whether regulatory reform like this is politically feasible.

A third step that Washington could take to guard against similar catastrophes in the future would be to resolve the conflict of interest that credit rating agencies face when they are paid by the same companies whose investment products they are hired to evaluate for risk. One way to do this would be to require investment firms to contribute annually to a general pool of funds from which credit rating agencies would be paid when rating derivatives and other financial products. In this way rating agencies would be paid from the collective pool of funds not by a particular firm with a personal stake in a rating. The idea of a *credit rating payment pool* is similar to what happened in the commercial nuclear power industry after the Three Mile Island disaster. Utility companies with nuclear facilities and industrial trade associations agreed to contribute to a new private organization designed to monitor and identify generic problems in utility operation, management, construction, and quality assurance practices. The basic idea was that by pooling their resources, industry members could facilitate better oversight of their operations and share important information among themselves (Campbell, 1989). The amount of money contributed each year to a credit rating payment pool could be based on how much money was spent the previous year by the industry on credit rating. Similarly, contributions could be prorated for each firm based on how many securities they had rated by agencies the previous year.

To ensure an additional degree of independence from the financial services industry the federal government could contribute to the payment pool. Moreover, in exchange for that contribution government representatives, perhaps from the SEC or FDIC, could participate in the rating process to ensure that ample caution and objectivity characterized the ratings being issued. That is, *government credit rating officers* trained professionally in investment credit rating techniques could serve along with traditional workers from the credit rating agencies as they conducted the research and calculated ratings for various offerings on the market. So credit rating would be a team effort consisting of public and private actors where at minimum a government official would have to sign off on all ratings issued by the credit rating agencies. This is a significant step beyond what the House Financial Services Committee passed recently – a bill that simply calls for more SEC oversight of the credit rating agencies (Nocera, 2009a). My idea would bring government credit rating specialists into the credit rating process itself rather than have them watch the process from the outside. In addition to the benefits described, this would infuse the credit rating system and thus the derivatives markets with an additional degree of transparency that might help mitigate excessively risky investing.

Prospects for Meaningful Regulatory Reform

As of this writing, virtually none of the Obama administration's reform proposals have been written into law. And I am not optimistic that these proposals will pan out as planned. Why? To begin with, enormous political forces have mustered against these proposals. Large and small banks and their trade associations in Washington have already waged a major lobbying campaign to kill or water down various parts of the administration's proposals (Labaton, 2009). Notably, Goldman Sachs, the large Wall Street investment bank, successfully lobbied the House Financial Services Committee to substantially dilute efforts to regulate over-the-counter derivatives markets (Kuttner, 2009). Special interest lobbying is built into the very institutional fabric of U.S. politics and will only accelerate moving forward in this area.

Beyond this, however, there are other factors that are likely to impede effective reform. One of the most important may be the often contradictory nature of new and old regulations themselves. For instance, under the federal Helping Families Save Their Homes Act of 2009, mortgage companies that agree to modify the terms of a mortgage in order to help financially distressed homeowners avoid foreclosure, such as by reducing their monthly mortgage payments, receive protection from liability arising from these loan changes. But in a suit brought against Countrywide, the big mortgage company now owned by Bank of America, a federal judge ruled that the firm must uphold its original contractual pledge to buy back loans from investors if it modifies those loans for troubled borrowers. The ruling is a win for holders of mortgage-backed securities who would typically see the value of their investment drop were mortgages renegotiated. Such institutionalized conflicts of interest are likely to bloom in the future (Morgenson, 2009a). The point is that new and old policies and laws may contradict one another such that the Obama administration's reforms may be hampered by the political–institutional legacies it has inherited, such as the edifice of contract law as this case illustrates.

Another looming obstacle to meaningful reform is bureaucratic infighting stemming from a regulatory architecture governing the financial services sector that is a complex patchwork of overlapping jurisdictions and laws at the state and federal levels. As reform plans unfold various government agencies are scrambling to protect or expand their regulatory turf. Notably, other regulatory agencies do not want to lose influence to the Fed, and the Fed does not want to relinquish its consumer protection responsibilities to a new agency although the Treasury Department has proposed both things (Blinder, 2009a). Obstructionist turf wars like this are to be expected because institutional fragmentation has caused similar problems in the past, such as when the SEC and CFTC vied for control of the stock-futures trading industry and ended up doing nothing (Paulson, 2009).

Other obstacles to reform are more ideational. For example, expertise in matters relating to the intricacies of how the financial markets and their complicated investment instruments operate lies squarely with the industry, not the government. This gives the industry an advantage in shaping whatever legislation is eventually passed as the government depends on the industry for advice on how to prevent such crises in the future. But Wall Street still seems locked into its old mind-set and remains devoted to the old way of doing things. Notably, investment banks are already devising new exotic investments that are reminiscent of those that got us into trouble in the first place. They are beginning to bundle and securitize life insurance policies as bonds and sell them to investors. And some firms are repackaging their money-losing securities, including real estate mortgage investments, into higher-rated ones. These innovations are simply a variation on the old asset-backed securities model and are fraught with some of the same risks (Anderson, 2009). Ideas on Wall Street about what constitutes appropriate risk-taking behavior do not seem to have changed much.

What all this points to is the strong possibility that, despite initial discussions among policymakers about rather bold regulatory change, we are likely to see something much less profound. This would not be surprising. Despite theoretical arguments about moments of crisis triggering radical institutional change, many scholars now recognize that political–institutional change tends to be much more incremental even at historical junctures like this one thanks to political resistance and other mechanisms of institutional path dependence (Campbell, 2004; Streeck & Thelen, 2005).

What is also troubling in the long run is that even many prominent economists continue to suffer from cognitive blind spots. For instance, Amartya Sen (2009), Nobel Prize winner in economics, wrote recently about the need now to remember the lessons of classical economists like Adam Smith, who stressed the importance of values and trust for efficient market performance, and Arthur Pigou, who theorized about the need for social welfare provisions to compensate for market failures. Sen's point was that we need to fortify the underlying institutions of capitalism as part of the fix for the current situation. Unfortunately, he provided no concrete suggestions about how to do that.

Similarly, in his latest book Paul Krugman (2009a), another Nobel Prize winner, argued that the crisis is largely a monetary and demand-side problem requiring a return to Keynesianism. He devoted only two pages to discussing the "prophylactic measures" for reforming the system so that a similar crisis does not happen again. Here he mentioned the need for regulatory change with a single guiding principle – anything that needs to be rescued during the crisis should be regulated in the future when the crisis is over (p. 189). But he offered only two specific ideas along this line: require more capitalization by banks and shadow banks, and beef up capital controls to prevent international currency crises (p. 184).

Krugman is an optimist. And his optimism is telling. As he put it: "I believe that the only important structural obstacles to world prosperity are the obsolete doctrines that clutter the minds of men" (p. 190). But might not the choice that he poses between Keynesianism and neoliberalism also constitute obsolete doctrine to a degree? Granted, there is need for Keynesianism at the moment to help resolve the current recession. But what about something new that is more appropriate for understanding the roots of the current situation, such as political–institutional analysis along the lines suggested by economic and political sociologists and historians? Economists are often at the ideational center of any paradigm shift when it comes to reforming economic regulation, which is why economic ideas matter so much (Fourcade, 2009). Hence, there is cause for concern that most economists – including Keynesians – have so little to say about political–institutional reform or institutional theory more generally. To be fair, although Krugman remains adamant that Keynesianism is our best framework for making sense of the current crisis, since his book was released he now calls for more attention among economists to some of the ideational factors that were involved in the crisis, such as those theorized in behavioral economics (Krugman, 2009b). This is a move in a more institutionally oriented direction. But more can be said.

For economic sociologists maintaining adequate state oversight in the financial markets is absolutely necessary to ensure that they operate properly. Similarly, economic historians have argued that the state must permanently engage the financial markets in order to mitigate their tendency toward booms and busts. For instance, Hyman Minsky (1986) theorized that financial markets are subject to slow movements from stability to crisis as speculative bubbles form and then burst causing banks and other lenders to tighten credit even to the most credit worthy companies and individuals. Recession follows immediately. He believed that without adequate state oversight through regulation, central bank intervention and other means the economy will be subject to severe business cycles. Similarly, Charles Kindleberger (1978) argued that financial crises occur when investors develop excessively optimistic expectations (i.e., irrational exuberance) and over estimate the future profitability of certain firms or markets. This leads firms and investors to devise and sell more securities than is prudent and take on more debt than they should. When their inflated expectations are not met, debt and stock values collapse, and markets for their heavily promoted financial assets dry up. Insolvency and economic recession or depression follows. The only way to avoid this, he argued, was for the state to intervene as the lender of last resort. All of this, of course, is evocative of the 2008 financial meltdown.

The point is that there are disciplines that take the political–institutional fabric of markets seriously. Economic sociology is one. Economic history is another. And institutional economics is a third (e.g., Hodgson, 1988).

However, they are all marginal to conventional economics in the United States. This is too bad because they warn of things that mainstream approaches miss – namely that markets are fragile and can only be protected from self-destruction through the state's supervision and protection. For markets to remain stable and avoid extreme booms and busts the state must limit how much risk market actors can take and when necessary intervene as the lender of last resort. This involves much more than a return to Keynesianism. The financial meltdown shows that when the state does not effectively manage risk taking it will eventually have to ramp up its lender of last resort function to fix the damage. This insight escaped neoliberals who sought to roll back or avoid financial market regulation. They failed to take seriously enough that state and market must always be intimately connected and that without the state markets cannot function properly. Because these insights are not central to mainstream economic thinking, and because the ideas of mainstream economics often inform economic policymaking, I worry that whatever regulatory reforms we see coming out of the current crisis will only be ad hoc and not sufficient to prevent more crises later on.

Indeed, skeptics have already charged that the administration's proposals for regulatory reform are not enough. For instance, they say that it fails to restore the separation of commercial and investment banking and it does not limit the possibilities of creating and selling new and ever more risky forms of derivative securities that carry with them the grave possibility of nasty spill-over effects (Morgenson, 2009b; Rich, 2009). The Obama administration won office campaigning on a theme of hope. We must now hope that it will fully appreciate the lessons of economic sociologists and others as well as the errors of the neoliberals as it tries to prevent future meltdowns.

NOTES

1. As is the convention among political sociologists and political economists, when I refer to the "state" I do not mean to imply that it is a monolithic whole. Rather it is a complex organization that consists of a number of branches, agencies, and departments.

2. Subprime mortgages are those typically made to borrowers with poor credit scores, histories of delinquent payments, foreclosures, or bankruptcies, poor debt-to-income ratios, and limited ability to cover monthly living expenses. Such easy credit often enticed prospective homeowners to buy houses that they would be unable to afford.

3. An asset-backed security is a financial instrument that is tradable like a stock or bond and whose value and income payments are derived from and backed (i.e., collateralized) by a specified pool of underlying assets. The pool is typically a group of small and illiquid assets that are unable to be sold individually. These might

include, for example, common payments from credit cards, auto loans, and mortgage loans, aircraft leases, royalty agreements, and movie revenues. Pooling the assets allows them to be sold as a bundle to general investors, a process called securitization. It allows the risk of investing in the underlying assets to be diversified because each asset-backed security will represent a fraction of the total value of the diverse pool of underlying assets. In short, an asset-backed security involves the bundling, underwriting, and selling of pieces of loans and other types of receivables as tradable securities. One incentive for banks to create and sell an asset-backed security is to remove risky assets from their balance sheets by having other investors buy them and, therefore, assume the credit risk, so that they (the banks) receive cash in return. This also allows banks to invest more of their capital in new loans or other assets and have a lower capitalization requirement. An asset-backed security is typically underwritten by an investment bank, which selects the portfolio of assets that constitute the security, sizes the pieces (or tranches), and works with credit rating agencies to establish the desired credit rating for each tranche.

4. Swaps are another type of security that is traded in the asset-backed security market. They are insurance policies against the possibility that an asset-backed security, including a securitized bundle of mortgages, or other derivative might default.

5. Some have argued that shoddy lending was facilitated by yet another institutional factor. Unlike many countries the U.S. legal system allows credit reporting to be widely shared, such as the well-known FICO score, which represents a numerical assessment of an individual's overall creditworthiness. These scores were initially developed to guide lending in credit card and other types of short-term debt markets, not mortgage markets. But because it is cheaper to rely on these scores than to do your own credit report on a prospective borrower, mortgage lenders became less likely to do their own in-house credit assessments and more likely to rely on these generic scores for evaluating the creditworthiness of prospective borrowers. The problem was that these scores were not always reliable indicators of long-term credit worthiness for large loans like mortgages (Ellis, 2008).

6. Years later former President Bill Clinton admitted that signing the Gramm–Leach–Bliley Act likely enabled some of these firms to become bigger than might otherwise have been the case and, thus, harder to manage (Baker, 2009, p. 80).

7. Over-the-counter derivatives involve much larger sums than do traded exchanges. In December 2005, the amount outstanding on all organized exchanges worldwide for both futures and options contracts was around $58 trillion. In over-the-counter markets, the sum was $248 trillion. Over-the-counter derivatives are often traded internationally. They are subject to a modicum of private self-regulation through the International Swaps and Dealers Association (ISDA). The problem with ISDA was that its standards were unconnected in any way with sanctions and hard law at the national and international levels (Morgan, 2008).

8. The regulation is known as "Alternative Net Capital Requirements for Broker-Dealers That Are Part of Consolidated Supervised Entities" (RIN: 3235-AI96).

9. The Act did not take effect before the largest rating agencies issued the ratings that contributed significantly to the financial meltdown. It was not until August 2007 that the SEC initiated an investigation of the large credit rating agencies and it was not until December 2008 that it adopted regulations governing credit rating agency transparency, competition, and accountability (Casey, 2009).

ACKNOWLEDGMENT

Thanks for helpful comments on an early draft go to Michael Allen, Jens Beckert, Fred Block, Bill Domhoff, John Hall, Peter Hall, Paul Hirsch, Michael Lounsbury, Ove Pedersen, Monica Prasad, Marc Schneiberg, and participants in seminars at the Copenhagen Business School, Harvard University, Dartmouth College, and Northwestern University.

REFERENCES

Abolafia, M. (1996). *Making markets: Opportunism and restraint on Wall Street*. Cambridge, MA: Harvard University Press.

Abolafia, M. Y. (2010). The institutional embeddedness of market failure: Why speculative bubbles still occur. In: M. Lounsbury & P. M. Hirsch (Eds), *Markets on trial: The economic sociology of the U.S. financial crisis: Part A*. Research in the Sociology of Organizations. Bingley, UK: Emerald.

Anderson, J. (2009). New exotic investments emerging on Wall Street. *The New York Times*, September 6, p. 1.

Baker, P. (2009). It's not about Bill. *The New York Times Magazine*, May 31, pp. 40–47, pp. 80–82.

Bank for International Settlements. (2008). *Part VII: The financial sector in the advanced industrial economies*. 75th Annual Report. Bank for International Settlements, Basel, Switzerland. Available at http://www.bis.org/publ/arpdf/ar2008e.htm

Blinder, A. S. (2009a). The wait for financial reform. *The New York Times* (Business Section), September 6, p. 4.

Blinder, A. S. (2009b). Six blunders en route to a crisis. *The New York Times* (Business Section), January 25, p. 7.

Blyth, M. (2002). *Great transformations: Economic ideas and institutional change in the twentieth century*. New York, NY: Cambridge University Press.

Braithwaite, J. (2009). *Regulatory capitalism*. London: Elgar.

Bruno, M. (2008). Money fund rescue smacks banks. *Financial Week*. Available at http://www.financialweek.com/apps/pbcs.dll/article?AID = /20081005/REG/810039951/1038/exclusives. Retrieved on October 5.

Campbell, J. L. (1987). Legitimation meltdown: Weberian and neo-Marxist interpretations of legitimation crises in advanced capitalist society. *Political Power and Social Theory, 6*, 133–158.

Campbell, J. L. (1989). Corporations, collective organization, and the state: Industry response to the accident at three mile Island. *Social Science Quarterly, 70*(3), 650–666.

Campbell, J. L. (2004). *Institutional change and globalization*. Princeton, NJ: Princeton University Press.

Campbell, J. L., Hollingsworth, J. R., & Lindberg, L. N. (Eds). (1991). *Governance of the American Economy*. New York, NY: Cambridge University Press.

Campbell, J. L., & Lindberg, L. N. (1990). Property rights and the organization of economic activity by the state. *American Sociological Review, 55*, 634–647.

98 JOHN L. CAMPBELL

Campbell, J. L., & Pedersen, O. K. (Eds). (2001). *The rise of neoliberalism and institutional analysis*. Princeton, NJ: Princeton University Press.

Carruthers, B. (2010). Knowledge and liquidity: Institutional and cognitive foundations of the subprime crisis. In: M. Lounsbury & P. M. Hirsch (Eds), *Markets on trial: The economic sociology of the U.S. financial crisis: Part A*. Research in the Sociology of Organizations. Bingley, UK: Emerald.

Carruthers, B., & Ariovich, L. (2004). The sociology of property rights. *Annual Review of Sociology, 30*, 23–46.

Casey, K. (2009). In search of transparency, accountability, and competition: The regulation of credit rating agencies. Speech by the Commissioner of the U.S. Securities and Exchange Commission, Washington. Available at http://www.sec.gov/news/speech/2009/spch020609klc.htm. Retrieved on February 6.

Conlan, T., Wrightson, J. M., & Beam, J. (1990). *Taxing choices: The politics of tax reform*. Washington, DC: Congressional Quarterly Press.

Cox, C. (2008). Chairman Cox announces end of consolidated supervised entities program. Press release 2008-230, U.S. Securities and Exchange Commission. Available at http://www.sec.gov/news/press/2008/2008-230.htm. Retrieved on September 26.

Dash, E., & Crewsell, J. (2008). Citigroup pays for a rush to risk. *The New York Times*, November 23, p. 1.

Ellis, D. (1998). *The effect of consumer interest rate deregulation on credit card volumes, charge-offs, and the personal bankruptcy rate*. FDIC Division of Insurance Paper no. 98-05 (March), Federal Deposit Insurance Corporation, Washington, DC. Available at http://www.fdic.gov/bank/analytical/bank/bt_9805.html

Ellis, L. (2008). *The housing meltdown: Why did it happen in the United States?* Working Paper no. 259. Monetary and Economic Department. Bank for International Settlements, Basel, Switzerland. Available at http://www.bis.org/publ/work259.pdf?noframes = 1

Federal Reserve Bank of Boston. (1980). *Depository institutions deregulation and monetary control act of 1980*. Boston, MA: Federal Reserve Bank. Available at http://www.bos.frb.org/about/pubs/deposito.pdf

Fligstein, N. (1990). *The transformation of corporate control*. Cambridge, MA: Harvard University Press.

Fligstein, N. (2001). *The architecture of markets*. Princeton, NJ: Princeton University Press.

Fligstein, N., & Goldstein, A. (2010). The anatomy of the mortgage securitization crisis. In: M. Lounsbury & P. M. Hirsch (Eds), *Markets on trial: The economic sociology of the U.S. financial crisis: Part A*. Research in the Sociology of Organizations. Bingley, UK: Emerald.

Fourcade, M. (2009). *Economists and societies: Discipline and profession in the United States, Britain and France, 1890s to 1990s*. Princeton, NJ: Princeton University Press.

Friedman, M. (1962). *Capitalism and freedom*. Chicago, IL: University of Chicago Press.

Geithner, T. (2008). *Reducing systemic risk in a dynamic financial system*. Speech to the Economic Club of New York, New York City by the President and Chief Executive Officer of the Federal Reserve Bank of New York. Available at http://www.newyorkfed.org/newsevents/speeches/2008/tfg080609.html. Retrieved on June 9.

Gourevitch, P. (1986). *Politics in hard times*. Ithaca, NY: Cornell University Press.

Gramlich, E. M. (2007). *Subprime mortgages: America's latest boom and bust*. Washington, DC: Urban Institute Press.

Guerrera, F. (2009). A need to reconnect. *Financial Times*, March 13, p. 9.

Guillén, M. F., & Suárez, S. L. (2010). The global crisis of 2007–2009: Markets, politics, and organizations. In: M. Lounsbury & P. M. Hirsch (Eds), *Markets on trial: The economic sociology of the U.S. financial crisis: Part A*. Research in the Sociology of Organizations. Bingley, UK: Emerald.

Gwinner, W., & Sanders, A. (2008). *The subprime crisis: Implications for emerging markets*. Policy Research Working Paper no. 4726, Financial and Private Sector Development Vice Presidency, Global Markets Non-Bank Financial Institutions Division, September, The World Bank, Washington, DC.

Hall, P. A. (1993). Policy paradigms, social learning and the state. *Comparative Politics, 25*, 275–296.

Hayek, F. (1944). *The road to serfdom*. Chicago, IL: University of Chicago Press.

Hodgson, G. M. (1988). *Economics and institutions: A manifesto for a modern institutional economics*. Philadelphia, PA: University of Pennsylvania Press.

Jickling, M. (2009). *Causes of the financial crisis*. CRS-7-5700, R40173. Washington, DC: Congressional Research Service.

Kindleberger, C. (1978). *Manias, panics, and crashes: A history of financial crises*. New York, NY: Basic Books.

Knight, J. (2001). Explaining the rise of neoliberalism: The mechanisms of institutional change. In: J. L. Campbell & O. K. Pedersen (Eds), *The rise of neoliberalism and institutional analysis* (pp. 27–50). Princeton, NJ: Princeton University Press.

Krippner, G. R. (2010). The political economy of financial exuberance. In: M. Lounsbury & P. M. Hirsch (Eds), *Markets on trial: The economic sociology of the U.S. financial crisis: Part A*. Research in the Sociology of Organizations. Bingley, UK: Emerald.

Krugman, P. (2009a). *The return of depression economics and the crisis of 2008*. New York, NY: Norton.

Krugman, P. (2009b). How did economists get it so wrong? *The New York Times Magazine*, September 6, pp. 36–43.

Kuttner, R. (2009). A tale of two Obamas. *The Huffington Post*. Available at http://www.huffingtonpost.com/robert-kuttner/a-tale-of-two-obamas_b_382061.html. Retrieved on December 7

Labaton, S. (2009). Regulators spar for turf in financial overhaul. *The New York Times* (Business Section), July 25, p. B1, p. B6.

Lanchester, J. (2009). Bankocracy. *The London Review of Books*, November 5, pp. 35–36.

Leicht, K. T., & Fitzgerald, S. T. (2007). *Postindustrial peasants: The illusion of middle-class prosperity*. New York, NY: Worth.

Levy, F. (1998). *The new dollars and dreams: American incomes and economic change*. New York, NY: Russell Sage Foundation.

MacKenzie, D. (2008). End-of-the-world trade. *The London Review of Books*. Available at http://www.lrb.co.ukk/v30/n09/mack01_.html. Retrieved on May 8.

Madrick, J. (2009). They didn't regulate enough and still don't. *The New York Review of Books*, November 5, pp. 54–57.

Minsky, H. (1986). *Stabilizing an unstable economy*. New Haven, CT: Yale University Press.

Mishel, L., Bernstein, J., & Allegretto, S. (2005). *The state of working America, 2004/2005*. Ithaca, NY: Cornell University Press.

Mizruchi, M. S. (2010). The American corporate elite and the historical roots of the financial crisis of 2008. In: M. Lounsbury & P. M. Hirsch (Eds), *Markets on trial: The economic sociology of the U.S. financial crisis: Part B.* Research in the Sociology of Organizations. Bingley, UK: Emerald.

Morgan, G. (2008). Market formation and governance in international financial markets: The case of OTC derivatives. *Human Relations, 61*(5), 637–660.

Morgenson, G. (2008). Was there a loan it didn't like? *The New York Times* (Business Section), November 2, p. 1.

Morgenson, G. (2009a). Countrywide loses ruling in loan suit. *The New York Times*, August 20, p. B1.

Morgenson, G. (2009b). Too big to fail, or too big to handle? *The New York Times* (Business Section), June 21, p. 1.

Nocera, J. (2009a). Cliffs notes of columns to come. *The New York Times*, October 31, p. B1.

Nocera, J. (2009b). Risk mismanagement. *The New York Times Magazine*, January 4, pp. 24–51.

North, D. C. (1990). *Institutions, institutional change and economic performance.* New York, NY: Cambridge University Press.

North, D. C. (2005). *Understanding the process of economic change.* Princeton, NJ: Princeton University Press.

Onaran, Y. (2007). Wall Street gets lift from SEC that may boost profit. Available at Bloomburg.com., http://www.bloomberg.com/apps/news?pid = 20601109&sid = aomFfZxHgzRA&refer = exclusive

Palmer, D., & Maher, M. (2010). A normal accident analysis of the mortgage meltdown. In: M. Lounsbury & P. M. Hirsch (Eds), *Markets on trial: The economic sociology of the U.S. financial crisis: Part A.* Research in the Sociology of Organizations. Bingley, UK: Emerald.

Paulson, H. (2009). Reform the architecture of regulation. *Financial Times*, March 17, p. 7.

Perrow, C. (2002). *Organizing America.* Princeton, NJ: Princeton University Press.

Polanyi, K. (1944). *The great transformation: The political and economic origins of our time.* Boston, MA: Beacon Press.

Pozner, J. E., Stimmler, M. K., & Hirsch, P. (2010). Terminal isomorphism and the self-destructive potential of success: Lessons from sub-prime mortgage origination and securitization. In: M. Lounsbury & P. M. Hirsch (Eds), *Markets on trial: The economic sociology of the U.S. financial crisis: Part A.* Research in the Sociology of Organizations. Bingley, UK: Emerald.

Prasad, M. (2006). *The politics of free markets.* Chicago, IL: University of Chicago Press.

Rich, F. (2009). Obama's make-or-break summer. *The New York Times* (Week in Review Section), June 21, p. 8.

Schmidt, V. A. (2002). *The futures of European capitalism.* New York, NY: Oxford University Press.

Schneiberg, M. (1999). Political and institutional conditions for governance by association: Private order and price controls in American fire insurance. *Politics and Society, 27*(1), 67–103.

Schneiberg, M., & Bartley, T. (2008). Organizations, regulation, and economic behavior: Regulatory dynamics and forms from the 19th to 21st century. *Annual Review of Law and Social Science, 4*, 31–61.

Sen, A. (2009). Capitalism beyond the crisis. *The New York Review of Books*, March 26, pp. 27–30.

Standard and Poor's. (2009). S&P/Case-Shiller home price indices. Available at http://www2.standardandpoors.com/spf/pdf/index/SP_CS_Home_Price_Indices_Factsheet.pdf

Stiglitz, J. (2003). *The roaring nineties.* New York, NY: Norton.

Strahan, P. E. (2002). *The real effects of banking deregulation.* Wharton Financial Institutions Center Working Paper no. 02-39. University of Pennsylvania, PA. Available at http:// fic.wharton.upenn.edu/fic/papers/02/0239.pdf

Streeck, W., & Thelen, K. (2005). Introduction: Institutional change in advanced political economies. In: W. Streeck & K. Thelen (Eds), *Beyond continuity* (pp. 1–39). New York, NY: Oxford University Press.

Surowiecki, J. (2008). Public humiliation. *The New Yorker.* Available at http://www.newyorker. com/talk/financial/2008/09/29/080929ta_talk_surowiecki. Retrieved on September 29.

Tett, G. (2009). Lost through creative destruction. *Financial Times,* March 10, p. 9.

The Economist. (2008). When fortune frowned: A special report on the world economy. October 11, pp. 1–33.

The Economist. (2009a). A special report on the future of finance. January 25, pp. 1–21.

The Economist. (2009b). Worse than Japan? February 14, pp. 81–82.

The New York Times. (2009). Draft of President Obama's financial regulation proposal. Available at http://documents.nytimes.com/draft-of-president-obama-s-financial-regulation-proposal/page/44#p = 1. Retrieved on June 26.

Vogel, S. K. (1996). *Freer markets, more rules.* Ithaca, NY: Cornell University Press.

Wade, R. (2008). Financial regime change? *New Left Review, 53*(September/October), 5–21.

Wolf, M. (2009a). Cutting back financial capitalism is America's big test. *Financial Times,* April 15, p. 9.

Wolf, M. (2009b). Seeds of its own destruction. *Financial Times,* March 9, p. 7.

THE AMERICAN CORPORATE ELITE AND THE HISTORICAL ROOTS OF THE FINANCIAL CRISIS OF 2008 [☆]

Mark S. Mizruchi

ABSTRACT

The events surrounding the financial crisis of 2008 are well known, and subject to a broad level of agreement. Less accepted are theories regarding the larger context within which this crisis was able to unfold. Much has been made of the financialization of the American economy and the lax regulation of new financial instruments, both of which stem from the trend toward a laissez-faire economic policy that has characterized the United States since the late 1970s. I do not take issue with these claims. Instead, I argue that these developments have an earlier and deeper source: a breakdown in the ability of large American corporations to provide collective solutions to economic and social problems, a phenomenon that I term "the decline of the American corporate elite." From a group with a

[☆]Earlier talks on which this article was based were presented at the conference on Understanding the Financial Crisis, University of Chicago, April 2009 and the Markets on Trial Workshop, Northwestern University, October 2009.

Markets on Trial: The Economic Sociology of the U.S. Financial Crisis: Part B
Research in the Sociology of Organizations, Volume 30B, 103–139
ISSN: 0733-558X/doi:10.1108/S0733-558X(2010)000030B008

relatively moderate political perspective and a pragmatic strategic orientation, this elite, through a series of historical developments, became a fragmented, largely ineffectual group, with a high degree of societal legitimacy but a paradoxical lack of power. I trace the history of this group, from its origins in the early 1900s, through its heyday in the post-World War II period, to its decline beginning in the 1970s and escalating in the 1980s. I argue that the lack of coordination within the American business community created the conditions for the crises of the post-1980 period – including the massive breakdown of 2008 – to occur.

In 2008, the American financial system experienced its most serious crisis since the Great Depression. Although some observers, most notably Paul Krugman and Nouriel Roubini, had been warning of the dangers being created by the real estate bubble, most appeared to be caught by surprise, just as they were in the dot-com crash of 2000, the stock market crash of 1987, and the crash of 1929. There has been no shortage of accounts of this event, and no shortage of attempts to explain it. The processes by which the crisis emerged have been well documented by several scholars, including the authors of this volume. My goal here is to examine this event from a different angle. Instead of focusing on the economic forces that led to the crisis, my goal is to discuss what I view as a major long-term determinant: the changing character of the American corporate elite. I do not claim that this is the only cause of the financial meltdown. I do believe that this development created the context within which the events of 2008 were able to occur. My aim in this article is to identify the historical roots of this phenomenon, in terms of the rise of the American corporate elite in the post-World War II period and its decline since the 1980s.

THE DILEMMA OF HISTORICAL EXPLANATION

Social scientists from the classical period to the present have made numerous attempts to understand the causes of individual events. Max Weber developed an account of the rise of capitalism. Karl Marx attempted to explain capitalism's presumed demise. American historians have debated the causes of the Civil War. And economists have debated the causes of the Great Depression.

The difficulties with attempting to account for singular historical events are well known, and have been the source of considerable debate among historical sociologists (see the chapters in Ragin & Becker, 1992 for an overview). The primary problem is what is called "overdetermination." Virtually all significant historical events have multiple causes, but with more causes than observations, it is not empirically possible to isolate a particular one.

The financial crisis of 2008 provides a good illustration of this predicament. Several causes have been suggested. Yet given the problem of overdetermination, how are we to adjudicate among these competing accounts? I shall avoid the temptation to wade into the debates on the nature of historical explanation. What I will do instead is the following. First, I will describe some of the proximate causes of the crisis. This discussion will provide little that is new in the way of explanation, since most of what I discuss is well known to those who have studied the crisis, and also relatively uncontroversial. This discussion will be used to set the stage for the main goal of the article. I shall argue that the context for the crisis can be traced to a process that began in the 1970s, and continued into the 1990s and beyond: what I have termed "the decline of the American corporate elite" (Mizruchi, 2007a). I argue that a group of pragmatic, forward-thinking corporate leaders emerged after World War II, that through its political moderation and high level of organization helped maintain a broad stability in the American economy (if not the society as a whole). This group experienced a major shift in focus during the 1970s, however, such that by the 1980s it had begun to dissipate. By the 1990s, I argue, the group had disappeared altogether.

This argument requires a relatively broad historical sweep, and operates at a highly general level. Before presenting it, however, I want to discuss the immediate causes of the crisis. From there, I will begin to frame the larger context within which the crisis occurred, drawing on the work of Davis (2009) and Krippner (2010) on the "financialization" of the American economy. I then discuss the context within which both financialization and the resulting crisis were primed to occur. My goal is to provide the broad historical and political context within which the recent crisis became possible. I must warn the reader that the term "broad" is to be taken literally. I will be covering a significant amount of history, and space considerations will prevent me from providing a level of detail sufficient to provide a fully documented demonstration. My aim is to provide an account that explains why a crisis that could have been prevented, and that would likely have been prevented in the previous generation, was allowed to occur.

WHAT HAPPENED?

There appears to be a general consensus about the sequence of events that precipitated the events of 2008. After the dot-com crash of 2000, many observers expected that the United States would experience a relatively serious recession. Instead, however, in part triggered by the low interest rates created by the Federal Reserve, a housing boom of unprecedented proportions (at least at the national level) transpired beginning in 2002. In response to the subsequent explosion in housing prices, banks rushed in to lend to home buyers. The circumstances under which this occurred were far different from those in earlier decades, however. In the traditional housing market, a single bank would issue a long-term loan to a home buyer and then hold the loan through its entire life, typically 25 or 30 years. In more recent years, the banks developed a different approach. Instead of holding a mortgage, the banks bundled together a group of loans and sold them to investors – including other banks – as securities.

These mortgage-backed securities, as they were called, were designed to reduce the risk experienced by lenders, since the combination of large numbers of mortgages meant that even if one borrower defaulted, it would have a negligible effect on the entire bundle. Instead of leading to a reduction of risk, however, this instrument led to what might be called "exploitation of risk." Because lenders knew that they would not be holding the mortgage but instead would sell it, there was less of a need to be concerned about the creditworthiness of the borrower. Moreover, borrowers with poor creditworthiness were in high-risk categories, so they could be charged a steep interest rate, thus yielding a high rate of return. These securities thus became extremely lucrative investments. This increased the competitive pressure on banks to make any and all loans, even to borrowers with faulty credit histories. It led to extremely high leveraging, which was possible in part because regulations placing limits on exposure levels in this market were not in place.

As seemingly precarious as this situation was, it remained feasible for the banks as long as housing prices continued to rise. Borrowers could continue to refinance, in the belief that their increased equity would provide a cushion for their ability to repay.[1] Lenders could be confident that even if a borrower defaulted, the increasing value of the property would allow them to recoup their investment. All financial bubbles eventually burst, however, and the housing bubble that began in 2002 was no exception. When the implosion occurred, the financial repercussions were worldwide, since the widespread sale of bundled mortgages had reached nearly every corner of the globe. Given the connectedness of the world financial system and its dependence in the post-9/11 period on the American housing market, the collapse of this market triggered a collapse of major proportions. The financial meltdown, beginning with the failure of Lehman Brothers in September 2008, plunged the worldwide economy into a downward spiral, which lasted well into 2009.

DEEPER ROOTS OF THE CRISIS

The events described above are well known, and have been described in far greater detail by others. There are several ways to approach the history of the crisis. Much of the story can be accounted for by developments within the banking system itself, as Fligstein and Goldstein (2010) have outlined. Much can be explained by the decisions (or nondecisions) of government policy makers, including the strikingly low interest rates promulgated by the Federal Reserve Bank in the post-9/11 period. But there were larger forces at work as well.

The United States was a largely manufacturing economy through the first half of the twentieth century. The manufacturing sector remained significant into the 1970s, although core industries, such as auto and steel, were experiencing significant declines by that point. Corporate profits in manufacturing had been falling since the late 1960s, and prospects for a reversal were not evident, given the rise of foreign competition, the energy crisis, and the resulting inflationary spiral, all of which hit during the 1970s. In the midst of this situation, corporations searched for alternative sources of investment. One such outlet was financial activity.

Finance during the post-New Deal period had been dominated by commercial banks. These banks earned their money through two primary means. First, they provided debt financing for corporations. Second, they held savings deposits for consumers, as well as other businesses, and invested these funds at rates higher than the interest they paid to depositors. Investment banks, which had played such a significant role in the early twentieth century, had been relegated to the sidelines following the passage of the Glass–Steagall Act in 1933. Prior to this law, commercial and investment banking could take place under a single roof, and the great financial institutions of the early 1900s, led by J. P. Morgan & Company, benefited significantly from this practice. In the stock market mania of the 1920s, investment banks had in many cases used the savings accounts of depositors to purchase stock under highly leveraged conditions, a phenomenon with obvious parallels to the situation of the early twenty-first century. This diversion of capital led to a number of bank failures when the stock market crashed, and many individuals lost their life savings. The Glass–Steagall Act was put into place to ensure that a repeat of this disaster did not occur. Investment banks were to specialize in the placement of securities, while commercial banks were to focus on saving and lending. Investment banks were prohibited from holding savings accounts, and commercial banks were prohibited from engaging in securities placement. Because this law required investment banks to forfeit their primary source of capital, these banks receded in significance in the following decades.

As we entered the 1980s, this situation began to change. After the deep drop in the stock market in 1974, stock prices remained low for several years, returning to the 1974 peak only in 1982. In response to this, corporations and investors began buying up what were viewed as "undervalued" corporate assets, and a massive takeover wave emerged, that Useem (1989) has termed the "revolt of the owners." This surge was led by investment banks, which as a result began to reassert their earlier prominence.

Meanwhile, a series of changes were occurring in the environment in which commercial banks operated. Alternative forms of investment, such as mutual funds and money market funds, became more widely available to consumers. This meant that consumers were no longer keeping their cash in passbook savings accounts, thus drying up a major source of bank capital. Corporations, for their part, increasingly turned to alternative sources of funding, such as commercial paper, in which nonfinancial firms loaned directly to one another. This led to a reduction in the banks' corporate lending business. As Jerry Davis and I have shown (Davis & Mizruchi, 1999), the banks responded to this situation by trying to operate more like investment banks, focusing less on traditional lending and more on services such as currency swaps, investment advice, and even investments themselves, in the form of derivatives.

I will have more to say on this development among the commercial banks later in this article. What is important at this point is that the shift in prominence from commercial to investment banking corresponded with an important development: the increasing focus on financial activities as a source of profit. As Krippner (2010) has shown, financial activities have become an increasingly significant source of corporate profits over the past four decades. In the 1950s and 1960s, profits from the financial sector (not including real estate) accounted for no more than 15 percent of the total profits in the American economy. By the mid-1980s, financial sector profits were accounting for approximately 30 percent of the total. By 2001 this figure had increased to over 40 percent. From a relatively "sleepy" field, in which bankers made loans to corporations and individuals, and were said to follow the "3-6-3" rule – borrow at 3 percent, lend at 6 percent, and be on the golf course by 3 – finance was now the center of economic activity, as MBA students flocked to Wall Street to make fortunes in the suddenly exciting world of investment banking. The investment banking world then witnessed a series of innovations, from the "junk bonds" that funded the 1980s takeover wave, to the collateralized debt obligations that fueled the housing bubble of the early 2000s.

Corresponding with the rise of financial activity was the move to a more laissez-faire economic policy. This reduction in government oversight and regulation had already begun in the late 1970s, under the Carter Administration, but it appeared in full force after Ronald Reagan was elected President in 1980. Not only did this shift facilitate the takeover wave of the 1980s, as antitrust regulation was relaxed, but it meant that the new financial instruments of the 1990s (derivatives) and 2000s (the mortgage-backed securities and collateralized debt obligations) were left largely unregulated. In 1998, in direct defiance of the Glass–Steagall Act, Citibank, the largest American commercial bank, merged with Travelers Insurance, one of whose subsidiaries was the investment firm Smith Barney. Glass–Steagall was repealed by Congress the following year.

A NEW DEPRESSION?

There are several accounts of what caused the Great Depression. Although it has fallen out of favor in recent decades, the explanation of the Depression provided by John Maynard Keynes was for many years the standard. Prior to Keynes, the accepted wisdom for how to handle an economic downturn was for the Federal Reserve to reduce interest rates to encourage investment. Keynes argued, to the contrary, that even if interest rates are low, firms will not invest if they do not believe that they will make a return on their investment. This seems to have been borne out in the crisis of 2008: the Fed reduced interest rates to virtually zero, yet it spurred neither borrowing nor investment. Even after the government bailout of several financial institutions, lending by those institutions was slow to follow. The problem at the root of the Depression, in the Keynesian view, was the tendency in capitalist economies for production to outstrip effective demand. When this occurs, there is insufficient purchasing power in the population to consume the goods that are produced. The result is a downturn, which, if sufficiently severe, can turn into a depression.

One consequence of the move toward a more laissez-faire economic policy, as well as the move away from a manufacturing economy, is that inequality in both income, and especially wealth, increased sharply, beginning in the late 1970s and continuing into the 2000s. Moreover, during the same period, productivity among American workers increased at a rate more than five times greater than wages (Harrison, 2009). This combination led to exactly the kind of situation that Keynes viewed as conducive to a depression. There is also a parallel between the recent historical period and the 1920s, when a rising level of inequality, combined with increased productivity, preceded the stock market crash and subsequent depression.

Even if the increasing inequality does not by itself explain the financial crisis – after all, inequality had already risen significantly years earlier yet the collapse occurred only in 2008 – it is difficult to discount it as a factor in the bursting of the housing bubble. It was precisely the lack of spending power that rendered so many consumers susceptible to the subprime mortgages that were at the heart of the meltdown. Consumers, heavily in debt because their incomes were insufficient to meet their expenses, were vulnerable to the kind of appeals made by the purveyors of subprime loans. Certainly a lack of disposable income, further exacerbated by the necessity of repaying high-interest loans, could have been a factor in reduced aggregate demand, a condition conducive to crises in market economies.

BUT WHY?

So we know what happened – the proliferation of bad bank loans spurred by the housing bubble was both the consequence of high-risk activity and a spur to continued activity. And we know something about the context within which this high-risk activity occurred – the decline of the manufacturing economy with its relatively high wages, the rise of finance as a source of corporate profits, and the lack of government regulation of new financial instruments. But how did we get to the point at which all of these forces coalesced? That is, was there a larger force at work that explains why and how we got to the point of having such a high level of inequality, back-to-back bubbles (the late 1990s and the mid-2000s), and a seeming inability to reign in the excesses that allowed these events to occur? I believe that there was such a force, and in the remainder of this article I propose an explanation for what I believe is behind the current crisis: the changing nature of leadership at the top of corporate America, that is, among the corporate elite. I shall argue that conditions that set the stage for the financial crisis of 2008 were a consequence of what I call the "decline of the American corporate elite."

BACKGROUND

A debate raged in political sociology during the mid- and late twentieth century over the extent to which the American business community constituted a coherent political actor. Some theorists, such as Floyd Hunter (1953), C. Wright Mills (1956), and G. William Domhoff (1967), argued that the leaders of the largest firms share a basic unity of interest and outlook that transcends whatever differences they may have over specific policy issues. Others, such as Robert Dahl (1961), Nelson Polsby (1963), and Arnold Rose (1967), argued that corporations are too broad and diverse, with too many competing or differing interests, to form anything resembling a cohesive community.

What most scholars agree on is that the vast majority of businesspeople in the United States have historically held views that we would classify as conservative: support for free markets, minimal government intervention in the economy, support for low levels of both business and personal taxes, and opposition to organized labor. This is reflected in the overwhelming (albeit not unanimous) support among businesspeople for the Republican Party. At the same time, several authors have argued that from the post-World War II period into at least the early 1970s, there was a small group of business leaders, representing the largest corporations, that had a relatively high degree of cohesiveness and that held political views (or engaged in political strategies) at odds with the traditional views of most American firms.

This small group of business leaders, whom Useem has called the "inner circle," sat on multiple boards of directors, tended to have a high level of involvement in civic activities as well as membership in national policy-making organizations, and tended to have a relatively cosmopolitan outlook, with a focus on the interests of the corporate community as a whole. In fact, in some cases, scholars argued, this group exhibited concerns about the well-being of the larger society, even in cases in which such views required corporations to place aside their own short-term interests (Kaysen, 1957; Bell, 1973; Useem, 1984). I shall refer to this group as the "corporate elite."

Members of this group did not necessarily disagree with their small-business brethren about the disadvantages of high taxes, regulations, and organized labor. They were more pragmatic about policy, however. Even though they would have preferred a world in which government regulation was minimal, these corporate leaders acknowledged that certain regulations, such as those enforced by the Federal Trade Commission and the Securities and Exchange Commission, were helpful to business because they helped enforce rules of "fair play" that helped the economy run more smoothly. Similarly, in an ideal world, perhaps labor unions would not exist. Yet unions did exist, these businesspeople acknowledged, and they were not about to disappear. Rather than attempt to destroy them, these relatively moderate corporate leaders decided that it was more feasible to attempt to work with union leaders to ensure that more radical elements within their ranks were kept at bay.

This pragmatism extended into social policy as well. Members of this moderate wing of the business community were prominent in elite social clubs and policy-making organizations such as the Committee for Economic Development (CED) and the Council on Foreign Relations (CFR), both of which consisted of academics and other intellectuals, and even some labor officials as well as corporate leaders (Domhoff, 1970; Soref, 1976; Useem, 1979). These groups tended to exhibit relatively moderate views toward political issues, and during the 1950s and especially the 1960s and early 1970s, these groups even advocated support for various government social programs. An example of this is evident in a 1971 position paper issued by the CED (Frederick, 1981). The report acknowledged the existence of serious social problems that required attention, including poverty, unemployment, unequal access to education, and violations of civil rights. Private voluntarism, or what today is called corporate philanthropy, can play an important role in alleviating these problems, the report noted. Such private action is not sufficient, however. Only the government has the resources and the public mandate to fully address these issues, the report suggested. Instead of simple voluntarism, the CED argued, solutions to these social problems required a "business–government partnership." This is a position that has rarely been heard in recent decades, yet it was commonplace in the postwar period, at least among the relatively small segment at the apex of the corporate world.[2]

Where did this group come from, and how important was it? The roots of the cosmopolitan leading edge of the American corporate community can be traced at least as far back as the turn of the twentieth century, with the formation of the National Civic Federation (NCF) in 1900 (Weinstein, 1968). The NCF was an organization that, like the later CED, drew from multiple sectors, including not only business but also labor and academia.

The group was formed during the rise of corporate capitalism, in a period in which the establishment of huge corporations, epitomized by United States Steel, was creating fears among academics and muckraking journalists, as well as populists and progressives. The concern, as expressed in a series of articles by future Supreme Court Justice Louis Brandeis, compiled in his book, *Other Peoples' Money, and How the Banks Use It* (1914), was that the concentration of power resulting from the rise of these large firms, connected into a cohesive community through interlocking boards of directors, posed a threat not only to the competitive market but to the democratic character of American society.

Members of the NCF saw a threat beyond the mere concentration of corporate power, however. The response to the rise of large corporations drew protest not only from populists and progressives, but from a growing group of socialists as well. Eugene V. Debs, running as a socialist in the Presidential election of 1912, received more than six percent of the popular vote, a significant increase from his showing in 1908. Without some attempt to reign in the negative excesses of capitalism, these business leaders believed, the increasing support for socialism among American workers could lead to the supersession of capitalism altogether. The goal of the NCF was thus to formulate and encourage a series of policies, mostly private at the time, designed to blunt the militancy of the workers. Given the relatively small size of the American government and its absence of any history of involvement in social welfare policies, most of these plans took the form of social welfare programs administered by the corporations themselves, including life insurance, pension, employee stock ownership, and worker representation (Mitchell, 1989). The NCF had largely disappeared from prominence by the early 1920s, but by that time, the policies it had recommended had become well established, and the threats posed by radical workers had, perhaps in part as a result, receded.

The Great Depression of the 1930s created another dilemma for American business, as the threat of worker revolt reappeared, attempts to organize unions reemerged on a mass scale, and for the first time in American history, the government engaged in a serious effort to institute large-scale social welfare programs. Most historical accounts of the period have suggested that American business was fiercely opposed to Franklin Roosevelt's New Deal, including especially Social Security and the Wagner Act, which greatly expanded workers' rights to organize (Collins, 1981), and many political sociologists have accepted these accounts (for a prototypical example, see Skocpol, 1980). Others, most notably Domhoff (1990) and Quadagno (1984), have argued that a segment of the corporate community not only supported, but actually helped to formulate the ideas behind these programs, although more in the case of Social Security than the Wagner Act. I shall not attempt to adjudicate between these two positions here, other than to note that there were indeed business leaders whose support for certain New Deal policies is well documented. The debate revolves primarily around the extent to which this group constituted an organized force, or merely a small number of idiosyncratic capitalists. Much more evident, however, is the rise to prominence of a moderate leadership of the business community in the postwar period. The CED was established in 1942 and the CFR, while dating from 1921, increased greatly in prominence after the war. The reasons in this case may have had less to do with concerns about worker militancy – although workers had indeed become more prone to strike during and shortly after World War II – than with concerns about the impending Cold War with the Soviet Union. Regardless of the source of its emergence, this moderate wing of the corporate community came to accept as inevitable both the institutions created by the New Deal, and the larger framework within which these reforms occurred: a broad acknowledgement that the state had a role to play in the economy, and that labor had a right to organize.

WHAT HELD IT TOGETHER?

The postwar period, from 1945 into the early 1970s, was the golden age of the moderate orientation of the American corporate elite. To reiterate, the vast majority of businesspeople continued to express conservative political positions during this period, positions that were reflected in the Taft–Hartley Bill, passed in 1947 – which contained a number of measures that unions found abhorrent – and the intense anti-communism that prevailed, reflected in the rise of Senator Joseph McCarthy. Yet although conservatism dominated among both business and the general public, a form of moderation emerged among the leaders of the largest corporations.

It is reasonable to question the extent to which this moderation represented an actual ideological position, or simply a strategic response to a particular set of circumstances. Consistent with the former view, a survey of attitudes among elites conducted in 1971 by Allen Barton (1985) suggested that the chief executives of the largest American corporations held relatively moderate views on a range of political issues. Among the modal positions held by the 120 CEOs who responded to the survey was support for Keynesian deficit spending and federal antipoverty programs, and even support for federal job creation programs for those unable to find employment in the private sector. These survey results suggest the possibility that the moderate positions held by corporate CEOs reflected genuine convictions. On the other hand, there is evidence that corporations exhibited strong opposition to labor unions when the opportunity presented itself, not only with the Taft–Hartley Bill, but also at the firm level (Gross, 1995), and there is considerable evidence that the new Environmental Protection Agency and the Occupational Safety and Health Administration faced significant opposition from large corporations prior to being signed into law by Richard Nixon (Vogel, 1989).

Even with the compelling findings presented by Barton, it is difficult to know the extent to which the views expressed by the CEOs represented deeply held convictions, as opposed to pragmatic responses to a seemingly immutable reality. For my purposes it is not necessary to resolve this issue. Rather, even if these attitudes, whether expressed in Barton's survey or in the CED's 1971 report on solutions to pressing social problems, were mere ploys for public support – and that would seem much more likely in the case of the CED report than in responses to Barton's survey – they still demonstrate the accommodation to a situation that was only partly of their own making. Corporate leaders were relatively moderate in the postwar period, but they were moderate under a specific set of conditions. Three forces contributed to this response, I argue: a relatively active state, a relatively powerful labor movement, and a financial community whose interests transcended those of particular firms or sectors.

The State

As has been well documented, the U.S. government played a relatively small role in the national economy until the 1930s. During that decade, with the rise of New Deal reforms, the state began to play a much larger role in the economy. With the development of programs such as Social Security, agencies such as the Securities and Exchange Commission and the Federal Deposit Insurance Corporation, and projects such as the Tennessee Valley Authority, the federal government became a major player in the economy. It was with World War II that the expansion of the state became fully institutionalized, however.

I noted earlier that there was considerable opposition among business leaders to the New Deal reforms. Even before the war came to an end, business leaders were debating the appropriate role for the state in the postwar economy. There was widespread agreement that the massive spending for the war had provided a significant economic stimulus that vaulted the American economy out of the Depression. There were equally widespread concerns that with the end of the war the economy would again sink into a depression. Under these conditions, moderate business leaders, including members of the CED, were reluctant to support severe reductions in the role of the state (Collins, 1981). The corporate elite instead gave grudging support to Keynesian economic principles, which included deficit spending to stimulate the economy, acceptance of certain transfer payments, and even support for full employment, which, as Collins notes, reduced the need for welfare. Although it is true that much of the state's role in the economy involved its continued high level of postwar military spending, support for nonmilitary federal spending existed as well.

The ability of the state to maintain economic stability as well as the high level of prosperity that existed in the postwar period made it difficult to oppose the state's role in the economy. The relatively high degree of legitimacy enjoyed by the state thus acted as a constraint on the ability of corporations to advocate a return to the more free-market orientation that existed prior to the 1930s. Regardless of what corporate leaders believed about the value of the Social Security system, for example, the abolition of Social Security was simply not an achievable goal in the postwar period.[3] Whatever corporate leaders believed about the need to avoid deficit spending, there was also an acknowledgement that such spending had economy-wide consequences that benefited them as well. The success of government economic action thus provided a constraint on the political behavior of business. Although the majority of businesspeople continued to prefer a smaller economic role for government – in some cases with great vehemence – the moderate leaders of the corporate elite came to accept, as a necessity, that the state had a significant role to play in managing the economy.[4]

Organized Labor

In addition to the state, the corporate elite was constrained in the postwar period by the relative power and legitimacy of organized labor. The history of labor relations in the United States is one of intense conflict (Lichtenstein, 2003). From the earliest days, unionization triggered fierce opposition from businesses. Yet as we have seen, even in the early 1900s, with the formation of the NCF, more moderate and accommodationist views prevailed among the leaders of the corporate community. The most widely held view among labor historians is that in the period following World War II, in the wake of extensive labor militancy, management and workers reached an accommodation, subsequently referred to as the "capital–labor accord" (McIntyre & Hillard, 2008). The key turning point, according to the conventional view, was the agreement reached between the United Auto Workers and General Motors in 1950, which has sometimes been referred to as the Treaty of Detroit. Management provided workers with significant wage increases over a five-year period, along with improved benefits and working conditions. The union promised to prevent strikes, and to eliminate the influence of its more radical elements.

Some labor economists and historians have viewed the accord as an ideological phenomenon, in which management genuinely accepted the idea of unions and saw them as partners in the pursuit of increased productivity and profit (Bowles, Gordon, & Weisskopf, 1983). Others have suggested that the existence of such an accord was a myth. Instead, they argue, it was the result of a temporary truce in an ongoing class war during which strike activity was high and management continued its attempts to thwart unions at every turn (McIntyre & Hillard, 2008). For my purposes, it is less important that corporate managers ideologically accepted the legitimacy of labor unions, than that they were compelled to deal with them. In other words, corporate leaders were faced with a set of strategic options during the postwar period. One option was an aggressive assault on unions. Another option was accommodation. Members of the more conservative (and more small business) National Association of Manufacturers preferred the former option. Members of the largest and more moderate firms, as represented in the CED, preferred the latter option. The result was a period in which unions remained relatively strong, and antiunion legislation with the exception of the bitterly opposed Taft–Hartley Bill (passed in 1947) was relatively dormant.

The Financial Community

A third source of constraint that contributed to the moderate and pragmatic stance of large corporations was the financial community, in particular, the largest commercial banks. In the early twentieth century, a broad range of commentators ranging from muckraking journalists and future Supreme Court Justice Louis Brandeis in the United States to Marxist theorists such as Hilferding and Lenin in Europe argued that the corporate world in developed capitalist countries was dominated by large financial institutions. In the United States, the most notable of these were

J. P. Morgan & Company, the First National Bank of New York, and the National City Bank. Major insurance companies such as Equitable and Metropolitan Life were also seen as highly powerful.

Beginning with the publication of the classic work by Berle and Means (1932), most observers of the corporate world in the United States came to believe that the inside managers who ran the day-to-day affairs of the firm came to dominate, while financial institutions receded in importance, especially after the passage of the Glass–Steagall Act of 1933, which forced commercial and investment banks to separate their functions. Scholars ranging from Daniel Bell (1960) and John Kenneth Galbraith (1967) to Marxist economists Paul Baran and Paul Sweezy (1966) all accepted the idea that the days when banks exercised control over nonfinancial corporations were long past. In the 1970s, a group of social scientists, most notably Maurice Zeitlin (1974), David Kotz (1978), and Michael Schwartz (Mintz & Schwartz, 1985) began to reassert the idea that nonfinancial corporations were beholden to financial institutions, although only Kotz argued that banks "controlled" corporations in a traditional sense. In retrospect, it is likely that the claims of bank power were exaggerated. On the other hand, as Mintz and Schwartz argued, the banks played an important role independent of any control that they might have exercised: they functioned as meeting places for the leadership of the corporate elite as a whole, in some cases mediating disputes between various sectors of business. The banks were a logical site for this role because of their neutral stance with regard to particular industries. Banks are concerned with the viability of the corporate system as a whole, not with the success of any individual sector or industry. They are thus uniquely positioned to represent the interests of business as a whole. Moreover, even in the absence of direct control, the banks could, and occasionally did, provide discipline for individual firms or capitalists who engaged in erratic behavior. One well-documented example was the case of Saul Steinberg, an entrepreneur, who in 1968 attempted to acquire Chemical Bank, at the time one of the six leading New York money market banks. Within two weeks of his announcement of his plan, the stock in Steinberg's firm, Leasco, lost nearly one-third of its value, precipitated by the simultaneous selling of Leasco stock by the trust departments of all six major New York banks (Glasberg, 1989). This massive action was remarkable, given that Chemical Bank was a direct competitor of the other five banks that "dumped" their Leasco stock. It sent a clear message, however, to anyone considering overstepping the bounds of his position.

WHY THIS MATTERS

I have argued that the leadership of the American business community in the postwar period was constrained toward a set of moderate political positions as a result of three forces: a relatively active state, a relatively powerful labor movement, and a financial community that, because of its mediating role, favored moderate solutions. But what relevance does this have to the financial crisis of 2008?

In 1907, in the midst of a severe financial panic, J. P. Morgan assembled a group of bankers and managed to stabilize the system. Morgan and other leading bankers used their own money as well as that of their banks to stave off a catastrophe. Morgan's ultimate act, facilitating the acquisition of the Tennessee Coal and Iron Corporation by U.S. Steel, has been viewed by some observers as a self-serving act that allowed a firm under his control to acquire a major competitor while avoiding antitrust action, all under the guise of solidifying the system. Nevertheless, the crisis was averted, although to ensure that a repeat did not occur, several businessmen, including Morgan, supported the formation of the Federal Reserve Bank, which was established in 1913. Morgan at the time was praised for the leadership he exhibited in averting a more serious crisis.

By the 1930s, in the midst of the greatest financial crisis in American history, an overhaul of the nation's financial system was engineered by Franklin D. Roosevelt, with the support of leading businesspeople. In addition to the aforementioned Glass–Steagall Act, the most important development with relevance to the financial system was the creation of the Securities and Exchange Commission in 1934. From the end of the Great Depression – facilitated by American entry into World War II – into the early 1970s, the American economy exhibited a high level of stability, as well as generally consistent growth. Recessions did occur, but significant financial crises were avoided. This stability was accompanied by the rise of a large middle class, and a reduction in income inequality. Although the share of income drawn by the top one percent of the population declined in the postwar period, absolute incomes and wealth, adjusted for inflation, increased significantly. Whatever the specific problems that occurred, the system was functioning at a high level.

As we moved into the 1970s this situation began to change. The roots of the problems of the 1970s are many, and some were clearly evident during the 1960s. In that decade, the simultaneous increase in government social spending, as part of Lyndon Johnson's Great Society program, along with the high expense involved in fighting the Vietnam War, created significant inflationary pressures. Income taxes were increased in 1968 to stave off a budget deficit, but inflation continued through the transition from the Johnson to the Nixon presidencies.

By 1973, the economic situation had become increasingly precarious. The first of two major energy crises occurred, either a cause or consequence, depending on one's viewpoint, of rapid increases in the price of oil. Foreign competition had begun to create serious problems for American companies, particularly in heavy industries such as auto and steel. The high level of concentration in these industries allowed firms to pass cost increases onto consumers. The firms found these cost increases necessary in part because of the formation of two major new regulatory agencies, the Environmental Protection Agency and the Occupational Safety and Health Administration. These agencies, both signed into law by President Nixon, had been the source of intense opposition by American corporations, even those that had been supportive of (or not strongly opposed to) regulation in the past.

Meanwhile, several decades of high concentration had stifled innovation, and left large American corporations unprepared to compete with upstart foreign producers. The combination of increasing costs for labor as well as those necessary to comply with the new regulations, plus the difficulties brought on by foreign competition, left American corporations in an increasingly difficult state. In addition, the social movements of the 1960s and early 1970s, as well as the Watergate scandal, created an environment in which major societal institutions faced a severe legitimacy crisis. This crisis affected business as well as government, and large corporations saw themselves as under siege.

The response to this crisis by American business has been extensively documented (see, among others, works by Ferguson & Rogers, 1986, and Vogel, 1989). Spurred on by a memo written by future Supreme Court Justice Lewis Powell, business began to organize on a level that dwarfed its earlier efforts. This time, however, rather than promoting moderation and a concern with the well-being of the society as a whole, corporations turned inward, focusing now on advocacy of pro-business positions rather than sober, balanced analyses of social problems. Whereas the CED had included academics and other non-business actors, whose members shared the view that objective social science research could be used in the service of society, the groups that emerged in the 1970s, including the newly formed Business Roundtable (an organization consisting exclusively of *Fortune* 500 chief executives), focused their attention on funding unabashedly partisan scholarship. Groups such as the Heritage Foundation and the American

Enterprise Institute provided forums for scholars to engage in pro-business analyses of contemporary issues (Judis, 2001).

It was also during this period that the traditional Keynesian economic framework came into question. President Nixon had stated in 1970, "I am now a Keynesian in economics."[5] A fundamental component of this approach was the notion that unemployment and inflation were inversely related. This relationship held with great consistency in the postwar period. In fact, the inflationary pressures of the late 1960s may have been triggered by the low levels of unemployment at the time. By 1973, however, the United States began to witness an unprecedented increase in both inflation and unemployment. None of the policies enacted by the state during the period were sufficient to address the problem. In this context, an alternative view emerged. The idea that advanced capitalist economies exhibited a chronic tendency toward insufficient aggregate demand was a central feature of Keynesian analysis. Now, however, the problem seemed to be not insufficient demand, but a lack of supply. Because an increase in scarcity leads to price increases, this supply-side account seemed to provide an explanation for the unprecedented levels of inflation that the nation was experiencing. The lack of supply could also be attributed to a lack of productivity, which in turn could be blamed on excessive regulation and the cumbersome work rules experienced by unionized firms. This led to the rise of alternatives to Keynesianism, including the controversial position, later adopted as policy by Ronald Reagan, known as "supply-side economics."

Among the positions that emerged by the late 1970s, then, were strong aversions to both government regulation and organized labor. As business organized, intensive lobbying efforts ensued, leading to the surprising defeats of both the proposed Consumer Protection Agency and a bill designed to weaken the most antilabor provisions of the Taft–Hartley Act (Vogel, 1989). Although federal policy was already becoming increasingly pro-business during the Carter Administration, the election of Reagan in 1980 signified a culmination of the business political activity of the 1970s. The moderate, accommodationist leadership of the American business community had by this point largely disintegrated. Whether this occurred as a result of a conservative shift by the existing leaders or as a consequence of succession, both cohort wise (as a younger generation of business leaders entered the scene) and geographic (the replacement of those from the Northeast with those from the South and West), there was clearly a change in orientation among the largest corporations.

Still, the pragmatic segment of business leaders had not entirely disappeared. In the late 1970s, a series of interviews conducted by Michael

Useem (1984) indicated that business leaders who sat on multiple boards of directors continued to hold relatively moderate positions. As if to confirm this point, in 1983, in response to growing deficits due to the Reagan tax cuts, the Business Roundtable issued a position paper advocating a tax increase to balance the budget, a decision I discuss below. But two developments were occurring that would ensure that whatever moderation and pragmatism remained within the corporate elite would become further diminished.

THE DECLINE OF THE BANKS, AND THE RISE OF FINANCIALIZATION

By the early 1980s, then, one could argue that the rightward shift of the corporate elite had helped to reshape the political landscape. Government regulation had been significantly scaled back and labor unions had been significantly weakened. Paradoxically, I will argue, the very success that business elites experienced in freeing themselves from the constraints of labor and government became the source of their ultimate undoing as a coherent political actor. But I am getting ahead of the story. There were two other developments during the 1980s that require discussion before returning to my main argument.

I suggested earlier that the large commercial banks, although not necessarily in control of major nonfinancial corporations, were in a position to mediate disputes as well as to discipline recalcitrant elements of the corporate community. As we moved into the 1980s, this situation began to change. As Davis and I have argued (Davis & Mizruchi, 1999), a series of events occurred in this decade that led commercial banks to abdicate their role as arbiters of inter-industry disputes. The banks' influence had come primarily from their control of capital, a necessary resource for corporations that had become even more necessary during the 1970s, as firms were increasingly less able to draw on retained earnings for their financing (Stearns, 1986). But the rise of commercial paper by the late 1970s, in which nonfinancial firms made loans directly to one another, began to reduce the latter's dependence on banks for capital. Moreover, as alternatives such as mutual and money market funds began to proliferate, individuals began to shift their funds away from passbook savings accounts. The banks thus began to lose a significant source of their capital. The upshot of this was that lending was no longer a significant source of profit for the major commercial banks.

Faced with this situation, the banks responded in two ways during the 1980s. First, they moved into increasingly risky lending, in particular, with a series of bad real estate and foreign loans that led some of the leading banks, including Citicorp, into serious trouble by the early 1990s. The second strategy that the banks adopted, however, was to move away from lending as a source of revenue, and instead shift into service-oriented activities, for which they received fees and which were thus risk-free. These activities led commercial banks to increasingly resemble investment banks. Corresponding with this (and perhaps resulting from it), the boards of leading commercial banks became less likely to serve as hosts for the CEOs of the largest nonfinancial firms. From the early part of the twentieth century into the early 1980s, one of the most consistent features of the corporate world was the continuously high centrality of commercial banks in the network of interlocking directorates (Mizruchi, 1982). In the postwar period, much of this centrality was a function of nonfinancial CEOs sitting on the boards of the major banks (Mintz & Schwartz, 1985). In 1982, to take one example, 14 CEOs of *Fortune* 500 corporations sat on the board of the Chase Manhattan Bank. As we moved through the 1980s, this situation changed. For the first time, the banks moved away from the center of the interlock network. In 1982, 8 of the 11 most interlocked firms were commercial banks. By 1994, only 4 of the 13 most central firms were banks (Davis & Mizruchi, 1999).

The shift of the banks away from commercial lending and toward fee-for-service activities, and the corresponding decline in bank centrality in interlock networks meant that the banks were no longer in a position to serve as the arbiter of inter-sector disputes. Nor were they in a position to discipline aberrant capitalists. This may have been one reason that the innovators of the 1980s, who, with the use of low-grade "junk bonds" created a revolution in the financial world, were as successful as they were. Had the banks played the conservative role that they had occupied back in the 1960s, the use of junk bonds for major acquisitions might have never gotten off the ground.

By the mid-1980s, then, all three of the major forces that had contributed to the relative moderation of the corporate elite in the postwar period had dissipated. The state had sharply reduced its role in regulating corporate activities, including what in earlier decades might have been viewed as antitrust violations. The labor movement had become a shadow of its former self, focusing increasingly on public employees while continuing to decline in the private sector. And the commercial banks, the final source of constraint for the corporate elite, had morphed into increasingly investment bank-like actors. This shift foreshadowed the ultimate end of the Glass–Steagall Act itself, repealed by Congress in 1999.

But how, given the widely cited financialization of the American economy described by both Davis (2009) and Krippner (2010), can we reconcile the decline of the banks with the presumed increasing power of the financial sector during the same period? The answer is twofold: first, the commercial banks did in fact resuscitate themselves, at least until the 2008 meltdown, but as we have seen, they did so by significantly altering their role; second, along with the shifting orientation of commercial banks came the reemergence of investment banks, as well as the rise of a series of other financial actors. Finance did indeed become the major source of corporate profits, and its institutions became increasingly powerful in a collective sense, in that the actions of key players now had an increasing impact on not only the rest of the society, but the rest of the world as well. Unlike the postwar period, however, this impact was not the result of any collective action, but rather an aggregate consequence of the individual dealings of actors who controlled enormous sources of wealth.

THE TAKEOVER WAVE

The real start to this development was the takeover wave of the 1980s. The roots of this wave rested with the stock market decline in 1974 and the continuing economic malaise of the 1970s. Stock prices remained low through the remainder of the decade, in part because of weak performance but also due to a lack of optimism about future economic prospects. The rise of agency theory in financial economics during this period also appears to have played a role, in that investors came increasingly to use these ideas as justifications for their actions (Zajac & Westphal, 2004). The theory implied that corporations were "undervalued" during the 1970s, as managers, insulated from stockholders and the market from years of high profits and low competition, found themselves unable to compete once their market power declined. The relatively low stock prices created an opportunity for investors to wrest control from the managers, and the 1980s takeover wave can be seen as a manifestation of this process. The wave was further facilitated by generous tax laws that allowed the interest on debt used for acquisitions to be written off, as well as by an absence of antitrust enforcement by Reagan Administration officials, who seemed instead to actually encourage the wave of acquisitions, perhaps as a means of restoring efficiency to the economy.

The result of this wave was that one-third of the *Fortune* 500 disappeared within a single decade. Corporate CEOs, heretofore the kingpins of the system, were now in an increasingly vulnerable position, as their firms were gobbled up by investors, who often chopped them into pieces and sold off the separate components, rendering the sum of the parts greater than the whole. Many firms attempted to legislate their way to safety from takeovers, through the use of "poison pill" defense programs (Davis, 1991), but even these did not stem the tide. Although there are some differences among scholars regarding the magnitude of the change, there is widespread agreement that CEO tenure declined substantially between the early 1980s and the turn of the century (Neff & Ogden, 2001; Kaplan & Minton, 2006). One could argue that it was precisely the high degree of security experienced by CEOs in the postwar period that provided the space to consider the long-term interests of both the larger business community and the society as a whole. Such security may not have been a sufficient condition for such behavior, but it undoubtedly was a necessary one. Useem (1984) has provided an example of the consequences of this turnover at the top of large corporations. A CEO of a retail firm lost his position as an outside director on the board of an insurance company after his firm was acquired by another company. In an interview conducted by Useem, a director of the insurance company explained why the retail CEO was not reappointed to the insurance company's board: "He was suddenly without a job; he devoted his time to working with the local art museum, but he didn't keep up with the business community because he hadn't any base ... His being on the board does not add anything" (Useem, 1984, p. 39).

CONSEQUENCES FOR THE CORPORATE ELITE

Let us now consider the glacial changes that the American corporate elite had experienced over a period of less than two decades. At the beginning of the 1970s the elite included a small group of leaders from the largest corporations, who held relatively moderate views on political issues and adopted an accommodationist, pragmatic strategy toward labor and the state. This group was constrained to act in this way by the relatively powerful positions of both the government and organized labor, as well as the disciplining force of the banking community. In the late 1970s a major corporate offensive greatly weakened the labor movement, and led to a significant reduction in government regulation. In the 1980s the United States witnessed a decline in the power of commercial banks, which abdicated their role in mediating inter-corporate disputes. Finally, the massive takeover wave of the 1980s decimated the position of management, who now found themselves under pressures that exceeded any faced by this group since before the Great Depression.

The CEOs who remained faced additional pressures as well. The threat of takeover was only one of the external forces the CEOs now experienced. Useem (1993, 1996) has argued that the growth of institutional stockholders has placed an entirely new set of constraints on CEO actions. Because of their large holdings, it is no longer feasible for these owners to simply sell their shares if they disagree with the policies of management. As a result, Useem argues, institutional stockholders have become increasingly aggressive in attempting to influence managerial decision making. Because of pressures that institutional investors face for quick returns, these owners have made it increasingly difficult for CEOs to engage in long-term planning. Interestingly, however, these institutional investors, according to Useem, are a far cry from the inner circle of his earlier writings. Rather than exhibiting concerns for the larger interests of the business community, the personnel who make decisions for the institutional investors are financial professionals, interested in returns on their investment, but with no concerns beyond those narrow confines.

Dobbin and Zorn (2005) go a step further, arguing that control emanates from an even lower level. Among the most important concerns facing contemporary CEOs is the quarterly profit projections issued for their firm by financial analysts. Regardless of whether the firm is highly profitable or experiencing deep losses, what matters for much of the investment community is how well the firm performs relative to expectations. In other words, even a highly profitable firm may see its market value decline if its profits come in under the projected rate. This has led many firms to adjust their books in such a way as to meet, virtually exactly, their quarterly projections. For our purposes, what is important is the significance attached to these projections. In Dobbin and Zorn's view, the ability to meet these projections dwarfs all other management concerns.

Finally, Davis (2009) has argued that the capital market itself has become the new source of corporate control. A number of scholars have noted the distinct shift beginning in the 1970s toward an ideology of "shareholder value" (see Zajac & Westphal, 2004). Prior to this time, corresponding with the ascendance of management, managers were seen as skilled professionals whose legitimacy in running the firm was largely unquestioned. As the economy suffered in the 1970s and stock prices declined, leading to significant losses for investors, criticism of management mounted. The rise of agency theory in financial economics, noted earlier, was accompanied by an ideology that stressed first and foremost the importance of the firm's stock price, as a means of appealing to investors. As Zajac and Westphal show, the ideology of shareholder value grew in significance during the 1980s, and it remained the dominant narrative into the twenty-first century.

Given the importance attributed to stock price, and the increasingly active role of investors – both in direct influence on running the firm as well as in corporate acquisitions – CEOs found themselves focusing not on the long-term concerns of the firm per se, but rather on the short-term value of the firm's stock. Too great a depression of a firm's stock price could leave a firm vulnerable to a takeover, or its CEO vulnerable to replacement. In some cases it even led to radical, possibly reckless, actions, such as Ross Johnson's ill-fated attempt at a leveraged buyout of RJR Nabisco in 1988 (Burrough & Helyar, 1990).

Each of the above three accounts suggests a different source of corporate control: institutional stockholders, financial analysts, and the general capital market, respectively. What all three have in common is the view that corporate CEOs no longer sat atop the business world, with both high prestige and security. Rather, they faced increasing external pressure, as well as a loss of legitimacy. What replaced them, however, was not a new coherent group of actors, but instead a void. The corporate community, increasingly run by the vicissitudes of Wall Street investors out for nothing more than spectacular returns on their investment portfolios, now faced a vacuum of leadership. The group was fragmented, with no cosmopolitan leading edge able to speak for the community as a whole. It is not that the networks had disappeared. On the contrary, connections to the inner circle within Wall Street provided the key to enormous riches. But these connections were used as instruments for very specific goals, and not as the basis of institutional or societal leadership, as the corporate elite of the postwar period had done.

This created an enormous paradox. On one hand, the overall legitimacy of business had reached an apex unequaled since at least the 1920s. The best and brightest from leading universities dreamt not of careers as scientists, in government, or even in corporate management, but rather of careers as Wall Street hedge fund operators. Free market ideology had returned to its pre-Depression dominance. Government intervention that would have been taken for granted in the Nixon Administration became far too radical for the Clinton and Obama Administrations to even consider. The political triumph of business could not have been more complete. And yet as a collective actor, business had become increasingly ineffectual.

TWO EXAMPLES

Two examples will illustrate this decline of the American corporate elite. After Ronald Reagan's election, Reagan managed to persuade Congress to enact a significant across-the-board tax cut, while at the same time rapidly increasing military spending. The result was record deficits, in the midst of an already severe recession. In 1983, concerned that the deficit was out of control, the Business Roundtable reluctantly chose to advocate a tax increase to balance the budget (*Wall Street Journal*, 1983). Given the popularity of the tax cuts, and the fact that corporations and wealthy individuals were major beneficiaries, the Roundtable was exercising an enormous level of responsibility in pursuing this position. One could argue, as I have elsewhere (Mizruchi, 2007a), that such an action was consistent with those of the moderate, forward-thinking corporate elite of the postwar period. In fact, the support for tax increases might even be viewed as the corporate elite's "last stand."

Two decades later, George W. Bush similarly enacted significant across-the-board tax cuts, again leading to record deficits. In addition, the nation was at war and was still recovering from the September 11 attacks. In other words, it was a time in which asking the public to make a sacrifice by agreeing to a tax increase to finance the Iraq War could certainly have been justified based on historical precedent. Yet despite a situation that mirrored that of the early 1980s, with the added wartime conditions, the Business Roundtable was nowhere to be heard on the issue. In April 2004, I attended a talk at the Detroit Economic Club by John Castellani, the president of the Business Roundtable. Departing from his prepared text, Castellani spoke for several minutes about the severity of the deficit and the dangers it posed for the long-run viability of the American economy. And yet at no point in this discussion did Castellani mention the Bush tax cuts as a possible cause of the deficit, or suggest the possibility of even a temporary rescinding of the cuts as a possible solution.[6] The contrast between the Roundtable's call for a tax increase in 1983 and its silence on the issue in 2004 is striking. The exact reasons for the group's unwillingness to suggest a tax increase during the George W. Bush Administration are unclear. As Krippner (2010) notes, during the 1980s, foreign governments and investors responded to high U.S. interest rates by investing in American Treasury Bills, thus in effect financing the U.S. government's deficit. This may have led American business leaders to view deficits as a less serious problem than they had in earlier decades. On the other hand, Castellani, in speaking for the Business Roundtable, expressed grave concern about the deficit, suggesting that it remained every bit as serious in 2004 as it had in 1983. This rendered his silence on the issue of taxes even more notable. This refusal to even consider the possibility of a tax increase reflects an absence of leadership, in terms of an unwillingness to take an unpopular position for the larger national interest, an absence that characterizes contemporary American corporations, and distinguishes them from their predecessors of earlier decades.

A second example of the ineffectual nature of the contemporary business community is its inability to come up with a health care proposal that would benefit not only the larger society but corporations themselves. The largest 500 American corporations alone spent more than $375 billion dollars in 2009 on health care for their employees, a cost that firms in other developed nations do not have to bear.[7] Although a single-payer health care system such as that in Canada would most likely lead to an increase in corporate taxes, this increase would also likely be more than offset by the cost savings that employers would receive from being released from the responsibility for their employees' health care. It is true that a number of corporate groups have called for health care reform. Even the Business Roundtable has issued a statement noting the enormous toll that high health care costs have taken on American corporations' ability to compete.[8] But none of these groups has been willing to introduce a comprehensive solution that would absolve corporations of this responsibility, despite the apparent financial benefits they would receive from doing so. This is one case in which the business community may be acting against its own interests, in a way that harms not only the larger society but the corporations themselves. It is true that the health insurance industry and other elements of the health care industry may have an economic incentive to preserve the existing system, but the majority of industries have no economic stake in preserving it, and a considerable stake in dismantling it. Yet neither the Business Roundtable nor any other business-wide group has been able or willing to propose any kind of coherent plan that would address the interests of the community as a whole.[9]

THE FINANCIAL CRISIS

The reactions of the business community to the financial crisis of 2008 provide a further illustration of the inability of this group to coordinate its interests in a coherent and effective fashion. The 1907 crisis was solved by private means, not by the state, but as a result of the crisis, corporate leaders, including Morgan himself, advocated the creation of the Federal Reserve Bank. The stock market crash of 1929 and the ensuing Great

Depression led to an enormous expansion of regulation, from the establishment of the Securities and Exchange Commission to the passage of Glass–Steagall. The financial community may have initially opposed some of these regulations, but they later came to accept them as at least an unchangeable reality.

The crisis of 2008 was different. Several observers have argued that the lack of regulation of new financial instruments played a major role in the crisis (Krugman, 2008). Subprime mortgages, the real estate equivalent of the junk bonds in the 1980s, had associated with them no rules regarding maximum exposure levels that the banks could endure. Derivatives were not required to be publicly listed. Because of their novelty, ratings agencies experienced difficulty in identifying an appropriate risk level for mortgage-backed securities. This contributed to charges that the services were providing an inappropriately rosy picture of the risk levels associated with them, driven in part by the fact that the agencies' customers owned the securities that the agencies were rating. As the Obama Administration took office, critics lobbied for increased regulation of several financial instruments. Historically, American corporations have accepted a certain level of regulation on the ground that, like a referee in a sporting event, the regulators helped to ensure that the players kept within the rules. Yet despite the enormous negative repercussions of the 2008 meltdown, there has, as of this writing, been nothing but resistance from the financial community for any further regulation. One possible reason for this has been the view that the largest financial institutions are "too big to fail," that after the collapse of Lehman Brothers in September 2008, the government made it a point to step in and rescue large institutions such as Citigroup and AIG, because of fears that their failure might have led to a complete implosion of the financial system. It was precisely this knowledge that the government would not allow them to fail that led these banks to engage in such high-risk activities, critics have argued.

The seemingly out-of-control behavior of even the most venerable financial institutions raises a question, however: would such a situation have occurred four decades earlier? From the end of the Great Depression until the mid-1980s, the American financial system experienced not a single episode that might be termed a "crisis." The stock market had its ups and downs to be sure, in 1974 losing nearly 50 percent of its value within a brief period. But there were no bubbles or abrupt collapses resembling 1929, or 1907, or 1893. Beginning with the one-day stock market crash in October 1987, we have witnessed at least three significant collapses: the 1987 crash, the dot-com bubble of the late 1990s and its collapse in 2000, and the real estate bubble of the early 2000s and its collapse in 2007–2008. In other words, is it an accident that as the primary source of profit shifted from the creation of tangible products to the creation of arguably fictitious wealth based on moving money from one place to another, using techniques that were increasingly mysterious even to those who engaged in them, the system became increasingly vulnerable to the booms and busts of the past two decades? And would this have occurred had there been a well-organized, trans-industry corporate elite able to work with the state to ensure that the system operated in an orderly and predictable manner? I believe that the answer to both questions is no.[10]

CONCLUSION

In *The Eighteenth Brumaire of Louis Bonaparte*, Karl Marx alluded to the floundering of the French bourgeoisie, which, unable to coordinate its actions in any coherent form, took on the character of a disorganized, ineffectual mob. Only the willingness of the French state to step in and "save" the bourgeoisie from itself prevented the complete destruction of French capitalism. In this case, state power manifested itself in the form of a coup. Yet, according to Marx, the French bourgeoisie seemed to understand that at times only the state can do for capitalists what they are unable to do for themselves. As Marx put it ([1852] 1972, pp. 473–474):

> "... the bourgeoisie therefore confesses that its own interest dictates that it should be delivered from the danger of *governing in its own name*; that, in order to restore tranquility in the land, its bourgeois parliament must, first of all, be given its quietus; that in order to preserve its social power inviolate, its political power must be broken; that the private bourgeois can only continue to exploit the other classes and to enjoy undisturbed property, family, religion, and order on condition that their class be condemned along with the other classes to a like political nullity; that in order to save its purse, it must abandon the crown ..." (emphasis in the original).

In this case Marx is referring to a very specific instance, in which Louis Bonaparte dissolved the capitalist-dominated French National Assembly in order to consolidate his power. But this formulation later became the basis of what was known as the structuralist theory of the capitalist state. This view, advanced most forcefully by Poulantzas (1972), suggested that left to their own devices, the business community was incapable of acting collectively to reach a coherent political position. Because there were situations in which different sectors of business experienced conflicts of interest, it was necessary for the state to be able to pursue policies that were in the best interest of business as a whole, even if it meant acting against the interests of particular sectors. Mintz and Schwartz (1985) argued that the financial community played this role. But a number of theorists, drawing on Poulantzas, saw this as a way to understand the passage of programs such as Social Security and the Wagner Act (Quadagno, 1984). Although these were understood to be opposed to the specific short-term interests of several sectors of the corporate community, they could also be seen as conducive to the preservation of the system as a whole.

In the post-World War II period, a leading segment of American capitalists came to accept, at least on strategic grounds, the role of the state in maintaining the system. This group, of course, attempted to influence the state to act in the interests of large corporations, but its members also understood that the state would require a degree of autonomy to be able to engage in such actions. I have argued that a series of events occurred that led to the breakdown of this arrangement. As a result of the economic turmoil and structural changes of the 1970s, large American corporations began to reject their earlier accommodation with the state and with organized labor. By the early 1980s business had achieved its goals, as state regulation receded and labor was greatly weakened. Yet the very success that the corporate elite experienced during this period ultimately led to its undoing, I have argued. No longer constrained by the state and labor, and increasingly independent of the banks as well, the corporate elite became increasingly fragmented, its members focused primarily on their specific short-term interests. This can be seen in the corporate response to the 1986 Tax Reform Act, in which corporations formed several different groups, each with a relatively narrow set of concerns (Martin, 1991). The highly organized collective action of the corporate community in earlier years had receded into the past. As a final coup de grace, the takeover wave of the 1980s decimated corporate management, the core of the old corporate elite, as one-third of the 500 largest manufacturing firms disappeared during the decade. By the early 1990s, despite the continued existence of groups such as the Business Roundtable, what remained of the American corporate elite bore little resemblance to that of the previous generation. Instead, power had shifted to the financial community. But this community was not the small group of leading, old-line New York commercial banks, as in earlier years. Rather, the financial community was now a mélange of professional investors working in the service of institutional stockholders, financial analysts, hedge fund managers, and arbitrageurs. Bankers remained, to be sure, but as Stearns and I found in a study of a leading commercial bank in the late 1990s, these bankers were mere sales people, providing a variety of financial services to corporate clients, but with no pretense to either influence over the firms' activities or any sense of the collective interests of the business community as a whole (Mizruchi & Stearns, 2001).

It was under these conditions that the real estate bubble, the proliferation of subprime mortgages, and mortgage-backed securities sold worldwide to investors who had little idea of what they were buying, were allowed to flourish. And it was the lack of rules, the nonexistence of restraints, which provided a context for them. Business, having won the war to free itself from the state and the workers, and having regained a level of legitimacy and admiration unlike anything since the 1920s, was now unable to prevent the collapse of its own system. "Power without efficacy" is the phrase I have used to describe this state of affairs (Mizruchi, 2007a). At the risk of immodesty, I believe that the term provides an appropriate description.

Implications for Policy

Given the historical nature of my argument and its relatively broad scope, it might be presumptuous to offer any suggestions for current policy. And yet the example with which we began this section – Marx's discussion of the French bourgeoisie during the reign of Louis Bonaparte – may provide a solution to the current morass. As noted earlier, American corporations have often accepted government regulation as a means of reducing destructive competition and maintaining a stable environment. This occurred in industries ranging from airlines to coal, and oil to sugar. It also occurred among financial corporations. Financial regulation, as we have seen, corresponded with a period of nearly half a century during which the American economy managed to avoid a single major financial disaster.

Correlation is not necessarily causation, of course. It may be that the coincidence of financial regulation with the avoidance of financial crisis was actually a function of an unmeasured third factor, perhaps general economic health. And even if regulation did benefit the economy during the earlier period, there is no assurance that it would have similar benefits in the present. On the contrary, to take one example, there were good reasons that deregulation occurred in the airline industry, even if the outcome has generated problems of its own (Lawrence, 2004). On the other hand, the correspondence of financial regulation with the absence of crisis is unmistakable: nearly five decades without a severe financial episode in the United States. What characterized the volatility that we have experienced since the 1980s – the savings and loan crisis, the 1987 stock market crash, the bursting of the dot-com bubble in 2000, and the financial collapse of 2008 – is an environment in which longstanding regulations were either lifted or unenforced, while a range of new financial instruments went unregulated. As of this writing, the financial industry has strongly opposed attempts to impose new regulations. And yet the absence of regulation may not only have played a significant role in the most recent crisis, but it may render the system vulnerable to future meltdowns in which large segments of the financial industry will suffer. The unwillingness or inability of the financial industry to act may be in part a collective action problem: why should any member of the financial community support regulation when its competitors refuse to do so? Yet this is precisely why it may be necessary for the state to step in, to save the financial industry (and with it, the rest of the nation) from itself. If major American corporations lack the effective internal organization to address their own problems, then there seems to be little alternative but for the state to exercise whatever autonomy it has, to do for the corporations what they are apparently incapable of doing for themselves.

Meanwhile, we sociologists have an obligation as well. In both economic and political sociology, our preoccupation with the state has in many cases blinded us to the role that non-state actors play in government policy. The study of the political activity of business emerged on a large scale in American sociology by the 1980s, but it has slowed to a trickle since that time (Mizruchi, 2007b). If sociologists are going to contribute to under-standing the economic issues of our time – the growing inequality of wealth, the declining role of the state, and the increasing incidence of financial crises among them – then we will have to refocus our lens on the actors whose actions (or nonactions) have played the largest role in affecting them. This means that we need to return to studying the corporate elite: its structure, its ideologies, its internal organization, and its relations with external actors. Why, given the hundreds of billions of dollars they spend, do American corporations continue to oppose efforts for health care reform? Why, despite the enormous losses they incurred, do members of the financial industry continue to oppose regulation? Are the problems ideological? Are they organizational, an inability to sustain an effective effort at collective action? Are they a simple consequence of individual actors pursuing their short-run interests without regard for the long-term consequences? Without the study of American corporations, arguably the most powerful actors in the society, we will remain unable to provide a clear understanding of the contemporary American economy.

NOTES

1. An example of this practice could be seen in a widely viewed television commercial for LendingTree.com, featuring the fictitious "Stanley Johnson." "I'm Stanley Johnson," the actor intones. "I've got a great family. I've got a four-bedroom house in a great community. Like my car? It's new. I even belong to the local golf club. How do I do it? I'm in debt up to my eyeballs. I can barely pay my finance charges." All of this is conveyed by the actor with a carefree smile on his face, which adds to the irony. After the narrator extols the virtues of securing a home equity loan through LendingTree.com, Mr. Johnson pleads, with the same blank smile, "Somebody help me." This commercial, which ran during the peak of the housing bubble, disappeared from the air almost immediately after the bubble burst. The commercial can be viewed at http://www.youtube.com/watch?v = hn5EP9StlVA, or by going to www.youtube.com and searching on "Stanley Johnson commercial."

2. A *Time* magazine article published shortly after President Eisenhower's reelection in 1956, and reprinted in full in an advertisement for the magazine in the *Wall Street Journal* (November 21, 1956:13) provides further evidence of this view. After describing the Eisenhower administration's policy of "conserving" and enlarging the social programs inherited from the "New and Fair Deals," the article quotes several leading business executives who express their support for this more moderate approach. "Says Gaylord A. Freeman, vice president of the First National Bank of Chicago: 'I think social security is good. I think unions are good. Unemployment compensation is desirable. Social legislation can add to the totality of freedom, increase the dignity of the individual.'" "Businessmen who once decried government meddling in the economy also recognize that most federal police powers, e.g., regulation of the stock market, benefit business as well as the consumer," the article continues. "Most businessmen agree today with DuPont chairman Walter S. Carpenter Jr. that the antitrust laws, under which his company has been haled [sic] into court 22 times, 'are fair and should be vigorously enforced.'" The article goes on to describe corporate leaders' support for the broadening of educational opportunity, as well as their aim to encourage their employees to become well-rounded citizens who live "in the world, not just the company." I thank Todd Schifeling for uncovering this reference.

3. There is evidence that even in the period right after its passage, most American business leaders had come to accept the existence of Social Security. In a poll conducted by *Fortune* in 1939, cited by Quadagno (1984), only 17 percent of the businesspeople sampled favored repeal of the system, and none of those who favored repeal were from large manufacturing firms.

4. This corporate acceptance of an active state extended beyond economic policy to limited acceptance of regulation as well. Business support for such regulation in both the pre- and post-World War II period was plentiful, particularly at the industry level. Members of the sugar industry supported the Sugar Act of 1948. Oil company executives supported the Interstate Oil Compact instituted in 1935 (Berle, 1954, pp. 44–45). The airline industry supported the regulations of the Civil Aeronautics Board that provided a steady stream of profits from the 1940s into the 1970s (Lawrence, 2004). And coal producers supported the government's attempts to enforce an industry-wide price (Bowman, 1989, pp. 203–210). Moreover, beyond

support for these industry-specific regulations, American business leaders expressed considerable support for a broad-based antitrust policy. See the discussion of this in Krooss (1970), especially pp. 313–314, as well as the *Time* magazine story described above.

5. The quote usually attributed to Nixon is "we are all Keynesians now." In fact, however, that statement was actually made by the militantly free-market economist Milton Friedman in an interview in *Time* magazine (Krugman, 2009). Friedman's full quote, which he clarified in a letter to the editor of *Time* (February 4, 1966), and which conveyed a very different meaning, was "In one sense, we are all Keynesians now; in another, nobody is any longer a Keynesian."

6. The text of Castellani's speech appeared on the Business Roundtable website for several years after the talk, which took place on April 26, 2004, but it no longer appears to be available. The discussion of the deficit did not appear in the publicly distributed text. Whether the published version was Castellani's intended speech and the material on the deficit was extemporaneous, or whether the material on the deficit was a part of the original prepared remarks but was excised from the published version is unclear.

7. I arrived at this figure as follows: A recent report by Hewitt Associates, commissioned by the Business Roundtable and available on the organization's website, estimated the average per employee cost of health insurance for "large employers" at $10,743 per year. According to the Business Roundtable, in March 2009 the group represented firms with more than 35 million employees. The product of the two yields the figure cited in the text.

8. See http://www.businessroundtable.org/initiatives/health.

9. A question raised by this discussion is why, if the American corporate elite held a moderate, pragmatic orientation in the postwar period, did its leaders not push for comprehensive health care reform at that time? One possible reason is that health care costs during the 1950s and 1960s were simply not a significant economic problem. According to the Congressional Budget Office, health care expenditures constituted approximately 17 percent of the U.S. gross domestic product by 2009 (with a projected rise to 25 percent by 2025), but only 4.9 percent in 1960 and approximately 6 percent in 1970. See http://www.cbo.gov/ftpdocs/87xx/doc8758/MainText.3.1.shtml.

10. One possible exception to this lack of regulation was the passage of the Sarbanes–Oxley Act of 2002. This law, which was passed in the wake of the Enron and Worldcom scandals at the turn of the century, put into place a series of regulating boards, reporting requirements, and rules prohibiting conflicts of interest between firms and their auditors. The bill was passed despite considerable opposition from the financial firms, and continues to inspire criticism. Although this case does demonstrate that it is possible to institute regulations even in the contemporary period, it does not change the fact that the activities at the root of the far more serious 2008 crisis remain unregulated at this writing. Commentators and scholars continue to debate the effectiveness of Sarbanes–Oxley (see, e.g., Cherry, 2004), and whether it led to fundamental changes in corporate governance. Even if it did have a nonnegligible impact, the absence of anything of comparable scope related to the more recent financial crisis suggests that Sarbanes–Oxley could be viewed as the exception that proves the rule.

ACKNOWLEDGMENTS

I thank the conference organizers, Paul Hirsch and Mike Lounsbury, as well as Greta Krippner, Monica Prasad, and the other conference participants, especially Bruce Carruthers, for their comments on an earlier draft. Research for the article was supported in part by the National Science Foundation, grant SES-0922915.

REFERENCES

Baran, P. A., & Sweezy, P. M. (1966). *Monopoly capital*. New York: Monthly Review Press.
Barton, A. H. (1985). Determinants of economic attitudes in the American business elite. *American Journal of Sociology, 91*, 54–87.
Bell, D. (1960). *The end of ideology*. New York: Collier.
Bell, D. (1973). *The coming of post-industrial society*. New York: Basic.
Berle, A. A., Jr. (1954). *The 20th century capitalist revolution*. New York: Harcourt, Brace, & World.
Berle, A. A., & Means, G. C. (1932). *The modern corporation and private property*. New York: Harcourt, Brace, & World.
Bowles, S., Gordon, D. M., & Weisskopf, T. E. (1983). *Beyond the wasteland: A democratic alternative to economic decline*. Garden City, NY: Anchor Doubleday.
Bowman, J. R. (1989). *Capitalist collective action: Competition, cooperation, and conflict in the coal industry*. New York: Cambridge University Press.
Brandeis, L. D. (1914). *Other people's money*. New York: Frederick A. Stokes.
Burrough, B., & Helyar, J. (1990). *Barbarians at the gate: The fall of RJR Nabisco*. New York: Harper & Row.
Cherry, M. A. (2004). Whistling in the dark? Corporate fraud, whistleblowers, and the implications of the Sarbanes-Oxley Act for employment law. *Washington Law Review, 79*, 1029–1122.
Collins, R. M. (1981). *The business response to Keynes, 1929–1964*. New York: Columbia University Press.
Dahl, R. A. (1961). *Who governs?* New Haven, CT: Yale University Press.
Davis, G. F. (1991). Agents without principles? The spread of the poison pill through the intercorporate network. *Administrative Science Quarterly, 36*, 583–613.
Davis, G. F. (2009). *Managed by the markets: How finance reshaped America*. New York: Oxford University Press.
Davis, G. F., & Mizruchi, M. S. (1999). The money center cannot hold: Commercial banks in the U.S. system of corporate governance. *Administrative Science Quarterly, 44*, 215–239.
Dobbin, F., & Zorn, D. (2005). Corporate malfeasance and the myth of shareholder value. *Political Power and Social Theory, 17*, 179–198.
Domhoff, G. W. (1967). *Who rules America?* Englewood Cliffs, NJ: Prentice-Hall.
Domhoff, G. W. (1970). *The higher circles*. New York: Vintage.
Domhoff, G. W. (1990). *The power elite and the state*. New York: Aldine De Gruyter.

Ferguson, T., & Rogers, J. (1986). *Right turn: The decline of the democrats and the future of American politics*. New York: Hill and Wang.

Fligstein, N., & Goldstein, A. (2010). The anatomy of the mortgage securitization crisis. In: M. Lounsbury & P. M. Hirsch (Eds), *Markets on trial: The economic sociology of the U.S. financial crisis: Part A*. Research in the Sociology of Organizations. Bingley, UK: Emerald.

Frederick, W. C. (1981). Free market vs. social responsibility: Decision time at the CED. *California Management Review, 23*(3), 20–28.

Galbraith, J. K. (1967). *The new industrial state*. New York: New American Library.

Glasberg, D. S. (1989). *The power of collective purse strings*. Berkeley, CA: University of California Press.

Gross, J. A. (1995). *Broken promise: The subversion of U.S. labor relations policy, 1947–1994*. Philadelphia: Temple University Press.

Harrison, P. (2009). *Median wages and productivity growth in Canada and the United States*. Centre for the Study of Living Standards Research Note 2009-2, Ottawa, Canada.

Hunter, F. (1953). *Community power structure*. Chapel Hill, NC: University of North Carolina Press.

Judis, J. B. (2001). *The paradox of American democracy*. New York: Routledge.

Kaplan, S. N., & Minton, B. A. (2006). *How has CEO turnover changed? Increasingly performance sensitive boards and increasingly uneasy CEOs*. Unpublished manuscript, Graduate School of Business, University of Chicago.

Kaysen, C. (1957). The social significance of the modern corporation. *American Economic Review, 47*, 311–319.

Kotz, D. M. (1978). *Bank control of large corporations in the United States*. Berkeley, CA: University of California Press.

Krippner, G. R. (2010). *Capitalizing on crisis: The political origins of the rise of finance*. Cambridge, MA: Harvard University Press.

Krooss, H. E. (1970). *Executive opinion: What business leaders said and thought, 1920s–1960s*. Garden City, NY: Doubleday.

Krugman, P. (2008). *The return of depression economics and the crisis of 2008*. New York: W. W. Norton.

Krugman, P. (2009). How did economists get it so wrong? *New York Times Magazine*, September 2.

Lawrence, H. (2004). *Aviation and the role of government*. Dubuque, IA: Kendall Hunt Publishing.

Lichtenstein, N. (2003). *State of the union: A century of American labor*. Princeton: Princeton University Press.

Martin, C. J. (1991). *Shifting the burden: The struggle over growth and corporate taxation*. Chicago: University of Chicago Press.

Marx, K. ([1852] 1972). The eighteenth Brumaire of Louis Bonaparte. In: R. C. Tucker (Ed.), *The Marx-Engels reader*. New York: Norton, pp. 436–525.

McIntyre, R., & Hillard, M. (2008). The 'limited capital-labor accord': May it rest in peace? *Review of Radical Political Economics, 40*, 244–249.

Mills, C. W. (1956). *The power elite*. New York: Oxford University Press.

Mintz, B., & Schwartz, M. (1985). *The power structure of American business*. Chicago: University of Chicago Press.

Mitchell, N. J. (1989). *The generous corporation: A political analysis of economic power*. New Haven, CT: Yale University Press.

Mizruchi, M. S. (1982). *The American corporate network, 1904–1974*. Beverly Hills, CA: Sage Publications.

Mizruchi, M. S. (2007a). *Power without efficacy: The decline of the American corporate elite*. Unpublished manuscript. Department of Sociology, University of Michigan. Available at: http://www-personal.umich.edu/~mizruchi/seminar-paper1.pdf

Mizruchi, M. S. (2007b). Political economy and network analysis: An untapped convergence. *Sociologica*, 2, 1–27. Available at: http://www.sociologica.mulino.it/doi/10.2383/24765

Mizruchi, M. S., & Stearns, L. B. (2001). Getting deals done: The use of social networks in bank decision-making. *American Sociological Review*, 66, 647–671.

Neff, T., & Ogden, D. (2001). Anatomy of a CEO: Chief executive officer research. The Chief Executive. Available at: http://findarticles.com/p/articles/mi_m4070/is_2001_Feb/ai_71579494

Polsby, N. W. (1963). *Community power and political theory*. New Haven, CT: Yale University Press.

Poulantzas, N. (1972). The problem of the capitalist state. In: R. Blackburn (Ed.), *Ideology in social science* (pp. 238–253). London: Fontana.

Quadagno, J. S. (1984). Welfare capitalism and the Social Security Act of 1935. *American Sociological Review*, 49, 632–647.

Ragin, C. C., & Becker, H. S. (1992). *What is a case?* Cambridge: Cambridge University Press.

Rose, A. M. (1967). *The power structure*. New York: Oxford University Press.

Skocpol, T. (1980). Political response to capitalist crisis: Neo-Marxist theories of the state and the case of the New Deal. *Politics and Society*, 10, 155–201.

Soref, M. (1976). Social class and a division of labor within the corporate elite: A note on class, interlocking, and executive committee membership of directors of U.S. industrial firms. *Sociological Quarterly*, 17, 360–368.

Stearns, L. B. (1986). Capital market effects on external control of corporations. *Theory and Society*, 15, 47–75.

Useem, M. (1979). The social organization of the American business elite and participation of corporate directors in the governance of American institutions. *American Sociological Review*, 44, 553–572.

Useem, M. (1984). *The inner circle*. New York: Oxford University Press.

Useem, M. (1989). The revolt of the corporate owners and the demobilization of business political action. *Critical Sociology*, 16, 7–25.

Useem, M. (1993). *Executive defense: Shareholder power and corporate reorganization*. Cambridge: Harvard University Press.

Useem, M. (1996). *Investor capitalism: How money managers are changing the face of corporate America*. New York: Basic.

Vogel, D. (1989). *Fluctuating fortunes: The political power of business in America*. New York: Basic Books.

Wall Street Journal. (1983). Business Roundtable urges that U.S. raise taxes, cut spending. March 3, p. 34.

Weinstein, J. (1968). *The corporate ideal in the liberal state, 1900–1918*. Boston: Beacon.

Zajac, E. J., & Westphal, J. D. (2004). The social construction of market value: Institutionalization and learning perspectives on stock market reactions. *American Sociological Review*, 69, 433–457.

Zeitlin, M. (1974). Corporate ownership and control: The large corporation and the capitalist class. *American Journal of Sociology*, 79, 1073–1119.

THE POLITICAL ECONOMY
OF FINANCIAL EXUBERANCE [☆]

Greta R. Krippner

ABSTRACT

This article argues that the financial crisis has brought to the surface a series of dilemmas that have their origins in the declining affluence of the U.S. economy in the late 1960s and 1970s. When growth faltered beginning in the late 1960s, policymakers confronted difficult political choices about how to allocate scarce resources between competing social priorities. Inflation offered a means of avoiding these trade-offs for a time, disguising distributional conflicts and financing an expansive state. But the "solutions" that inflation offered to the end of growth became increasingly dysfunctional over the course of the 1970s, setting the stage for the turn to finance in the U.S. economy. Paradoxically, the turn to finance operated as the functional equivalent of inflation, similarly allowing policymakers to avoid difficult political choices as limits on the nation's prosperity became more constraining. But the turn to finance no more resolved these underlying issues than did inflation, and as a result the

[☆]Portions of this article are reprinted by permission of the publisher from Chapters 3 and 4 of the forthcoming title, *Capitalizing on Crisis; the Political Origins of the Rise of Finance* by Greta R. Krippner, Cambridge, MA: Harvard University Press, Copyright © 2011 by the president and Fellows of Harvard College. All Rights Reserved.

Markets on Trial: The Economic Sociology of the U.S. Financial Crisis: Part B
Research in the Sociology of Organizations, Volume 30B, 141–173
Copyright © 2010 by Emerald Group Publishing Limited
All rights of reproduction in any form reserved
ISSN: 0733-558X/doi:10.1108/S0733-558X(2010)000030B009

recent financial crisis likely augurs the return of distributional politics to center stage in American political and social life.

1. INTRODUCTION

Writing about the inflation crisis of the 1970s, the British sociologist John Goldthorpe (1978, pp. 211–212) made the following observation: "Free market relations will in themselves be unable to provide a basis for their own stable continuance, [and] further ... they will be a source of social divisions and antagonisms which may then lie at the root of what are experienced as economic problems." Goldthorpe wrote these words three decades ago, but they must appear almost prophetic today. In fact, Goldthorpe's thesis that what superficially appear as "economic problems" rest on a series of deeper social and political conflicts offers a very useful point of departure for understanding the recent turmoil in U.S. financial markets. Yet the underlying social divisions and antagonisms that Goldthorpe pointed to have not been central to most discussions of the financial crisis to date.

The omission is striking for two, closely related reasons. First, the connections between our current predicament and the inflation crisis of the 1970s are not merely a matter of coincidence. Rather, there are important historical continuities that link the present crisis to the social and political conflicts that Goldthorpe so pithily described. In this article, I will argue that the financial crisis has brought to the surface a series of dilemmas that have their origins in the inflation crisis of the 1970s. In this sense, my goal is not to provide an account of the causes of the financial crisis per se (an objective taken up by many other contributors to this volume), but rather to place recent developments in financial markets in the context of a longer historical evolution in which potentially disruptive distributional tensions were deferred over several decades.[1] I will further argue that the key to this "deferral" lies in the broad-based turn to finance that has characterized the U.S. economy since the 1970s,[2] a development that allowed policymakers to avoid confronting the social and political realities of slowing growth after inflation itself failed to achieve this same purpose. Second, while economists have recognized that asset price bubbles represent a form of inflation, and have even belatedly acknowledged that some of the economic lessons learned about managing inflation in product markets should perhaps also apply to financial markets (Trichet, 2005), sociologists and political scientists have made no analogous discovery. A rich literature written in the 1970s and 1980s described social and political features of inflation and embedded this discussion in a political economic framework (e.g., Alexander, 1974; Bell, 1976; Goldthorpe, 1987; Greider, 1987; Hirsch & Goldthorpe, 1978; Hirschman, 1980; Lindberg & Maier, 1985). But these insights have not been extended to periods of financial exuberance, with the result that the sociological understanding of such episodes lags considerably behind the state of economic knowledge.

Instead, many sociologists have tacitly signed on to the conventional account of the developments in financial markets that preceded the current crisis. This view, widely circulated in the media and in certain prominent academic treatments (see especially Shiller, 2008), suggests that our current predicament reflects the emergence of a speculative bubble in real estate markets that swept unsuspecting homebuyers into its swirling vortex. The conventional account rests on a venerable academic literature that describes *intrinsic* properties of financial markets that make these markets prone to episodes of what Alan Greenspan famously called "irrational exuberance."[3] In particular, the tendency of economic agents to become overconfident during a period of prosperity creates a sense of euphoria among investors. In this context, the belief that asset prices will continue their upward trajectory becomes a self-fulfilling prophecy as investors acting on this belief propel markets higher. In addition, credit standards tend to deteriorate during a boom, allowing speculators to leverage their bets and further inflating asset prices (Kindleberger, 1978; Minsky, 1986). Paradoxically, the same self-fulfilling tendencies that propel the boom on the way up can quickly give way to panic on the way down should optimism turn sour on the news of a bankruptcy, a financial scandal, or any other event that causes investors to revise their expectations (Kindleberger, 1978).

Notably, a focus on speculative dynamics in financial markets seems to fit well with the experience of the U.S. economy, and there is little doubt that the emergence of an asset price bubble has shaped (or more aptly, distorted) patterns of economic activity in recent years. But there are also some problems with this way of understanding the nature of recent developments in the U.S. economy. Most importantly, in focusing on dynamics internal to financial markets, the conventional view leaves the event that triggers a speculative mania *outside the frame* of what is to be explained. In economic historian Charles Kindleberger's (1978) well-known theory of financial manias, for example, a manic episode begins when a "displacing" event – a bumper harvest or crop failure, a technological innovation, a war or the cessation of war, or a policy mistake – changes profit opportunities in the economy.[4] Once the displacing event occurs, whatever it is, speculative tendencies intrinsic to financial markets inflate the bubble. In the case of our own recent speculative mania, the displacing event is typically understood as a policy mistake in the form of Alan Greenspan's decision to leave interest rates at very low levels for an extended period after 2001. The important point here is that, from the perspective of the theory of speculative bubbles, the displacing event is more or less arbitrary. Alan Greenspan's decision to cut interest rates following the stock market decline of 2001 might as well have been a meteor falling to earth from outer space.

As a result, the conventional view cannot explain why some *historical* periods seem to be more prone to episodes of financial exuberance than others. A related difficulty is that this view tends to create the impression that our current difficulties might have been avoided in the absence of policy errors, or that they will yield to merely technical solutions once these errors are corrected. In contrast, if the policy choices that set the stage for financial exuberance are not left outside the frame of what is to be explained (as in the "policy mistake" formulation), but analyzed as integral to a social and political process in which state actions and market responses evolved in tandem, then we can begin to situate recent events in terms of broader patterns of historical development. Such an approach requires, of course, relaxing the boundary between the political and the economic, between state officials and market actors, and exploring the mutual constitution of these spheres of activity rather than treating one as "inside" and the other "outside" the analysis. To return to Goldthorpe's (1978) opening observation, this perspective suggests that our current predicament is not exclusively – or even primarily – economic in nature, but rather reflects a series of social and political dilemmas carried underneath apparently technical problems.

In order to understand the precise nature of these dilemmas, it is necessary to revisit the problems that confronted U.S. society as postwar affluence faltered beginning in the late 1960s and 1970s. Economic growth has long been the traditional American remedy for distributional conflict (Collins, 2000), a means of avoiding zero-sum competition between social groups by continually expanding the resources available to be divided. When the seemingly boundless growth of the immediate postwar decades slowed, inflation reflected an attempt to escape these zero-sum constraints through other means (Crouch, 1978; Hirsch, 1978; Wojnilower, 1980). In particular, inflation served to mask open distributional conflict, allowing competing social groups to dissipate social tensions in a game of leapfrog in which it was impossible to determine who was ahead and who was behind at any given moment (Goldthorpe, 1987; Hirschman, 1980; Tobin, 1972). Similarly, inflation allowed the state to appear to accommodate the proliferating demands of social groups while in reality *denying* them (Hirschman, 1980): social expenditures could increase in nominal terms while rising prices eroded the real value of these claims. But critically, the solutions that inflation offered to the end of growth became increasingly dysfunctional over the course of the 1970s, exacerbating rather alleviating social conflict as inflation accelerated, and contributing to deteriorating state finances as a poor economic climate eroded tax revenues. Thus, policymakers faced a choice between allowing inflation to accelerate and imposing austerity through fiscal and monetary restraint – but without the benefit of any broad social consensus regarding how the burden of declining affluence should be shared (Bell, 1976).

These developments created the context for the turn to finance in the U.S. economy. If inflation had temporarily offered an answer to the dilemmas posed by slower growth, the turn to finance would answer the dilemmas posed by inflation, similarly allowing policymakers to avoid difficult choices between competing social priorities. But just as inflation was not a conscious "strategy" to accomplish this end, neither did the turn to finance reflect a well worked out plan to escape the constraints imposed by declining affluence. On the contrary, policymakers initially embraced financial markets not to escape those constraints, but to *conform* to them, believing that it would be possible to discipline proliferating social wants more effectively by relying on market mechanisms rather than through direct state action (see Krippner, 2011). But in pursuing this course of action, policymakers inadvertently eliminated internal and external restraints on the expansion of credit in the U.S. economy, transforming the emergent scarcities of the 1970s into a new era of abundant capital. In this regard, the turn to finance offered policymakers a resolution of the dilemmas posed by declining affluence not because policymakers successfully transferred the task of imposing discipline to the market, but because the market *failed* to impose the discipline that policymakers sought. In short, in freeing the expansion of credit from institutional constraints, policymakers would dissipate latent social and political conflicts into an apparent return to prosperity. Of course, as we now know, the turn to finance did not so much remove the resource scarcities of the 1970s as suspend them, while introducing a number of fragilities into the economy that have periodically threatened to revisit previous dilemmas upon policymakers – at no time more ominously than at the present moment.

In the following text, I proceed by examining two key episodes in which policymakers' attempts to avoid difficult political choices as growth slowed beginning in the late 1960s eliminated internal and external[5] restraints on the expansion of credit in the U.S. economy. This was consequential because increased credit flows fed the growth of the financial sector, and rendered the broader economy increasingly vulnerable to asset price bubbles (Borio & Lowe, 2002; Cooper, 2008; Minsky, 1982, 1986). The first of these two episodes involved the deregulation of domestic financial markets in the 1970s, culminating in the removal of interest rate ceilings in the U.S. economy in 1980. The second key episode traces the Reagan Administration's efforts to gain access to global capital markets in order to avert a looming fiscal crisis in the early 1980s. Taken together, these episodes marked the transition from an economy in which the expansion of credit was subject to definite limits, to one in which no such limits prevailed, preparing the ground for our own era of free-flowing credit, financial manias, and panics some three decades later.

One important caveat to the argument should be noted before proceeding. In discussing the "state" and "policymakers" here and below, I compress what in reality are multiple state agencies and polyvalent state actors into what appears to be an undifferentiated whole. This compression is necessary in an abbreviated presentation of a complex historical reality, but it should be emphasized that no such unified whole is presumed to exist. Rather, I understand the state to be comprised by multiple agencies and actors, with distinct and often (as we will see) conflicting objectives. In the first episode examined below, the "policymakers" that are central to the narrative are the Congressional legislators who sought to deregulate domestic financial markets; in the second episode, the Reagan Administration officials who pursued the liberalization of global financial markets take center stage, with the Federal Reserve officials who attempted to impose restraint on Reagan's expansive program cast in a supporting role. While these policymakers are not presumed to share the same objectives, what they hold in common – and what unifies a multistranded narrative – is the set of problems to which they were responding. As a general matter, state actors sought to avoid the social and political conflicts engendered by the emergence of new limits as postwar prosperity turned to stagnation beginning in the late 1960s and 1970s. The narrative in the following pages tells the story of how policymakers learned to tap into first domestic and then global financial markets in order to evade these limits, setting the stage (in the still quite distant future) for our own recent financial calamity.

2. THE SOCIAL POLITICS OF DOMESTIC FINANCIAL DEREGULATION

The difficulties faced by the state beginning in the late 1960s and 1970s encompassed a number of dimensions, but the common denominator of these various problems was inflation. Inflation refers to the general rate of price increases in a given economy (Flemming, 1978, p. 13). Economists and sociologists have debated the causes of inflation endlessly, but in a generic sense inflation reflects a situation in which claims on resources exceed the actual output of the economy, with the result that individuals competing for goods and services bid up prices. Claims on resources may exceed the actual productive potential of the economy for a variety of reasons, including excessive government spending, the ability of wage-earners to successfully press demands for higher compensation, and the expansion of the money supply (Alexander, 1974). Economists tend to collapse all of these mechanisms into the final one – the celebrated claim of monetarists that "inflation is always and everywhere a monetary phenomenon" (Friedman, 1970, p. 24). In a technical sense, this may be correct, but as sociologists have observed, it is not particularly illuminating as it hardly explains why governments succumb to pressures to expand the money supply (Maier, 1978, p. 38; Goldthorpe, 1978, p. 188; Crouch, 1978, p. 225). In this sense, sociological accounts have placed greater emphasis on the intergroup conflicts and demands for redistribution that are the ultimate source of inflationary episodes (even if fed to the economy through monetary channels) (Hirsch & Goldthorpe, 1978).[6]

Of course, if all prices in the economy scaled up and scaled down in lockstep, inflation would be of no consequence for distribution: it should make no difference whether transactions are denominated in dollars or dimes, as long as *relative* prices remain fixed (Tobin, 1972). But because price changes occur unevenly across sectors (and social groups), inflation has significant distributional consequences, although these consequences are typically somewhat veiled. A trade union that secures a favorable wage settlement from employers momentarily advances its position, until these higher wage costs translate into higher prices, eroding the real value of the goods and services that the wage can purchase. Once these price increases become generalized across the economy, workers whose real wage has decreased push for another wage increase, turning the wheel again. This cycle can repeat endlessly, with each group securing only temporary gains, and yet the sequence of moves and countermoves tends to vent distributional tensions as it is never totally clear who is winning and who is losing (Goldthorpe, 1987, p. 373).

Critically, inflation dissipates tensions not only between social groups, but also between the state and its citizens. Hirschman (1980, p. 202) notes that for political authorities lacking the will or the ability to directly deny resources to particular groups in society, inflation is an indirect means of "saying no": by eroding purchasing power, inflation lowers living standards without requiring any explicit agreement that it is appropriate to do so. Of course, by the same token, the lack of an explicit social compact regarding distribution means that, when exposed, inflation can itself become the focus of rather intense social conflict rather than a salve to ease such tensions (Hirsch & Goldthorpe, 1978). But in general, inflation allows societies facing a deterioration in their economic position to avoid, at least for a time, internal divisions about how the burdens of declining affluence are to be distributed (Wojnilower, 1980, pp. 325–326).

Inflationary pressures first emerged in the U.S. economy beginning in the mid-to-late-1960s, marking the transition from a period of easy abundance to an era defined by increasingly severe limits on the nation's prosperity. President Johnson's failure to squarely face these limits by choosing between financing the Vietnam War and funding the Great Society's antipoverty programs was widely blamed for initially unleashing the inflation demon as the nation struggled to meet its financial commitments. Further adding to inflationary pressures, a vigorous trade union movement refused to scale back its demands as growth faltered in the late 1960s. In this context, policymakers confronted the possibility that, as Charles Maier (1978, p. 60) observed, "Disputes over the allocation of national income [would] raise ugly confrontations or [require] increased dosages of inflation." Only a few years after Johnson demurred, President Nixon reflected a new sobriety in policymaking, creating a National Goals Research Staff that was charged with defining a social agenda that could be achieved with strictly limited means (Collins, 2000, p. 146).

Financial regulators were especially cognizant of this imperative; capital appeared to be among the most scarce of national resources – and the most vital to the nation's future well-being. As such, policymakers saw themselves as overseeing the rational distribution of credit between competing social priorities.[7] Through most of the postwar period, New Deal financial regulations had been an aid in accomplishing precisely this goal, but beginning in the mid-1960s, the system began to exhibit perverse effects. Under the New Deal system, the key mechanism regulating the flow of credit in the economy was a device called Regulation Q, a regulation that imposed a ceiling on the rate of interest that depository institutions could pay for funds. The express purpose of Regulation Q, which had been legislated as part of the Banking Act of 1933, was to prevent ruinous competition between depository institutions. In the wake of spreading bank failures in the 1930s, it was widely believed that a bidding war for deposits in the boom years of the 1920s had caused financial institutions to pay too much for funds, drawing bankers into reckless lending. By suppressing competition between depository institutions, policymakers hoped they could prevent another financial collapse.

But in addition to this explicit function, Regulation Q also served as a convenient tool for stabilizing the economy over the course of the business cycle (Knodell, 1994). When inflationary pressures in the economy stirred, market interest rates would rise above the regulated ceilings on savings deposits, prompting households and corporations alike to pull their funds out of depository institutions in order to invest in Treasury bills and other financial instruments offering a market rate of return. The predictable result was that, in periods of high market interest rates, capital would flow out of depository institutions. As a result, lending from these institutions would come to an abrupt halt. These episodes of *disintermediation* – so called because they interrupted the traditional function of the banking system to intermediate between suppliers and users of funds – contracted the capital available for new lending, affecting long-term mortgage loans especially severely. An acute recession in the housing and construction industries would quickly restrain the broader economy. As the economy gradually slowed, the mechanism would go into reverse, with funds returning to depository institutions as market interest rates fell back below regulated ceilings, restarting lending and economic expansion.

One could question the equity of this system – the burden of restraint fell heavily on the housing sector – but not its effectiveness. These "stop-valves in the plumbing of finance," as journalist William Greider (1987, p. 177) referred to the Regulation Q ceilings, pumped with hydraulic efficiency. Unlike what happens in a deregulated economic environment, in which credit becomes more expensive during periods of economic expansion, it was simply unavailable in the pre-deregulation era. Interest rates only had to edge above the regulated ceilings and the flow of credit to the economy was quite literally shut off. As a result, Regulation Q ceilings had the significant advantage of imposing restraint on the economy at relatively low interest rates, and the typical postwar recession was mild and mercifully brief (Wojnilower, 1980). That housing bore the brunt of every economic downturn generated some resistance from the building industry and from organized labor, but housing's special role as countercyclical weight to the expansion and contraction of the economy was more or less accepted at the time as sound economic management.

The social tensions embedded in this mechanism would become increasingly pronounced, however, as inflation became a persistent feature of the postwar economy. With inflation not just a cyclical occurrence but a *permanent* condition in the 1970s, the role of Regulation Q in stabilizing the economy began to malfunction. In such an environment, market interest rates remained continuously above Regulation Q ceilings, with the result that the depository institutions supporting housing experienced not a temporary outflow of funds but a hemorrhage. In addition to the routine angst of mortgage lenders and builders suddenly short on funds, policymakers now faced a much broader, and deeper, anger from individuals who found carrying out the mundane tasks of living without access to credit an unbearable hardship.[8] As inflation accelerated, policymakers found themselves standing at the center of an increasingly bitter distributional struggle that pitted large corporations against urban residents, suburban homeowners, and proprietors of small business.

The key to this evolving drama was the fact that Regulation Q did not bind all financial institutions equally. Savings and loan associations (or "thrifts") – specialized financial institutions dedicated to mortgage lending – were tightly constrained by the regulation, as were smaller banks lending to small business and consumers. But larger banks – and by extension their large corporate customers – increasingly found ways to evade the interest rate ceilings.[9] As a result, tight credit affected homeowners, consumers, and small business disproportionately, denying these sectors access to credit while large corporations could continue borrowing without constraint. Adding insult to injury, unrestrained corporate borrowing was *contributing* to inflationary pressures in the economy, further tightening the vise around thrifts and the housing sector.

In addition, by the late 1960s, another victim of inflation had joined the thrifts, and also began clamoring for relief. State and municipal governments, whose bond sales were regulated by strict usury limits, discovered that they too confronted their own version of disintermediation. In Los Angeles, for example, the city charter placed a limit of six percent on the interest rate at which the city could market its debt. As market interest rates surged past this limit, bond issues to finance various infrastructure projects in Los Angeles failed to raise even a single bid. Construction of new facilities at the airport, improvements to the Los Angeles harbor, programmed expenditures for the water and power departments, and street repairs were all abruptly suspended as funds evaporated from the city's coffers.[10]

In cities across the nation, the scenario was repeated, draining capital from the public sector. In New York City, Mayor Lindsay complained that it had become almost impossible for the city to borrow to finance its public housing programs.[11] Although the cities had received an infusion of federal money following racial riots in the 1960s, now inflation was effectively washing the money away, leaving urban centers in as degraded a condition as ever. "There are emotions in the cities that can be as disruptive as 1967, 1968, 1969," Mayor Alioto of San Francisco warned. He added, "It would be a serious mistake to think the cities cannot erupt."[12]

As legislators examined the problem, conducting a seemingly endless series of hearings, they kept coming back to what seemed to be the very essence of the matter: *there was only so much money*. Only so much money for business. Only so much money for housing. Only so much for the cities. As such, legislators directed their efforts toward locating new sources of capital that could be channeled toward housing, urban problems, and small business. "Unless we find some money, *big money*, there is not much we can do about housing," Chairman Patman soberly assessed.[13] But legislators' most innovative attempts to tap new sources of financing sooner or later ran into the same inescapable reality: capital was available in strictly limited supply.

A particularly telling episode was Congress's creation in 1968 of a new federal agency, the Government National Mortgage Association (GNMA), to support a market for mortgage-backed securities.[14] Mortgages are long-term loans; as such, they are not attractive to investors, such as pension funds that require liquidity in their portfolios. In this regard, policymakers reasoned that one way to bring new capital into housing would be to transform the mortgage instrument from a loan into a *security* that could be traded in the capital markets. This was done by assembling a pool of mortgages, standardizing them by requiring that they meet certain criteria, and then selling participations entitling each investor to a pro-rated share of the cash flow generated by the underlying mortgages (Sellon & VanNahmen, 1988, p. 9). The securitization of housing finance was enormously successful, and as policymakers had hoped, it helped to stabilize the mortgage market. But, as always, there was a catch: Policymakers soon realized that rather than drawing *new* capital into housing, mortgage-backed securities were pulling money out of the thrifts.[15] In addition to Treasury bills or corporate bonds, savers could now choose among a range of agency securities in which to invest when market interest rates rose above regulated rates on passbook savings accounts. *There was only so much money*.

In fact, the inexorable logic of inflation suggested that even had legislators somehow managed to conjure up new capital for housing, small business, or the cities, they would have only added to inflationary pressures. In a world in which capital was inherently scarce, increasing housing expenditures meant cutting other expenditures, with the implication that some form of credit allocation would be necessary. Reflecting this imperative, credit allocation schemes were continually on the legislative agenda between the mid-1960s and mid-1970s, with nearly 100 separate bills under consideration in the 1974 legislative session alone.[16] While the details of these schemes varied, ranging from voluntary credit restraint programs such as had been used in the Korean War to the imposition of penalties on banks that made loans in "nonpriority" areas, the basic premise was the same: If government controls in the form of Regulation Q ceilings were distorting flows of credit in the economy, then government actions could be devised to counteract the distortion, directing scarce capital where it was needed. But there was a basic problem with all of these initiatives. Even when policymakers agreed that allocation was necessary, they also agreed it was better for *someone else* to do it. Congress insisted that the Federal Reserve was using the "Nation's credit" and therefore had an obligation to establish priorities.[17] The Federal Reserve countered that setting priorities was the proper responsibility of the Congress or the President.[18] Federal Reserve Chairman Arthur Burns was especially adamant that involvement in credit allocation would turn the Federal Reserve into a "political instrument,"[19] forcing policymakers "to determine that some groups in our economic society were more worthy than other groups." [20] These were matters, Burns suggested, in which the Federal Reserve had no special expertise or jurisdiction.

This game of hot potato continued for several years, with Congress repeatedly authorizing the Federal Reserve and the President to exercise various forms of credit allocation, only to later discover that these new powers went untapped.[21] One exasperated legislator asked his colleagues in frustration: "If [credit allocation] is such a neat idea, why doesn't the Congress do it itself?"[22] No answer was necessary: Congress was no more eager to thrust itself into pitched battles between those who had access to credit and those whose demands for credit went unmet than was the Federal Reserve or the Treasury Department. But, of course, this only raised the question: Wasn't credit *already* being allocated under the existing system of regulatory controls? The iconic liberal economics professor, Lester Thurow, whose application for a mortgage loan was denied in the credit crunch of October 1974, thought so: "The banking system at the moment is in the process of credit allocation, and the questions is, should there be some public guidelines in this credit allocation, not should we have credit allocation or no credit allocation, because that is not the choice."[23]

For his part, Treasury Secretary William Simon rejected this suggestion, warning that explicit public guidelines along the lines that Thurow recommended would create "a national credit police state."[24] The Treasury Secretary proceeded to paint a chilling portrait of a totalitarian society in which a "credit czar"[25] controlled all citizen initiative, dictating financial choices down to the last minute detail. Simon queried:[26]

> Would a businessman who wanted to add a wing to his store and hire a dozen people be able to obtain a loan? Under this [credit allocation] law, he would have to stand in line behind low-income housing, even though the tenants in low-income housing might be looking for a job.

> Would a housewife who wanted to buy a new refrigerator at a department store be denied the use of her charge account because someone in Washington thinks she can do just as well with the old refrigerator?

> Would a family of six that wanted a station wagon be able to borrow the money, or would it be limited to a smaller car that Federal officials thought would be better for the country?

The answers to Simon's questions were clear. As Simon explained, "Some borrowers could not obtain funds at any price, creating serious hardships for them, while others could obtain larger amounts of money than they actually needed."[27] But, ironically, as Thurow had suggested, these questions were already being answered in much the same way, day after day, under the existing system of financial regulation. In the context of inflation, Regulation Q constrained some borrowers severely, while providing others virtually unlimited access to credit. In fact, Simon had gone to the crux of the matter: either policymakers would have to tighten restraints on the large banks that had escaped regulation, or housing, state and local governments, and other similarly constrained sectors would have to be unshackled from these restraints. The former choice would place policymakers in the position of continually having to decide how to allocate the burden of restraint – with access to credit becoming increasingly politicized as policymakers weighed the claims of competing social groups. The latter choice meant that, at least within certain limits, the *market* could do the choosing, relieving policy-makers of an unpalatable task.

Given this calculus, it is perhaps not surprising that policymakers endorsed the removal of interest rate ceilings – against significant opposition from segments of the financial sector, the housing industry, and organized labor.[28] After nearly a decade long struggle, Congress passed the *Depository Institutions Deregulation and Monetary Control Act* in the spring of 1980,[29] establishing a framework and timetable for the phasing out interest rate ceilings over a period of six years.[30] Central to legislators' support of deregulation was the notion that the price mechanism would ration credit in much the same way as had been achieved through interest rate ceilings. As the economy accelerated, the cost of credit would be bid up, discouraging would-be borrowers from seeking access to loans and thereby imposing restraint on the economy. Willingness to pay, rather than rickety interest rate controls, would determine access to funds. But one of the great surprises of deregulation was that prices largely *failed* to ration (Wojnilower, 1985, p. 352). As it turned out, Americans were insensitive to the cost of credit in their borrowing decisions – they would continue borrowing except at *very* high levels of interest. The result was free flowing, but expensive credit, as the money taps were turned wide open.

Thus, deregulation presented a kind of paradox. Policymakers had hoped that in removing interest rate ceilings they would relieve themselves of responsibility for overseeing the distribution of scarce capital between competing uses, leaving this politically difficult task to the market. The unforgiving logic of the price mechanism would serve as a source of discipline where the state failed to do so, forcing businesses and households to live within their means. But ironically, rather than offering an indirect means to allocate credit between uses, deregulation made the entire problem of allocating scarce capital a moot issue. In a deregulated environment, capital would no longer be scarce, but available in ample supply.

But if it seemed that all the grim certainties of the 1970s had been somehow suspended, this judgment was still premature. As the decade closed, two nagging worries lingered on the horizon. The first was that inflationary pressures would accelerate in a deregulated environment, once again forcing difficult political decisions on policymakers who appeared to have momentarily escaped them. Indeed, financial economists who observed credit working itself free from institutional constraints predicted that inflation would accelerate sharply in the 1980s (Kaufman, 1986; Wojnilower, 1980).[31] The second worry was closely related. While financial deregulation allowed policymakers a reprieve from decisions about how capital should be distributed between competing uses, large projected government deficits in the early 1980s threatened to revisit these pressures on policymakers with a vengeance. Observers feared that government demands for capital would swamp financial markets, forcing the cost of credit so high that the market's rationing mechanism would finally slam into place, excluding all other users of capital. As it turned out, neither of these two scenarios materialized. The tenuous balance would hold, although the resolution to each of these problems would deepen and extend the turn to finance in the U.S. economy.

3. THE REAGAN ADMINISTRATION DISCOVERS THE GLOBAL ECONOMY

If policymakers were first presented with the problem of capital scarcity in the late 1960s and 1970s, this problem would reemerge in the 1980s in the context of a looming fiscal crisis. Fiscal strains on the state were of course not new in the Reagan era – the state's budget position had been steadily deteriorating since the Vietnam War when President Johnson's failure to choose between "guns and butter" created a sizable gap between the state's revenues and its expenditures (Collins, 2000). As we have seen, it was the erosion of the state's fiscal position during the Vietnam era that had first ignited inflation, forcing a belated recognition among policymakers that painful choices would be necessary in the context of slowing growth. But whereas in the late 1960s and 1970s, the government had been one of a number of borrowers competing with business and housing for funds in crowded capital markets, in the 1980s government deficits on an unprecedented scale threatened to preempt all other borrowers.

The Reagan deficits were the result of a series of blunders that have been well chronicled in the existing literature (e.g., Greider, 1987; Murphy, 1997; Stockman, 1986). Prior to being elected President, Reagan had come under the sway of supply-side economics, a radical new economic theory then circulating in conservative circles. Supply-side economics suggested that the most important obstacles to economic growth reflected institutional features of markets that interfered with incentives to invest rather than insufficient demand, as under the Keynesian paradigm. Initially, the supply-side program encompassed a broad range of policies, from worker training programs to deregulation schemes, which aimed at removing these obstacles to the smooth functioning of markets. Nevertheless, during the Reagan administration the term came to refer more narrowly to the proposition that tax cuts would release pent-up entrepreneurial energies and drive an investment boom. Under the most extravagant claims of the supply-siders, tax cuts would generate sufficient new economic activity to offset revenue losses to the government.[32] Of course, the presumption was that tax cuts would be accompanied by an aggressive program of expenditure reductions. But so certain was President Reagan that the tax cuts would "pay for themselves" that the 1981 tax bill was signed into law even when the needed expenditure reductions failed to materialize. The result, as Budget Director David Stockman (1986, p. 370) famously put it, was "deficits as far as the eye can see."

While the supply-siders remained confident that Reagan's tax proposals would spur a vigorous recovery and that the economy would "outgrow" the deficits, the financial markets were less certain. The forecast that haunted Wall Street – and increasingly, policymakers inside the administration who fell off the supply-side bandwagon – was that of an imminent collision between the federal government and private borrowers in the capital markets. Under this "crowding out" scenario, the government would preempt capital from private borrowers; as private borrowers bid amongst themselves for the remaining funds, interest rates would rise so high as to price these borrowers out of the market. That unhappy outcome, analysts feared, would grind economic activity to a halt, suffocating the nascent recovery by making it impossible for firms to obtain financing for new investment. For most of 1981 and 1982, the stock and bond markets lurched along in anticipation of this crowding out scenario, causing considerable consternation among Reagan officials.[33]

But, to the surprise of both Washington and Wall Street, no such scenario materialized. Several factors kept the dreaded calamity in the capital markets at bay. First, recovery proved elusive for many months, and private demand for investment funds remained sluggish well into 1983. Second, firms were able to fund investment projects directly out of retained earnings, which had received a significant boost as a result of the liberalized depreciation allowances associated with the 1981 tax cut.[34] Finally, most importantly, just as the recovery was finally underway in mid-1983, a major new source of capital emerged, quite unexpectedly, to finance the federal budget deficit: International – especially Japanese – investors had developed a voracious appetite for Treasury securities.

Reagan administration officials did not anticipate this development for a number of reasons. In the early 1980s, policymakers had not fully adjusted to thinking of the world in terms of a sea of open capital flows. International financial integration was a work in progress, the implications of this process still unfolding. David Stockman later admitted that no one among Reagan's close advisers had foreseen the role that foreign capital flows would come to play in financing the budget deficits (Murphy, 1997, p. 148). Even Federal Reserve Chairman Paul Volcker, perhaps more attuned to the international economy than any central banker before or since, did not predict the magnitude of the capital flows that would emerge, out of nowhere and seemingly overnight, to finance the budget deficits (Volcker & Gyohten, 1992, pp. 178–179).

To be sure, the economists in the Treasury Department and at the Council of Economic Advisers (CEA) were equipped with the familiar macro-economic formula that suggested that a savings shortfall (in the form of a budget deficit) would, by definition, be offset by (negative) net exports, and hence a capital inflow, but these linkages were stated rather tenuously.[35] In a memo written in the fall of 1981, for example, CEA Chairman Murray Weidenbaum noted that "foreign portfolio flows are *potentially* useful in easing deficit financing pressures in domestic markets."[36] Similarly, in December of 1981, during a speech given at the American Enterprise Institute, CEA member William Niskanen (1988, p. 110) hypothesized that the opportunity to import capital meant that the deficits then on the horizon might not place the strong upward pressure on interest rates that observers at the time were expecting. Niskanen recalled that his audience was highly skeptical that capital inflows of any significant magnitude were possible. Moreover, while these relationships may have been understood – in abstract terms, at least – by the economists on Reagan's staff, the notion that in an open economy, a deficit could be financed by importing capital from abroad did not penetrate far into the broader cabinet. As late as October of 1984, Niskanen wrote a memo for the Cabinet Council on Economic Affairs, explaining that the gap between domestic saving and domestic investment was necessarily equal to foreign borrowing.[37] Niskanen recalled, "That was a surprise to nearly everybody in the Cabinet meeting!"[38]

Another reason that many members of the Reagan administration did not fully anticipate the role that foreign capital inflows would come to play in financing the budget deficit was that these flows were drawn in by the extraordinarily high interest rates associated with Volcker's embrace of monetarism.[39] Policymakers believed that the monetarist experiment would be short-lived and that interest rates would soon return to more normal levels. But contrary to expectations, high interest rates in the U.S. economy persisted even after the monetarist experiment was abandoned. While this was in part a result of structural change in the economy associated with financial deregulation,[40] the persistence of higher rates also reflected Volcker's resistance to the Reagan program. Volcker observed the budget wrangling going on inside the administration and feared that the large deficits would reverse the progress he was making on inflation (Volcker & Gyohten, 1992). As a result, he stubbornly refused to do what central bankers before him had done in similar circumstances – to "monetize" the deficit by steering the economy toward a more accommodative monetary policy that would create inflation and thereby reduce the current-dollar value of the debt (Greider, 1987, p. 560).[41] Instead, Volcker ratcheted up interest rates higher, determined to smother any inflationary spark.

What Volcker failed to realize was that this policy would backfire in the context of open global capital flows. As Jane D'Arista, a senior staff economist on the U.S. House Committee on Banking, Housing, and Urban Affairs explained, "Volcker wanted to counter the effects of the easy fiscal policy, but *compounded* them by an interest rate policy that encouraged capital inflows."[42] Rather than producing the "crowding out" that would force the administration back on to the path of fiscal austerity, high interest rates – as much as five percentage points higher than comparable risk-free government securities sold in Japan (Murphy, 1997, p. 144) – brought capital pouring into the U.S. economy: $85 billion in 1983, $103 billion in 1984, $129 billion in 1985, and a staggering $221 billion in 1986.[43] As a result, the dreaded collision of private and public borrowers in the credit markets never occurred.

But if crowding out was not occurring in the textbook fashion, another, more insidious form of "crowding out" was reshaping the American economy. In the 1980s, the textbook form of crowding out was mitigated by the fact that rising interest rates attracted funds from abroad, allowing private borrowers continued access to capital even as the deficit grew. But the capital pouring in from abroad introduced another distortion into the economy of the 1980s: the dollar began to appreciate rapidly. In order to invest in the U.S. economy, foreigners had to exchange their currencies – yen, marks, francs, etc. – into dollars, with the result that the demand for the dollar on foreign exchange markets increased, driving up its price. This, in turn, placed American exporters at a competitive disadvantage in foreign markets for the reverse reason: in order to sell in those markets, exporters converted dollar prices into local currencies, which became more expensive as the value of the dollar rose.[44] The results of this process were soon evident in the intense pressure on U.S. manufacturing and agriculture as American producers steadily lost market share to foreign competitors.

Domestic opposition to the strong dollar came from all quarters, but was spearheaded by the Business Roundtable and its very vocal leader, Caterpillar Tractor Chairman, Lee Morgan (Destler & Henning, 1989). In 1982, Morgan commissioned two academics, David Murchison and Ezra Solomon, to study the causes of the strong dollar and propose appropriate policy responses. Their report, officially released in September of 1983 but widely circulated in the year prior, argued strongly in favor of the view that the Japanese had taken deliberate steps to hold down the value of the yen in order to gain a competitive advantage in U.S. markets. In particular, they argued that restrictive capital market policies discouraged *inflows* of capital into Japanese markets, thereby suppressing demand for the yen, and increasing demand for other currencies, such as the dollar. As such, the Caterpillar report called for correcting the strong dollar by further opening Japanese financial markets.

This analysis turned out to be erroneous. In fact, the most significant controls in the Japanese capital market restricted *outflows*, not inflows, of capital.[45] As a result, liberalizing Japanese financial markets would have the effect of increasing capital flows from Japan to the United States, strengthening rather than weakening the dollar. As Paul Krugman, then a staff economist at the CEA, noted in a memo, "It is hard to believe that liberalization of Japan's capital markets would make Japan a major importer of capital. Japan has the world's highest savings rate. With free movement of capital we would expect it to invest some of these savings abroad, i.e., become a capital exporter rather than a capital importer."[46] Nevertheless, prompted by the Caterpillar report, the Treasury Department launched a diplomatic offensive aimed at liberalizing Japanese financial markets in November of 1983 (Frankel, 1984).

It is difficult to know whether Treasury adopted the Caterpillar report knowing that its conclusions were faulty, or whether Treasury, like the Caterpillar economists, simply miscalculated the effect of liberalizing Japanese markets on the direction of capital flows. What is certain is that the convoluted economic logic of the Caterpillar report solved a number of problems for the Reagan Administration. Perhaps most importantly, the Caterpillar report allowed the Reagan Administration to appear to respond to the increasingly vociferous complaints of the business community without compromising a strict laissez faire orientation.[47] It is here that the interpretation of events becomes somewhat challenging, for the public and private pronouncements of the Treasury Department regarding the likely effect of Japanese capital market liberalization diverge. In public – especially in the statements of Treasury Secretary Donald Regan – the Treasury appeared to adopt the view expressed in the Caterpillar report that steps taken to liberalize Japan's capital markets would result in increased capital flows to Japan, putting upward pressure on the yen and downward pressure on the dollar.[48] In private, Treasury knew better. At a Cabinet Council meeting in which Krugman's memo was discussed, Beryl Sprinkel, Treasury Undersecretary for Monetary Affairs, agreed with the CEA that the immediate result of pressuring the Japanese to further open their financial markets would be to *weaken*, not strengthen, the yen (with converse effects on the dollar).[49]

In addition to allowing Treasury officials to loudly proclaim that it was dealing with the overvalued exchange rate – while likely realizing that the effect of capital market liberalization would be the *opposite* of what the business community believed – the Caterpillar report was welcome at Treasury for another reason. Critically, the analysis developed in the Caterpillar study deflected attention away from the explanation of the strong dollar articulated within the Council of Economic Advisors (CEA). The CEA argued that the dollar had appreciated because the budget deficit contributed to high interest rates; high interest rates, in turn, made the dollar a desirable asset, attracting a capital inflow.[50] For Treasury, this analysis – with its unpleasant emphasis on the budget deficit – amounted to "selling short" the Reagan program.[51] From Treasury's perspective, foreign capital was attracted to the U.S. economy because the rate of return on investment was higher here than elsewhere.[52] Even if the logic was a little erroneous, then, the Caterpillar study at least put the emphasis where it belonged: the dollar was strong because deregulated U.S. markets drew capital in, whereas shackled markets abroad repelled capital. For the Treasury economists, if not for Caterpillar Tractor, the soaring dollar was a sign not of some underlying pathology but of all that was right in Reagan's America.

But there was one thing on which Treasury and the CEA could agree: whatever their cause, the capital inflows associated with the high dollar represented a beneficial development. This position was elaborated most explicitly in what came to be known as the "Feldstein Doctrine," after CEA Chairman Martin Feldstein.[53] Feldstein argued that foreign capital inflows provided a significant supplement to national savings. Thus, taking the budget deficit as given, the rise of the dollar and associated capital inflow acted as a "safety valve" for the U.S. economy, avoiding the crowding out of domestic investment.[54] Treasury concurred: "The capital inflows to the United States ... will permit interest rates to be lower here than they otherwise would be, preserving jobs in interest rate sensitive industries, and [allowing] more capital formation than would otherwise be the case."[55]

In short, over the course of two years, the Reagan administration economists had learned that they lived not in a closed national economy, but in a world of global capital. Consequently, when the Reagan recovery began to accelerate in mid-1984 and fears again turned to an imminent "crowding out" of private borrowers in the capital markets,[56] Treasury was prepared. While Volcker startled the financial markets by repeating his earlier warnings that he would not under any circumstance accommodate deficits – and hence that "the day of reckoning" was close at hand – administration economists calmly analyzed the role that foreign capital would play in financing the coming investment boom.[57]

Whether efforts to liberalize Japanese financial markets represented a deliberate attempt on the part of the Treasury to harness Japanese capital flows to finance U.S. deficits – or, as some have argued, was simply a policy "mistake" – there can be no ambiguity about Treasury's intentions as economic recovery progressed.[58] Beginning in July of 1984, Treasury took several concrete steps to make U.S. financial instruments more attractive to foreign borrowers (Frankel, 1994, pp. 301–302). First, the 30 percent withholding tax imposed on interest earned by foreigners on U.S. investments was eliminated. *Business Week* (July 23, 1984) remarked, "A desire to expand the pool of buyers of U.S. government debt was a major reason the [tax] was finally repealed." Second, in the fall of 1984, Treasury initiated its foreign-targeted securities program, in which several special issues were prepared for European and Japanese markets. In September, David Mulford, Under-secretary of the Treasury for International Affairs, traveled to Europe in order to generate interest in the new issue. Beryl Sprinkel similarly visited Tokyo to market the bonds to Japanese investors. The auction was extremely successful; Destler and Henning (1989, p. 29) called the Reagan Treasury Department, "[T]he greatest bond salesmen in history." Finally, in October, after a battle with Congress, Treasury obtained permission to issue so-called "bearer bonds," consistent with the preference of international investors for unregistered securities that could be held anonymously.[59]

The result of these various initiatives was to transform the zero-sum relationship between the government and all other borrowers competing for capital in crowded markets. Remarkably, only a few years had passed since the perennial capital shortages of the 1970s, and yet the dilemmas confronted by policymakers in that decade seemed to belong to another era entirely. Reagan's record deficits notwithstanding, *fiscal crisis had been averted*. At least for the moment, the stock market ceased to gyrate on every budget number. As *Business Week* noted, in an incredulous tone:

> The nation's financial foundation was supposed to shake when a growing economy collided with the huge budget deficit. Credit demand would soar, driving interest rates into the stratosphere. Instead, after being intimidated for two years, the stock market is pressing boldly ahead to record levels. ... The experience of the last two years [has] shown that the U.S. does not have a closed system. Inflows of foreign capital can sustain private and public borrowers alike.[60]

What the Reagan policymakers discovered in the early 1980s, then, was that they lived in a world in which capital was available in potentially limitless supply. In this sense, Reagan-era economic policies completed – and in a sense, *perfected* – the process begun with the deregulation of domestic financial markets in the previous decade. Financial deregulation had removed barriers to the free flow of credit in the U.S. economy, but the resulting expansion of credit threatened to contribute to accelerating inflation. Volcker assumed leadership of the Federal Reserve with a mandate to suppress inflation, and his policy regime was intended to force a bitter pill down the throats of American businesses and households by squeezing credit *hard*. This was a policy designed for a closed economy, however, and foreign capital inflows washed out any effect high interest rates might have had restricting the growth of total credit in the U.S. economy (Greider, 1987; Konings, 2008). But while Volcker's punitive monetary regime did not restrict the growth of credit, high interest rates *did* suppress inflation by drawing capital out of the productive economy and into financial markets. Critically, with inflation vanquished to the financial markets – where it was not visible (or conceptualized) as such[61] – the state would no longer confront seemingly impossible trade-offs between imposing austerity and facing ever mounting price pressures. In this regard, if the deregulation of domestic financial markets allowed policymakers to momentarily escape politically difficult decisions regarding how the burden of declining affluence would be shared, access to liberalized global capital markets would allow policymakers to defer these choices indefinitely.

4. CONCLUSION

In this article, I have explored the longer-term historical developments that, by removing structural constraints on the flow of credit, created conditions that rendered the U.S. economy vulnerable to financial crisis. More specifically, I have argued that the broad-based turn to finance that set the stage for the recent financial crisis grew directly out of responses to the *preceding* economic crisis more than three decades ago. But these events are linked not only through the chain of historical events that I have traced in the preceding narrative, but also through the underlying logic that connects both inflation and the turn to finance to the declining affluence of the U.S. economy. Numerous commentators writing about the inflation crisis in the 1970s observed that inflation offered a kind of "solution" to the end of growth, disguising the deterioration in living standards and allowing the state to avoid the consequence of its eroding finances. But only for a time: as inflation accelerated, it ceased to act as a social lubricant and instead exacerbated underlying social and political conflicts (Maier, 1978, p. 71). This change of phase arguably occurred in the mid-to-late 1970s as inflation climbed into the double-digits and Americans wearied of the constant struggle to keep up with rising prices. It was widely expected at the time that distributional conflicts that had been submerged would now rise to the surface, where they would demand political solutions. Samuel Brittan (1978, p. 185) captured the prevailing mood when he wrote, "We have come to the end of the period of grace."

But remarkably, the "period of grace" lasted much longer than Brittan could have imagined. In fact, the turn to finance offered further means to put off difficult political decisions associated with declining affluence. In this sense, the turn to finance has operated as the functional equivalent of inflation, allowing U.S. society to sidestep the resource constraints that first began to impinge on standards of living in the late 1960s. The mechanisms, of course, differ, but the effects are parallel: rather than inflation allowing social actors to (temporarily) lay claim to greater resources than warranted by the underlying performance of the economy, now the expansion of credit would serve this same function. Rather than inflation dissipating distributional tensions in a dizzying dance between competing social groups, now free-flowing credit would ease latent social conflicts by displacing debts and obligations far into the future. But while the turn to finance has proven much more durable than inflation as an answer to the declining affluence of the U.S. economy, the unavoidable lesson of the current crisis is that this strategy too has now run its course. Whether this suggests that distributional conflicts will once again return to center stage, or policymakers will stumble upon some novel method for deferring these conflicts even further into the future remains to be seen.

It is difficult to know what the future holds in this regard in part because the "strategies" relied upon in the past to avoid the dilemmas of declining affluence have been largely inadvertent. In this regard, if inflation and the turn to finance represent parallel responses to the same underlying problems in U.S. society, this was hardly by design. Rather, the turn to finance resulted from a series of ad hoc decisions taken in response to the inflation crisis whose outcome was very nearly the *opposite* of what policymakers expected. This is evident in both of the key episodes examined in this article: While policymakers' reliance on market mechanisms initially reflected efforts to restrain the state, corporations, and consumers all vying for scarce capital, policymakers soon discovered that in fact financial markets imposed *no such restraint.* Policymakers eliminated interest rate ceilings intending to pass the politically difficult task of allocating capital between competing social priorities to the market. Instead, policymakers freed the expansion of credit from institutional constraints, avoiding the need for allocation altogether. In a closed economy, of course, freeing borrowers to compete for a finite amount of capital would have eventually pushed the price of credit so high as to force some borrowers to drop out of the market, or failing this would have contributed to accelerating inflation. But in a newly open economy, such an outcome was forestalled, as high interest rates drew abundant foreign capital to U.S. financial markets, suppressing inflation while also avoiding credit rationing in domestic capital markets. In short, neither the mechanism of disintermediation from the banking system, nor the "crowding out" of private borrowers from capital markets functioned to choke off seemingly limitless demands for credit.

No wonder that policymakers succumbed to the temptations of unfettered markets, even though free-flowing credit would subject the U.S. economy to the spasms of financial markets. Under the policy regime put in place in the 1970s and 1980s, credit would be available in ample supply, with the result that incipient political conflicts over how to distribute limited resources between competing social priorities could be effectively *depoliticized*. Rather than making the state the arbiter in zero-sum struggles, the expansion of credit allowed policymakers to dissolve emerging political tensions into what for the moment appeared to be a return to prosperity. Policymakers would no longer be placed in the position of having to decide which social groups should receive preferential access to credit, nor would they confront difficult political choices about which social priorities to fund as the state's budget position deteriorated. Put simply, the crisis conditions of the late 1960s and 1970s were washed away in a sea of capital.

My objective in presenting this narrative has been to suggest that this transformation in U.S. political economy provides important insights into the longer-term social and political conditions that created the context for the current financial crisis. There is, to be sure, a more fine-grained account of the origins of the crisis that complements and extends the story I tell here. This more proximate account would trace in detail events that are not given full consideration in the preceding pages – in particular, the development of the market for mortgage-backed securities, the creation of credit default swaps, lax regulators, loose monetary policy, and foreign central banks eager to finance U.S. deficits in order to maintain access to the insatiable American consumer (see Morris, 2008). All of these developments contributed to a powerful bubble in the real estate market that, once underway, continued its dizzying ascent propelled by speculative dynamics internal to financial markets (Shiller, 2008). But before these events could occur, and setting the context for them, the U.S. economy made the transition from a system in which credit flows were subject to strict controls internally and externally to one in which all such constraints had been removed.

It should be emphasized that the point of this exercise is not to engage in a sterile debate regarding whether distant or near historical events should be considered more "important" in understanding the current crisis. The key point is rather that distinct issues come into and out of view at different temporal scales. In particular, while proximate accounts of the crisis demonstrate convincingly that the apparent prosperity generated by free-flowing credit rested on fragile economic foundations, what emerges clearly from a longer historical perspective is that the *normative* underpinnings of our recent financial euphoria were equally flimsy. In particular, the historical analysis presented in this article suggests that a series of unresolved distributional questions lurk just below the surface of the credit expansion that has occurred in the U.S. economy in the decades since the 1970s. The important implication is that the problems confronting U.S. society, then as now, will not yield to merely technical solutions.

This is not, of course, to underplay the significance of the various policy failures that have contributed to the financial crisis – or the urgency of seeking remedies to these failures by reforming the regulatory structure of U.S. financial markets. It is to suggest that such remedies, no matter how well conceived, will not be sufficient to address the more fundamental questions raised by the current crisis. Some three decades ago, in the crucible of inflation, the sociologist Daniel Bell (1976, p. 230) observed, "The problem of capital will *always* be with us." Policymakers at the time concurred, and they viewed it as their responsibility to allocate scarce capital between competing social priorities. But in turning to the market, policymakers not only sidestepped this responsibility, they also avoided the question that Bell (1976, p. 278, emphasis added) suggested must be confronted: "How much do we want to spend, and *for whom?*" The market could not resolve such matters because these are questions for which the price mechanism has no metric. Indeed, it was the state's role as arbiter – to return to our point of departure – that threatened to plunge the state into ever more divisive conflicts in a society in which boundless economic growth no longer provided easy answers to distributional dilemmas. This was precisely the predicament presented by organizing allocation around political rather than economic power: political decision making *concentrated* responsibility, whereas the market *dispersed* it (Bell, 1976, p. 197, p. 226). Accordingly, if free-flowing credit has in the last three decades allowed policymakers to avoid overtly political decisions about how resources are allocated and rewards distributed in our society, there will be no alternative in the years ahead to the political management of the economy, with its attendant conflicts and crises.

NOTES

1. This is not to suggest that redistribution has not occurred in recent decades, as the post-1970s period has witnessed a dramatic increase in income and wealth inequality in the U.S. economy. It is merely to suggest that issues of distribution have not been politicized in recent years, and they remain relatively absent from public discourse.

2. Space considerations prevent me from providing a full discussion of the "turn to finance," but I use this phrase to refer to the growing importance of financial activities in the U.S. economy beginning in the 1970s. There is no one single determinant of the turn to finance, but my focus here is on the expansion of credit in the U.S. economy associated with the liberalization of domestic and global financial markets in the 1970s and 1980s. See Krippner (2011) for a more elaborate discussion.

3. For useful surveys of the voluminous economic literature on bubbles, see Evans (2003), Shiller (2000), and Shleifer (2000). It should be noted that not all accounts of bubbles require the types of cognitive distortions that Shiller in particular emphasizes, and some theories of speculative bubbles presume fully rational behavior.

4. Kindleberger's formulation represented a popularization of heterodox economist Hyman Minsky's writings on speculative manias (Minsky, 1975, 1982, 1986).

5. The removal of *formal* external constraints on credit flows was accomplished with the elimination of capital controls in the U.S. economy in 1974 (see Abdelal, 2007). Rather than focus on this formal change, my emphasis here is on the gradual liberalization of the markets of foreign *suppliers* of capital (especially Japan) to the United States. Arguably, it was this latter change that made the formal elimination of capital controls from the U.S. economy meaningful in terms of the effect of this policy in relaxing financing constraints on the U.S. government.

6. What neither of these two perspectives initially gave much attention to was inflation caused by shortages of key commodities. This type of inflation took center stage with the oil price hikes of the 1970s, and in some ways rendered the debate between economists and sociologists irrelevant. But while the oil price hikes transmitted a significant inflationary shock to the economy, it is important to note that it was only by virtue of being fed through a wage–price–wage spiral that this shock contributed to accelerating inflation in the U.S. economy (see Tobin, 1974).

7. See, for example, hearings conducted on the *Report of the Commission on Credit and Money* before the Joint Economic Committee, August 14–18, 1961.

8. See, for example, the letter from Vivian Cates to Representative Wright Patman, September 14, 1973 (U.S. House of Representatives, Committee on Banking and Currency, *The Credit Crunch and Reform of Financial Institutions, Part II*, September 17, 18, 19, and 20, 1973, p. 1094).

9. One key development in this regard was the development of the negotiable certificate of deposit, a financial instrument that effectively allowed banks to secure continual access to funds. Commercial banks' increasing reliance on the commercial paper market to finance lending was also significant in this regard. Finally, access to the Eurodollar market gave banks a source of capital that was entirely outside the reach of the U.S. regulatory system. See Krippner (2011) for elaboration on these points.

10. Testimony of Sam Yorty, Mayor, City of Los Angeles, *Grassroots Hearings on Economic Problems*, House Committee on Banking and Currency, December 1, 1969, pp. 126–129.

11. Testimony of John V. Lindsay, Mayor, City of New York, *Emergency Home Financing*, House Committee on Banking and Currency, February 2, 1970, pp. 21–25.

12. Testimony of Joseph Alioto, Mayor, City of San Francisco, and President, U.S. Conference of Mayors, *The Growing Threat of a Domestic Financial Crisis*, August 7, 1974, p. 2.

13. Statement of Chairman Wright Patman, *Emergency Home Financing*, House Committee on Banking and Currency, February 3, 1970, p. 89, emphasis added.

14. GNMA (or "Ginnie Mae") was formed from the Federal National Mortgage Association (FNMA or "Fannie Mae"), which had been created in 1938 to finance mortgage purchases during the depths of the Depression. FNMA was privatized in 1968, while GNMA remained a public corporation. In 1970, the private Federal Home Loan Mortgage Corporation (FHLMC or "Freddie Mac") was created to provide competition to Fannie Mae.

15. Testimony of Kenneth Wright, Chief Economist, Life Insurance Association of America, *Emergency Home Financing*, House Committee on Banking and Currency, February 3, 1970, p. 87.

16. "Congress Tries to Strongarm the Fed," *Business Week*, February 24, 1975, p. 23.

17. Statement of Chairman Wright Patman, *Emergency Home Financing*, House Committee on Banking and Currency, February 3, 1970, p. 90.

18. Testimony of Arthur Burns, Chairman, Federal Reserve Board, *Selective Credit Policies and Wage-Price Stabilization*, Senate Banking Housing and Urban Affairs, March 31, 1971. See also Eastburn (1970).

19. Testimony of Arthur Burns, Chairman of the Federal Reserve Board, *To Lower Interest Rates: The Credit Allocation Act of 1975*, February 19, 1975, p. 28.

20. Testimony of Arthur Burns, Chairman of the Federal Reserve Board, *To Lower Interest Rates: The Credit Allocation Act of 1975*, February 19, 1975, p. 38.

21. See *Interest Rates and Mortgage Credit*, Senate Banking and Currency Committee, August 4, 1966; Statement of Senator William Proxmire, *Purchase of Treasury Securities and Interest on Savings Deposits*, Senate Banking and Currency Committee, April 3, 1968, pp. 1–2; Testimony of William McChesney Martin, Chairman, Federal Reserve Board, *Deposit Rates and Mortgage Credit*, September 10, 1969, pp. 86–87; *Deposit Rates and Mortgage Credit*, Senate Banking and Currency Committee, September 9, 10, 22, 1969; *Selective Credit Policies and Wage-Price Stabilization*, Senate Banking Housing and Urban Affairs, March 31, April 1, 7, 1971.

22. Statement of Representative Willis Gradison, *To Lower Interest Rates: The Credit Allocation Act of 1975*, February 19, 1975, p. 41.

23. Testimony of Lester C. Thurow, MIT Professor of Economics, *An Act to Lower Interest Rates and Allocate Credit*, House Banking, Currency, and Housing Committee, February 4, 1975, p. 83.

24. Testimony of William E. Simon, Treasury Secretary, *An Act to Lower Interest Rates and Allocate Credit*, House Banking, Currency, and Housing Committee, February 4, 1975, p. 19.

25. Testimony of William E. Simon, Treasury Secretary, *An Act to Lower Interest Rates and Allocate Credit*, House Banking, Currency, and Housing Committee, February 4, 1975, p. 18, p. 20.

26. Testimony of William E. Simon, Treasury Secretary, *An Act to Lower Interest Rates and Allocate Credit*, House Banking, Currency, and Housing Committee, February 4, 1975, p. 19.

27. Testimony of William E. Simon, Treasury Secretary, *An Act to Lower Interest Rates and Allocate Credit*, House Banking, Currency, and Housing Committee, February 4, 1975, p. 20.

28. See Krippner (2011) for the story of this opposition to financial deregulation – and how it was eventually overcome.

29. Interest rate decontrol was the most significant aspect of this mammoth piece of legislation, but the new law also gave thrifts greater flexibility in lending and investment activities, expanded membership in the Federal Reserve System, and authorized negotiable order of withdrawal accounts and automatic transfers between savings and checking accounts. See Florida (1986) for an excellent account of the history of the legislation.

30. The phase-out of interest rate ceilings was dramatically accelerated with the passage of the Garn-St. Germain Act in 1982.

31. The mechanism linking financial deregulation to inflation is that easy access to credit allows demand to be transmitted to the market without restraint, enabling businesses and consumers to bid up prices for goods and services.

32. Some of the most ardent supply-siders, such as Paul Craig Roberts, later denied that they had ever endorsed the idea, embodied in the famous Laffer Curve, that the tax cuts would be revenue-neutral (or even revenue-enhancing). But as Feldstein (1994, p. 25) notes, the supply-siders – Roberts included – left behind a substantial paper trail making subsequent attempts to distance themselves from Laffer appear somewhat disingenuous.

33. Lawrence Kudlow and Beryl Sprinkel, "Financial Warnings," April 28, 1981, *Cabinet Councils*: Box 12, Ronald Reagan Presidential Library; Jerry Jordan, "Economic Summary," October 6, 1981, *Cabinet Councils*: Box 16, Ronald Reagan Presidential Library; L. Kudlow, "Financial and Economic Outlook," January 21, 1982, Cabinet *Councils*: Box 19, Ronald Reagan Presidential Library; L. Kudlow, "Financial Markets Update," August 6, 1982, *Cabinet Councils*: Box 26, Ronald Reagan Presidential Library.

34. "Recovery Shrugs off the Deficit," *Business Week*, June 6, 1983, pp. 24–26.

35. Private Saving + Budget Surplus – Domestic Investment = Exports – Imports. This formula became the basis of the famous debate over the "twin deficits" – i.e., the notion that the trade deficit was caused by the budget deficit.

36. Murray Weidenbaum, "The United States and the International Economy," September 16, 1981, *Cabinet Councils*: Box 13, Ronald Reagan Presidential Library (emphasis added).

37. William Niskanen, "Characteristics of the Current Recovery," October 5, 1984, *Cabinet Councils, Restricted Materials*: Box 31, Ronald Reagan Presidential Library.

38. Interview, July 18, 2002.

39. Monetarism refers to the theory that the rate of growth in the money supply is the sole determinant of real economic outcomes (see Friedman, 1968). According to monetarist doctrine, the role of the central bank should be confined to controlling the money supply rather than attempting to directly stimulate growth or create employment. While in theory monetarism prescribes only a constant rate of growth of the money supply (neither stimulating nor contracting the economy), monetarist policies tend to be quite restrictive in practice, as was the case during the Volcker years.

40. As explained in the preceding section, without interest rate ceilings rationing borrowers out of the market, *all* could seek access to credit, with the result that interest rates in the economy were bid sharply higher.

41. During a period of rising prices (i.e., inflation), money loses value: it takes more of a given unit of currency to purchase the same quantity of any commodity. As inflation proceeds, then, the real value of debt is eroded as the dollars used to retire debt are worth less than the dollars in which the debt was originally accumulated. Thus, inflation is a boon to debtors, and therefore tends to ease the fiscal burden of the government.

42. Interview, July 16, 2002.

43. Data is from the *1989 Economic Report of the President*. The size of the federal budget deficit in these years was $208 billion in 1983, $185 billion in 1984, $212 billion in 1985, and $221 billion in 1986. Thus, the share of the federal budget deficit financed by foreign capital ranged from slightly under half in 1983 to *all* of the budget deficit in 1986.

44. Suppose that an American firm needs to sell its widget for $10 in order to realize a profit. Further suppose that the yen is trading ¥150 to $1. This means that the American widget sells in Tokyo for ¥1500. Now suppose that the dollar appreciates so that, under the new exchange rate, one dollar is worth ¥300. The widget now sells for ¥3000 in Tokyo. Assuming that local producers' costs are unchanged, they are in a position to undersell the American producer, whose price has doubled. The example may seem extreme, but these values are in line with the magnitude of the change in the dollar/yen exchange rate over the 1980s.

45. Paul Krugman, "Is the Yen Undervalued?" September 30, 1982, *Martin S. Feldstein, Files*: Box 1, Ronald Reagan Presidential Library.

46. Paul Krugman, "Caterpillar Tractor's Yen Study: An Evaluation," October 25, 1982, *Martin S. Feldstein, Files*: Box 1, Ronald Reagan Presidential Library.

47. Interview with Jeffrey Frankel, July 12, 2002.

48. In a November 10, 1983 interview published in the *Washington Post*, for example, Regan remarked, "They won't share [their] savings with anyone else. Any Japanese company can come over here and borrow in our markets and take our savings; we cannot go over to their markets with impunity and borrow whatever we

want over there, so what we're saying is, open up your capital markets and learn to share. *And in that way you will help to strengthen your yen and our dollar won't be nearly as strong"* (Quoted in Frankel, 1984, p. 27, emphasis in original). This analysis by the Treasury Secretary is remarkable in two respects. First, it was arguably the United States, with its growing dependence on foreign capital, that needed to learn to "share." Second, Regan demonstrates a rather weak understanding of economics by asserting that increased outflows (i.e., borrowing) from Japan would strengthen the yen. A correct analysis is that if U.S. residents are borrowing from Japan, then Japanese residents are purchasing U.S. assets, increasing the demand for – and hence the value of – the dollar.

49. "Minutes of the Cabinet Council of Economic Affairs," October 27, 1982, *Cabinet Councils, Restricted Materials*: Box 23, Ronald Reagan Presidential Library.

50. "Minutes of the Cabinet Council of Economic Affairs," April 12, 1983, *Cabinet Councils, Restricted Materials*: Box 26, Ronald Reagan Presidential Library.

51. Frankel Interview, July 12, 2002.

52. Treasury also stressed the "safe haven" view: that capital was flowing to the United States because U.S. markets offered investors a refuge from political and economic turmoil elsewhere in the world. Similar arguments resurfaced in the 1990s, when they were somewhat more plausible. See Frankel (1988) for an attempt to adjudicate between the various explanations offered for the capital inflows into the United States in the 1980s.

53. The term "Feldstein Doctrine" was coined by Fred Bergsten.

54. Martin Feldstein, "Is the Dollar Overvalued?" April 8, 1983, *Cabinet Councils, Restricted Materials*: Box 26, Ronald Reagan Presidential Library. Council of Economic Advisers, "The U.S. Trade Deficit: Causes, Prospects, and Consequences," October 4, 1983, *Cabinet Councils*: Box 42, Ronald Reagan Presidential Library.

55. Treasury Department, "Causes and Consequences of U.S. Deficits on Trade and Current Account," October 4, 1983, *Cabinet Councils*: Box 42, Ronald Reagan Presidential Library.

56. William Poole, "Interest Rates, Stock Prices, and Monetary Policy," June 19, 1984, *Cabinet Councils*: Box 52, Ronald Reagan Presidential Library.

57. J. Gregory Ballentine, "International Capital Flows," October 26, 1984, *Cabinet Councils, Restricted Materials*: Box 31, Ronald Reagan Presidential Library; Sidney Jones, "Report of the Working Group on International Trade on the Probability of Large Merchandise and Current Account Deficits Continuing for Several Years," December 14, 1984, *Cabinet Councils*: Box 55; Roger Porter, "Minutes of Cabinet Council on Economic Affairs," January 22, 1985, *Cabinet Councils, Restricted Materials*: Box 31, Ronald Reagan Presidential Library. Volcker's comments – and their effects on the financial markets – are reported in *Business Week* (February 20, 1984; March 5, 1984; March 19, 1984; October 15, 1984).

58. See Destler and Henning (1989) for the former view and Frankel (1994) for the latter.

59. "Why the Treasury's Plan to See Debt Overseas May Not Fly," *Business Week*, October 22, 1984, p. 129.

60. "The Markets Bet Against Henry Kaufman," *Business Week*, February 11, 1985, p. 88.

61. Until recently, the Federal Reserve has not considered asset price inflation as a form of inflation that it should attempt to counter using the tools of monetary policy (see Bernanke & Gertler, 1999). This view has been revised in the aftermath of the current financial crisis, obviously.

ACKNOWLEDGMENT

I gratefully acknowledge the contributions of Paul Hirsch, Michael Lounsbury, Mark Mizruchi, Monica Prasad, and the participants of the Economic Sociology Seminar in the Sociology Department at the University of Michigan for their helpful comments on this article.

REFERENCES

Abdelal, R. (2007). *Capital rules: The construction of global finance*. Cambridge, MA: Harvard University Press.

Alexander, K. (1974). The politics of inflation. *The Political Quarterly*, *45*, 300–309.

Bell, D. (1976). *The cultural contradictions of capitalism*. New York, NY: Basic Books.

Bernanke, B., & Gertler, M. (1999). Monetary policy and asset price volatility. *Economic Review*, *84*, 17–51.

Borio, C., & Lowe, P. (2002). *Asset prices, financial and monetary stability: Exploring the nexus*. Working paper no. 114. Bank for International Settlements, Basle.

Brittan, S. (1978). Inflation and democracy. In: F. Hirsch & J. H. Goldthorpe (Eds), *The political economy of inflation* (pp. 161–185). Cambridge, MA: Harvard University Press.

Collins, R. (2000). *More: The politics of economic growth in postwar America*. New York, NY: Oxford University Press.

Cooper, G. (2008). *The origins of financial crises: Central banks, credit bubbles, and the efficient markets fallacy*. New York, NY: Vintage.

Crouch, C. (1978). Inflation and the political organization of economic interests. In: F. Hirsch & J. H. Goldthorpe (Eds), *The political economy of inflation* (pp. 217–239). Cambridge, MA: Harvard University Press.

Destler, I. M., & Henning, C. R. (1989). *Dollar politics: Exchange rate policymaking in the United States*. Washington, DC: Institute for International Economics.

Eastburn, D. (1970). Federal reserve policy and social priorities. *Business Review of the Federal Reserve Bank of Philadelphia*, November Issue, pp. 426–432.

Evans, L. (2003). *Why the bubble burst: U.S. stock market performance since 1982*. Cheltenham, UK and Northampton, MA: Edward Elgar.

Feldstein, M. (1994). American economic policy in the 1980s: A personal view. In: M. Feldstein (Ed.), *American economic policy in the 1980s* (pp. 1–79). Chicago, IL: National Bureau of Economic Research.

Flemming, J. S. (1978). The economic explanation of inflation. In: F. Hirsch & J. H. Goldthorpe (Eds), *The political economy of inflation* (pp. 13–36). Cambridge, MA: Harvard University Press.

Florida, R. (1986). *Banking on housing: The political economy of financial deregulation and the reorganization of housing finance*. Ph.D. Dissertation, Columbia University, New York, NY.

Frankel, J. (1984). *The yen/dollar agreement: Liberalizing Japanese capital markets*. Washington, DC: Institute for International Economics.

Frankel, J. (1988). International capital flows and domestic economic policies. In: M. Feldstein (Ed.), *The United States in the world economy* (pp. 559–627). Chicago, IL: National Bureau of Economic Research.

Frankel, J. (1994). The making of exchange rate policy in the 1980s. In: M. Feldstein (Ed.), *American economic policy in the 1980s* (pp. 293–341). Chicago, IL: National Bureau of Economic Research.

Friedman, M. (1968). The role of monetary policy. *American Economic Review, 58*, 1–17.

Friedman, M. (1970). *The counter-revolution in monetary theory*. London: Institute of Economic Affairs.

Goldthorpe, J. (1978). The current inflation: Towards a sociological account. In: F. Hirsch & J. H. Goldthorpe (Eds), *The political economy of inflation* (pp. 186–214). Cambridge, MA: Harvard University Press.

Goldthorpe, J. (1987). Problems of political economy after the postwar period. In: C. S. Maier (Ed.), *Changing boundaries of the political* (pp. 363–407). New York, NY: Cambridge University Press.

Greider. (1987). *Secrets of the temple: How the federal reserve runs the country*. New York, NY: Simon and Schuster.

Hirsch, F. (1978). The ideological underlay of inflation. In: F. Hirsch & J. H. Goldthorpe (Eds), *The political economy of inflation* (pp. 263–284). Cambridge, MA: Harvard University Press.

Hirsch, F., & Goldthorpe, J. (1978). *The political economy of inflation*. Cambridge, MA: Harvard University Press.

Hirschman, A. (1980). The social and political matrix of inflation: Elaborations on the Latin American experience. In: *Essays in trespassing: Economics to politics and beyond* (pp. 177–207). New York, NY: Cambridge University Press.

Kaufman, H. (1986). *Interest rates, markets, and the new financial world*. New York, NY: Times Books.

Kindleberger, C. (1978). *Manias, panics, and crashes: A history of financial crises*. New York, NY: Wiley.

Knodell, J. (1994). Financial institutions and contemporary economic performance. In: M. A. Bernstein & D. E. Adler (Eds), *Understanding American economic decline* (pp. 114–160). New York, NY: Cambridge University Press.

Konings, M. (2008). The institutional foundations of U.S. structural power in international finance: From the re-emergence of global finance to the monetarist turn. *Review of International Political Economy, 15*, 35–61.

Krippner, G. (2011). *Capitalizing on crisis: The political origins of the rise of finance*. Cambridge, MA: Harvard University Press.

Lindberg, L., & Maier, C. (1985). *The politics of inflation and economic stagnation: Theoretical approaches and international case studies*. Washington, DC: Brookings Institution.

Maier, C. (1978). The politics of inflation in the twentieth century. In: F. Hirsch & J. H. Goldthorpe (Eds), *The political economy of inflation* (pp. 217–239). Cambridge, MA: Harvard University Press.

Minsky, H. (1975). *John Maynard Keynes*. New York, NY: Columbia University Press.

Minsky, H. (1982). *Can "It" happen again? Essays on instability and finance*. Armonk, NY: M.E. Sharpe.

Minsky, H. (1986). *Stabilizing an unstable economy*. New Haven, CT: Yale University Press.

Morris, C. (2008). *The trillion dollar meltdown: Easy money, high rollers, and the great credit crash*. New York, NY: Public Affairs.

Murphy, R. T. (1997). *The weight of the yen*. New York, NY: W.W. Norton.

Niskanen, W. (1988). *Reaganomics: An insider's account of the policies and the people*. New York, NY: Oxford University Press.

Sellon, G., & VanNahmen, D. (1988). The securitization of housing finance. *Economic Review* (July/August Issue), 3–20.

Shiller, R. (2000). *Irrational exuberance*. Princeton, NJ: Princeton University Press.

Shiller, R. (2008). *The subprime solution: How today's financial crisis happened, and what to do about it*. Princeton, NJ: Princeton University Press.

Shleifer, A. (2000). *Inefficient markets: An introduction to behavioral finance*. Oxford: Oxford University Press.

Stockman, D. (1986). *The triumph of politics: How the Reagan revolution failed*. New York, NY: Harper and Row.

Tobin, J. (1972). Inflation and unemployment. *American Economic Review, 62,* 1–18.

Tobin, J. (1974). There are three types of inflation: We have two. *New York Times,* September 6, p. 33.

Trichet, J. C. (2005). *Asset price bubbles and monetary policy*. Mas lecture, Singapore, June 8.

Volcker, P., & Gyohten, T. (1992). *Changing fortunes: The world's money and the threat to American leadership*. New York, NY: Times Books.

Wojnilower, A. (1980). The central role of credit crunches in recent financial history. *Brookings Papers on Economic Activity, 2,* 277–339.

Wojnilower, A. (1985). Private credit demand, supply, and crunches – how different are the 1980s? *American Economic Review, 75,* 351–356.

SECTION IV
CRISIS PRODUCTION:
SPECULATIVE BUBBLES AND
BUSINESS CYCLES

THE INSTITUTIONAL EMBEDDEDNESS OF MARKET FAILURE: WHY SPECULATIVE BUBBLES STILL OCCUR

Mitchel Y. Abolafia

ABSTRACT

This article identifies the institutional factors behind both the emergence of a highly vulnerable financial system and the housing bubble that devastated it. The underlying premise is that the financial crisis was a market failure embedded in and caused by an institutional one. The failing institutions were academic, political and regulatory. The article shows how these institutions were fatally undermined, suggesting limits to the rationalization of finance capitalism. The perspective on financial crisis developed here recognizes the pressing need for reform of the financial markets, and also recommends institutional reforms as critical protections against future system failure.

Most speculative bubbles are not disasters for society. Their fallout is usually limited to the group of speculators who bought the asset and a somewhat wider group of exchange partners. Even the consequences of the dot.com bubble at the turn of the millennium were relatively contained.

Markets on Trial: The Economic Sociology of the U.S. Financial Crisis: Part B
Research in the Sociology of Organizations, Volume 30B, 177–200
Copyright © 2010 by Emerald Group Publishing Limited
All rights of reproduction in any form reserved
ISSN: 0733-558X/doi:10.1108/S0733-558X(2010)000030B010

But the collapse of the housing bubble set off defaults in subprime mortgages and related securitized instruments, leading directly to bank failures and a credit freeze that sent the economy into the worst recession since the Great Depression. Bubbles are a societal problem when the relevant asset is tied to a broad swath of the economy, the financial system is so complex that its operators and regulators do not understand it, and the relationships between its parts are so tightly coupled that a failure in one part is not easily contained (see Palmer & Maher, 2010; Schneiberg & Bartley, 2010). In the context of a complex and tightly coupled financial system, speculative bubbles in widely held assets constitute an unacceptable systemic risk.

This article argues that advanced industrial societies have the knowledge to prevent crippling speculative bubbles. But it will also argue that we are unlikely to put an end to such man-made disasters. The reason, I will show, lies less in our understanding of the economics of speculative bubbles than it does in our understanding of the institutional factors shaping the formulation of economic policy. It is not a failure of knowledge about our economy, rather it is a failure of knowledge about our academic, political, and regulatory institutions and their interpenetration. It is a failure to understand the extent to which economic policy and, in fact, the market system, is embedded in this institutional field. More specifically, it is a failure to predict the corrosive impact of a radical ideology on the robustness of those institutions.

The ideology in question may at first be hard to recognize because of its ubiquitous nature. The idea that financial markets are self-regulating, requiring only minimal state intervention, has appeared throughout the history of capitalism. Each time it is adopted by the state, it leads to a period of innovation and opportunism. As the economic historian Karl Polonyi explained, low levels of market restraint yield both profits and "pernicious effects" (Polonyi, 1944). These pernicious effects include increased frauds, defaults, and bankruptcies. Markets contain a "self-destructive mechanism" that societies eventually protect themselves against. (See my discussion of Polonyi cycles in Abolafia (1996).) From an historical perspective, the question would seem to be what level of dislocation and systemic risk is a society willing to tolerate in return for financial innovation?

But this choice is not a simple rational calculation. This article develops an analytic framework in which academic, political, and regulatory entrepreneurs take advantage of events to socially construct what they believe to be "market friendly" institutions. Difficult economic conditions, such as the Great Inflation of the 1970s, create opportunities for political and regulatory entrepreneurs to unravel the existing regime of stability and restraint in favor of increased profits. The enactment of weakened social institutions leads to the kind of system failure discussed here. This article identifies three institutions in particular that contributed significantly to the disastrous societal effects of the recent speculative bubble. These institutions are (1) the profession of academic economics, (2) the ruling political discourse of the era, and (3) vulnerable regulatory structures. The failure of these institutions to moderate the "self-destructive mechanism" in markets calls their legitimacy into question. It also suggests that the solution to speculative bubbles lies in the difficult path of institutional change.

FRAMING THE PROBLEM

"Bubbles generally are perceptible only after the fact. To spot a bubble in advance requires a judgment that hundreds of thousands of informed investors have it all wrong. Betting against markets is usually precarious at best." Alan Greenspan (June 1999)[1]

"Those of us who have looked to the self-interest of lending institutions to protect shareholder's equity (myself especially) are in a state of shocked disbelief" Alan Greenspan (October 2008).[2]

These two quotes may be seen as bookends to the bubble economy of the last decade or so. They indicate the Federal Reserve's reluctance to inhibit the irrational exuberance of investors at the beginning and its alarm that market forces had allowed two successive bubbles to happen at all. This faith in the judgment of the market and self-interest of bankers as a self-regulating force will be referred to as market fundamentalism in this essay. Market fundamentalism, I will argue, is poorly suited to diagnose or prescribe a remedy for bubbles. I will argue further that it is market fundamentalism that underlies the Fed's role in inflating the bubble economy and its reluctance to restrain it. My goal is to explore how such an ideology was adopted, and the confluence of ideas, interests, and events that explain its adoption.

The underlying premise of the essay is institutional, i.e. that organizations are constituted by the narratives, logics of action, and ideologies that exist in a particular field (Phillips, Lawrence, & Hardy, 2004). My argument relies on work in organizational and historical institutionalism that shows how economic and managerial theories come to be adopted in both private and public sector policy making (Weir & Skocpol, 1985; Hall, 1989; Guillen, 1994; Campbell, 1998). Following Campbell (1998), the argument shows how an idea, in this case market fundamentalism, can both constrain and enable the policy-making process. Although this argument has echoes of

Keynes' famous observation that policy makers "are often the slaves of some defunct economist" (Keynes, 1936, p. 383), it does not grant sole influence to talented academics and their ideas. Rather, it explores how the choice of ideas adopted may also be affected by the nature of national political discourse, the receptiveness of state structures, and the goals of ruling political parties. These institutional pressures, when taken together, help to explain why a bubble economy may still occur despite the existence of the knowledge and organizational capacity needed to inhibit it.

This essay is organized around three questions: Where do bubbles come from? Why do they still occur? Can they be managed? Before proceeding to explore the latter two questions, however, I will introduce three analytic perspectives that have been used to explain speculative bubbles. For our purposes, bubbles will be defined simply as a condition in which "prices are high ... only because investors believe that the selling price will be high tomorrow – when 'fundamental' factors do not seem to justify such a price" (Stiglitz, 1990, p. 13). I will argue in the following section that market fundamentalism obscures what we know from historical experience and alternative models.

WHERE DO BUBBLES COME FROM?

Market Fundamentalism

The most influential approach to understand asset markets today may be referred to as market fundamentalism. As stated above, it is an exaggerated faith in the ability of the market to achieve socially optimal outcomes. It is not one idea, but a system of interrelated ideas that offer predictions, diagnosis, and solutions. This faith is seen in its strongest form regarding financial markets. In finance it has become a stylized conventional wisdom. Recently, the British Financial Services Authority, in describing the intellectual assumptions underlying its regulatory philosophy before the financial crisis, has usefully articulated this conventional wisdom.

1) Market prices are good indicators of rationally evaluated economic value.
2) The development of securitized credit, since based on the creation of new and more liquid markets, has improved both allocative efficiency and financial stability.

3) The risk characteristics of financial markets can be inferred from mathematical analysis, delivering robust quantitative measures of trading risk.
4) Market discipline can be used as an effective tool in constraining harmful risk.
5) Financial innovation can be assumed to be beneficial since market competition would winnow out any innovations which did not deliver value added (cited in Skidelsky, 2009, p. 38).

The focal actor here is the invisible hand. It determines value, creates efficiency, reduces risk, and ensures valuable innovations. In sum, the market is optimally self-regulating. Government can only interfere with the market mechanism, making it less efficient. It assumes that the market can price risk correctly. The flaw in all of this is uncertainty, the kind of uncertainty where the future is unknowable or at least unpredictable. In the face of uncertainty, risk is not normally distributed and the mathematical analysis of risk creates the illusion of security.

In the strong form of market fundamentalism, often associated with the efficient markets hypothesis (EMH), asset prices always reflect the asset's true value, leaving no room for the existence of bubbles. Any major price swing is explained as a response to an exogenous shock that changed the fundamental underlying value of the asset. This position is reflected in the works of Flood, Garber, and Hodrick (Flood & Garber, 1980; Garber, 1990; Flood & Hodrick, 1990). They studied the Tulipmania in Holland and the South Sea Bubble in France and England, two of history's most famous bubbles. They found that they were not bubbles at all, but rational responses to changing conditions. But this triumph of market fundamentalism over economic history has not gone uncontested. Following the critiques of this work by Canterbury (1999) and Baddeley and McCombie (2001), it does not appear that rapidly rising prices reflected a sudden increase in the desire for tulips or the rational expectation of earnings by the South Sea Company. Also, the collapse in prices over a period of days and the government intervention that followed suggest a crash rather than a standard pattern of price depreciation. In sum, prices did not reflect a rational assessment of fundamental value and the concept of bubbles cannot be so easily dismissed.

In its weak form, market fundamentalism, as seen in Alan Greenspan's quotes above, generally accepts that bubbles may occur in rare instances. In these instances, values are distorted by some exogenous shock to the market. But as Greenspan explains, you cannot tell that it was a bubble until after it is burst and it is better to trust the judgment of investors and bankers than to act to inhibit the exuberance. The weak form is best represented by the work of Kindleberger who argues that bubbles are the result of exogenous shocks leading to a mania fueled by destabilizing changes in the supply of credit (Kindleberger & Aliber, 2005). The three major weaknesses in this kind of thinking are (1) its reliance of exogenous shocks obscures the endogenous weaknesses in the market, (2) its assumption of equilibrium leads to a functionalist search for the source of disturbance, and (3) its psychological reductionism that conceals the role of institutions in speculative bubbles. The next two theories speak to these weaknesses.

Financial Instability Hypothesis

This model was developed by Hyman Minsky (1986, 1993)[3]. Only since the collapse of the housing bubble in recent years has it come to prominence. The congruence of current events with Minsky's model has made "Minsky moment" a catch phrase on Wall Street. Rather than assuming that bubbles require an exogenous shock, Minsky saw that such instability was part of the internal dynamics of capitalist economies, i.e. endogenous to the system[4]. Minsky posited that the economy has financing regimes that range from prudent to Ponzi (Minsky, 1986, p. 230). "Over periods of prolonged prosperity, the economy transits from financial relations that make for a stable system to financial relations that make for an unstable system" (Minsky, 1993, p. 8). Periods of stability encourage more risk taking and innovation that increases income even as it disrupts the conditions that generated the system coherence and stability. This is not a system in which the individual pursuit of self-interest leads an economy to equilibrium. Rather, "tranquility" encourages more risk taking and innovation, which, in turn, creates endogenous, deviation-amplifying destabilizing forces.

Recently, Papadimitriou and Wray (2008) have applied Minsky's model to the current financial meltdown. As they explain, "the financial innovations of the past decade greatly expanded the availability of credit, which then pushed up asset prices. That, in turn, not only encouraged further innovation to take advantage of profit opportunities but also fueled a debt frenzy and greater leveraging." They show how a series of profit opportunities increased the appetite for risk and "tipped the balance of sentiments" from fear toward greed. The greatest strength of the Financial Instability Hypothesis is its recognition that instability is the result of internal processes of the finance capital. Minsky shows that 20 years of postwar stability from 1945 to 1965 were followed by a series of near crises (1970, 1974–1975, 1979–80, 1982–1983) that reflected the system's increasing fragility. Although the Financial Instability Hypothesis has much to recommend its explanatory power, it contains two weaknesses. First, is the model's psychological reductionism. Minsky tended to rely, especially in his early versions of the hypothesis, on terms such as euphoria, mania, distress, and other Keynesian "animal spirits" to explain the instability and deviation and amplification. A second weakness is an economic function-alism that makes bubbles seem overdetermined. These issues are addressed in a third model.

Social Construction Perspective

This model was first developed in Abolafia and Kilduff (1988) and Abolafia (1996). In its current version it also draws on Akerlof and Romer (1993), Barron (2007), and Ferguson (2008). It shares with Minsky's model the sense that bubbles are endogenous to the system and that the economy or, in this case political economy, goes through different financing regimes. But in the social construction perspective, individual economic activities, such as speculation, are enacted in the context of social relationships, cultural idioms, and political and economic institutions. These social phenomena define the market, rather than the reverse. Thus, it is the market professionals pushing innovations, and insider speculators who create the bubble, rather than the irrational herd of manic victims.[5] These institutional entrepreneurs redefine the cognitive maps and normative restraints of the trading community, most recently by marketing subprime mortgages and derivatives with no transparency. In the same vein, it is state sponsorship of easy credit and lax regulation that enacts instability, rather than the deterministic consequences of too much stability. In other words, markets work because of the structure of formal and informal constraints constructed to tame them. Without this social infrastructure, financial markets are self-immolating.

The social construction perspective emphasizes the speculogenic enactments by market professionals and insider speculators. This model predicts that people are likely to produce bubbles in asset markets wherever these speculogenic conditions exist, a proposition supported by work in experimental economics (Smith et al., 1988; Haruvy et al., 2007; Hussam et al., 2008). Comparative historical research suggests that speculative bubbles have three recurrent features. The first is the creation of financial innovations, such ase those mentioned above, that have forms of information asymmetry that the insiders can exploit fraudulently (Ferguson, 2008; Akerlof & Shiller, 2009). In recent years these have included subprime mortgages and off-balance sheet accounting. Such deviant innovations become "normalized" in the institutions that operate financial markets (Palmer & Maher, 2010).The second feature is the active deregulation of financial markets. These policy decisions signal market professionals that they are free to test the limits of opportunism. The final necessary feature is easy money. All bubbles occur under conditions of easily available credit. In the current bubble economy, this has meant prolonged periods of low interest rates. Both an excessively expansionary Federal Reserve policy and the glut of Chinese investment have contributed to this.

WHY DO BUBBLES STILL OCCUR? THE INSTITUTIONAL EMBEDDEDNESS FRAMEWORK

I have no illusions that the social construction perspective is going to be adopted by our economic policy makers, although I believe it offers guidance for the inhibition of speculative excess. Even if these ideas remain outside the dominant paradigm, policy makers would still have economic history and institutional memory to remind them of the legacy of past bubbles and their consequences. But history is notoriously ignored and institutional memory is undependable as older members leave the organization. Although policy makers were fixated on not repeating 1929 during the postwar years, by 1980 it was the Great Inflation rather than the Great Depression that was foremost in their minds. It was at this historical moment that market fundamentalism came to be the dominant ideology. How, then, does such an ideology come to be adopted and what accounts for its pervasive influence?

The answer lies in understanding not only the bubble, but also the institutional pressures in which it is embedded. This is an argument about the role of ideas in policy making. But, it will not claim that ideas alone determine policy. Rather, I will show that ideas are in a constant interplay with interests and events. Ideas, as Weber indicated, can often embody the interests and events of the moment, creating a new image of the world and switching the direction of history (Gerth & Mills, 1946). The institutional approach used here identifies three factors influencing the adoption of ideas. These factors reflect the power of organized actors, e.g. professions, political parties, and technocrats, to create institutional pressures on national economic policy. In this essay I focus on monetary policy in the United States. During the recent bubble economy, the Fed has been responsible for controlling the money supply and regulating the largest bank holding companies. It is central to understanding the enactment and management of the bubble economy.

The Role of Professional Economics

Economic concepts and models play an important role in economic policy making. Like management theories, these concepts and models are used in at least two different ways (Guillen, 1994). First, they offer policy makers a body of technical knowledge that can provide a filter for sifting through information and a script for identifying and selecting among policy alternatives. Second, the concepts and models constitute an ideology "aimed at establishing legitimacy and reinforcing credibility" (Guillen, 1994, p. 3). They contain the basis for agreement on the justice and reasonableness of policy decisions (Heilbroner & Milberg, 1995). This second use is of particular importance when policy making is highly visible and controversial.

Economics as a discipline had already established a legitimate, even dominant, role in public affairs by the mid-twentieth century. The discipline's own internal dynamics were reflected in changing policy regimes in the United States. As Marion Fourcade (2009, p. 127) explains, the mathematization of economics offered technical abilities that gave their work an air of "impartiality in the eyes of political audiences" and made it seem "less prone to arbitrariness." The advantage of the appearance of technical neutrality was augmented by the congruence between economics and the laissez-faire political philosophy with which Americans are most comfortable.

Economic policy is always reflective of a set of beliefs about how the economy works. For most of American history, the preference for minimal government involvement in the economy has been dominant. During the Great Depression, Keynesian theories about the role of government in increasing aggregate demand and stabilizing the economy became dominant. Keynes had argued that financial markets were a "casino" and that active regulation was critical to inhibiting their worst excesses. The dominance of Keynesianism was supplanted by market fundamentalism in the 1980s. Such ideas usually lie in the background of policy debate as tacit assumptions (Campbell, 1998), although they may rise to the foreground when economic circumstances call these assumptions into question, as in the following excerpt from a Federal Reserve policy meeting from the 1990s in which an unresponsive economy forced policy makers to reconsider the current orthodoxy.

> **Mr Lindsey**: Twenty years ago I was sitting in freshmen economics with Samuelson's Eighth Edition, and the first thing we were taught was something called the "paradox of thrift." The paradox of thrift was the 1972–or probably the 1952–way of saying "balance sheet restructuring will lead to less economic activity." … Well, we've been trying to unlearn Keynesian economics for the last 20 years and that may have been a mistake because, in fact, I think it's probably very close to the situation we're in now … (FOMC, 1992, p. 37).

This questioning of assumptions reflects the fact that the Keynesianism consensus had dissolved in the 1970s and competing versions of market fundamentalism had risen to fill the vacuum. Heilbroner and Milberg (1995) identify four analytical weaknesses in Keynesianism that led to its unraveling within the academic field of economics. First was its inability to offer a theory of inflation. Its one effort, the Phillips curve, was thoroughly discredited in a series of papers by Friedman (1968), Phelps (1967), and Gordon (1972). Second was its failure to predict or explain the stagflation that plagued the United States in the 1970s. Third was the relatively limited efficacy accorded monetary policy. Monetarists and other market fundamentalists took this as a direct challenge, especially in a period of inflation. Finally, Keynesian behavioral assumptions about the macroeconomy, the animal spirits referred to earlier, are at odds with previous and current rational actor assumptions of microeconomics. All these weaknesses opened the door to an assault on Keynesianism, an effort by policy makers to "unlearn" it, and a return to the market rather than the state as the solution to problems.

At the same time that academic economics was in transition, its applied sister, academic finance, was achieving new coherence through quantification. The first step was the use of longitudinal data on stock prices to develop the EMH. EMH basically says that the invisible hand works in financial markets, i.e. that the price of financial instruments reflects all available information and reflects the best possible estimate of risk. This, of course, became the prime directive of market fundamentalism. Perhaps the most important development in the new quantitative finance for understanding the bubble economy was the development of approaches to portfolio diversification that allowed the investor to "know" the level of risk he or she was assuming. Simple measures of risk and a panoply of new investment instruments were the result. Bankers, brokers, investors, and regulators came to believe that you could use securities, options, and other derivatives to reduce the worst risks and choose the level of risk you were willing to take. As Alan Greenspan said in 2004, "These increasingly complex financial instruments have contributed, especially over the recent stressful period, to the development of a far more flexible, efficient, and hence resilient financial system than existed just a quarter century ago" (quoted in Cassidy, 2009, p. 227). The market had itself become the solution to market risk. Although this return to market solutions might well be expected from America's history of economic policy, its character was shaped by the political and organizational factors discussed below.

The Conventions of National Political Discourse

Policy making takes place within the context of prevailing political ideas (Hall, 1989). These ideas reflect culturally popular notions about such things as the appropriate role of government, the efficacy of markets vs. the state as solutions to social issues, the salience of competing values, and the shared interpretation of past successes and failures. There are times when a dominant discourse emerges. At its most coherent, such discourse becomes a program (Campbell, 1998), a policy prescription that guides policy makers to a course of action. Such a program, in the hands of skilled leaders, may become a tacit part of public sentiments, a set of normative assumptions about what is politically acceptable and legitimate (Campbell, 1998).

Starting in the mid 1970s, during the Carter administration, the nature of political discourse began to shift toward deregulation of the economy and market-centered policy making. This discourse was a response to the steep recession of 1974–1975 and the stagflation mentioned above. There was a congruence between ideas and circumstances. Milton Friedman released his book and TV show, *Free to Choose*, an antigovernment, pro-market manifesto in 1980. Far right think tanks rose to new prominence. Under President Reagan, a master communicator, these ideas had a skilled interpreter. The deregulation movement escalated into frenzied antistatism (Block, 1996). Market fundamentalism represents the interpenetration of the neoclassical revival in the economic sphere and the ascendance of conservative ideology in the political sphere. Economic policy rhetoric reflected the Panglossian view that market outcomes are optimal when left alone.

The discourse of the "free" market and antistatism held sway for nearly 30 years. At the Fed, policy makers adopted a form of monetarist policy to bring down inflation. The policy had newfound legitimacy because it presumably reduced the discretion of policy makers and trusted the rationality of the market. Later, under Greenspan, the Fed loosened regulation of the banking sector and took a laissez-faire attitude toward irrational exuberance as described in the quote at the beginning of the essay. Greenspan was a master of framing, explaining the soaring value of stocks in the dot-com bubble as reflective of increases in productivity. National political discourse became resolutely market fundamentalist and skeptics were marginalized.

Receptiveness of State Structures

Economic policy is most often understood as the outcome of interest groups or class politics. Institutional theorists (Hall, 1989; Weir & Skocpol, 1985; Campbell, 1998) suggest how the state and the structure of its agencies may become vehicles for the adoption of ideas and models in their effort to create coherent reactions to policy problems. In a recent work (Abolafia, in press), I argue that monetary policy is increasingly the work of relatively autonomous technical experts in government. Control over Fed policy making has shifted over the course of its history from bankers to economists. From its establishment in 1913 to the Great Crash, the Fed was controlled by the regional reserve banks, especially the one in New York. During the Depression and the Second World War, the Fed dutifully responded to the policy needs of the Treasury. In 1951, the Treasury–Federal Reserve Accord gave it relative autonomy from the executive branch. The Fed had to learn to operate in this new, more discretionary environment. In 1960, none of the governors of the Federal Reserve were economists. In 1970 four of the seven were and by 1980 all but one were economists. By the time of the bubble economy, the shift from bankers to technical experts who were partisans of economic orthodoxy was accomplished.

With the Keynesian unraveling, particularly the discrediting of the Phillips curve, the technical experts at the Fed fell back on the standard tool kit of the neoclassical paradigm, just as their colleagues in academia did. At the same time, the discrediting of fiscal policy seemed to leave the Fed in charge of the economy. The critique of Keynesian demand management was congruent with the Fed's capacity for managing the money supply. This unintentionally concentrated more authority in the Fed and put it at the center stage. In 1987, President Reagan appointed Alan Greenspan, a market fundamentalist by inclination, as chairman of the Fed. By 1999, with the passage of the Financial Services Modernization Act, this Act and the leadership of Greenspan insured that banks would enjoy lax regulation and bubbles would not be spotted in advance. The Fed became increasingly reluctant to follow former Chairman Martin's dictum that its job was to "take away the punchbowl just when the party gets going."

From 1996 to 1998 the Fed followed an accommodative monetary policy and the Standard and Poors' (S&P) Index of 500 stocks rose from 740 to 1229. This exuberant market hit a bump when the Russian ruble and Long-Term Capital Management (LTCM), a hedge fund, collapsed. In response, the Fed lowered interest rates three times. This was widely viewed as an effort to bail out hedge funds that were in trouble. Many in the market came to believe that the Fed would intervene to protect asset prices. In the year following these cuts, the S&P index rose 35 percent and the Nasdaq Index that was heavily laden with technology and new Internet stocks doubled. Chairman Greenspan explained the behavior of stock prices as a result of technology-driven increases in productivity. The business press extolled a new economy fueled by technology. The Fed began to slowly raise interest rates in late 1999 because of fears of inflation. The stock market bubble broke in March 2000. The Nasdaq index stood at 5048. By May 2000 it was down to 3164. It had declined 47 percent from its high, reflecting the end of a speculative bubble in high-tech stocks fueled by easy money.

As the effects of the collapse began to ripple through the economy in 2001, the Fed began to lower interest rates. In light of the Fed's action in 1998 and now again in 2001, market professionals began to refer to the Fed's willingness to cushion the fall as the "Greenspan Put," referring to an option that keeps investors from losing money. After the terrorist attack of September 11, 2001, the Fed began to lower rates aggressively. The economy continued to decline and Greenspan announced in speeches that he feared deflation. The Fed lowered interest rates all the way to 1 percent by 2003, believing that this would lead to a surge in housing that would inhibit deflation. As interest rates reached historic lows, home sales and housing prices took off. During this time, the Fed signaled that it would maintain accommodative interest rates "for a considerable time." Tightening, when it came in 2004, proceeded at a slow pace. When the supply of qualified buyers in the housing market was exhausted, the banks offered teaser rate (subprime) mortgages to the less qualified. Sales and prices of homes continued to soar until the bubble finally broke 2007. This time, the collapse led to the demise of several major financial institutions, a credit freeze, a very steep recession, and a massive infusion of money by both the Fed and the Treasury.

By the period of the bubble economy, the late 1990s to 2007, the Fed was operating under what Fed governor Don Kohn has referred to as "the Greenspan Doctrine." This doctrine, referenced earlier, was based on the belief that new financial instruments flooding Wall Street reduced systemic risk. As Kohn described the doctrine, "By allowing institutions to diversify risk, to choose their risk profiles more precisely, and to improve the management of the risks they do take on, they have made institutions more robust" (Cassidy, 2009, p. 22). This doctrine, a variant of market fundamentalism, made the Fed highly receptive to what turned out to be very high-risk strategies. It allowed the Fed to keep its key interest rate below 2.5 from November 2001 to February 2005, setting off the greatest borrowing binge in American history, without concern for the excessive leverage and risk taking by major bank holding companies under its purview. The Fed did not seem to notice that risk had been concentrated in a small number of firms that had become too big to fail.

Finally, it should be clear by now that the success of market fundamentalism came in large part from the interpenetration of the three institutional spheres discussed above.[6] There is a high degree of mobility between academia, the Fed, and investment banks. The disciplines of economics and finance have supplied the staff of the Fed as well as the vast majority of MBA's at investment banks. The banks have supplied an increasing number of presidential advisors and cabinet officers. This interpenetration by a cadre of technical experts led to an increasing homogeneity of analysis, exacerbated by the declining empiricism and increasing mathematization of the reigning orthodoxy. The consequence of this interpenetration was to make market fundamentalism hegemonic. As Mary Douglas has written, "An answer is only seen to be the right one if it sustains the institutional thinking that is already in the minds of the individuals as they try to decide" (Douglas, 1986, p. 4).

DISCUSSION: ALTERNATIVE MODES OF INSTITUTIONAL THINKING

It would be tempting to blame the financial crisis of 2008 on a system design problem. By creating instruments whose risk was poorly understood, by eliminating firewalls and permitting banks to become large holding companies attracted to such risk, and by failure to properly regulate the riskiest parts of the financial sector, we have designed our way into failure. This explanation, as far as it goes, is a good one. But the explanation does not go far enough. It does not examine the institutional factors and critical events that unhinged the old system of regulation. It misses the common academic, political, and regulatory pressures shaping both the decisions at the Fed and the redesign of the financial system. Finally, it overlooks the need for an ideological shift away from market fundamentalism through the sponsorship of alternative modes of institutional thinking.

If we stop our analysis at the level of system design, then the financial crisis may be seen as an accident. Several articles of this volume frame the financial meltdown of 2008 as a normal accident (Palmer & Maher, 2010, Schneiberg & Bartley, 2010). But, normal accidents are, by definition, not preventable (Perrow, 1984). Their complexity and coupling lead to interactions that are beyond human ability to predict. But the recent financial meltdown *was* preventable. The flaws in the system were understood. Whether it is labeled a casino (Keynes, 1936), Ponzi finance (Minsky, 1986), or the "pernicious effects" of capitalism (Polonyi, 1944), the consequences of extremes of financial innovation and leverage were predicted by both scholars and financial pundits. Given the existing knowledge, how did we design our way into this failure? My answer to this question has been to examine the ideological blinders created by the institutional infrastructure.

A greater danger in stopping our analysis at the level of system design is that we would offer no recommendations for reforming the deep-seated problems in the institutional infrastructure. This article has argued that the principal underlying cause of the failure was an exaggerated faith in a bankrupt ideational regime that captured key institutions in which markets are embedded. We designed our way into this system failure by the adoption and implementation of a radical ideology at odds with the historical record of American capitalism. Prevention of similar failures will require institutional reflexivity: the ability of institutional actors to question their own practice. This, in itself, may seem unlikely, but learning organizations *do* exist, parameters for a more stable system can be legislated, and policy makers and regulators can be better and more broadly trained.

Trading the Perfect for the Imperfect

The first policy question suggested by the above analysis is "What do we do about the overwhelming hold that market fundamentalism has on economic policy?" While heterodox voices, such as Paul Krugman, Joseph Stiglitz, and some behavioral economists shout from the sidelines, the true believers are still in control. At this writing, populist anger is rising, but the defenders of the faith have shown little in the way of remorse or doubt in their faith.

More ominous than this is the fact that the economy has been significantly redesigned in market fundamentalism's image. Financial markets have been deregulated and financial assets have been securitized. As Jerry Davis explains, the EMH has been transformed into an organizing principle of society in which financial capital is the central actor rather than a supporting player in the economy.

> As the American economy has come to orbit financial markets like planets around the sun, entire categories of social life have been securitized, turned into a kind of capital. It is not the company or the government that will take care of us in our old age, but our 401(K). Home is not simply a place to live, but an option on future housing price increases. We now refer to education, talent, and personality as "human capital" – not ironically, but as an obvious fact. Friends, families, and neighborhoods are now "social capital," investments that might pay off down the road (Davis, 2009, p. 236).

These new ways of thinking and acting are insidious and not easily changed. Market fundamentalism's hold on our collective psyche is unobtrusive and thorough.

But this troubling condition should not stop one from discussing, even promoting, policy alternatives that might introduce a more balanced view of markets and their relation to society. Breaking the hold of market fundamentalism calls for an interdisciplinary challenge. As part of this challenge, competitive funding would be offered to universities to create programs in financial regulation at the Masters and Ph.D. levels. These programs would be interdisciplinary, requiring courses in the history of financial markets (Bubbles, Panics, and Bank Runs 101), the politics of regulation, comparative regulatory systems, administrative and regulatory law, economic sociology, and behavioral finance, as well as finance and the economics of regulation. Electives would provide concentrations in securities, banking, risk analysis, etc. The central premises of such programs would be that markets are institutionally embedded and that good regulation balances market growth with stability and discipline. Students would participate in internships in several financial regulatory agencies before graduation. The objective would be the creation of a professional cadre with a positive view of regulation.

A competitive funding stream would be created at NSF for studies of financial market failures in disciplines ranging from history, political science, and information science to sociology, psychology, and economics. These studies would contextualize our understanding of markets. They would highlight information asymmetries, market externalities, and their consequences for social welfare. They would develop diverse indicators of market failure. And they would begin to question the key assumptions of market fundamentalism. While economics and finance should either increase their recognition of market failure or loosen their claim on the analysis of public policy, the other social sciences must note their enhanced responsibility as policy sciences here as well.

Favoring Society over Markets

The second major policy question is "How might we rebalance our political discourse?" In the 1980s, Margaret Thatcher was famous for declaring that there is no such thing as "society." As a true market fundamentalist, she saw only atomized individuals. At roughly the same time, Ronald Reagan was saying that government was the problem, not the solution. It is exactly such discourse that undermines the market's ability to operate. By belittling individual's responsibility to each other as members of a common society and by signaling the weakening of regulatory enforcement power, opportunism and fraud are invited. Ironically, the normative underpinnings of market exchange, e.g. trust and cooperation, are debased. By belittling government as a solution to problems, the excesses of market exchange are not curbed, a weakened inclination to regulate is signaled, and enforcement of existing laws is delegitimated.

Market fundamentalist discourse, which has become a taken-for-granted part of our political culture, must be exposed to critical examination, its failures publicly discussed and analyzed. Surprisingly, this has not happened in the wake of the financial meltdown. Although numerous journalists have covered the bank failures and bailouts, there has been too little discussion, either in the press or by politicians, of root causes of the meltdown, including a discrediting of the political and economic regime that got us here. The Great Depression was marked by the Pecora hearings of 1932 to 1934 that led to New Deal financial regulation. "Hooverism" became a synonym for bad economic policy. We have seen no equivalent. At this writing, hearings have been mild affairs exhibiting little investigatory zeal. Politicians have shown little interest in attacking the status quo ideology. A spirited public discussion of our institutional failures, public and private, would help build the necessary coalition for reform as well as discrediting of market fundamentalism's hegemony.

Most important, a new political discourse that embeds markets in society, not the other way around, is needed. This discourse should be informed by heterodox theories that question market fundamentalism and its implicit values. Politicians need to promote values of fairness and security to rebalance the drive for profit at any cost that has dominated the current era. Politicians need to create a logic of action that can inoculate existing regulatory institutions against the excesses of market fundamentalism. The first step would be the creation of new rules, policies, and institutions that can search out and mitigate financial risks for society as they develop.

Enhancing State Capacity and Effectiveness

Even if the reform of the two previously discussed institutional spheres were to occur, it would not be enough without strengthening the state's capacity to mitigate the risk of an inherently fragile financial system. To do this the state must become less vulnerable to academic fads and political discourse and more effective at implementing its legislative responsibility. Given the fads in macroeconomic theory, the Fed is at its best when ruled by hard-headed pragmatism tied to its mandate to maintain price stability and economic growth (Abolafia, 2004). It needs to maintain a greater ability to define and interpret problems apart from other institutional spheres. This idea is reflected in the Fed's structural independence from the executive branch of government, but it has not gone far enough. Structural autonomy does not confer cultural autonomy (Carruthers, 1994). The Fed must be able to "think" outside of market fundamentalist orthodoxy in order to protect its mandate of balancing growth and stable prices (Abolafia, 2010).

Cultural autonomy can be enhanced by increasing the heterogeneity among both the economics staff and FOMC members. The schools of regulation, mentioned above, should have monetary policy concentrations that serve as feeders to the Fed staff. The FOMC should be redesigned to include graduates of these programs who have served in academia, government, and business, as well as orthodox economists. The current efforts to increase Congressional oversight of monetary policy are mistaken as they are likely to further politicize policy making and reduce structural and cultural autonomy.

At the same time that I would increase cultural autonomy, I would also increase accountability to the Fed's legislative mandate The first step to increased oversight and accountability would be to focus the Fed on monetary policy by removing the regulation of bank holding companies from its purview. As banking has concentrated in fewer and fewer bank holding companies, these entities require special oversight. Although a system of smaller banks seems preferable from a system failure perspective, it also seems politically unlikely. We therefore need to ensure enhanced capacity for bank regulation. The Fed's failure to oversee these banks properly suggests that its eye was far from the ball. Also, there is some danger of conflicting interests between bank regulation and monetary policy. Focusing on its other critical tasks, especially monetary policy, is a wide enough domain.

The increased need for accountability in the financial system also calls for the creation of an independent system regulator (ISR). The belief that financial markets should be self-regulating must be replaced by the belief that the state has a responsibility for risk control. The fundamental idea here is that as the financial system increases in complexity and coupling, the state has an increasing responsibility in protecting society from the attendant risk. The state needs the expertise and resources to keep pace with financial innovation as well as the analytic skill to assess its risk. The recent meltdown has taught us that the risks were poorly understood by the firms involved and by their regulators. Just as society empowers intelligence agencies to show discretion and analytic skill in fighting domestic and international terrorism, we should empower a financial regulator that searches the financial system looking for threats. This agency would be independent of existing bank and securities regulators as well as the Fed, but would also perform a coordinating function focused around systemic risk.

An ISR would have, as its primary mission, control of systemic risk. The ISR would oversee the interconnections of the component parts of the financial system so that it can scan, assess, and prioritize risks. Following Sparrow (2000), an agency with a risk control focus does not have just a few units at the top of the organization concentrating on risk, but rather has a project-based infrastructure dedicated to picking important problems (areas of risk) and appointing teams to resolve developing risks in the system. There would be a range of projects underway that would oversee the major components of the financial system but all would be intent on risk control.

Such an oversight agency would need to be particularly innovative in creating a learning system in which information from existing agencies and their own intelligence is searched, shared, and integrated. Treating financial crisis as a matter of national security, it would need to be more alert and responsive than the SEC and the Fed were in the recent crisis. If we are to have institutions that are "too big to fail" then we must protect society's interests by giving the ISR a mandate to assess the risk of financial innovations and the authority to create orderly resolutions, i.e. liquidation of assets, at the expense of stock and bond holders, when large institutions fail. The ISR would provide a significant enhancement in state capacity.

These recommendations above are meant to have a dual purpose. On the organizational design level, we need to reengineer the financial system so that it produces lower levels of systemic risk. This should be accomplished both by making risk more transparent (e.g. separating hedge funds from bank holding companies) and by creating new state capacity for risk control. On the institutional level, we need to engineer ideological change across major institutions in our society. This is not as radical as it sounds. It only recommends a return to the Depression-era thinking; a time when it was widely recognized that financial markets require adequate regulation to moderate their excesses and maintain their legitimacy. It is in this spirit that I have proposed an ISR that is linked to funding for alternative education and research and a discourse of regulation grounded in a rhetoric of fairness and economic stability.

CONCLUSION: CAN SPECULATIVE BUBBLES BE MANAGED?

The causal factors and solutions discussed in this article suggest that our society needs a broad discussion of the institutional failure displayed in the recent financial meltdown. This is necessarily a discussion about interests and values, about the ways our institutions "think" about the social good. How do we balance the trade-off between innovation and profit opportunities on the one hand while protecting families and firms from the worst excesses of the financial markets on the other? This article argues that we have lost our balance in this perpetual question of modern capitalism and that we have lost sight of the critically important goal of economic stability. The hegemony of market fundamentalism moved the balance too far in the direction of uncontrolled and unsustainable risk. The failure to protect citizens from this instability has eroded trust in our major institutions.

This conclusion, of course, assumes that stability and trust are societal values worth protecting and enhancing. The gains made toward stability and trust after the Great Depression were real. The establishment of a functioning regulatory sector reduced the risk of financial markets for society. As financial markets have continued to innovate and globalize these gains need to be reclaimed and extended. The unraveling of these gains by a failure to keep up with changing markets was mistake. It is time to admit this mistake and rectify it. At the same time, the goals of stability and trust require a renewed willingness on the part of the Fed to moderate extremes of irrational exuberance.

The best approach to reform would be to initiate system redesign in the markets and reform of academic, political and regulatory institutions at the same time, thereby dealing with the most complete set of causal factors. System redesign would include such things as compartmentalizing different levels of risk into separate types of financial firms, the movement of derivatives trading onto exchanges, and the increase of capital reserves in banks. But given the current direction of reform efforts and the political power of the financial sector, substantial redesign of the financial sector seems improbable.

Significant reform will require a shift in focus from markets to the institutions in which they are embedded. Economists are still engaged in an absurd debate between approaches that assume markets are perfect and those that admit imperfections (inefficiencies). This debate has proven ineffective in addressing the system's tendency toward crisis. An institutional focus asks if professionals, such as those discussed in this article, and major agencies, such as the Fed, have used their power effectively for the general social welfare. It asks if the institutions in which these professions and regulators are embedded are doing their jobs. Such an approach is designed to appraise an institution's legitimacy. Although effectiveness and efficiency are both to be valued, the former has received too little attention.

This brings us to our final question, "Can speculative bubbles be managed?" My answer is yes and no. "Yes," because we have the knowledge needed to inhibit the worst excesses of a speculative binge. We know that extremes of lax regulations with low penalties, information asymmetries in financial innovations, and easy money are the conditions making economies susceptible to bubbles. Indicators of trading volume, proliferation of new instruments, leverage levels of firms, and market participation by newcomers can all be monitored. Creating an ISR would extend these capabilities into new areas. Strengthening existing regulatory agencies to oversee the dramatically expanded markets, requiring derivatives to be exchange traded, and practicing more vigorous countercyclical monetary policy are well within the current organizational capabilities of government.

But, in the end, I will favor "no" because it seems likely that the institutional factors identified here have not been extinguished and will be a repeating motif in the American version of capitalism. The discourse of market fundamentalism may be repressed, as it was in the Keynesian revolution, but it is likely to reemerge and be championed by institutional entrepreneurs like Ronald Reagan and Margaret Thatcher, backed by political and economic actors who favor unfettered business interests. There is no labor movement or other social movement with the power to countervail the institutional forces of professional economics and state-sponsored fundamentalism. Given the current state of campaign finance, it is the financial industry itself that will decide on any redesign of its regulatory system.

In the end, I fear that despite the housing bubble of 2008, we have not seen the end of market fundamentalism in the United States. It is too deeply embedded in the individualist culture and political rhetoric of America. The inertial strength of this discourse may be seen in the current political difficulties of the Obama administration in the areas of health, energy, and the environment. Institutional factors, as we know, do not change easily. Major changes in economic policy call for shifts in academic economics and regulatory practice supported by an institutional entrepreneur with consummate rhetorical skill and impeccable timing. At this point, significant institutional change does not seem probable.

NOTES

1. This quote is taken from Greenspan's appearance before the Joint Economic Committee of Congress in June of 1999 (Zandi, 2009, p. 70).
2. Testimony of Alan Greenspan, Committee on Government Oversight and Reform, U.S. House of Representatives (October 23, 2008).
3. Minsky reworked this model many times over his career. As a Keynesian, Minsky's early models assumed exogenous shocks (displacements). We rely, therefore, on the later work.
4. It is worth noting that a considerable body of research in experimental economics supports Minsky's contention that bubbles are endemic to asset markets (Smith, Suchaneck, & Williams, 1988; Haruvy, Lahav, & Noussair, 2007; Hussam, Porter, & Smith, 2008).
5. This finding is supported by the research in experimental economics cited above.
6. I owe this observation to comments made on the article by Klaus Weber.

ACKNOWLEDGMENTS

I thank Frank Dobbin, Mike Lounsbury, Paul Hirsch, Amy Svirsky, Tim Lytton, and Klaus Weber for their insightful comments.

REFERENCES

Abolafia, M. Y. (1996). *Making markets: Opportunism and restraint on Wall Street.* Cambridge, MA: Harvard University Press.

Abolafia, M. Y. (2004). Making sense of recession: Toward an interpretive theory of economic action. In: V. Nee & R. Swedberg (Eds), *The economic sociology of capitalism*. Princeton, NJ: Princeton University Press.

Abolafia, M. Y. (2010). Narrative construction as sensemaking: How a Central Bank thinks. *Organization Studies, 31*(2), 1–19.

Abolafia, M. Y. (in press). The interpretive power of central banks. In: K. Knorr-Cetina & A. Preda (Eds), *The handbook of the sociology of finance*. Oxford: Oxford University Press.

Abolafia, M. Y., & Kilduff, M. (1988). Enacting market crisis: The social construction of speculative bubbles. *Administrative Science Quarterly, 33*(2), 177–193.

Akerlof, G. A., & Romer, P. M. (1993). Looting: The economic underworld of bankruptcy for profit. *Brookings Papers on Economic Activity, 2*, 1–73.

Akerlof, G. A., & Shiller, R. J. (2009). *Animal spirits*. Princeton, NJ: Princeton University Press.

Baddeley, M., & McCombie, J. (2001). An historical perspective on speculative bubbles and financial crises. In: P. Arestis, M. Baddeley & J. McCombie (Eds), *What global economic crisis?* London: Palgrave.

Barron, M. (2007). *Speculative bubbles and the dot-com era*. Doctoral Dissertation, Sociology Department, Stony Brook University.

Block, F. (1996). *The vampire state*. New York: The New Press.

Campbell, J. (1998). Institutional analysis and the role of ideas in political economy. *Theory and Society, 27*, 377–409.

Canterbury, E. R. (1999). Irrational exuberance and rational speculative bubbles. *The International Trade Journal, 13*, 1–32.

Carruthers, B. G. (1994). When is the state autonomous? Culture, organization theory, and the political sociology of the state. *Sociological Theory, 12*(1), 19–44.

Cassidy, J. (2009). *How markets fail: The logic of economic calamities*. New York: Farrar, Strauss, and Giroux.

Davis, G. F. (2009). *Managed by the markets: How finance reshaped America*. Oxford: Oxford University Press.

Douglas, M. (1986). *How institutions think*. Syracuse, New York: Syracuse University Press.

Ferguson, N. (2008). *The ascent of money: A financial history of the world*. New York: Penguin.

Flood, R. P., & Garber, P. M. (1980). Market fundamentals versus price-level bubbles: The first tests. *Journal of Political Economy, 88*, 745–770.

Flood, R. P., & Hodrick, R. J. (1990). On testing for speculative bubbles. *Journal of Economic Perspective, 4*, 85–101.

FOMC. (1992). *Federal open market committee meeting October 6, 1992*. Board of Governors of the Federal Reserve, Washington, DC.

Fourcade, M. (2009). *Economists and societies: Discipline and profession in the United States, Britain, and France, 1890s to 1990s*. Princeton, NJ: Princeton University Press.

Friedman, M. (1968). The role of monetary policy. *American Economic Review, 58*, 1–17.

Garber, P. M. (1990). Famous first bubbles. *Journal of Economic Perspectives, 4*, 35–54.

Gerth, H. H., & Mills, C. W. (1946). *From Max Weber: Essays in sociology*. New York: Oxford University Press.

Gordon, R. (1972). Wage-price controls and the shifting Phillips curve. *Brookings Papers on Economic Activity, 1972*(2), 385–421.

Guillen, M. (1994). *Models of management*. Chicago, IL: University of Chicago Press.

Hall, P. (1989). *The political power of economic ideas*. Princeton, NJ: Princeton University Press.

Haruvy, E., Lahav, Y., & Noussair, C. (2007). 'Traders' expectations in asset markets: Experimental evidence. *American Economic Review*, *97*(5), 1901–1920.

Heilbroner, R., & Milberg, W. (1995). *The crisis of vision in modern economic thought*. Cambridge: Cambridge University Press.

Hussam, R. R., Porter, D., & Smith, V. L. (2008). Thar she blows: Can bubbles be rekindled with experienced subjects? *American Economic Review*, *98*(3), 924–937.

Keynes, J. M. (1936). *The general theory of employment, interest, and money*. New York: Harcourt Brace.

Kindleberger, C., & Aliber, R. (2005). *Manias, panics, and crashes: A history of financial crisis*. Hoboken, NJ: Wiley.

Minsky, H. (1986). *Stabilizing an unstable economy*. New Haven, CT: Yale University Press.

Minsky, H. (1993). The financial instability hypothesis. In: P. Arestis & M. Sawyer (Eds), *Handbook of radical political economy*. Aldershot, UK: Edward Elgar.

Palmer, D., & Maher M. (2010). A normal accident analysis of the mortgage meltdown. In: M. Lounsbury & P. M. Hirsch (Eds), *Markets on trial: The economic sociology of the U.S. financial crisis: Part A*. Research in the Sociology of Organizations. Bingley, UK: Emerald.

Papadimitriou, D., & Wray, L. R. (2008). Minsky's stabilizing an unstable economy: Two decades later (Preface). In: H. Minsky (Ed.), *Stabilizing an unstable economy*. New York: McGraw Hill.

Perrow, C. P. (1984). *Normal accidents: Living with high-risk technologies*. New York: Basic Books.

Phelps, E. S. (1967). Phillips curves, expectations of inflation and optimal employment over time. *Econometrica*, *34*, 254–281.

Phillips, N., Lawrence, T. B., & Hardy, C. (2004). Discourse and institutions. *Academy of Management Review*, *29*, 635–652.

Polonyi, K. (1944). *The great transformation: Political and economic origins of our time*. Boston: Beacon Press.

Schneiberg, M., & Bartley, T. (2010). Regulating and redesigning finance? Market architectures, normal accidents, and dilemmas of regulatory reform. In: M. Lounsbury & P. M. Hirsch (Eds), *Markets on trial: The economic sociology of the U.S. financial crisis: Part A*. Research in the Sociology of Organizations. Bingley, UK: Emerald.

Skidelsky, R. (2009). *Keynes: The return of the master*. New York: Public Affairs Press.

Smith, V. L., Suchaneck, G. L., & Williams, A. W. (1988). Bubbles, crashes, and endogenous expectations in experimental spot asset markets. *Econometrica*, *56*(5), 1119–1151.

Sparrow, M. K. (2000). *The regulatory craft: Controlling risks, solving problems, and managing compliance*. Washington, DC: Brooking Institution Press.

Stiglitz, J. (1990). Symposium on bubbles. *Journal of Economic Perspectives*, *4*, 13–18.

Weir, M., & Skocpol, T. (1985). State structures and the possibilities for Keynesian responses to the Great Depression in Sweden, Britain, and the United States. In: P. Evans, D. Rueschmeyer & T. Skocpol (Eds), *Bringing the state back in*. Cambridge: Cambridge University Press.

Zandi, M. (2009). *Financial shock*. Upper Saddle River, NJ: FT Press.

THE SOCIAL CONSTRUCTION OF CAUSALITY: THE EFFECTS OF INSTITUTIONAL MYTHS ON FINANCIAL REGULATION

Anna Rubtsova, Rich DeJordy,
Mary Ann Glynn and Mayer Zald

ABSTRACT

In this article, we consider the evolution of the US stock market from the 1770s through the early 20th century. Adopting an institutional lens, we conceive of the stock market as an institutional field constituted by socially constructed cultural logics and myths. We focus on the role of the US government as an actor embedded in the stock market field and sharing in the prevailing field logics. Tracking the dominant logics of the stock market field at different historical periods, we examine how these logics impacted government regulatory action upon the stock market, and how those government regulations affected the subsequent logics of the stock market field. Our research included both quantitative content analysis of articles in historical newspapers and qualitative historical analysis of multiple primary and secondary accounts of stock market problems and solutions across more than 150 years. We document how government regulatory action both reflects and shapes the logics of the stock market field.

Markets on Trial: The Economic Sociology of the U.S. Financial Crisis: Part B
Research in the Sociology of Organizations, Volume 30B, 201–244
ISSN: 0733-558X/doi:10.1108/S0733-558X(2010)000030B011

One side effect of the much-debated Troubled Assets Relief Program (TARP) in the United States is that its debate, passage, and execution have dispelled, at least temporarily, any illusions that the federal government is somehow an exogenous actor in the financial markets that underpin the economy. Bailouts of banks, insurers, manufacturers, and other principal players in the economy belie a mythical separation of political and economic action, at least when such extreme action is required. Yet, such interdependence itself is not a crisis-induced anomaly; only its visibility and conscious recognition are. Monetary policy, securities regulation, and a multitude of other linkages (Baum & Oliver, 1991) embed the US Federal and State Government within the institutional field of the capital markets. Even beyond these resource-based linkages, however, the government itself is also embedded in the cultural/cognitive institutional context of the economy and the financial markets that underpin it. Yet, institutional research often treats the government and its actions as either exogenous to and/or unaffected by the field (e.g., Hoffman, 1999), or focuses on explicit, coercive, or resource-based forms of institutional pressures such as lobbying (e.g., Greenwood & Suddaby, 2006; Haveman & Rao, 1997) or cooptation (Selznick, 1966).

In this article, we expand on Friedland and Alford's (1991) call to "bring society back" by focusing specifically on how the government itself is subjected to the same socially constructed and taken-for-granted meaning systems as other actors in the field. Specifically, we show that the government is influenced by the dominant institutional logic of the field at any given time, adopting Thornton and Ocasio's definition of institutional logics as "the socially constructed, historical pattern of material practices, assumptions, values, beliefs, and rules by which individuals produce and reproduce their material subsistence, organize time and space, and provide meaning to their social reality" (1999, p. 804). We focus specifically on how historically situated assumptions, values, and beliefs, especially those related to appropriate market practices, shape the socially constructed theories of causality for market crises and subsequent regulatory action taken by the government.

By doing so, we make contributions to both institutional theory and the literature on securities regulation. We show not only how government affects the field of the financial markets, but also how government actions are affected by the field's historical development and by its dominant logic as embodied in institutional myths and professional norms. Further, this endogenous conceptualization of the government allows us to examine the institutional factors affecting the development, form, and content of governmental regulation.

We examine how regulatory action arises endogenously within an organizational field; more specifically, we focus on state and federal securities law in the US stock market from 1770 to 1934. This time period allows us to track the complete historical development of the US stock market through the creation of the Securities and Exchange Commission (SEC) in the wake of the Great Depression. The oft-asserted parallels between our current economic challenges and those faced between 1929 and 1934 suggest that a nuanced understanding of the effect of context on regulation enacted in that time period may help us not only to better understand the forces at work in our current situation but also, potentially, to make more informed choices about the nature and content of future regulation as we face our current challenges.

Some of the most influential work on the diffusion of new organizational practices (e.g., Dobbin, Sutton, Meyer, & Scott, 1993; Hoffman, 1999; Sutton & Dobbin, 1996) shows how legal changes prompt field-level changes. For instance, Baron, Dobbin, and Jennings (1986) show how the national crisis predicated by WWII caused the US government to promote employment stabilization policies, which then facilitated the institutionalization of new employment policies, and Hoffman (1999) shows how the creation of the environmental protection agency influenced the institutional development of the emergent field of environmental practices. Independent of whether the government is explicitly conceptualized as internal or external to the field, an implicit assumption in such models of change is that the government is insensitive to the noncoercive institutional forces affecting the field being regulated; this approach is consistent with state-centric accounts in political sociology, which view the state as a bureaucracy whose routines and structures affect policies and laws, but is unaffected by society at large (e.g., Evans, Rueschemeyer, & Skocpol, 1985). More specifically, little research has examined the effect of the taken-for-granted cultural/cognitive aspects of the dominant institutional logic on the regulatory action undertaken by the government.

Importantly, a long tradition of institutional work has recognized that government action is subjected to explicit pressures from the institutional fields and the actors, which constitute it. For example, Haveman and Rao (1997) explain that actors lobbied for regulatory support of various forms of thrifts at both the state and federal levels, and Greenwood and Suddaby (2006) detail the active and explicit role of the "Big Five" accounting firms in effecting regulatory changes in public accounting. Further, more recent work has started to probe the degrees of interdependence between the government and the institutional fields in which it operates. For example, in addition to mapping out the macro-structural impact of financial regulation on societal and corporate organizing in the United States since the turn of last century, Davis's work (2009) also elaborates on how the logic of the financial markets, and particularly the stock market, have become more prominent in public policy debates. We adopt and extend this perspective by examining an alternative assumption: that the government agencies and actors enacting legal and regulatory change are fully endogenous to the institutional field, both impacting the field through the regulations they enact, but also explicitly impacted by the full complement of institutional pressures and logics prevailing in the field being regulated, including the implicit, taken-for-granted assumptions about appropriate practices and values.

We theorize and empirically demonstrate that in addition to helping to constitute the larger field, the regulations enacted by government regulatory bodies are, in part, simultaneously constituted by the field and the prevailing institutional logic. We propose that the socially constructed beliefs and practices that comprise the stock market field logic at any time (e.g., stock valuations, efficient theories of the market, the appropriateness of certain practice such as short-selling) subsequently shape the government's regulatory responses to various market crises. We find that legal solutions, typically in the form of regulation, are formulated in terms of the institutional logic dominant in the field as a whole. Further, as socially constructed institutions, stock markets are subject to contradictions and delegitimization in the form of crisis episodes, which allow for various forms of corrective, restorative (DeJordy, 2010), or change-oriented action. Such episodes serve to focus policy-makers' attention on the market, who then socially construct both the problem definition and the legal solutions, from a "primeval soup" (Kingdon, 1984) of institutional litter (Schneiberg, 2007) that comprises historical experiences of past "problems" and "solutions," aborted paths, media portrayals, and industry analyses among other sources. Mutability (Clemens & Cook, 1999), transposability (Sewell, 1992), and recombination (Powell, 1991) through the revival, reassembly, redeployment, and elaboration of alternative logics (Schneiberg, 2007) allow a fully endogenous regulatory agent to enact novel forms of legislation which reflect, to varying degrees, past and present institutional logics.

Conceptualizing the government as an actor embedded in the logic of stock market field, subject to all forms of institutional pressures, reasserts DiMaggio and Powell's (1983) classic definition of a field, in which they explicitly enumerate regulatory agencies among the field constituents. Proceeding from that definition, we conceptualize government agencies, such as the Banking and Currency Commission and the Federal Trade Commission (FTC) – even Congress as a whole – as integral actors in the stock market and thus sharing the same institutional logic, albeit with different structural and political positions, power and agency, and interests. We empirically examine these ideas through an historical analysis of stock market crises, the construal of the causes that led to the crisis, and the legal solutions that were implemented, as well as abandoned. We use both quantitative and qualitative data and methods to address our core research questions: What values and beliefs constituted the dominant institutional logic of the stock market field at different historical periods? How did these logics, and specifically the underlying professional and cultural sentiments, impact government regulatory action? And finally, how did government action affect the subsequent dominant institutional logics of the field?

Through addressing these questions, we make two primary contributions to the literature. The first extends our current understanding of the role of government in institutional theory. Often neoinstitutionalists view government regulations as jolts, shocks, or disruptive events exogenous to the field under consideration (e.g., Baron et al., 1986; Hoffman, 1999; Dobbin et al., 1993; Sutton & Dobbin, 1996). However, this conceptualization implicitly assumes a unidirectional flow of influence – government action influences the institutional field, but is not influenced by it. Other work recognizes the explicit influence of coercive forms of institutional pressure on governmental action (e.g., Greenwood & Suddaby, 2006; Haveman & Rao, 1997), but is less attentive to the implicit, cultural-cognitive aspects of the institutional logics, such as the implicit belief systems and values, which dominate the field. By considering the government itself an actor embedded in the stock market field, we theorize how it is exposed to, and wrapped in, all aspects of prevailing field logic, including these taken-for-granted aspects. When prompted by crisis episodes, the subsequent responses of the government are not those of actors unencumbered by such context, but rather, they are shaped by the prevailing institutional logics as understood from the governmental actors' unique but *embedded* position within the field.

Second, we extend work that explains the emergence and content of various state and federal securities regulations (Burk, 1985; Galbraith, 1972; Khademian, 1992; Mahoney, 2001). Extant research typically views securities regulation as the product of rational response to market failures or political conditions (e.g., political group lobbying, the drive for state expansion). However, very little attention has been paid to how the securities regulations are affected by the taken-for-granted institutional myths and normative pressures that surround and permeate government agencies. Although a number of scholars (e.g., Abolafia & Kilduff, 1988; Mezias, 1990; Zajac & Westphal, 2004; Zuckerman, 2000) apply an institutional perspective to the stock market and related practices, they typically do not consider the effect of institutional forces on the enactment of securities regulation as we do here. By assessing the impact of socially constructed institutional myths and normative forces, we contribute to a more complete understanding of the emergence and content of securities regulation in the United States.

GOVERNMENT REGULATION AND THE STOCK MARKET AS AN INSTITUTIONAL FIELD

In his recent book, Davis (2009) outlines the evolution of the financial markets in the United States and some of the impacts of that evolution on society at large. In particular, he draws linkages between the "investment"-centric logic of the market and the mortgage meltdown and credit crisis of recent years. This relationship, he proposes, is mediated by a shift in American society from a Puritan ethic of frugality and savings to an "investment"-based logic, where valuation is based primarily on economic investments, permeating all aspects of culture from education ("human capital") to friends and social activities ("social capital"). In particular, he notes how the shift in attitudes toward homeownership – from the early perspective as the basis for "putting down roots" in a community to the more recent perspective as just another asset in one's portfolio – contributed to both the real estate boom and the subsequent crash. Homes, while increasing in value, became assets, which could be leveraged to fuel consumption, and, if declining, could be as readily abandoned as a poorly performing stock. This evolution was not spontaneous or deterministic, however, and was facilitated by public policy (as evidenced by a long, bipartisan history of presidential initiatives to create an "ownership society") and, of course, regulatory action (and inaction) in the financial markets, including a trend toward deregulation.

But Davis (2009) goes further still. Not only does he show how policy and regulatory action becomes manifest in the day-to-day functioning of financial markets, he also discusses how the behavior of financial markets influences those same policy debates, and extrapolates to speculate on possible future implications of this trend. By doing so, Davis raises questions about the effects of the larger context on public policy in general, and regulation of financial markets in particular. He suggests that government actors are also members of the institution and subject to the same institutional forces, albeit from a different structural position. This recalls DiMaggio and Powell's (1983) original definition of an organization field, which included specific reference to regulatory bodies as constituents embedded in the field. We take up these questions by adopting an institutional perspective on the enactment of securities regulation to explore not only how the institutional context is shaped by regulatory action, but also how that same context simultaneously shapes the activities of governmental regulators. In doing so, we contribute to the literature on both institutional theory and on securities regulation.

The Institutional Perspective

Our research contributes to the literature addressing several interrelated problems noted in institutional theory. First, there is an ambiguity in the definition of one of the key notions produced by this literature – that of a field. On the one hand, the "classic" definition by DiMaggio and Powell proposes that an organizational field consists of "those organizations that, in the aggregate, constitute a recognized area of institutional life: key suppliers, resource and product consumers, *regulatory agencies*, and other organizations that produce similar services and products" (1983, p. 148, *emphasis added*). In practice, however, many researchers have equated the field to an industry, excluding many other relevant actors, such as regulatory agencies and consumers. For example, Fligstein (2001, p. 242) conceptualizes the stock market as an institutional field, "in that a market consists of firms who orient their actions toward one another," thus excluding both regulatory agencies and audiences. Others (e.g., Baron et al., 1986; Dobbin et al., 1993; Sutton & Dobbin, 1996) explicitly see government legislative action as exogenous to, or at least unaffected *by*, the field under consideration.

In parallel, there is a body of literature that explicitly considers the state as an actor within the institutional field (e.g., Dobbin & Sutton, 1998; Greve, Pozner, & Rao, 2006) and subject to various institutional forces. Most of this research focuses on explicit and overt forms of institutional pressure or resource dependence (Greenwood & Suddaby, 2006; Haveman & Rao, 1997). Our findings extend this perspective. We find that the state is not only an actor in the institutional field, but subject to both explicit and implicit forms of institutional pressures embodied in the field's prevailing institutional logic. Hence, the changes in the legislation occur not only due to the activities of institutional entrepreneurs and lobbying efforts on the part of the interest groups but because government decision-makers are subject to the cultural/cognitive assumptions embedded in the dominant field logic.

A second widespread critique of the institutional perspective points to its overemphasis on the exogenous models of change (Barley & Tolbert, 1997; Farjoun, 2002) and the role of superhuman agents (often institutional entrepreneurs) in institutional change. Seo and Creed (2002) resolve the paradox of embedded agency by theorizing that by leveraging institutional contradictions, embedded actors can affect change to the institution from within; a perspective supported empirically by recent work investigating how the elite US accounting firms used multidisciplinary logics to drive a change in institutional form (Suddaby & Greenwood, 2005). Yet this conceptualization still requires powerful, "hyper-muscular" change agents, such as institutional entrepreneurs or lobbying groups (e.g., Lounsbury, 2007; Marquis & Lounsbury, 2007). However, conceptualizing the government as part of the field offers an opportunity to also see field-level change through regulatory action as an endogenous process occurring as a result of dialogue among the actors sharing in the same prevailing logic, yet having different structural positions and interests. Recognizing the government's unique structural and political position allows theorists to model more veridically a range of endogenous action from preservation to both radical and incremental change.

Finally, this article contributes to the growing stream of literature that examines how institutions and institutional logics evolve. Although Thornton and Ocasio (1999) imply a somewhat linear process of field logic change over time, whereby one logic is supplanted by the next, other researchers (e.g., Schneiberg, 2007) has shown that institutions are littered with "flotsam and jetsam" of previous forms or aborted excursions. Our research builds on that perspective, showing that newer institutional logics in the stock market do not completely eradicate older ones; the disconnected elements of earlier field logics (e.g., stock market problems, solutions, theories of value; legitimation of stock market functions and practices) become retained in the "primeval soup" (Kingdon, 1984) or cultural toolkit (Swidler, 1986) available for use by actors, including the media, stock market professionals, and the governments. Thus, debates and proposals about regulation designed to address any current problem are infused with meanings and myths from those prior problems and times. Although one logic may be dominant in the field at any point in time, since logics are "the socially constructed, historical pattern of material practices, assumptions, values, beliefs, and rules" (Thornton & Ocasio, 1999, p. 804), the history of their development is embedded in the field, and available as resources to institutional actors. In our case, this impacts the emergence of securities regulation in the field of the stock market, to which we now turn.

Securities Regulations

The literature on emergence of the securities regulation is dominated by the realist (or rational choice) models. Several authors promote a "market failure" hypothesis, arguing that regulatory action at the state or federal level emerges to solve specific failures of the market, such as fraud or excessive speculation; the resulting regulations are purportedly efficient, producing net social wealth (e.g., Carosso, 1970; Galbraith, 1972; Seligman, 1983). Others view securities regulations as the result of lobbying by various interest groups. In this view, the group which most effectively solves the free rider problem (Macey & Miller, 1991) is thought to win. To that, Mahoney (2001) adds a political hypothesis, which attributes regulatory action to broad political movements, such as populism and progressivism, without implying economic efficiency of the specific securities regulations. In addition, Burk (1985) introduces a structural contingency hypothesis, whereby securities regulations are seen as the result of the expansionist tendencies of the state and a political contingency hypothesis, which states that the emergence of the securities regulations is not inevitable but is contingent on specific political conditions. Finally, Khademian (1992) shows that the federal securities regulations are the result of a rational choice process but, somewhat similarly to Burk (1985), argues that these rational decision-making processes are influenced by the routines of the state bureaucracy. Specifically, she argues that legislation is a response to functional deficiencies in the market, but internal routines and processes of the SEC have an independent causal influence on the resulting legislation. On balance, this literature primarily employs functional-realist and rational choice models to explain the contents and emergence of various securities regulations, and considers regulatory agencies as exogenous to the financial markets they regulate, with their own, independent institutional logics (e.g., bureaucracies).

Supplementing these views, we conceptualize securities regulation as emerging *within* the context of the changing institutional logics of the stock market field. We theorize that, in addition to having their own bureaucracies and internal logics, regulatory agencies are also simultaneously embedded within the larger institution of the financial markets. Their patterned interaction with the market exposes them to the prevailing cultural and professional logics of the market, which subsequently shape the enacted regulations.

OUR THEORETICAL FRAMEWORK

Following Fligstein (2001), we conceptualizes the stock market as an institutional field, consisting of firms who orient their behaviors toward each other, are structurally connected by patterns of power and control, and share a common cultural framework. However, we extend Fligstein's conceptualization (2001) of the stock market field to include a wider range of actors – not only firms, but also the government, regulatory agencies, and the media, consistent with DiMaggio and Powell's (1983) definition. Stock market fields, consequently, are socially constructed and reconstructed through historically contingent processes of social interaction among different actors – stock market professionals, governmental agencies, "lay" audiences as well as media, who have different structural positions and interests but share in the dominant logic of the stock market field. Like other fields, the stock market field embodies institutional logics which endow the actors and actions in the stock market with meaning and legitimacy. The logic of the field may change through gradual processes such as new trading techniques that emerge as a result of technological advancements, or more revolutionary shifts in actors, power structures, cultural understandings, or environmental contingencies.

In particular, we theorize that deep changes in logics are prompted by periodic market crises, originating either endogenously within the stock market field (e.g., stock market panics and crashes) or exogenously to the stock market field (e.g., droughts, natural disasters). These crises situations draw attention to stock market problems and possible solutions by various actors in the field, including government agencies, "lay" investors, stock market professionals, and media. Overall, the crises episodes serve to question the legitimacy of the existing cultural accounts and trigger the telling of new accounts or the retelling of previous ones. However, we note two important foundational ideas: (1) different actors in the field occupy different structural positions and, consequently, serve different roles in the generation of field logics, and (2) the resulting logics are not entirely new, but reflect or retain some elements from the past because the residual elements of the previous logics circulate in the field as a part of the "cultural toolkit" always at disposal for future uses by actors in the field.

By considering the government agencies, and the actors which constitute them, as embedded within the larger institutional field of the stock market, we allow for the possibility that other aspects of the institutional environment influence the way regulation is enacted.

To explore this possibility, we examined the history of securities regulation in the United States from colonial times until the creation of the SEC in 1934. The frequency with which our most recent wave of economic crises have been compared with the Great Depression and the Market Crash which preceded it suggests some fundamental similarities between the two periods, so a nuanced understanding of how regulations were enacted then should provide useful understanding into the mechanisms and forces most likely to be at work as we struggle with enacting regulations that address our current situation.

DATA AND ANALYSES

Because our research questions focus on understanding the social construction of historical institutions, we employed qualitative, historical analyses (Farjoun, 2002), as is customary in institutional research (Brint & Karabel, 1991; DiMaggio, 1991; Galaskiewicz, 1991; Leblebici, Solancik, Copay, & King, 1991). We follow Jones (2001) in using qualitative, historical analyses based on the procedures outlined by Miles and Huberman (1984), combined with the general premises of grounded theory (Strauss & Corbin, 1998) as well as recommendations for historical analysis offered by Farjoun (2002, p. 854), i.e., striving to (1) obtain accurate data from contemporaneous sources, (2) triangulate data using multiple sources, (3) perform constant comparison across cases (time periods in our case), (4) organize the data into intermediate forms such as data displays tables that facilitate data reduction, (5) synthesize and extract the most relevant material from the data, (6) remain constantly mindful of distinguishing between evidence and interpretation, (7) read history forward in constructing our narrative, and (8) present the data in order to allow the reader to derive a chain of evidence.

We gathered qualitative data from primary and secondary sources regarding the actions of three categories of actors: Government, Wall Street, and the Media representing a broader cultural/societal perspective in which the market and its actors are embedded. Table 1 provides a description of the primary and secondary data sources for each of the three categories of actors.

Table 1. Data Sources.

Actors	Primary Data Sources	Secondary Data Sources
Government (State & Federal)	Congressional hearings, debates, committee reports, including: US Congress Gold panic investigation of 1870 • US Congress investigation into Silver Pool of 1891 • Hughes Committee Investigation of "Speculation in Securities and Commodities" • Pujo Committee Money Trust Investigation of 1909 • US Congress Investigation of 1929 panic	Historians' accounts of securities legislation, including: • Banner, 1998 • Cowing, 1965 • Fraser, 2005 • Smith, 2001 Contemporary legal treatises written by various lawyers describing various legal doctrines and practices concerning the stock market in the 19th century, including: • Cook, 1898 • Dos Passos, 1882 • Helliwell, 1903 • Lewis, 1881 • Parker, 1911
Wall Street/ NYSE	Documents produced internally by New York Stock Exchange, including: • NYSE Constitutions and amendments (1817, 1902, 1914, 1925, 1931) • Committee Reports (e.g., from Committees on Publicity and Library) • Responses to investigations (e.g., Milburn & Taylor, 1913) • Testimony at state and federal investigations • NYSE public relations publications (e.g., Clews, 1900; Martin, 1913; Van Antwerp, 1914; Meeker 1922) Articles published in the Wall Street Journal (1900-1936)	Historians' accounts of the stock market and stock market regulation, including: • Banner, 1998 • Cowing, 1965 • Fraser, 2005 • Geisst, 2004 • Ott, 2004 • Seligman, 1995 • Smith, 2001
Public/Media	Contemporary media reporting from general circulation newspapers, especially those in cities with active exchanges. In particular, we focus on articles published between 1800 and 1940 in the following: • New York Times • Chicago Tribune These were supplemented by searches in the broader Index of Historical Newspapers (ProQuest)	Historians' accounts of popular opinion and media representations of the same, including: • Banner, 1998 • Cowing, 1965 • Fraser, 2005

We worked to compile an exhaustive list of legislative action on securities exchange, from Colonial times (circa 1770s) until 1935. Here, secondary sources provided a useful starting point for identifying legislative activity (e.g., Banner, 1998; Cowing, 1965; Fraser, 2005; Smith, 2001). In addition, we studied original documents produced by US Federal and State government, that is, US Congress Gold Panic Investigation of 1870 (Garfield, 1870); US Congress Investigation into Silver Pool (Committee on Banking and Currency, 1891); Hughes Committee Investigation of "Speculation in Securities and Commodities" (New York (State) Committee on Speculation in Securities and Commodities, 1909); Pujo Committee Money Trust Investigation (Committee on Banking and Currency, 1913; Pujo, 1912, 1913); US Congress Investigation of 1929 panic (e.g., Pecora, 1939). To verify and supplement the resultant list, we conducted extensive searches on a variety of databases (e.g., Wolrdcat; Hein Online and Thomas Gales, databases specializing in historical legal documents; and the US Congressional Serial Set 1817–1980). Contemporary legal treatises and articles by legal scholars (e.g., Cook, 1898; Dos Passos, 1882; Helliwell, 1903; Lewis, 1881; Parker, 1911) also helped to identify which acts were deemed relevant contemporaneously (see Table 1).

The process employed to identify professional and cultural sentiments was more straightforward. In particular, we used the *Wall Street Journal* and multiple publicity documents produced by the New York Stock Exchange (e.g., Van Antwerp, 1914; Clark, Bernheim, Dewhurst, & Schneider, 1934; Clews, 1900; Committee on Public Relations, 1936; Committee on Publicity, 1929, 1934; Martin, 1913, 1919; Meeker, 1922; Milburn & Taylor, 1913). To explore the media representations of the stock market, we examined articles on stock market problems and solutions that appeared between 1800s and 1940s in the *New York Times, Chicago Tribune*, and an Index of Historical Newspapers in the ProQuest database. These were again validated against secondary sources to ensure the completeness of our data and also informed our understanding of their historically situated meaning. The data generated across all sources were then tabulated into several displays.

The first display captured stock market problems and solutions as conceived by various bodies of government. The display included: (1) date of the legislative act (either an enacted law or measures of various forms discussed but not enacted), (2) a description of the problem the legislative act was intended to address, (3) a description of the proposed solution, and (4) detailed information about both the legislative component of the solution and the agents involved, as well as the data source(s). Our major conceptual categories of stock market problematizations emerged from iteratively coding and reviewing the data in this display. In particular, by attempting to create a label for what problem each legislative act was addressing, and constantly comparing these labels with other acts, we eventually identified three categories that comprehensively described all of them: (1) excessive speculation, (2) manipulation/fraud, and (3) government revenue. The third of these appears relatively infrequently and is irrelevant to our interest in regulatory change and so we dropped this from our analyses (for a shortened version of this data display, see Tables 2 and 3). More detailed displays were constructed to capture the richness of data gleaned from our analyses of Hughes and Pujo committee investigations.

Yet another data display captured the analysis of articles in the *Wall Street Journal* between 1900 and 1935. We collected data through ProQuest database keyword searches, employing the themes identified from the analyses of the legislative acts, specifically "manipulation," "fraud," "speculation," and their synonyms, that occurred within three words of "stock market." For each article identified by the search, qualitative analyses were conducted as described above.

Finally, we supplemented these data with quantitative content analysis counting the number of articles referring to stock market manipulation, speculation, and fraud, which appeared in the *New York Times, Chicago Tribune*, and an Index of over 1,000 US periodicals published between 1796 and 1940. For these purposes, we conducted key word search in the ProQuest Multiple database. Because of the large number of articles this generated, we conducted searches in five-year intervals (e.g., 1801–1805, 1806–1811).

Our analyses relied on our immersion into the history of US stock markets through engaged readings of history books (e.g., Banner, 1998; Burk, 1985; Cowing, 1965; Fraser, 2005; Geisst, 2004; Khademian, 1992; Kindleberger, 1989; Prechel, 2000; Seligman, 1995; Smith, 2001); different authors read partially overlapping sets of historical accounts and engaged with each other and with other colleagues (particularly in financial and legal studies) to avoid unacknowledged biases (Vaughn, 1992).

Creating and referencing these data displays informed our emergent theorizing about the interaction between governmental actors, professionals, and societal perceptions in the evolution of stock market regulation in the United States. We present our findings in the following section.

Table 2. State and Federal Legislative Acts, 1789–1899.

Year	Government Actor	Problem	Solution
1789	US federal	Corruption	The Congress passed the Treasury Act, which had a section, which prohibited the Treasury officials and clerks to deal in the stock market under the penalty of $3000 and removal from the office
1789	US federal	Excessive speculation	The idea to slow down the speculation by introducing the tax on stock transfer was first proposed in 1789 by William Bingham but declined by a vote. Temporary transfer taxes existed during the war time in 1898
1792	Pennsylvania	Excessive speculation	After the panic of 1792, there was issued a Bill "to prevent the practice of stockjobbing" modeled on English Barnard's act. The act required that the seller owned the stock to be sold. The bill never made through legislature
1792	New York	Manipulation and fraud Excessive speculation	"An Act to prevent the pernicious practice of stock jobbing, and for regulating sales at public auctions." Paragraph 2 of an Act forbade the sale of securities in the public auctions because auctions were seen as especially susceptible to manipulation and were thought to be among the cause of the crash of 1792. Paragraph 3 was copied from the bill debated at Pennsylvania and made void all contracts for the sale of stock, which the seller did not possess at the time of the sale (to prevent speculative time bargains)
1836	Massachusetts	Excessive speculation	Similar to Paragraph 3 of New York Act of 1792: required to own the stock to be sold, thus curbing most speculating time sales
1837	New York	Excessive speculation	Introduced a requirement for a three-month holding period before the stocks in banks could be resold
1840	Mississippi	Excessive speculation	Prohibited banks to deal in the stock markets
1841	Pennsylvania	Excessive speculation; Government revenue	Introduced a requirement that all the deliveries on time bargains be executed within the five days after the sales. Also, introduced licensing for stock brokers in order to generate revenues. Repealed in 1862
1842	Maryland	Overspeculation, government revenue	Introduced the same requirements as Pennsylvania in 1841
1845	Illinois	Government revenue	Broker licensing

Table 2. (*Continued*)

Year	Government Actor	Problem	Solution
1847	Indiana	Government revenue	Broker licensing
1851	Kentucky	Government revenue	Broker licensing
1862	US federal	Government revenue	Broker licensing as a wartime measure to generate revenues
1870	US federal	Manipulation/fraud	US Congress Gold panic investigation
1879	California	Excessive speculation	California banned futures trading in its constitution
1882, 1885	Ohio	Fraud	Ban on option sales, spreading false rumors to influence the market
		Excessive speculation	Ban on futures trading
1882	Mississippi	Overspeculation	Law, which makes void time bargains that do not foresee actual delivery
1883	Tennessee	Overspeculation	Ban on futures trading
1883	Arkansas	Overspeculation	Ban on futures trading
1885	Texas	Overspeculation	Ban on futures trading
1885	South Carolina	Overspeculation	Ban on futures trading
1886	Iowa	Overspeculation	Ban on futures trading
1887	Michigan	Overspeculation	Ban on futures trading
1889	Missouri	Overspeculation	Ban on futures trading
1890	Massachusetts	Overspeculation	Passed the following act: "Whoever contracts to buy or sell upon margins, without intent to actually receive or deliver, may sue for any payment made"
1890	North Dakota	Corruption	Prohibited public officers to speculate while in office
1891	US federal	Manipulation/fraud	US Congress investigation into Silver Pool
1892	US federal	Overspeculation	The Congress had hearing on Hatch bill, which proposed to introduce a 10% tax on futures trade in commodities
1898	US federal	Government revenue	As a wartime measure to generate revenues, government introduced a temporary tax on securities transfer
1898	Louisiana	Overspeculation	Act prohibiting futures sales with no intention of delivery

Table 3. State and Federal Legislative Acts, 1900–1930.

Year	Government Actor	Problem	Solution
1905	North Carolina	Excessive speculation	Ban on futures sales
1905	North Dakota, Minnesota	Fraud	Ban on bucket shops
1906	Georgia	Excessive speculation	Enforced penalty for dealing in futures
1907	Arkansas, Nevada, Nebraska	Fraud	Ban on bucket shops
1907	Vermont	Excessive speculation	Act to restrain stock gambling
1908	Mississippi, New York, Oklahoma, Rhode Island, Virginia	Fraud	Ban on bucket shops
1908	Arkansas, Florida, Alabama, Mississippi, Montana	Excessive speculation	Ban on futures sales
1908	New York state	Manipulation and fraud	Hughes committee investigation
1909	Kansas, New Hampshire, Arizona, Iowa, Tennessee	Fraud	Ban on bucket shops
1910	US federal	Excessive speculation	Representative Charles F. Scott proposed to ban from interstate commerce futures trading in cotton. The bill failed
1911	Kansas	Fraud	Blue sky laws
1912	Arizona, Louisiana, Vermont	Fraud	Blue sky laws
1913	Arkansas, California, Florida, Georgia, Idaho, Iowa, Maine, Michigan, Missouri, Montana, Nebraska, North Carolina, North Dakota, Ohio, Oregon, South Dakota, Tennessee, Texas, West Virginia, Wisconsin	Fraud	Blue sky laws
1913	US Federal	Overspeculation	Clarke amendment – Senator Clarke proposed to introduce tax on futures sales in cotton. The amendment failed
1913	US Federal	Excessive speculation	Senator Cummings proposed to introduce 10% tax on short sales of securities and commodities. The proposal failed
1913	US Federal	Manipulation, excessive speculation	Pujo Committee investigation

Table 3. (Continued)

Year	Government Actor	Problem	Solution
1914	US Federal	Manipulation, fraud	Owen's bill was drafted based on the results of Pujo investigation. Proposed to empower Postmaster to censor messages concerning speculation in the stock markets. The bill failed
1914	US Federal	Excessive speculation	The Cotton Futures Act was enacted. It was less drastic than Cummings and Clarke proposals; introduced government grading standards, and reduced the number of grades available for futures contracts
1914	US Federal	Revenue	Temporary stock transfer tax
1917	US Federal	Excessive speculation	Permanent stock transfer tax
1915	South Carolina	Fraud	Blue sky laws
1916	Mississippi, Virginia	Fraud	Blue sky laws
1917	Minnesota, New Hampshire	Fraud	Blue sky laws
1919	Alabama, Ilinois, Oklahoma, Utah, Wyoming	Fraud	Blue sky laws
1920	Indiana, Kentucky, Maryland, New Jersey	Fraud	Blue sky laws
1921	Massachusetts, New Mexico, New York, Rhode Island	Fraud	Blue sky laws
1921	New York	Fraud	Martin act gave power to state attorney general to investigate fraudulent securities practices
1921	US federal	Excessive speculation	Futures Trading Act
1922	US federal	Excessive speculation	Futures Trading Act was supplanted by Grain Futures Act, which required that the seller of futures must be producer
1922	US federal	Fraud	Congressman Denison proposed to introduce the national blue sky law, which would standardize the multitude of state blue sky laws. The bill failed
1922	US federal	Excessive speculation	Grain futures act
1923	Colorado, Pennsylvania, Washington	Fraud	Blue sky laws
1929	Connecticut	Fraud	Blue sky laws

FINDINGS

In the following sections, we provide a stylized history of the origin of the US Stock Market, followed by an analysis of its evolution divided by major shifts in institutional logics. Our discussion is organized chronologically, identifying the initial conditions under which the stock market and New York Stock Exchange emerged, then an initial period which lasted through most of the 19th century, and finally the period culminating in the crash, Great Depression, and subsequent regulation. Within each time period, we discuss the role of each of the three major aspects of the institution: regulation and the government, professional norms and Wall Street, and the popular cultural perceptions comprising the larger societal context represented through the mass media.

The New York Stock Exchange: Early History

Although a formally organized stock exchange in New York did not emerge until the 1790s, the marketplace existed since the 1600s. Being a Dutch colony, New York "aped the mother country in its ability for trade and lucre" (Fraser, 2005, p. 8). Also, like other seaboard cities, by the 18th century, New York was increasingly immersed in the market economy with its instruments of credit and debt. However, the first items traded were not stocks but slaves and commodities, such as lumber, fur, and flour (Smith, 2001, p. 3). Some rudimentary trading in stocks began around the 1770s; however, even before securities trading emerged in Colonial America, some wealthy colonists had experience investing in English securities, and many others heard about South Sea Bubble of 1720. As a result, many colonists inherited the negative attitudes the English held toward "stock-jobbing," the buying and near immediate selling of stocks to turn a quick profit (Banner, 1998). Consequently, short-term ownership of stocks was regarded as inappropriate and inconsistent with the Protestant Ethic. In North America, "[b]efore the second half of the century, widespread investment in small shares of an enterprise was a phenomenon largely limited to the shipping industry, where large amounts of capital were necessary to finance individual vessels" (Banner, 1998, p. 128). By the second half of the 18th century, however, several colonies in America began to copy the English practice of issuing shares in government debt. In 1751, Massachusetts was the first colony to raise money by issuing transferable bonds, and the practice diffused to other colonies – Connecticut,

New Hampshire, Rhode Island, and North Carolina – throughout the 1770s (Banner, 1998).

After the war of American Independence, the newly formed federal government deliberately assumed the debts incurred during the war and the prior debts of the colonies-turned-states in an effort to strengthen and centralize a national monetary policy. Yet, the federal government found itself with no immediate source of revenue. Although, it was hard-pressed to honor those debts, doing so was critical to establishing its legitimacy as a nation. Weary of increasing taxes, which had served as a rallying cry for independence, the federal government opted instead to raise $80 million by issuing bonds; thus, "the American capital markets, however humble, were born" (Geisst, 2004, p. 10). In 1791, daily public auctions of federal government debt started to be held on Wall Street (Banner, 1998).

Even at this early stage, Wall Street became an arena for political scandal and market manipulation. In particular, a number of politicians, most notably the Assistant Treasury Secretary William Duer, used insider knowledge of government plans for personal benefit when trading bonds (Banner, 1998), even sharing this knowledge with others in the commercial community (Fraser, 2005). These practices precipitated the 1789 Treasury Act, prohibiting Treasury officials from directly or indirectly engaging in commerce and speculation (Banner, 1998), effectively banning this form of "insider trading." However, there was market manipulation as well: "Together with a secret circle of fellow grantees, Duer put together the "6% Club" to manipulate the price of the new national government's securities. The conspirators plotted as well to corner the stock of the new Bank of the United States and the Bank of New York" (Fraser, 2005, p. 7), and even used government moneys to finance these plans. In "March 1792, when an audit uncovered a $250,000 discrepancy in the government accounts Duer had controlled in his Treasury job, confidence in him was lost and the prices of securities he was heavily involved in tumbled" (Smith, 2001, p. 4). The first Wall Street panic and crash ensued.

The crash of 1792 had important consequences on legislation. New York (as well as Pennsylvania) enacted "An Act to prevent the pernicious practice of stock jobbing, and for regulating sales at public auctions" (Banner, 1998). The act attempted to address both manipulation and excessive speculation – the former by prohibiting the sale of securities in public auctions, which were thought to be especially susceptible to manipulation, and the latter by forbidding short sales (selling of securities one does not own at the current price, with the intention of buying them later at a lower price).

In addition, there was an effort to formalize securities trading on Wall Street (Burrows & Wallace, 1999). The earliest efforts at self-regulation occurred in September 1791 when several dealers agreed to be governed by 14 rules (Banner, 1998). However, because these rules dealt with securities sold through public auctions, they became obsolete after public auctions were prohibited in 1792. Subsequently, 24 New York brokers signed the Buttonwood Agreement in May 1792, which established a fixed minimum commission rate and contained a promise that the signed brokers would give preference to each other in negotiations. More formalization occurred in 1817, when 27 brokers constituted themselves as the New York Stock and Exchange Board, adopting a set of 17 rules, or the first Constitution, which was the genesis of the New York Stock Exchange (NYSE). The crash of 1792 precipitated the first wave of attempted regulatory action in the financial markets in the United States, and serves as the starting point for our analysis of stock market as an institution.

1790–1890: Initial Imprinting of Stock Market Logics

Contributions of Popular Perceptions
Early on, few American colonists had personal experience of stock markets, typically limited to the wealthy with access to the stock exchanges in Holland and Britain, but more were aware of the famous European stock market panics and crashes, such as the South Sea Bubble of 1720. Banner (1998) and Fraser (2005) reveals that the American Protestant ethics, amplified by Revolutionary sentiments, regarded quick enrichment gained through stock speculation as morally inferior to wealth gained through methodical daily hardwork. However, although they tended to view speculation as a form of morally reproachful gambling that served no economic function, it was nevertheless widely practiced (Banner, 1998).

In addition to this morally grounded critique of the market, it was feared the bonds of government debt, initially widely distributed among the population, would quickly become concentrated in the hands of the rich merchants and financiers trading on Wall Street, raising concerns about the influence of a new "aristocracy," the Robber Barons (Fraser, 2005). Almost a century later, the populist movement, emerging after the panic of 1873, provided another American contribution to the cultural accounts around stock exchanges. The farmers' alliance was formed to act against the brokers, railroaders, and merchants whom agrarians saw as the source of their economic troubles. During this period, commodity speculators in

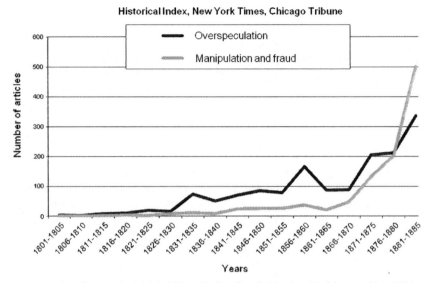

Fig. 1. Popular Press Articles Mentioning Stock Market Problems, 1801–1885.

particular were seen as villains who affected the prices for the harvest (Cowing, 1965), reflecting a cultural rift between the agrarian and financial sectors of the economy.

Thus, the theme of speculation as dangerous and morally reproachful dominated popular cultural accounts of the US stock market between 1770s and 1870s. Starting in the 1850s, professional speculators first appeared on the market, including Jay Gould, Daniel Drew, Jacob Little, and Commodore Vanderbilt, who saw stock market manipulation as a trick of their trade. As a result, incidents of fraud and manipulation increased during this time[1]. Nonetheless, the cultural accounts of the stock market were still dominated by attention to excessive speculation, as shown graphically in Fig. 1, which plots the number of articles in two major metropolitan newspapers which dealt with excessive speculation (the black line) and manipulation or fraud (the gray line) during this time. As can be seen, gambling and excessive speculation dominated the cultural accounts for the majority of the century, and it is not until the first half of the 1880s that manipulation and fraud surpass excessive speculation in the media.

Contributions of Government Action
In addition to creating the market by issuing bonds to finance the debt it assumed after the American Revolution, the government continued to

influence the prevailing logic of the stock market, through both action and inaction. Because participation in the early market was minimal (Smith, 2001), both the size of the market compared to the national economy and the limited number of people directly affected by market activities severely limited the scope of potential danger from excessive speculation. At the same time, however, the smaller size made it arguably more prone to manipulation by powerful actors in privileged structural positions. Yet government activity during the time focused more on excessive speculation, seemingly reflecting the cultural sensibilities outlined above. Of the 31 federal and state legislative acts between 1789 and 1900, only six deal with manipulation, fraud, or corruption; seven dealt with generating revenue from securities exchange, but 21 dealt directly with excessive speculation (see Table 2).

During this time nearly 68% of the legislative action concerning the stock markets was aimed at limiting speculation. Moreover, the legislative measures adopted were, for the most part, not novel solutions but rather adopted from existing laws, either in England or in several states, and generally employed one or more of the following five basic approaches to hindering excessive speculation (1) requirement to own the stock to be sold; (2) fixed holding period before the stock could be resold; (3) prohibiting banks from dealing in securities; (4) limiting time period of time sales; (5) ban on futures sales. It is also interesting to note that although the popular perceptions of the stock market logics, as reflected in the popular press, shifts around 1880 with increasing focus on manipulation and fraud, government action does not transition at this same time. We will see, however, a similar shift in legislative action emerge subsequently, suggesting that popular perception is a leading indicator of governmental action.

Contributions of Stock Market Professionals
Early organizational efforts by Wall Street seemed to imprint the logic of the field. The first constitution, that is, the Buttonwood Agreement, was modeled on a cartel, with its fixed minimum commission rates and mutual preference by the member-brokers. Despite successive constitutional changes, the logic of a "private club" where members had obligations to each other (but not to the outside public) survived until 1929, despite both critics and government investigations (e.g., Pujo Committee). Government action and policy contributed to the establishment of this logic.

For example, the New York state law outlawing short sales and banning public auctions precipitated the adoption of a "private club" logic for the stock market. Since the law outlawed public auctions, such activities were privatized as those auctioning securities looked for new ways to organize legally. Further, the illegitimacy of the bidding mechanism at the heart of securities exchange meant normal legal recourse was unavailable for those dealing in securities. They could not, therefore, create legally binding contracts around such mechanisms, as they would be unenforceable in the courts. As a result, the major means of their enforcement became the laws of honor in the stock market itself: a private club with private rules and private enforcement. The Buttonwood agreement, as well as the subsequent agreement of 1817, made the enforcement of the laws of honor simpler as it circumscribed the number of stock brokers participating in the "club" and made their reputations more transparent to other members, thus reinforcing the "private club" logic. Arguably, the logic of the private club was also strengthened by the US government's implicit sanctioning of cartels until 1897, when it adopted an antitrust policy (Dowd & Dobbin, 2001).

The stock market professionals also resisted societal reproach of speculation as immoral and, instead, tried to legitimate it. In 1892 when the US Congress was debating the Hatch bill, which proposed a federal ban on futures trading, financiers, and brokers advanced legitimating accounts for speculation, arguing that futures trading served to stabilize the prices, to transfer risk from the producers to the speculators, and to establish price quotations which, when cabled across the country, helps to lower price variation (Cowing, 1965). Also, in 1896, Henry Crosby Emery, an economist from Columbia University, wrote that speculation served important economic functions – namely it provided world-wide price quotations and stabilized prices – and cannot lead prices to below or above an objective value, but rather that values are subjectively determined in the marketplace (Cowing, 1965). Wall Street leverages these legitimating accounts, and they reemerge and influence the government logic in the next historic period.

Summary
In this early period of stock market emergence, the government over-whelmingly addressed issues of stock market speculation, seemingly in response to cultural sentiments 'rather than the potential consequences of such activity, since its small size limited the scope of danger from speculation. The stock market professionals respond to cultural accounts demonizing speculation by advancing legitimating counter accounts. An important side effect of government action in the period, and particularly the New York ban on public auctions, was the development of a *private club* logic for the stock market. In the next historic period, we show how this private club logic and the legitimating accounts from this period shape the legislative acts undertaken to regulate the market.

1900–1929: Shifting Perceptions

Contributions of Popular Culture

Fig. 2 shows that the relative emphasis on manipulation and fraud, begun in the previous period, continues and dominates cultural accounts in this period. Even when stock market troubles received minimal attention (notably, in the decade following World War I), nearly twice as many accounts dealt with manipulation and fraud rather than excessive speculation. Furthermore, there were up to six times as many of these at both the beginning and the end of this period. This period also was one that saw a growing cultural acceptance of speculation, as it became decoupled from Puritan indignation (Fraser, 2005).

In addition, a large and popular literature romanticizing and mythologizing Wall Street had emerged, including Dreiser's popular trilogy (*The Financier, The Titan, The Stoic*) as well as the novels by Will Payne (*The Money Captain*) and H. K. Webster (*The Banker and the Bear*) and *The Winning by Barbara Worth* by Harold Bell Wright (Fraser, 2005). As well, the notion of "risk" was also transformed. In the 19th century, speculation was equated with gambling; however, in the early 20th century, it came to be viewed more mathematically, through concepts of "probability," "standard deviation," and "risk assessment" (Fraser, 2005, p. 251). Finally, speculation became more acceptable due to greater middle-class exposure to

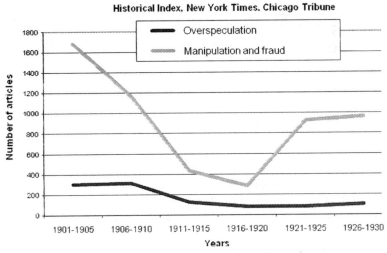

Fig. 2. Popular Press Articles Mentioning Stock Market Problems, 1900–1930.

the stock market, which followed World War I both through programs like the government massive Liberty Loan campaign that introduced many people to the idea of owning securities and because the employment boom created by the war generated household surpluses that could be channeled into securities (Smith, 2001). Through these mechanisms, speculation in the market had undergone democratization: although only about 4 million people were invested in the stock market in 1900, ten years later this number had increased to about 7 million (Fraser, 2005, p. 250), and by 1922 it was about 14.4 million (Smith, 2001, p. 65).

While increased acceptance of speculation accounts for the decline in its presence in cultural accounts, there is a simultaneous increase in accounts pointing to manipulation and fraud in the stock market, which became favorite targets of muckrakers and the growing force of the progressive movement (Cowing, 1965). In particular bucket shops[2] became popular targets of muckraking journalists, and concerns over the potential negative impact of the concentration of money and power of the financiers on the democratic process became a target of the progressives (Cowing, 1965).

Contributions of Government Actions
Corresponding to cultural sentiments of the period, legislative action was overwhelmingly focused on stock market manipulation and fraud. At the state level, attention to excessive speculation is not significant; although there is some early activity surrounding excessive speculation, this seemed to result from mimetic diffusion of regulations banning futures sales by late-adopting states. However, as outlined in Table 3, most other legislative actions on the state level concerned securities fraud, for example, blue sky laws, which prohibited fraudulent representation of securities (i.e., prevent them from promising "the blue sky"). Interestingly, Mahoney (2001) shows that the adoption of blue sky laws by a particular state did not necessarily reflect the proliferation of stock fraud in this state but was connected to the strength of populist and progressive movements and lobbying by banks, suggesting not only the influence of the dominant cultural accounts on government action, but also the influence of professional norms as well.

The situation with the US federal government is somewhat more complex. First, the federal government seems to follow the patterns set by the states. Thus, while the state movement to ban futures sales was the most pronounced in the 1880s, with a few laggard states adopting after 1900, the first attempts to ban the futures sales at the federal level did not occur until 1914 in the form of federal Cotton Futures Act and then strengthened in 1922 when the Grain Futures Act was enacted at the federal level.

Although these acts targeted excessive speculation, which had fallen out of the prominence in the cultural accounts, their enactment at the federal level lags behind the shift in cultural perceptions and state legislative action.

Bans on bucket shops and blue sky laws constitute the bulk of the state legislative acts in this period and again show a pattern of diffusion through the states culminating in federal legislation. In the specific case of blue sky laws, due to federal jurisdiction over interstate commerce, many of the state-enacted laws were ruled unconstitutional or unenforceable. Consequently, in 1922 Congressman Denison introduced federal blue sky legislation. Although this proposal failed at this time, parts of it are taken up again when something akin to a national blue sky law appears in the 1930s.

Between 1900 and 1929, there were 83 separate legislative acts adopted by the state and federal governments. Only one focused on revenue generation; 17 focused on excessive speculation, most of which represent the trailing diffusion bans of futures sales previously adopted by the bulk of the states. However, 66 acts addressed issues of manipulation and fraud, again reflecting the dominant cultural accounts of the time. The numbers total to 83 instead of 84 because one act, the Pujo Money trust investigation of 1913, dealt with both excessive speculation and manipulation and deserves special attention. This federal investigation followed, and in certain ways mimicked, the Hughes Committee's informal investigation of commodity and stock exchanges conducted in 1908 by New York State.

The Hughes committee was grappling with issues of incorporation of stock exchanges and attempting to differentiate between speculation and gambling, but did not have power to call witnesses under oath, and its major conclusions were based on written responses provided by the authorities of the New York Stock Exchange. Its only concrete recommendations concerned improvements in the state's legislation against bucket shops. However, the Pujo Committee conducted a far more extensive investigation of Wall Street and uncovered numerous monopolistic practices of the New York Stock Exchange, instances of stock market manipulation and fraud, as well as a lack of investor protections. The committee also grappled with the function of the exchanges, and specifically the New York Stock Exchange within the US economy, deliberating over whether NYSE was just a private association or an institution endowed with public functions integral to the US economy, which implicate questions of the legitimacy of stock market manipulation. Repeatedly, the committee asks exchange members how they justify instances of manipulation and under which conditions manipulation is legitimate.

As a result of investigation, the committee offered a number of recommendations for curbing manipulation, fraud, and excessive speculation, including that exchanges (1) require full disclosure from corporations; (2) require a margin of not less than 20%, (3) prohibit wash sales; (4) prohibit brokerage firms from using securities pledged by customers as collateral for bank loans (rehypothecating); (5) prohibit members from lending to one another customers' securities; (6) state in its charter the conditions of admitting/removing securities from the list; and (7) require its members to keep books recording the actual names and transactions of customers. Importantly, the Committee regarded the exchanges as self-regulated "private clubs" and denied a role for the federal government in their regulation. To stimulate the exchanges to adopt the above recommendations in their constitutions, the Committee recommended the incorporation of the exchanges at the state level and, drawing on the only jurisdiction they believed existed at the federal level, proposed a bill that would prohibit the exchanges from transmitting information through the mails, telegraph, or telephone unless they follow committee recommendations. However, the bill was never enacted.

In sum, although the Pujo investigation took place in a political climate with strong antitrust sentiments, the private club logic of the exchange, originally precipitated by 18th century laws banning public auctions of securities, was so well institutionalized by the beginning of the 20th century that the committee accepted it as the taken-for-granted nature of the exchange. Proceeding from that assumption, more drastic regulatory measures, such as regulation at the federal level, was inconceivable, since the federal government had no regulatory role in such private clubs, as evidenced by their attempts to leverage federal control over the mails in dealing with the exchanges. However, one important consequence of Pujo investigation was further development of stock market logic by Wall Street professionals, as discussed below.

Contributions of Stock Market Professionals
Once again, Wall Street did not passively succumb to either cultural or governmental accounts about the nature of the stock market, but responded with publicity campaigns, promoting its own logic (Ott, 2004). During the Pujo Investigation, Wall Street responded with an official brief (Brief on Behalf of the New York Stock Exchange by John G. Milburn and Walter F. Taylor), presenting its own view of the situation and arguing against the incorporation of exchanges the government sought, as well as for the inevitability and economic necessity of speculation.

Over this period, Wall Street was especially active promoting the distinction they saw between useless and dangerous gambling and useful and necessary speculation (in the stock market), potentially contributing to the increased acceptance of speculation outlined earlier. This theme emerges from the analysis of the *Wall Street Journal* in the period 1900–1929. A number of articles discuss the difference between gambling and speculation, arguing that the distinction lies only in quality: while gambling is based on ignorance and wild guesses, speculation involves consideration, is done by professionals, and implies an almost scientific prediction of future events based on probabilities and risk assessment. Speculation thus defined is integral to the stock market and has useful function for the economy in general. Several articles draw on economists, such as Henry Crosby Emery discussed above, to support this view. Further, even stock market manipulation was supported by legitimating accounts. Such accounts attempted to reclassify certain behaviors categorized as manipulation as a form of exercising professional discretion, where experts acted in the best interest of the market as a whole. In this case, the distinction was made between the dangerous kinds of self-serving manipulation of the stock market and useful types of manipulation by benevolent stock market elites working to stabilize prices and prevent either steep falls or increases in the prices. The argument was that in these useful kinds of manipulation, the elites went against the crowd and traded in the direction opposite the rest of the market to promote stability.

The 1930s: The Role of Context in Responding to Crises

In our previous analysis, we suggest that although the market was arguably more vulnerable to fraud and manipulation when smaller, that is prior to 1900, the legislative acts of the time reflect the contemporary cultural accounts which focused on gambling and excessive speculation. Further, the government legislative acts prohibiting short sales and public auctions, as well as government's implicit sanctioning of cartelization before the 1890s, facilitated the development of the private club logic for the stock market. After 1900, participation in the market grew dramatically and the exposure to potential dangers from speculation grew considerably, both in terms of impact on the overall economy and in the number of citizens potentially affected; however, the major government concern switched to manipulation and fraud, again mirroring but trailing the popular cultural acceptance of speculation but growing concern over manipulation and fraud.

Further, the private club logics of the stock exchanges institutionalized in the earlier period were so deeply ingrained that they interfered with the government's ability to enact incorporation or federal regulation of the exchanges. Yet, even investigations that made no proposals of federal regulation promoted stock market professionals to engage in guardianship activities, advancing legitimating accounts justifying speculation and manipulation when undertaken by stock market elites. These tendencies also explain the federal securities regulation subsequent to 1929 (DeJordy, 2010).

In 1933, federal securities regulation was enacted for the first time. Notably, the first investigation of the 1929 crisis did not uncover any organized market manipulation or fraud that could be blamed for the crash. In contrast to earlier crises (e.g., 1907) the crash of 1929 did not have immediately obvious causes, and could not be easily attributed to market manipulation or fraud. Government investigations, begun in 1932 as hearings of the Senate Banking and Currency Committee, eventually uncovered a great deal of fraudulent, manipulative, and speculative activity in the market; however, linking cultural accounts from both prior and subsequent to 1900, many forms of manipulation were framed in terms of promoting speculation, and subordinated to it (Pecora, 1939). In a sense, the definition of speculation was expanded to include various activities previously considered to be forms of manipulation, when such manipulation stimulated speculation (e.g., pools, wash sales). Consequently, excessive speculation, and not the manipulation that precipitated it, was framed as the proximal cause for the market crisis. This connection has proven resilient. For example, in 1972 economist Kenneth Galbraith famously argued that depression was caused by the crash, and the crash of 1929 was caused by excessive speculation. However, other scholars alternatively contended that both the crash and depression had similar underlying causes (e.g., Fed's tight money policy) that were different from overspeculation.

It is clear, though, that in contrast to earlier panics or crashes (e.g., 1907) the crash of 1929 did not have immediately obvious causes, and could not be easily or immediately attributed to market manipulation or fraud. It would be logical to assume, given the emphasis on excessive speculation in committee reports, that federal legislation would be designed primarily to prevent overtrading and only secondarily to address manipulation and fraud. Nonetheless, the federal securities regulations actually enacted deal primarily with manipulation and fraud and only secondarily with speculation. For example, the Securities Act of 1933 is centered on the notion of *disclosure*-companies issuing new securities were obliged to register with the FTC, providing detailed financial data (Khademian, 1992). Disclosure implied greater transparency, which impeded fraud. The Act also had explicit antifraud provisions (e.g., Section 17(a)) aimed against market manipulation and securities fraud (Ratner, 1998). Provisions against overtrading were minimal, but gained some attention in the Securities Exchange Act of 1934 which has two provisions (Sections 7 and 8) designed to regulate the overall operations of the market by authorizing the Fed to limit the amount of available credit and regulate borrowing by brokers and dealers (Ratner, 1998). However, its primary purposes were to extend disclosure requirements to all securities exchanged on the markets, not only new issues, and to establish the SEC to enforce those requirements.

Although such regulations appear "illogical" based on the problematization offered by the Senate investigation into the stock market decline of 1929 to 1932, commonly referred to as "The Pecora Commission" after lead counsel Ferdinand Pecora, they are more understandable when the institutional logic is taken into account. First, as we have already noted, the popular cultural accounts relating to stock market troubles from 1900 to 1929 focus on manipulation and fraud, and these continue into the 1930s as shown in Fig. 3. Second, we have already noted that in the period between 1913 and 1929, Wall Street made a concerted effort to promote legitimating accounts justifying stock market speculation and manipulation as economic necessities. Although justifying accounts coincided with, and perhaps contributed to, growing popular acceptance of speculation, the growing repudiation of stock market manipulation and fraud made its justification more challenging. Further, the key argument legitimating manipulation was that stock market elites traded against the crowd and stabilized prices;

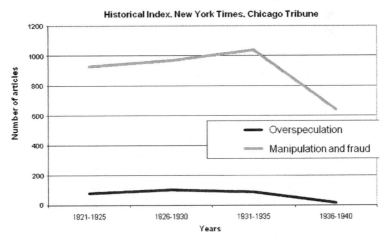

Fig. 3. Popular Press Articles Mentioning Stock Market Problems.

however, the Pecora investigations made very public that the opposite occurred – in slumping markets, the elites followed (or led) the crowed, turning bearish and playing short, exacerbating the pace of collapse instead of stabilizing the prices (Cowing, 1965).

Yet, the effects of increased cultural acceptance of speculation, now framed in the scientific language of probabilities and risk assessment as an appropriate part of the institutional logic combined with, or resulting from, Wall Street's attempts to legitimize speculation, have proven quite successful. From our analysis of the history of US stock market from 1789 through 1935, we identified the following solutions, either proposed or enacted, to curb excessive speculation: (1) banning short sales; (2) constraining the time period for short sales (e.g., the speculators could remain in short position no longer than 3 days); (3) taxing short sales; (4) taxing stock transfer; (5) demanding physical delivery of stocks after each transaction to a Clearing House; (6) introducing margin requirements; (7) banning rehypothecating securities; (8) banning lending securities; (9) introducing a fixed holding period during which the stock cannot be resold. From all these possible measures, the Securities Exchange Act of 1934 implemented only one – the establishment of margin requirements. This suggests that the growing cultural acceptance of speculation had a direct impact on the focus of securities regulation.

Importantly, however, the enactment of securities legislation of any sort, whether aimed at curbing speculation or at manipulation and fraud, signaled that government actors no longer accept the private club logic of the stock market as taken-for-granted. Both President Roosevelt and the Pecora Commission draw on the federal government's role in interstate commerce and in securing a national economy for the common good as justifications for federal jurisdiction over stock exchanges.

Lastly, it must be noted that in its legislative actions of the 1930s, the government followed its earlier patterns. As noted before, the federal bans on futures trading of 1914 and 1922 followed and were modeled on prior state legislation. Federal regulation was often enacted only once there was near complete adoption of similar regulation across the states. Similarly, by the 1930s, the state antifraud legislation was relatively well developed and the stage was set for similar legislation at the federal level. In contrast, the state legislation against excessive speculation in stock markets was relatively less developed because most state legislation focused on commodity trading rather than the stock markets, and most of the acts that concerned excessive speculation securities trading (such as the New York law of 1792) had been repealed. Given both the cultural accounts and the mimetic forces, it is little wonder that federal securities regulation in the 1930s was modeled on recently diffused state blue sky laws (Cowing, 1965).

DISCUSSION

Our empirical research helps to refine our theoretical framework. Following other authors, such as Fligstein (2001), we conceptualized the stock market as an institutional field, which consists of interacting social actors connected by patterns of power and control and sharing common cultural frameworks. As with other fields, the stock market is endowed with institutional logics which imbue the actors and their actions in the stock market with meaning and legitimacy (Meyer, Boli, & Thomas, 1987). Lastly, we assumed that the stock market logics are socially constructed and reconstructed through historically contingent processes of social interaction among various social actors.

The focus of this article, however, is not only on the historical processes of construction of the US stock market logics, but specifically on the role and embeddedness of the US and state governments in this process. In contrast to some views in the neoinstitutional literature, which understand government regulations as forces exogenous to the fields under consideration (e.g., Baron et al., 1986; Dobbin et al., 1993; Sutton & Dobbin, 1996), we view government itself as an actor embedded in the stock market field and wrapped in the prevailing field logic. In other words, we argue that there is a dualism between the government actions and the stock market field. On the one hand, government responses to the stock market behavior, such as the new legislative acts, may cause changes in the prevailing logics of the stock market field. On the other hand, government responses to the stock market behavior, such as excessive speculation, fraud, or crises episodes, are not exclusively rational, but also reflect their tacit acceptance of the prevailing socially constructed field logics. In sum, our theoretical model addresses both government responses to stock market behavior and how the processes of social construction of the US stock market field also affect those responses.

Government Responses to Stock Market Behavior

In the empirical part of our article, we have considered the US, state, and federal government responses to the stock market behavior from the 1770s to 1930s. In general, we have argued that the state or federal securities regulations were not just rational reactions to stock market failures as assumed by the rational choice models (e.g., Carosso, 1970; Galbraith, 1972; Seligman, 1983). Neither are these regulations wholly explained by the lobbying of various interest groups (Macey & Miller, 1991), expansionist tendencies by the state (Burk, 1985), or routines by state bureaucracy (Khademian, 1992). Rather, we advance an institutional model in which government legislative action, albeit triggered by stock market behaviors and crises episodes, is both path- and context-dependent, both reflecting historically available policy solutions and also imbued with the prevailing field logics as shown in Fig. 4.

For example, we have shown that in the period between 1770 and 1900, government legislative acts concerning the stock market were mostly aimed at preventing excessive speculation. However, due to the small size of the stock market – about four million corporate shareholders by the year 1900 (Fraser, 2005) as compared to 14.4 million in the year 1922

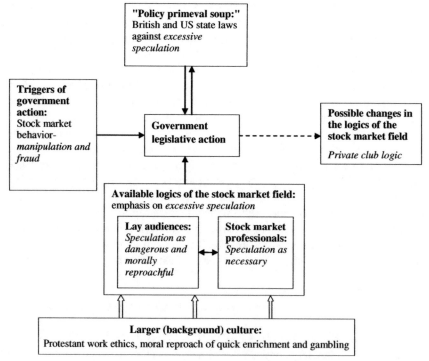

Fig. 4. Theoretical Model Applied to 1770–1900.

(Smith, 2001) – the threat posed by excessive speculation was very limited, both in terms of affecting the national economy and the small numbers of investors, but such small markets were arguably more susceptible to manipulation and fraud. Thus, the rational choice theories do not offer much insight as to why government action was focused on excessive speculation instead of manipulation or fraud. Similarly, theories that stress bureaucratic routines and expanding structuration may explain the states' copying each others' legislation, but they leave unclear why, in the 1770–1900 period, legislation specifically targeting excessive speculation achieved legitimacy and diffused readily. Theories stressing political pressures upon the government partially explain government actions in this period, however. For example, after 1873, the populist movement emerged as an influential force and affected government action; however, such pressures still do not explain the consistent emphasis on excessive speculation that dominated from 1770 to 1900, despite changes in the political pressures and forces. We argue that the institutional explanation fills the gap.

As shown in Fig. 4, we argue that the institutional field of the stock market is embedded in the larger cultural context. As outlined by DiMaggio and Powell (1983) and elaborated by Scott (1995), we allow for several institutional forces to impact the field. Specifically, we examine institutionally embedded regulatory forces, manifest primarily through government actions, cultural forces at the societal level; and normative pressures from field professionals. We focus on the interplay among these forces and, in particular, how cultural and normative forces help to shape the regulatory action undertaken by the government, as indicated by the arrows connecting the cultural context to the government legislative action in Fig. 4. Independent of whether the government has been included in the field of study, most institutional accounts only posit an effect from the government to the field, not an impact from the field back onto the regulatory agencies and governing bodies, except in overt or coercive forms such as lobbying. Yet, we have shown that in the period 1770–1900, the US culture emphasized the Protestant work ethic and moral reproach of gambling and quick enrichment. And this cultural context had an impact on the social construction of the logics of the stock market field. Within the stock market field, the moral imperatives of the Protestant ethic translated into the focus on curbing excessive speculation, which was considered a morally reproachful form of gambling. We also argued that depending on their positions and interests, different actors in the field had different interpretations of excessive speculation. Thus, media and "lay" audiences interpreted excessive speculation as dangerous, but the stock market professionals went to great pains to redefine speculation as economically necessary.

By the same token, in the period 1770–1900 the US state/federal government was imbued with the same field logic emphasizing excessive speculation. We can thus explain the US state/federal legislation in the period of 1770–1900 as following cultural accounts rather than economic rationality. The same explanation applies to the second period that we considered, 1900–1930. We have argued that although the stock market behavior was characterized by excessive speculation accompanying considerable growth of the US stock market, the US state/federal legislation targeted stock market manipulation and fraud, following the new logic of the stock market field. We also noted that government legislative actions may cause changes in the logics of the stock market field. Thus, in the period 1770–1900 the New York State laws outlawing public auctions contributed to the development of the "private club" logic of the stock market. We show how, as an embedded actor, the government both affects and is affected by the cultural/cognitive as well as the normative and coercive aspects of institutional fields in which it operates.

Social Construction of the Stock Market Field

The second part of our theoretical model is concerned with larger processes of social construction of the stock market field. The US government is an important but not the only social actor having an impact on the emergence and change of the stock market field logics. We have argued that multiple events, such as stock market crises or public scandals, connected to such stock market behaviors as excessive speculation, manipulation, or fraud may serve as triggers leading to the changes in the prevailing field logics (see Fig. 5). According to our theoretical model, these triggers of change provoke dialogue and sense making by social actors in the field. In their sense-making processes, the actors in the field share similar cultural schemes or logics, but have different positions and interests, which afford somewhat different interpretations of stock market problems and solutions. Out of this dialogue, the winning interpretations emerge and become the new field logics. Which interpretations win is a matter of power and specific historical circumstances (Berger & Luckmann, 1967). Finally, the field logics do not change completely but retain the elements from the past as well as the wider cultural context; the changes may either be revolutionary or accumulate over time.

A similar theoretical explanation applies to the crisis of 1929. As we have argued, different social actors interpreted the crisis through the cultural

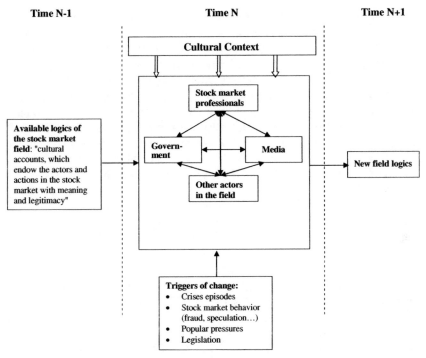

Fig. 5. The Evolution of Field Logics.

lens of manipulation/fraud, even though the government investigation found that, if anything, it was excessive speculation to be blamed. Again, these interpretations differed by actors' positions and interests. Stock market professionals tried to define manipulation as economically necessary, whereas media and lay audiences believed manipulation and fraud to be the causes of the stock market crisis. The government, although drawing on the prior cultural accounts condemning excessive speculation in framing the results of its investigation, enacted the federal securities regulation in 1933 aimed to prevent manipulation and fraud. The revolutionary consequence of this legislation was the end of the "private club" logic of the stock market.

CONCLUSION

Our research shows that different social actors in a field respond differently to particular crisis episodes. The media and other "lay" audiences (which are not professionally connected to the stock exchange) serve to problematize the exchange practices and draw the government attention to the stock markets. The government responds by formulating policy concerns, and designing policy solutions to the stock market problems. However, the government responses are not simply rational and efficient solutions to the nascent stock market problems, nor are they simple responses to cooptation or lobbying. Instead, the policy-making processes are also shaped both by the dominant field logic of the stock market field (e.g., as to the functions and purposes of the stock market) and policy solutions to stock market problems generated in the earlier historic periods and forming the "policy primeval soup" (Kingdon, 1984). Despite the fact that policy-makers operate within the same institutionalized logics and available problems and solutions, revolutionary decisions are possible because of mutability of schemas (Clemens & Cook, 1999), transposability of schemas (e.g., when a policy-maker applies his/her experience with commodity markets to stock markets) (Sewell, 1992), recombination of schemas (Powell, 1991), and reviving or recombining previously aborted institutional forms (Schneiberg, 2007).

Finally, the stock market professionals work to influence the institutional logics with legitimating accounts for current practices that come under threat in the cultural accounts, as in defending certain types of market manipulation (DeJordy, 2010). Interestingly, in counteracting the government, the stock market professionals draw on similar cultural resources, but draw different arguments based on their different position and interests (Creed, DeJordy, & Lok, in press). As a result, the changes to the field are introduced in compromised and sometimes ambiguous forms that accommodate a broad array of cultural accounts as a result of a dialogue between the different parties. Although these changes may be revolutionary in their effect, they do not completely eradicate previous logics of the field, since parties to the dialogue drew on the existing cultural schemas to generate the new ones. Finally, our research shows that different disconnected elements of the older field logics (e.g., stock markets problems and solutions, theories of value, and stock market functions) are retained in the stock market cultural toolkit and reemerge throughout history.

Policy Implications

We can see this interplay between cultural accounts, professional legitimating accounts, and governmental action revived in the performances of the respective actors in our most recent financial crises. Although no dominant cultural account for the crisis has clearly emerged, some major themes in the popular press echo previous accounts. On one hand, irresponsible consumers taking on mortgages they could not service echoes the Protestant ethic of hardwork and living according to ones means, a seeming parallel to the moral reprehensibility of gambling. On the other hand, Wall Street greed and indecipherable financial instruments harkens back to the vilification of market manipulations and fraud. In this sense, both popular cultural accounts from the 19th and 20th century are evident here in the 21st century.

It is our hope that by better understanding the mechanisms by which government regulations are enacted, we can subsequently identify ways to decouple our understanding of market problems from the cultural and professional myths at work in the institutional environment, freeing actors in all arenas to more clearly assess, understand, resolve, and prevent market crises and their underlying causes in the future. To that end, our research suggests the following recommendation: *The government must recognize and fulfill its regulatory role in the stock market field.*

As shown in our analysis, it is only in 1933, in the wake of the precipitating market events, when the federal government rejects the private club logic of the stock market and asserts its regulatory authority over the exchanges in the interest of securing the national economy for the common good and protecting its citizens. This role was asserted through the passage of federal regulations such as the Securities Act of 1933 (often called the "Truth in Disclosures Act"), the Securities Exchange Act of 1934 (establishing the SEC), and Banking Act of 1933 (more commonly known as the Glass-Steagall Act). Independent of the role of rational choice, political lobbying, or institutional myths in their enactment, the passage of these acts laid a foundation for government regulation of the financial markets.

However, in the lead up to our current crisis, there has been a systematic return to the self-regulated private club logic for financial markets. This return was the direct result of government action, including explicit deregulation of financial markets (e.g., the repeal of Glass-Steagall) as well as the government explicitly abdicating regulatory authority over trading of various asset backed securities (e.g., the Commodities Futures Modernization Act of 2000), both of which contributed to the current crisis. Independent of the appropriateness of any specific regulation, the role of federal regulation of financial markets to protect the investing public and ensure economic stability for the common good must not be abdicated.

NOTES

1. In very broad strokes, we use the terms *manipulation* and *fraud* to refer to activities designed to misrepresent or misuse information to hinder market functioning (e.g., using insider information or undermining the market pricing function through misinformation), and *speculation* to refer to activities relating to future or short-term trading focused on immediate profitability instead of investment. As we discuss later, since our analysis spans 150 years, the very definition of these terms evolves over this period, based on the prevalent cultural accounts, as discussed later.

2. Bucket shops offered a place for a form of betting run by brokers with their customers' money. The Hughes Committee investigation defined bucket shops as being "ostensibly brokerage offices, where, however, commodities and securities are neither bought nor sold in pursuance of customers' orders, the transactions being closed by the payment of gains or losses, as determined by price quotations." Bucket shops were notorious for many forms of fraud: e.g., it was common for the brokers to manipulate or delay quotations at will, and many shops operated "without even the benefit of a real 'wire' reporting the real prices of real securities, run by pretend brokers unconnected to any stock or commodity exchange" (Fraser, 2005, p. 250) and it was common for the owners of the bucket shops to eventually flee with their customers' money (Geisst, 2004, p. 158).

ACKNOWLEDGMENTS

We thank Don Palmer, Jo-Ellen Pozner, Mary Kate Stimmler, and Klaus Weber for their helpful comments; Kate Glynn-Broderick for her research assistance; Chris Marquis for his valuable contributions; and especially the volume editors, Michael Lounsbury and Paul Hirsch, for their encouragement and feedback. We appreciate the generous support of the Boston College Winston Center for Leadership and Ethics and the Joseph F. Cotter Professorship in enabling this research.

REFERENCES

Abolafia, M. Y., & Kilduff, M. (1988). Enacting market crisis: The social construction of a speculative bubble. *Administrative Science Quarterly, 33*, 177–193.
Banner, S. (1998). *Anglo-American securities regulation: Cultural and political roots, 1690–1860*. Cambridge: Cambridge University Press.
Barley, S. R., & Tolbert, P. S. (1997). Institutionalization and structuration: Studying the links between action and institution. *Organization Studies, 18*, 93–117.

Baron, J. N., Dobbin, F. R., & Jennings, P. D. (1986). War and peace: The evolution of modern personnel administration in U.S. industry. *American Journal of Sociology, 92,* 350–383.

Baum, J. A. C., & Oliver, C. (1991). Institutional linkages and organizational mortality. *Administrative Science Quarterly, 36,* 187–218.

Berger, P. M., & Luckmann, T. (1967). *The social construction of reality: A treatise in the sociology of knowledge.* Harmondsworth: Penguin.

Brint, S., & Karabel, J. (1991). Institutional origins and transformations: The case of American community colleges. In: W. W. Powell & P. J. DiMaggio (Eds), *The new institutionalism in organizational analysis* (pp. 337–360). Chicago: The University of Chicago Press.

Burk, J. (1985). The origins of federal securities regulation. *Social Forces, 63,* 1010–1029.

Burrows, E. G., & Wallace, M. (1999). *Gotham: A history of New York city to 1898.* Oxford: Oxford University Press.

Carosso, V. P. (1970). *Investment banking in America.* Cambridge, MA: Harvard University Press.

Clark, E., Bernheim, A. L., Dewhurst, F. J., & Schneider, M. G. (1934). *Stock market control: A summary of the research findings and recommendations of the security market survey staff of the twentieth century fund, Inc.* New York: D. Appleton-Century Company.

Clemens, E. S., & Cook, J. M. (1999). Politics and institutionalism: Explaining durability and change. *Annual Review of Sociology, 25,* 441–466.

Clews, H. (1900). *The Wall Street point of view.* New York: Silver, Burdett and Company.

Committee on Banking and Currency. (1891). *Silver pool investigation.* February 25, 1891 Report. G.P.O., Washington.

Committee on Banking and Currency. (1913). *Report of the committee appointed pursuant to House resolutions 429 and 504 to investigate the concentration of control of money and credit.* February 28, 1913. U.S. G.P.O, Washington.

Committee on Public Relations. (1936). *New York Stock Exchange: Its functions and operations.* New York: New York Stock Exchange.

Committee on Publicity. (1929). *The New York Stock Exchange: History, organization, operation, service.* New York: New York Stock Exchange.

Committee on Publicity. (1934). *The New York Stock Exchange: History, organization, operation, service.* New York: New York Stock Exchange.

Committee on Speculation in Securities and Commodities. (1909). *Report of governor Hughes' committee on speculation in securities and commodities. June 7, 1909.* New York.

Cook, W. W. (1898). *A treatise on the law of corporations having a capital stock.* Chicago: Callaghan.

Cowing, C. B. (1965). *Populists, plungers, and progressives: A social history of stock and commodity speculation, 1890–1936.* Princeton, NJ: Princeton University Press.

Creed, W.E., DeJordy, D., & Lok, J. (in press). Being the change: Resolving institutional contradictions through identity Work. *Academy of Management Journal.*

Davis, G. F. (2009). *Managed by the markets: How finance reshaped America.* New York: Oxford University Press.

DeJordy, R. (2010). *Fighting for the status quo: The role of institutional guardianship in the persistence and conformity of social systems.* Unpublished Dissertation. Boston College, Boston, MA.

DiMaggio, P. J. (1991). Constructing an organizational field as a professional project: U.S. art museums, 1920–1940. In: W. W. Powell & P. J. DiMaggio (Eds), *The new institutionalism in organizational analysis* (pp. 267–292). Chicago: The University of Chicago Press.

DiMaggio, P. J., & Powell, W. W. (1983). The iron cage revisited: Institutional isomorphism and collective rationality in organizational fields. *American Sociological Review, 48,* 147–160.

Dobbin, F., Sutton, J., Meyer, J. W., & Scott, R. W. (1993). Equal opportunity law and the construction of internal labor markets. *American Journal of Sociology, 99,* 396–427.

Dobbin, F., & Sutton, J. R. (1998). The strength of the weak state: The employment rights revolution and the rise of human resource management divisions. *American Journal of Sociology, 104,* 441–476.

Dos Passos, J. R. (1882). *A treatise on the law of stock-brokers and stock-exchanges.* New York: Harper.

Dowd, T. J., & Dobbin, F. (2001). Origins of the myth of neo-liberalism: Regulation in the first century of US railroading. In: L. Magnusson & J. Ottoson (Eds), *The state, regulation, and the economy: An historical perspective* (pp. 61–88). Cheltenham: Edward Elgar.

Evans, P. B., Rueschemeyer, D., & Skocpol, T. (1985). *Bringing the state back in.* Cambridge, NY: Cambridge University Press.

Farjoun, M. (2002). The dialectics of institutional development in emerging and turbulent fields: The history of pricing conventions in the on-line database industry. *Academy of Management Review, 45,* 848–874.

Fligstein, N. (2001). *The architecture of markets: An economic sociology of twenty-first-century capitalist societies.* Princeton, NJ: Princeton University Press.

Fraser, S. (2005). *Every man a speculator: A history of Wall Street in American life.* New York: HarperCollins.

Friedland, R., & Alford, R. R. (1991). Brining society back in: Symbols, practices, and institutional contradictions. In: W. W. Powell & P. J. DiMaggio (Eds), *The new institutionalism in organization analysis* (pp. 232–263). Chicago: University of Chicago Press.

Galaskiewicz, J. (1991). Making corporate actors accountable: Institution-building in Minneapolis-St. Paul. In: W. W. Powell & P. J. DiMaggio (Eds), *The new institutionalism in organizational analysis* (pp. 293–310). Chicago: The University of Chicago Press.

Galbraith, J. K. (1972). *The great crash, 1929.* Boston: Houghton Mifflin.

Garfield, J. A. (1870). *Investigation into the causes of the gold panic report of the majority of the committee on banking and currency, March 1, 1870.* Washington: G.P.O.

Geisst, C. R. (2004). *Wall Street: A history from its beginnings to the fall of Enron.* Oxford: Oxford University Press.

Greenwood, R., & Suddaby, R. (2006). Institutional entrepreneurship in mature fields: The big five accounting firms. *Academy of Management Journal, 49,* 27–48.

Greve, H., Pozner, J.-E., & Rao, H. (2006). Vox populi: Resource partitioning, organizational proliferation and the cultural impact of the insurgent micro-radio movement. *American Journal of Sociology, 112*(3), 802–837.

Haveman, H. A., & Rao, H. (1997). Structuring a theory of moral sentiments: Institutional and organizational coevolution in the early thrift industry. *American Journal of Sociology, 102,* 1606–1651.

Helliwell, A. L. (1903). *A treatise on stock and stockholders covering watered stock, trusts, consolidations and holding companies.* St Paul, MN: Keefe-Davidson Co.

Hoffman, A. J. (1999). Institutional evolution and change: Environmentalism and the U.S. chemical industry. *Academy of Management Journal, 42,* 351–371.

Jones, C. (2001). Co-evolution of entrepreneurial careers, institutional rules and competitive dynamics in American film, 1895–1920. *Organization Studies, 22,* 911–944.

Khademian, A. M. (1992). *The SEC and capital market regulation: The politics of expertise.* Pittsburgh, PA: University of Pittsburgh Press.

Kindleberger, C. P. (1989). *Manias, panics, and crashes: A history of financial crises.* New York: Basic Books, Inc., Publishers.

Kingdon, J. (1984). *Agendas, alternatives, and public policies.* Boston: Little, Brown.

Leblebici, H., Solancik, G. R., Copay, A., & King, T. (1991). Institutional change and the transformation of interorganizational fields: An organizational history of the U.S. broadcasting industry. *Administrative Science Quarterly, 36,* 333–363.

Lewis, F. A. (1881). *Law relating on stocks, bonds, and other securities, in the United States.* Philadelphia: Rees Welsh & Co.

Lounsbury, M. (2007). A tale of two cities: Competing logics and practice variation in the professionalizing of mutual funds. *Academy of Management Journal, 50,* 289–307.

Macey, J., & Miller, G. (1991). Origin of the blue sky laws. *Texas Law Review, 347.*

Mahoney, P. (2001). The origins of the blue sky laws: A test of competing hypotheses. In: *Law and economic workshop* (Vol. Paper 5). Berkeley, CA: University of California.

Marquis, C., & Lounsbury, M. (2007). Vive la resistance: Competing logics in the consolidation of community banking. *Academy of Management Journal, 50*(4), 799–820.

Martin, H. S. (1913). *The New York Stock Exchange and the "money trust"; a review of the report to the house of representatives by the Pujo committee.* New York: F.E. Fitch.

Martin, H. S. (1919). *The New York Stock Exchange.* New York: Francis Emory Fitch, Inc.

Meyer, J. W., Boli, J., & Thomas, G. M. (1987). Ontology and rationalization in the Western cultural account. In: G. M. Thomas, J. W. Meyer, F. O. Ramirez & J. Boli (Eds), *Institutional structure: Constituting state, society, and the individual* (pp. 12–37). Beverly Hills, CA: Sage.

Mezias, S. J. (1990). An institutional model of organizational practice: Financial reporting at the Fortune 200. *Administrative Science Quarterly, 35,* 431–457.

Meeker, E. J. (1922). *The work of the stock exchange.* New York: The Ronald Press Company.

Milburn, J. G., & Taylor, W. F. (1913). *Money trust investigation: Brief on behalf of the New York Stock Exchange.* New York: C.G. Burgoyne.

Miles, M. B., & Huberman, M. A. (1984). *Qualitative data analysis: A sourcebook of new methods.* Beverly Hills, CA: Sage.

Ott, J. (2004). The "free and open" "people's market": Public relations at the New York Stock Exchange, 1913–1929. *Business and Economic History On-Line, 2,* 1–43.

Parker, C. (1911). Governmental regulation of speculation. *Annals of the American Academy of Political and Social Science, 38*(2), 126–154.

Pecora, F. (1939). *Wall Street under oath: The story of our modern money changers.* New York: Simon and Schuster.

Powell, W. W. (1991). Expanding the scope of institutional analysis. In: W. W. Powell & P. J. DiMaggio (Eds), *The new institutionalism in organizational analysis* (pp. 183–203). Chicago: The University of Chicago Press.

Prechel, H. (2000). *Big business and the state: Historical transitions and corporate transformation, 1880s–1990s.* Albany, NY: State University of New York Press.

Pujo, A. P. (1912). *Money trust investigation: Investigation of financial and monetary conditions in the United States under house resolutions nos. 429 and 504.* Washington: G.P.O.

Pujo, A. P. (1913). *Report of the committee appointed pursuant to House resolutions 429 and 504 to investigate the concentration of control of money and credit. February 28, 1913.* Washington: G.P.O.

Ratner, D. L. (1998). *Securities regulation in a nutshell.* St Paul, MN: West Group.

Schneiberg, M. (2007). What's on the path? Path dependence, organizational diversity and the problem of institutional change in the U.S. economy, 1900–1950. *Socio-Economic Review, 5,* 47–80.

Scott, R. W. (1995). *Institutions and organizations.* Thousand Oaks, CA: Sage.

Seligman, J. (1983). The historical need for a mandatory corporate disclosure system. *Journal of Corporate Law, 9.*

Seligman, J. (1995). *The transformation of Wall Street: A history of the securities and exchange commission and modern corporate finance.* Boston: Northeastern University Press.

Selznick, P. (1966). *TVA and the grass roots* (original edition, 1949). New York: Harper Torchbooks.

Seo, M.-G., & Creed, W. E. D. (2002). Institutional contradictions, praxis, and institutional change: A dialectical perspective. *Academy of Management Review, 27,* 222–247.

Sewell, W. H., Jr. (1992). A theory of structure: Duality, agency, and transformation. *The American Journal of Sociology, 98,* 1–29.

Smith, B. M. (2001). *Toward rational exuberance: The evolution of the modern stock market.* New York: Farrar Straus and Giroux.

Strauss, A. L., & Corbin, J. (1998). *Basics of qualitative research: Techniques and procedures for developing grounded theory.* Thousand Oaks, CA: Sage Publications.

Suddaby, R., & Greenwood, R. (2005). Rhetorical strategies of legitimacy. *Administrative Science Quarterly, 50,* 35–57.

Sutton, J. R., & Dobbin, F. (1996). The two faces of governance: Responses to legal uncertainty in U.S. Firms: 1955–1985. *American Sociological Review, 61,* 794–811.

Swidler, A. (1986). Culture in action: Symbols and strategies. *American Sociological Review, 51,* 273–286.

Thornton, P. H., & Ocasio, W. (1999). Institutional logics and the historical contingency of power in organizations: Executive succession in the higher education publishing industry, 1958–1990. *American Journal of Sociology, 105,* 801–843.

Van Antwerp, W. C. (1914). *The stock exchange from within.* New York: Doubleday, Page & Company.

Vaughn, D. (1992). Theory elaboration: The heuristics of case elaboration. In: C. Ragin & H. Becker (Eds), *What is a case? Exploring the foundations of social inquiry.* New York: Cambridge University Press.

Zajac, E. J., & Westphal, J. D. (2004). The social construction of market value: Institutionalization and learning perspectives on stock market reactions. *American Sociological Review, 69*(3), 433–457.

Zuckerman, E. W. (2000). Focusing the corporate product: Securities analysts and de-diversification. *Administrative Science Quarterly, 45,* 591–619.

MESOECONOMICS: BUSINESS CYCLES, ENTREPRENEURSHIP, AND ECONOMIC CRISIS IN COMMERCIAL BUILDING MARKETS

Thomas D. Beamish and Nicole Woolsey Biggart

ABSTRACT

Both neoclassical and Keynesian economists have widely favored the use of equilibrium models to understand economic activity, but dramatic periods of change such as the current global economic downturn are poorly understood by assuming equilibrium. The economist Joseph Schumpeter tried to inject dynamism and disequilibrium into economic models by arguing for the role of entrepreneurs in creating microeconomic change, and for examining long-term macroeconomic change as represented in business cycles. No economist, including Schumpeter, has ever connected these two approaches to change and these approaches are not typically used as alternative and complementary ways of viewing transformation over time. We suggest that these theories can be connected in a "mesoeconomic" institutional analysis rooted in economic sociology; we demonstrate this connection by examining the US commercial building industry. This industry has changed in qualitatively distinct ways over

Markets on Trial: The Economic Sociology of the U.S. Financial Crisis: Part B
Research in the Sociology of Organizations, Volume 30B, 245–280
Copyright © 2010 by Emerald Group Publishing Limited
All rights of reproduction in any form reserved
ISSN: 0733-558X/doi:10.1108/S0733-558X(2010)000030B012

the past two centuries in what we call market orders, economic orders sometimes lasting for decades or more. In each market order, entrepreneurs of different sorts are able to flourish and push forward institutional changes that result in long-term economic shifts. Credit and finance have been pivotal influences in each market order, a factor supporting Schumpeter's focus on entrepreneurial action and speculation and one not largely discussed today. We view the recent disruption of financial markets as a signal of the destruction of a reigning market order.

INTRODUCTION

Neoclassical economics has been by far the dominant theoretical orientation for understanding our economy in recent decades, trumping institutional economics and a range of less widely known schools of thought, such as evolutionary economics. Neoclassical economics relies on general equilibrium models that aggregate the activities of many different presumably rational individuals, models that have proven extremely useful when the conditions assumed by them are approximated. Periods of change, however, are poorly understood through models predicated on stasis and a belief that markets are always in a process of self-correcting. The financial collapse that took place in 2008–2009 exposed the limits of equilibrium models to explain markets in crisis.

As a consequence, widespread criticism of neoclassical economists' inability to foresee the collapse and to articulate plans to mitigate the financial disintegration emerged. One noteworthy critic was former Federal Reserve Chairman Alan Greenspan, who admitted that he had expected market actors to conduct themselves according to the principles of neoclassical theory[1] and not as they actually had behaved. Nobel laureate Paul Krugman's recent *mea culpa* is among the recent statements but economic self-criticism goes back decades and reflects continuing conflicts between Krugman's own neo-Keynesian view and a more traditional neoclassical view expressed by the Chicago School (Krugman, 2009).

Keynesianism differs from neoclassical economics in its assumption that the actions of rational, private sector individuals and firms can lead to market failure and that markets therefore cannot be assumed to be self-correcting. Keynesians advocate activist fiscal policies on the part of central governments as critical for stimulating aggregate demand in times of crisis.[2] Keynes believed that governments could flatten economic downturns by stimulating the macroeconomic system as a whole.

Despite their macroeconomic differences, neoclassical and Keynesian theories make similar microeconomic assumptions. Both theoretical perspectives assume that economic agents are rational and independent, seek to maximize profits, and have equal access to full and relevant information. Moreover, these perspectives overlook qualitative changes in the economy, such as political, institutional, or technological changes, instead focusing only on economic variables amenable to quantitative description, such as supply, demand, and price.

One important economic theorist, Joseph Schumpeter, critiqued the inherently static assumptions of equilibrium models. Schumpeter seriously grappled with capitalist markets as dynamic systems at both the micro- and macroeconomic levels of analysis. At the microeconomic level, Schumpeter argued for attention to the role of entrepreneurs in creating change. He saw entrepreneurism as a category of economic action that both individuals and firms could pursue, and significantly, as a form of action that distinguished capitalism from previous economic orders. The capacity to innovate under capitalism allows entrepreneurs to break with established economic practices and arrangements, potentially resulting in fundamental transformation of an economic order, a process he termed "creative destruction."

Schumpeter also examined macroeconomic change by observing business cycles that take shape as interrelated "waveforms"[3] (Schumpeter, 1934; Schumpeter, 1939). Schumpeter's attention to business cycles reflected his critique of Walrasian general equilibrium economics. Though a fan of Walras, Schumpeter believed that elegant but static equilibrium models could not explain capitalism's hallmark: its progressive transformation over time (Ingham, 2003, p. 298).

Although not a central figure today, Schumpeter is the only prominent economic thinker who consistently engaged in both structural and agent-level theorizing in order to explain economic change. Schumpeter, however, never explicitly connected his microeconomic and macroeconomic theories. Indeed, no contemporary economic theory connects microeconomic and macroeconomic understandings; *there is no "mesoeconomics."*

We believe, however, that microeconomics and macroeconomics can be connected in an intermediate institutional analysis informed by economic sociology. A mesoeconomics founded on economic sociology and other forms of institutional social science can addresses the elements that underlie stability, change, and economic crisis. Sociologists, political scientists, economic anthropologists, and related thinkers utilize methods, which allow them to capture both temporal and qualitative change in the organization of economies, as opposed to simply the growth and contraction of an economy in waves over time (Block, 1977; Zelizer, 1983; Biggart, 1989;

Fligstein, 1996; Dobbin & Dowd, 1997). Our intent in this article is to suggest a way in which economic sociology can productively bridge the gap between microeconomics and macroeconomics, thereby providing insight into change in economic orders.

We view the sum total of a stable micro-, meso-, and macroeconomic continuity as a qualitatively distinct type of economy that we call a *market order*. Market orders are a collection of durable institutional arrangements and practices spanning individual levels to even supra-national levels and may include formal laws and regulations, government organizations, firms and investors, and conventional practices. Market order institutions share a logic that is sufficiently integrative so as to allow action without routine conflicts or misunderstandings. Institutional logics include material and cultural elements as well as concrete social practices (Alford & Friedland, 1985). Market order institutions' shared understanding of what is "normal" and "appropriate" permits routine interaction, although logics may be contested, weakly held or in the process of transformation (see Thornton & Ocasio, 2008 for a review).

Dramatic changes in previous forms of market organization, including those that preceded the current financial collapse, represent shifts toward new market orders. We view sociopolitical factors as critical bridges between macroeconomic and microeconomic explanations. We do not propose a theory, but instead illustrate how attention to middle range factors can enhance our understanding of microeconomic and macroeconomic market changes by examining the recent financial collapse of the commercial buildings market.

THE COMMERCIAL BUILDING MARKET

We examine the past 200 years of the US commercial building market, one of this country's largest economic sectors, to illustrate how middle-range institutional factors help explain both macroeconomic cycles (i.e., booms and busts) and microeconomic shifts caused by entrepreneurial action. We document three distinct mesoeconomic market orders in US commercial real estate. We term these utility, speculative, and hedge market orders and describe in detail the conditions that led to their rise and fall. Although other sectors of the building industry coexist and overlap with commercial real estate and construction, particularly residential, private owner driven, and the institutional (e.g., schools, government buildings, University, and hospitals), the market orders we examine are large, economically influential, and clearly distinct from these others.[4] Unlike some industries, building construction tends to be geographically limited to a few regional firms, with most lacking a national footprint. The sorts of global influences that one sees in industries such as manufacturing and even cultural industries (cf. Zeitlin & Herrigel, 2000) tend not to extend to commercial construction.[5] Change from one period to another represented different entrepreneurial opportunities that reflected emerging macroeconomic trends. Firms and actors involved in actually constructing buildings were more likely to reposition themselves in response to new opportunities than to develop wholly new relationships (see McDermott (2003) for an example of similar repositioning in another context). As buildings became commoditized, however, actors with new financial products such as commercial mortgage-backed securities (CMBS) entered the market. Intermediate-level factors, however, were critical in creating new opportunities and closing off others. Meso-level factors include material and technological changes, new skills and expertise, changing production networks, new urban development patterns, real estate taxes, and new sources and terms for investment capital. Alone, each factor was modest in its transformative effect, but collectively they created opportunities for entrepreneurs to dramatically alter the nature of commercial construction markets.

The collapse in the commercial building industry that is underway in 2010 and is likely to continue into 2011 and even beyond, we believe, is best understood as the outcome of institutional and technological factors – mesoeconomic opportunity structures for entrepreneurs that reflect macro-level economic, political, and social factors. Middle-range or "mesoeconomic" influences are critical for understanding the rise and fall of market orders. Classically conceived economic factors obviously play a significant role but the dynamic is more complex than an econometric model can demonstrate.

In what follows, we recount the creation and destruction of distinct market orders in the commercial construction industry. Strongly conventionalized conduct, entrepreneurial zeal, and dynamic business cycles are all characteristic of this industry (Eccles, 1981a; Eccles, 1981b; Stinchcombe, 1959). Through our historical examination of commercial construction we illustrate our larger point: *economic change reflects the conjuncture of macrostructural trends and micro agents situated in intermediate institutional contexts. Stable micro-, meso-, and macroeconomic arrangements represent a market order.* Our analysis also suggests another way to view those economic moments when "creation" runs second to "destruction": moments when entrepreneurial activity destabilizes established equilibrium and dramatic change, even financial crisis, results.

MARKET ORDERS: 200 YEARS OF
COMMERCIAL BUILDING

The commercial building market is one of the largest markets in the United States. In 2007, the total US construction industry represented by commercial, residential, and industrial accounted for 14 percent of the $10 trillion US GDP (McGraw-Hill Construction Research & Analytics, 2006). In 1995, commercial construction alone represented 9.5 percent of the US gross domestic product at $642 billion (Gause, 1998). In 2007, the nation's stock in commercial structures was valued at more than $3 trillion over one-tenth of US privately held wealth (Meeks, 2008). Since 1960, the industry has added more than 9.22 billion sq. ft. of floor space to its total US inventory of 11 billion sq. ft. (This translates into roughly 44 sq. ft. per capita or 200 sq. ft. per white-collar employee; see Goettsch, 1993, pp. 22–23.). What is more, commercial real estate provides one of the banking industry's central profit making activities. In 2008, loans for commercial real estate accounted for 24 percent of the banking industry's books, some $1.7 trillion, which is comparable to the now busted residential real estate loans that for the same period accounted for 28 percent of the industries books (Meeks, 2008). But this percentage is not spread equally among lenders. The smaller, regional banks are much more highly exposed with 40 percent of their loans represented in commercial real estate ventures while with the big domestic banks this figure drops to 17 percent (see Downs, 2009; Meeks, 2008 for extended discussion).

The level of exposure coupled with the severity of the recent economic downturn – originating both inside and outside the commercial buildings market – lead us to expect a new market order to emerge as economic growth commences sometime in the future. As of September 2009, the commercial building market stands humbled; nationally, commercial buildings on average have lost nearly 30 percent of their precrisis value (DallasNews.Com, September 30, 2009). Until 2005, commercial buildings were typically constructed in what we call a "hedge" market order, reflecting buildings' role as hedge investments in institutional investors' portfolios. In the 1980s, the hedge market order replaced the "speculative market order" which emerged in the late 1940s with the growth of the post-World War II economy. Before that, and extending back to the earliest commercial construction in the United States, construction was organized by a "utility" market order. These three market orders are distinct, if overlapping institutional regimes.

Buildings as Utilitarian Infrastructure

The earliest market order emphasized buildings' utility as a place to house workers and wares. Red brick factories and mills were typical manifestations of commercial buildings in the nineteenth century, a period of rapid industrial growth. The construction industry was transforming from a premarket, feudal system of local craft production to a nascent market with a local focus and an increasingly technical, professionalized division of labor. Changing building practices coevolved with societal changes including brisk population growth and urbanization, rapid concentration of capital, the expansion of professions and labor differentiation, and an accompanying increase in technical knowledge. When a steady market for buildings began to emerge, the profitability of constructing buildings increased as well. Profitability promoted the emergence of local entrepreneurs who took advantage of new advances in architectural and technological expertise to create structures more appealing to industrial firms and to corporations, which increasingly wanted buildings to symbolically represent their newfound economic power (Davis, 1999).

From antiquity through the early eighteenth century, a master builder[6] was hired to design and oversee a small coterie of tradespeople to construct an entire structure from start to finish. By the 1750s, however, intersecting trends were transforming the building trades, the buildings they built, and the reasons for building them. First, this period saw the first intensification of demand for buildings as cities in Europe and the United States began to grow. Architectural knowledge was being codified to the degree that schooled professionals – architects and master builders with specialized technical design and engineering knowledge – were increasingly involved in the construction process. As such building knowledge was applied, typical structures became larger and more complex. This had the added effect of increasing the capital intensity of such projects. The capital intensity, in turn, fostered higher profits for the master builders and led to the commensurate accumulation of capital in the hands of entrepreneurial builders. Finally, municipalities were playing an increasingly important role in overseeing and requiring that general standards be met, which also pushed builders toward a standardized building (Davis, 1999) (see Table 1).

By the middle of the nineteenth century, these trends had pushed building and construction processes in relatively formalized and technical directions and with that greater divisions of labor and specialization (Bourdon &

Table 1. The Utility Market Order.

Macroeconomic Developments	Mesoeconomic Market Order	Microeconomic Entrepreneurism
Banking and finance changes Rapid concentration of capital	Industry is almost entirely local/regional	Greater capital intensity means higher profit margins
Early capitalism follows boom-bust business cycles	Land prices and technological innovations increase the capital intensity of buildings and they are forced to go vertical	Local entrepreneurial activity begins
Capital circuits are mostly local/regional with some national and very little international investment	Market emergence begins	Late: Investment builder emerges – engages in partnerships to pool local capital
Demographic and labor market changes Rapid urbanization and increased central business district density	High demand for utilitarian buildings for administrative and production purposes	Early: Emergence of master builders
Rapid population explosion	In boom-bust environment, larger construction firms emerge, but industry retains craft-network structure	Local master builders and later investment builders populate industry looking for profitable opportunities
Rapid expansion and specialization of the labor force	Guilds expand and develop networks of "building trades" Quasi-formalization of building processes vis-a-vis networked role structures of professions	Small scale speculative construction emerges in preeminent urban centers (New York, London, Paris, Chicago)
Technological and infrastructural changes Rapid industrial growth; energy intensification; transport and communication technologies	Architectural and engineering designs are increasingly specialized and codified	Late: Overtime increasing capital costs pushes entrepreneurs toward partnerships and consortiums to build buildings
Rapid technological innovation in metallurgy, mechanics, steam power, electricity, and electrical lighting	Innovations in the use of steel "I" beams, ventilation, stink-trap toilet, and lifts allow buildings to exceed 10 stories	
Governance and regulatory changes Middle to late: Largest municipalities begin enforcing basic building standards; basic health and safety measures emerge during this period as well	Middle to late: Industry incorporates building, health, and safety standards into technical and design considerations; in conjunction with other technological and infrastructural changes this increases the capital intensity of buildings	Middle to late: Over time increasing capital costs push entrepreneurs toward partnerships and consortiums to build buildings

Levitt, 1980; Eccles, 1981a). Such trends, however nascent, distinguish this period from earlier ones for its development of those elements that enabled a true market for commercial buildings began to take shape. Despite these changes, the craft-guild system characteristic of the trades and the construction process were still largely in place as they had been since the Renaissance (Finkel, 1997).

The Emergence of Building Markets

Massive urban expansion between 1850 and 1930 both reflected and propelled the growth of local and regional economies in Europe and the United States. These, in turn, fueled further increases in population, capital accumulation, and consumptive demands, which promoted construction projects that were truly commercial in nature. Larger construction firms emerged as did the further division of the construction trades into ever more specialized and technical niches (Chandler, 1977; Miles & Snow, 1994). For a few entrepreneurial builders in the very largest industrial cities, these developments also opened the way for the speculative construction and sale of buildings for profit.

Certainly, greater economic activity added to the demand for commercial buildings, and entrepreneurs stepped up to take advantage of the opportunity. However, middle-range mesoeconomic developments were critical: urban expansion and industrial demand for buildings, a production organization conducive to entrepreneurial activity, and technological innovations that would both standardize the building form and propel buildings to new forms and heights.

Urban Expansion

By the late nineteenth century, incredible demand had developed for office buildings, warehouse space, and production facilities. The rise of water- and coal-powered energy production, mass-production techniques, and railroad transportation created opportunities for the growth of manufacture and market size. Communication and transport technologies drove economic agglomeration in the major cities, especially those that were "transfer points" for goods and services (Storper & Walker, 1989). The massive expansion of these cities further promoted a vast influx of people, jobs, and capital (Chandler, 1977; Heilbrun, 1963). Increased urban density reduced available space in what became the nerve centers of industrial capitalism – central business districts (CBDs). This precipitously raised the demand for real estate and the corresponding land values in these areas. The increased concentration of commercial enterprise in city centers forced those who could not afford them out and provided the motivation for those who could to pay the premium to build increasingly large, technically complex, and vertical buildings (Shlaes & Weiss, 1993).

A true market for buildings reflected economic cycles and development trends including urban expansion, capital accumulation, extensive industrialization, and corresponding corporate consolidation (Perrow, 2002; Roy, 1997). The period's economic expansion produced huge firms as well as a massively expanded state bureaucracy that required buildings to house their white- and blue-collar workers (MacCormac, 1992).[7] Reflecting the demand for functional work and production spaces, the first true office buildings began to appear in the 1830s, insignificant structures by today's standards at three to five stories, but impressive in their day. Buildings of this scale continue to provide the core of commercial office development (Willis, 1995). The reigning market order of the day reflected buildings' utilitarian purpose: *buildings were primarily financed and constructed for their functional utility as shelter, not as an end in and of themselves, nor was their construction a means of profit making per se* (Willis, 1995).

During this early period the emblematic importance of corporate headquarters developed, and the emergence of a nascent speculative market for office buildings began in industrial centers such as London, New York, and Chicago. Taking after the civic tradition of the official palazzo, corporate headquarters stand as symbolic representations of their owners (MacCormac, 1992). Epitomized in skyscrapers – officially buildings over 35–40 stories (Gause, 1998) – such as the Empire State (1930) and Chrysler buildings (1929) – office towers reflected corporate "egonomics" (Mattill, 1986) in which the big, extremely expensive structures signaled the wealth and power of a firm. Yet, even "trophy buildings" were built for their functional utility as well as their symbolic power as capitalist icons (Feagin & Parker, 1990; Landau & Condit, 1996; Lehman, 1974; Shales & Weiss, 1993; Shultz & Simmons, 1959).

While symbolically important, skyscrapers were and remain a peripheral form. For example, in Pittsburgh, a city rarely noted for its commercial business core, over 400 commercial office buildings were completed in the final years of the 1880s. The city would not have a single skyscraper until after WWII (Shultz & Simmons, 1959). Until 1960, only five cities in the United States had more than two buildings taller than 25 stories: New York, Chicago, Detroit, Philadelphia, and Pittsburgh. Skyscrapers continue to be relatively insignificant indicators of the larger industry's production even if they represent the technical achievements of the industry and the capital prowess of a firm or nation.

The trend was the growth of speculative investments in building developments (Harvey, 1985; Lefebvre, 1970, 1996). In the mid-nineteenth century, the speculative or "unit building," as it was then called, reflected the explosion in CBD construction and rapidly increasing real estate prices in New York and Chicago. For example, in the late nineteenth century, the entrepreneurial Brooks Brothers would be among the first to take advantage of this trend, commercially developing a new class of commercial office space and leasing it in Chicago and other regional CBDs (Gause, 1998). Theirs would become a building type and model copied by other entrepreneurs in New York, London, and continental Europe (MacCormac, 1992).

Networked Production
Fordist production proved uneconomical in commercial construction because of the cyclic nature of the business cycle for buildings: volume and product type varied with time and economic intensity, the geographic distribution of projects was wide (Eccles, 1981a, 1981b; Stinchcombe, 1959; Stinchcombe, 1965), and dependence on skilled and specialized labor all limited its centralized, vertical integration. Thus, unlike other economic sectors, which in the past were craft-based such as glass making, textiles, and smithing, the organization of the construction industry did not develop a formalized division of labor, integration, and centralized administration (Tushman & Anderson, 1997; Utterback, 1994).

As a consequence, building production maintained an independent guild-based character. Even today, specialists subcontract projects as they arise and are based on demand. Moreover, the networked relations of production that existed before 1850 continue in many ways to organize construction. Remnants of the "master builder" system, as embodied by such famous architectural figures as Frank Lloyd Wright and his studio of apprentices, and reflected in craft-based categories, norms, and network configurations, are relatively commonplace (Levine, 1996; Pogrebin, 2004; Sanvio & Konchar, 1999). The industry depends on communities of practice and networks of craft and trade specialists to produce buildings (Bensman & Lilienfeld, 1991; Biggart & Beamish, 2003; Granovetter, 1973; Van Maanen & Barley, 1984).[8] The industry's organization via informal quasi-market production networks of large and small firms has insulated it from other industries that are authoritatively organized.[9]

New Technologies
Ventilation, illumination, and structural integrity have long challenged architects, engineers, and skilled tradespeople who have met the challenges with new materials and techniques (Finkel, 1997; Sanvio & Konchar, 1999; Shales & Weiss, 1993). Technologies hold a dialogic relationship with other considerations – both pushing and pulling the shape the market takes, both literally and figuratively, and what motivates those who participate in it (Bijker & Law, 1997; Hargadon & Douglas, 2001; Hughes, 1983; Hughes, Pinch, & Bijker, 1987; Latour & Woolgar, 1986).

Between 1830 and 1920, technical and material changes in construction enabled the marketizing of the industry. The development of cast iron columns circa 1830 used in the lower floors of buildings, and subsequent development of the steel "I" beam around the 1870s improved the weight-bearing capacity beyond the four- to five-story limits of masonry foundations and cast iron technology. In the 1880s, improvements in cement and reinforced concrete also increased the potential size and complexity of commercial buildings and made possible more standardized building processes and more uniform buildings, thereby improving their market potential. Lifts (circa 1850) and steam-powered Otis elevators (circa 1890s) allowed buildings over 10 stories to become commonplace. The innovation of the 1875 stink trap toilet, electricity circa 1880, ventilation, and environmental controls all transformed the form and content of buildings by making them habitable over a greater range of conditions.

Each new technology also added to the commercial potential of buildings and supported the industry's transformation toward an investor-driven market order. That is, while these improvements greatly improved the rentable, leasable, salable qualities of buildings as material objects, they simultaneously vastly increased the capital intensity of buildings and standardized them, making them more appealing as tradable commodities.

Market Emergence and Market Crisis
The sustained economic expansion of CBDs in the 1920s, coupled with marked improvements in building technologies and the increased expertise of architects, engineers, and builders, enabled a surge in office construction (see Fig. 1). With the 1929 stock market crash, however, city center development was halted for another 20 years.[10] While the years immediately following World Wars I and II would be golden eras for "large-scale property development" (Feagin & Parker, 1990; Gause, 1998; Shales & Weiss, 1993), until then, commercial construction markets remained mostly local and regional, despite technological advances.

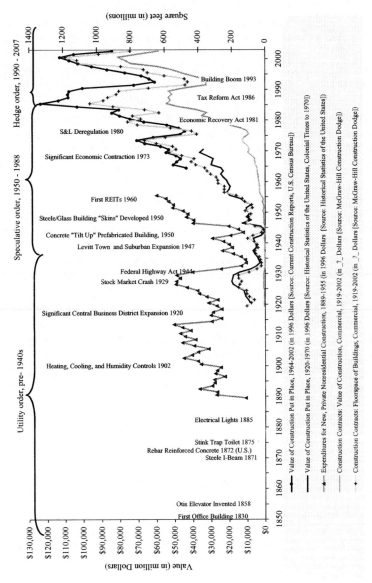

Fig. 1.   Market Trends and Market Orders.

By this time, exchange was governed by a production network embedded in a market context, but most activities were still relatively localized and conducted by individual developer-entrepreneurs who pursued small-scale building projects as "investment builders" (Gause, 1998). Investment builders typically constructed their properties with the intention of holding them for an indefinite period of time. Most of these commercial buildings were financed through relatively simple schemes such as partnerships that involved regional sources of capital (Davis, 1999). In especially ambitious projects that required great capital outlays and financial commitments, prominent and mostly local entrepreneurs would gather investors and pool resources or, rarer yet, long-term mortgages were arranged with insurance companies (called "takeout commitments"). These projects and financial schemes were unusual at this time and took place only in a handful of elite urban centers and the market order remained firmly rooted in a utility conception of buildings. Early speculators emerged and outside sources of capital were occasionally tapped, and custom corporate headquarters and skyscrapers were sporadically being commissioned. More typically, however, investment-builders either built buildings to occupy and use for manufacturing or they hoped to profit as landlords of commercial properties they themselves had constructed.

A market order characterized by a new type of entrepreneur who constructed buildings to quickly "flip" them for a profit, who raised outside capital from beyond their immediate partners, and who viewed commercial buildings as "strategic assets" would not emerge until after WWII. At that time, a new real estate entrepreneur emerged, which precipitated a change to a new market order. These entrepreneurs would become known as commercial developers.

A Speculative Market Order

With the close of WWII, the United States began an unprecedented economic expansion (Gans, 1967; Logan & Molotch, 1987; Molotch, 1976; Molotch, 1993; Rome, 2001). Unlike earlier commercial trends focused in CBDs, however, by the late 1950s, development was flowing out of the urban centers along the expanding federal and state highway systems. Financed through the Federal Highway Act of 1944, new roads and highways encouraged development areas away from cities, setting the stage for massive suburban migrations (Rome, 2001). The expansion invigorated the construction of offices and other commercial structures.

Schumpeter's claim that entrepreneurs are the dynamic force behind economic change (see Swedberg, 2002, 2006) is evident in the entrepreneurial efforts of a new form of businessperson, the "commercial developer." Real estate developers transformed the market for buildings away from a utility-based market order toward a speculative one (Feagin & Parker, 1990; Gause, 1998; Shales & Weiss, 1993). As a result, the market for commercial buildings quickly expanded from its local and regional focus toward a national and international marketplace that traded in buildings as products. A key aspect of the commercial developers' entrepreneurial success was increased access to credit and capital circuits. US tax laws also gave a powerful incentive to industry outsiders to invest in commercial real estate. Institutional investors such as insurance companies and pension funds, big national and international lenders, and wealthy individuals increasingly looked at commercial construction, especially office construction, for its profit potential and for tax benefits.

Buildings became financial assets and secondarily utilitarian products. Functional adequacy was all that was required of design and construction. A market order motivated to construct buildings as strategic financial assets became the dominant organizing logic and remained so until the mid-1980s (White & Adler, 1993). Commercial developers tried to profit from development trends by producing commercial structures that cashed in on the rapid appreciation of real estate holdings (Feagin & Parker, 1990; Rome, 2001; Squires, 2002).[11] While this market order followed the economic principles of buying low and selling high, what did change was the increasingly nonlocal character of investment interests within it. Commercial development firms were often geographic outsiders and they tapped national and international capital for their prospective projects (Feagin & Parker, 1990; Pygman & Kateley, 1985).[12] The commercial developer, reflecting Schumpeter's attention to the role of credit as a basic aspect of capitalist dynamism (Ingham, 2003; Schumpeter, 1936, pp. 70–72), provided a key linkage between the wider circulation of capital via money markets and the construction market that had not been fully realized (Harvey, 1985).

Taking advantage of the postwar economic boom and the suburban growth surge, by the 1960s developers found it profitable to take out loans in advance of construction and quickly build and sell buildings as speculators. Investors, in turn, often bought these properties with resale in mind as demand was so great that with each sale a profit could still be made. By the mid-1970s, speculative construction was the norm – a situation where a developer neither had clients ready to buy nor tenants ready to lease. This was the reverse of the previous market order and also contrasts with today's real estate market. Unlike builders in the previous utility order, speculative developers *assumed* market demand. By the early 1980s, a wide range of investors had entered the market wanting in on the profits and a bandwagon effect ensued: banks and others competed for stakes in projects and pushed the rigor and criteria for creditworthiness and developer personal stake to all time lows. At its zenith, lenders required as little as 10 percent personal equity stake by developers, virtually handing over capital in what became a speculative bubble (Abolafia & Kilduff, 1988).[13]

Indeed, it was during this period that developers learned to make their profits on the loans and highly leveraged equity arrangements rather than on the sale of buildings. Leveraging involves borrowing or acquiring equity commitments as a high percentage of the costs of a given project, in this era as much as 20–30 percent *more* than the actual out-of-pocket costs of a project. One ramification of the low developer stake and high appreciation rates that ruled development during this time was that developers could demand much of investors but were themselves insulated from the risks of their undertakings.

The dynamics of macroeconomic structures and micro-entrepreneurial activity also held consequences for the kind of commercial projects that were being conceived, designed, and built. Developers and other short-term investors were seeking ever-faster means of delivering buildings to the market as well as cheaper ways of constructing them to enhance their profits. This pushed standardization in both building design and building processes. Trends in prefabrication and reliance on cheaper materials such as rebar and concrete reflect buildings' reconceptualization under a speculative market order. Since developers had no long-term interest in these properties, attention to detail and the quality of the product declined. "Tilt-up" buildings made of preformed concrete slabs embodied the new market order's logic, reflecting the changed economic strategy and esthetics that developed after WWII (see Table 2).[14]

A massive influx of capital from new sources generated a "gold rush" mentality that, in turn, significantly expanded the volume and size of the market in a very short time. In the 1970s and 1980s, savings and loans associations, large pension funds, and insurance companies increased their presence in debt and equity investments and began purchasing properties outright. Especially important to this surge in investment capital was money from the newly deregulated banking sector. Banks and savings and loan associations were able to offer depositors competitive rates and federally backed deposit insurance as well as a new ability to invest in nonresidential

Table 2. The Speculative Market Order.

Macroeconomic Developments	Mesoeconomic Market Order	Microeconomic Entrepreneurism
Banking and finance changes		
Capital circuits expand to include national and international investors	National and eventually international investors target commercial real estate	National/international investment groups and commercial developers link up on large capital-intensive projects
Massive post-WWII economic expansion	New demand for office, warehouse, and industrial facilities	Late: Commercial developers use "leveraging" to maximize profits
Late: Financialization of US industry begins during the latter half of this period as national and international capital circuits seek investments to manage their liquidity problems. Specifically, institutional investors grow their stake in industrial/business enterprises	Late: Financialization of the industry begins. Non-local investment and investment competition lead to low interest loans that transform the market order with an emphasis on buildings as "financial instruments"	
Hyper growth and heady economic times	Speculation emerges with high demand and (virtually) free loan money	Late: Entrepreneurs build assuming demand; market eventually crashes
Demographic and labor market changes		Early: Emergence of new industry entrepreneur: *commercial developers* who take advantage of profligate real estate opportunities
Technological and infrastructural changes		
Federal and state highway construction and suburban infrastructural development	Creation of suburban transportation corridors fuels massive demand for buildings	
Rapid technological innovation across industries	Building production processes morph to match the speculative quick flip credo – reflected in standardized building designs, pre-fabrication, cheaper materials, and tilt-up construction	
Governance and regulatory changes		
Liberalization of tax and investment laws	New tax laws incentivize commercial development	Entrepreneurial use of buildings as financial assets (appreciation, depreciation, and tax write-offs) Demand coupled with US tax laws incentivize quickly flipping or losing money on buildings

properties. These changes promoted the boom in office construction that took place between 1980 and 1991 (see Fig. 1).

Real estate entrepreneurs also developed new sources of equity and debt in order to take advantage of the massive influx of capital presented by the period's rapid economic expansion. Real estate syndicates and real estate investment trusts (REITs) were created to pool and thus leverage smaller investor money that had yet to be tapped for commercial development (McCoy, 1988).[15] Financial instruments such as these, invented in the 1970s, were also very popular with investors because tax laws and liberalized rules governing real estate investment made it a very attractive tax shelter. REITS provide income tax relief so long as 90 percent of their taxable income is returned to shareholders.

The financialization of the industry also began during this period (Feagin & Parker, 1990; Krippner, 2005). Pension fund investors could write off federal taxes by investing in REITs, which significantly increased available capital for development purposes. Likewise, the liberal real estate tax laws of the 1970s and 1980s also encouraged the well off to invest in real estate mortgage investment conduits (REMICs) to shelter their incomes from taxation (Roulac, 1993).

The expansion of market-actor motives and relations based on these changes both mirrored and reinforced the rise of a market order that by the late 1970s was almost wholly speculative as reflected in industry investment decision making and practices. Hyper growth and high returns on investment had become an expectation, especially in markets for commercial office and commercial space.[16] In fact, from 1979 until 1989, the industry would engage in the greatest building boom in US history (see Fig. 1). As much as half of the office and commercial space ever built in the United States was constructed during this 10-year period (Gause, 1998).

Investors did not approach buildings as long-term commitments or in some cases even as profit-seeking investments. Ironically, losing money could be the inspiration behind investment in commercial development as it afforded significant tax advantages. "With so much money available, some developers ignored questions of economic viability of projects ..." (Feagin & Parker, 1990); bigger losses just meant bigger tax write-offs. In short, buildings were being built for reasons other than those typically attributed to merchant builders: entrepreneurial capital was so available and developers with good reputations and previous development successes were so insulated from risk that they could make money on the loans themselves without fear of loss, since there was little rigor and often poorly executed analysis of prospective projects (Gause, 1998). Others simply sought to lose money to protect their incomes through tax write-offs.

In the end, however, transformation away from a speculative market order would reflect the destruction of the associated speculative bubble. The massive influx of outside investor money into real estate worked to increase dramatically the capital available to property developers, which stimulated a building frenzy out of step with demand. It would lead to extraordinarily overbuilt CBDs and suburbs; even soaring demand could not absorb the incredible explosion in supply. Nevertheless, because the financial schemes that drove investment and construction insulated those developers and rewarded others for failure, the boom continued well past the capacity of local markets to absorb the new square footage of office and commercial space (Roulac, 1985, 1993). The speculative market order emphasized commercial structures less as physical artifacts that provided physical space and more as strategic financial assets constructed to be "flipped" for profit.

The real estate bubble of the late 1980s reflected both the organizational and normative power of the speculative market order to overshadow emergent market realities. At first this market order involved relatively risk-insulated developer-entrepreneurs who constructed and profited primarily on credit. Even as overbuilt cities and townscapes threatened to render investment money worthless, lenders and investors continued to channel money to developers to build new commercial properties. Thus, the prevailing market order promoted a "speculative bubble" (Abolafia, 1996; Abolafia & Kilduff, 1988) that led to a financial crisis in the industry. Investors seemed to pay little attention to the "objective state of market" as represented in vacancy rates, square feet being produced, and other indicators of "demand" because they relied on developers to assess the market and they shared an investment ethic with them that emphasized buildings as low risk, quick, and high yield sources of cash and/or as lucrative tax shelters. In this context, the signal that unrented, unleased, and empty buildings should have sent potential investors went unheeded. The speculative market order focused on getting money in and out quickly with the assumption that any building would sell once it hit the market.

By 1987, however, the boom was over and with it the speculative market order. First, changes to the federal tax code – a revision of the Tax Revision Act of 1986[17] – severely undercut real estate's attractiveness as a tax shelter by making financial losses in real estate unattractive (Bettner, 1990). Second, the inability to fill properties with tenants or to sell properties once constructed eventually reduced investor incentives when the tax revision act took full effect. In the end, the economic downturn and the acutely overbuilt CDB and suburban corridors left investors no returns and many vacant properties. Even syndicates and REITs, created to leverage capital from diverse sources, went from spectacular to flat and in some cases insolvency.

Buildings as Conservative Hedge Investments

Institutional scholars have observed in a range of settings that strategies and practices infused with symbolic value can persist well beyond their "technical merit" for reasons of legitimacy, uncertainty reduction, reliability, and accountability (DiMaggio & Powell, 1991; Hannan & Freeman, 1984; Meyer & Rowan, 1977; Selznick, 1957; Selznick, 1966). In the case of commercial construction, entrepreneurial speculators continued to pursue an economic trajectory that at its zenith was almost entirely detached from the "real economy" of building production, leasing and sales, and occupation. The outcome was a market crash. While boom and bust cycles are not uncharacteristic of commercial construction, the economic bust and recession of the late 1980s was transformative, altering the industry's underlying investment motives and with them the conceptualization of commercial buildings as investable products. By the 1990s, the commercial building industry had transitioned from a "get-rich-quick" speculative market order to its near opposite, a market order that redefined buildings as long-term conservative investments that could act as a hedge in portfolios with more volatile assets such as stocks. Buildings were no longer valued for their quick appreciation but rather for their ability to generate predictable rental income over a decade or more (see Table 3).

The 1980s crash in real estate markets was a major trough in the business cycle. A large number of commercial developers were in default as they could not sell or lease buildings in a glutted market (Miller, 1999). The market collapse tightened the availability of investment capital – debt, equity, and venture – for commercial building projects of all kinds. Entrepreneurial developers, who survived intact, had to develop new strategies for generating capital because their usual investors had largely disappeared. A new kind of investor-entrepreneur played a significant role in realigning this market around a new model with new financial performance criteria.

By the mid-1990s, pension funds, banking conduits or trusts, mutual funds, and REITS became the biggest source of investment capital in commercial building development. Their prominence worked to "financialize" the real estate sector, subtly and not so subtly reordering the reigning market order.[18] As institutional investors became the most important sources of capital in a recessional real estate market, their preferences reordered the market (McCoy, 1988). Institutional investment funds recognized that real estate is often countercyclical to other assets, and when compared to stocks, bonds and other fixed investments, delivered similar returns without the daily

Table 3. The Hedge Market Order.

Macroeconomic Developments	Mesoeconomic Market Order	Microeconomic Entrepreneurism
Banking and finance changes		
Globalization of capital flows	Globalization of industry investment	Globalization of entrepreneurial interests
Volatile capital markets, new forms of financial securities, and continuing liquidity problems	Brick-and-mortar buildings represent a place to safely park capital assets; demand skyrockets as other markets fail	Real estate used as a hedge against more volatile stocks and bonds in investment portfolios
Financialization of Wall Street	Financialization continues as pension funds, insurance, and REITS become dominant	Change in basic siting, design, and financing options reflective of conservative "hedge" ethos
Capital looking for safe landing	Institutional investors emphasize conservative hedge ethic; other investors follow their lead	
Technological and infrastructural changes		
Overbuilt CBD and suburban environments	Demand continues to skyrocket	Massive entrepreneurial investment pushes market over cliff; bubble bursts, market losses one-third of its value
Governance and regulatory changes		
US Tax Revision Act of 1986; Financial Services Modernization Act of 1999	Speculative development deincentivized	Loss of income security through tax sheltering

fluctuation in market value. Real estate was reinterpreted as a tangible asset that promised more stability over the long term.

The attractiveness of commercial real estate increased in the mid-1990s as the high-tech boom surged because it promised to fill overbuilt urban and suburban properties and to generate the need for new buildings. This made commercial office buildings and real estate appealing to institutional investors who typically favored mid-term and longer-term investments, but who could now also benefit from the traditional trifecta of real estate booms: rapid appreciation rates; tax sheltering depreciation; and if dealing with leased properties, enhanced revenue streams.

As one of the few available sources of capital in a capital-strapped industry, the trend toward increased financialization of real estate accelerated during this time (Collier, Collier, & Halperin, 2002; Feagin & Parker, 1990; Muldavin, 1999). By 2000, fully 89.9 percent of all commercial construction loans originated with institutional lenders (Collier et al., 2002).[19] This had the associated effect of tying real estate markets more tightly to both Wall Street and global capital flows (Roulac, 1993). In turn, this also expanded the influence that these investors had in ordering the commercial building market, given the types of risks they were willing to take, the benefits they sought to secure, and thus what a commercial building was to them (Black, 1994).

Institutional investors were delighted to invest in this new market order; buildings were prized for their "brick and mortar" materiality in contrast to most financial assets. On the other hand, commercial buildings are not merely physical artifacts, since they were seen as strategic hedges in a portfolio of diversified investments. As strategic hedges, commercial buildings are conceptualized as stable products that reap predictable income streams over 5, 10, or 20 years, that guard investment portfolios against inflation, and that counter the perceived short-term volatility of stocks, bonds, and other securities (Miller, 1999).

The hedge market order is an inherently conservative outlook that framed industry decisions at all levels including siting, design, and financing, and the choice of contractors involved in the actual construction of buildings. Indeed, the hedge-based market order influenced the material form office buildings take, explaining the industry's emphasis on what they term "function and flexibility" (Beamish & Biggart, 2010). This market order's buildings are typically nondescript, rectangular structures, three-to-five stories in height, of modest size (50,000–100,000 sq. ft. of floor space), and with open floor plans that can accommodate the widest possible set of future tenants (Gause, 1998). They are also typically designed and constructed by developers, architects, and construction managers with proven credentials since these building are typically not "flipped" but must be refinanced after short-term construction loans come due (Coverdale, 1993). Given this market order, buildings constructed by novice developers, purely for their symbolic value, or entirely for speculative reasons are marketplace anomalies. The norm is a proven developer with a conventional design that can accommodate a wide variety of tenants over the life of a building (Miller, 1999; Steele & Barry, 1988).

The 1990s and early 2000, hedge market order reflected investors, designers, and builders that shared assumptions and expectations about the product as a financial hedge in a portfolio. Buildings that did not conform with the hedge market order – for example, "trophy buildings" that demonstrate singular features and atypical designs – were looked at with skepticism. "Special" buildings were typically privately financed by owner-occupants who wanted to have their business identified with, for example, a "green" building.[20]

2000 to Date: From Hedge to "Financialized" Crisis

By 2000, the stock market, led by high-tech stocks, had crashed but so had commercial construction contracting by nearly 18 percent, leaving the market both ready for investment and reinforcing the conservative investment ethic (Meeks, 2008). To avert a recession, central banks around the world slashed interest rates and flooded their economies with liquidity. The search for investments that could outpace inflation and avoid the declines experienced on Wall Street made real estate investment properties very attractive. The massive influx of capital into commercial building markets in the United States and other developed nations began as gains made in other economic sectors led investors to seek the stability of "real" estate to stabilize their portfolios. The inflow generated investment imbalances in US real estate markets: there was far greater demand than supply of desirable investment properties. Intense competition among investors and lenders to acquire or lend against properties fueled both a drop in lender vigilance and a sharp increase in real estate prices.

In addition to the flood of financial capital from investors fleeing the stock market after the 2000 dot-com crash, banking deregulation in the 1990s radically reorganized the real estate lending processes used by commercial banks and many insurance companies and further contributed to massive inflows of capital into US real estate markets (Downs, 2009). In the mid-1990s, financial innovators, typically math graduates from top universities such as MIT, hired by investment banks like J.P. Morgan, devised new ways for banks to mitigate the risks associated with lending money, and ultimately enabled the industry to push for banking deregulation. One of these innovations was the credit default swap (CDS), one of the most widely used new financial derivatives. CDS can be understood as a form of third-party insurance against loan defaults. In exchange for regular payments from banks, insurance companies like AIG assume the risk of borrower defaults (Philips, 2008).

These new insurance schemes enabled lenders to push for deregulation such as the Financial Services Modernization Act of 1999. This law allowed for the creation of bank holding companies that could set up new, affiliated organizations that were largely unregulated. Unlike the banks, these new organizations could make loans against real properties without holding substantial reserves against the loans until they matured or were repaid. These unregulated new divisions made real estate-related loans, packaged many of these loans together in the form of securities similar to bonds, sold

268 THOMAS D. BEAMISH AND NICOLE WOOLSEY BIGGART

those securities to investors, and then used the funds generated from the sale of the securities to make new rounds of real estate loans, and the process was repeated manifold (Downs, 2009).

CDS, also almost entirely free of government regulation, were sold in vast quantities to supposedly offset the risks associated with complex and nontransparent securities such as the CMBS. The total nominal value of outstanding CDS securities can only be grasped in comparative terms. In 2008, the total nominal value of outstanding CDS securities exceeded $62 trillion. This is three times larger than the total value of all stocks on all American exchanges (at $21 trillion) and 4.4 times larger than the US annual GDP (at $14 trillion). On a global scale, this $62 trillion exceeds the total value of bonds throughout the world at $61 trillion and the total value of all stocks on all world stock markets in May 2008 at $57.5 trillion (Downs, 2009).

By the time it was bailed out by American taxpayers last year, AIG, the country's largest insurance company, held $440 billion of CDS and had defaulted on $14 billion worth of these securities (Philips, 2008). Insurance against loan defaults is unlike other forms of insurance: if one rate payer gets in an automobile accident, it does not necessarily increase the risk of another insured getting into an accident. But when one bondholder defaults on a bond, it can result in a chain reaction because so many financial institutions were linked together through deals. Ultimately, the "insurance" purchased by these financial institutions was rendered meaningless because no insurer can hold sufficient reserves against widespread, reckless lending behavior. Warren Buffett called CDS "financial weapons of mass destruction." Less than a decade after regulations on lending reserves were dismantled, the US government is providing reserves by bailing out financial institutions.

Rising vacancy rates, declining property values, and the collapse of the CMBS market are expected to exacerbate the current economic crisis. According to Reis, a New York-based commercial real estate research firm, the US office vacancy rate increased to 15.9 percent during the second quarter of 2009, the highest level in four years. In the first half of 2009, reflecting the massive layoffs and business closures associated with the economic downturn, tenants vacated 45.2 million sq. ft. of office space nationwide. Because of rising vacancy rates, a growing number of commercial properties fail to generate sufficient cash to make principal and interest payments. Most US commercial properties have declined in value from the time they were first financed. According to Mark Dotzour, chief economist of the Real Estate Center at Texas A&M University, "Every commercial real estate building in the nation has lost 30 percent of its value" (DallasNews.Com, September 30, 2009). In mid-September 2009, New York City-based Real Estate Econometrics predicted that the default rate for bank-held commercial mortgages will increase from 2.8 percent in the second quarter to 4.2 percent in the fourth, and will not peak until 2011. The number of US commercial properties in default, foreclosure or bankruptcy has more than doubled since the end of 2008. Most owners with loans bundled into CMBS (which represent 20 percent of outstanding commercial mortgages) have been unable to refinance (Wei & Grant, 2009).

It is widely anticipated that commercial real estate will be "the next shoe to drop" in the current economic collapse. Ironically, the motives behind recent commercial real estate investments were conservative in nature – they were to be a means to protect investors from the wild and short-term swings of the stock market.

DISCUSSION AND CONCLUSIONS

In our socio-historical account of the commercial real estate industry, we have shown that endogenous changes along with exogenous forces have led to market order transformations over the past 200 years. We have sought to demonstrate that these should be understood at multiple levels of analysis: macro, meso, and micro. Commercial real estate is an industry known for its macroeconomic boom and bust business cycles. Business cycles have reflected diverse causes such as state initiatives like the Highways Act of 1944 and the Tax Reform Act of 1986, and also investment trends that originate on Wall Street such as the financialization of many industries including real estate beginning in the 1980s (Krippner, 2005; Useem, 1996). Commercial real estate is also an industry characterized by entrepreneurial actors who have pressed and generated transformation to their marketplace. Entrepreneurial efforts have been variously led by master builders, owner-occupants, regional business elites, commercial developers, spec-ulators, and most recently, pension fund executives. In this regard, Schumpeter was correct to identify both business cycles and entrepreneurial action as reflecting, expressing, and animating capitalist dynamics.

However, what he and others have missed is that the nexus of exogenous and endogenous factors and forces generate mesoeconomic contexts whose dominant logic and shape play an indelible role in shaping economic action that cannot be reduced to either the macro or micro level of analysis. Thus, elements as diverse as technological and material standards, available knowledge and skills, industry social organization, state initiatives, and variant investment motives reveal the impact that mesoeconomic issues have played in this market's reconfigurations over time. They also reveal, as evidenced by the financial meltdown of 2007 – which was centered in both residential and commercial real estate – the wider impact such mesoeconomic conditions hold and thus have for understanding of larger economic trends and ruptures as well (see Table 4).

The last mesoeconomic market order before the current financial crisis emphasized real estate as a hedge investment and differed from the previous market orders in its financial conservatism (see Table 3). Even earlier market orders were based on commercial buildings as utilitarian objects meant to house workers and production processes (see Table 1), and then after WWII as speculative entrepreneurial endeavors meant to provide relatively quick investor returns or tax shelters for wealth (see Table 2). Each institutional transformation reflected a complex mixture of exogenous environmental factors and endogenous opportunities driven by entrepreneurial interests. In short, mesoeconomic market orders are the institutional nexus of macro and micro conditions that supply a common point of departure from which market actors plan, negotiate, and reproduce buildings as products whether primarily material or financial in conception. Economic action in any given mesoeconomic market order, then, is best conceived of as institutionally embedded behavior – *environmentally influenced, network structured, socially*

Table 4. Mesoeconomic Market Factors.

Mesoeconomic Factors	Role in Order and Change	Examples
1. Technological and material standards	Stability/innovation in technical and material elements	Structural and mechanical materials, codes, and conventions
2. Knowledge and skills	Social heuristics, communities of practice, credentialing promote order; new skills, novel ideas challenge status quo	Engineering, architectural, and financial norms; career traditions and trajectories
3. Social organization	Division of labor and authority; distribution of expertise; forms of interdependence and networks	(Pure) Markets, formal hierarchy, production networks
4. State structures	Government requirements and incentives	Health and safety regulations, zoning and building laws, tax policies and governance requirements
5. Investment motives	Qualitative and quantitative investor preferences define general industry conceptions of product and organize actors	In CC, demand characteristics emanate from investors such as "invest to own," "invest to flip," and "invest to hedge"

organized, and materially present. Market orders, as active social and material constructs, organize the means and ends defined as legitimate and likely to lead to success. Market orders generate social stability for ongoing economic transactions, but may eventually collapse as intermediate conditions such as new motivations, knowledge, targeted tax laws, or technologies shift.

This was indeed the case with commercial construction in the run up to the 2007 financial crisis, even though the dominant ethic before the collapse was ostensibly conservative with investors often approaching commercial properties as hedge investments. Indeed, the rapid financialization and subsequent boom of this market after 2001 reflected its status as a place to *protect profits* gained in this industry and other economic pursuits and sectors. This partly reflected exogenous macroeconomic conditions. In early 2000, to prevent recession, central banks made capital readily available to markets. Many sought a safe landing for their capital by investing in US commercial real estate. The search for investments that could outpace inflation and avoid Wall Street's volatility also made commercial real estate very attractive to domestic investors in the form of pension funds, insurance, banking conduits, mutual funds, and REITS.

Another key development that explains the rapid influx of capital into the commercial real estate market was the banking and investment deregulation of the preceding 40 years, which culminated in the repeal of the Glass–Steagall Act in favor of the Financial Services Modernization Act in 1999 (a.k.a. the Gramm–Leach–Bliley Act). The relatively radical expansion in investment potential this provided banks and investment houses reflected newfound freedom to invest savings deposits into profit making vehicles coupled with the deposit protections provided by the FDIC, which encouraged banks to embrace levels of risk formerly unavailable to them and thus uncorked a great deal of capital for investment. This rapidly took form in new investment vehicles such as CMBS that proliferated in the early 2000s in both residential and commercial real estate sectors and that further amplified the massive flow of investment into these sectors. For example, like residential mortgage-backed securities, CMBS's went from less than $5 billion in the US commercial real estate market in 1995 to over $200 billion in 2005 (Meeks, 2008).

Based on the intense competition, high rates of return, and an increasingly reified, dematerialized, and financialized conception of commercial real estate as a "stable hedge investment," demand far exceeded available supply of "real" brick and mortar buildings. This led to the intensification of entrepreneurial activity and with it competition among investors that fueled further invention and the subsequent proliferation of increasingly arcane investment vehicles that sought to tap the flood of investment dollars.

A corollary trend that also reflected the intense competition for investment was the precipitous drop in lender vigilance and a sharp and sustained increase in real estate prices. Add to this lax governmental oversight that accompanied market deregulation and the making of a mesoeconomic catastrophe was at hand; a "hedge bubble" ensued in commercial real estate that began to unravel in 2007 along with the rest of the economy, but is only now beginning to be felt as defaults on commercial real estate leases mount and the number of vacant properties increases (circa 2009–2013). This is because the business cycle for commercial real estate tends to run 18 months to 2 years behind the larger economy, reflecting lease terms and the delayed economic impact of recession (and growth) on those who typically occupy commercial buildings.

Understanding the interconnected nature of the "inside" and "outside" and the macro and micro aspects of markets in scenarios like those related above requires that one attend to the logics that prevail within the mesoeconomic market orders that describe where economic plans are made and carried out. Market orders are best conceived as mesoeconomic constructs that reflect the intermediate and intersubjective components present at both moments of economic stasis and change, factors not easily captured by Neoclassical, Keynesian, or Schumpeterian models of economic contexts. Even Schumpeter's heroic conceptualization of entrepreneur-driven action does not do so. And while Schumpeter did recognize what Weber called "the spirit of capitalism" and embodied it in his conceptualizations of entrepreneurism, he never developed a fully sociological conceptualization of the economy and economic change. Schumpeter's understanding of entrepreneurism retained a methodological individualist set of presumptions: the efforts of entrepreneurs were essentially antisocial and reflected nothing less than Herculean efforts to resist the collective economic status quo. While we concur that entrepreneurial activity and the economic creativity and destruction those activities can provoke indeed provide capitalism with its dynamic nature, we disagree that entrepreneurism is an individual psychological orientation. Rather, it reflects the social and institutional context within which economic action is carried out. Entrepreneurial action can only be achieved through the successful understanding, conceptualization, and exploitation of intermediate institutional arrangements we have termed mesoeconomic market orders.

By looking at the long-term changes in the market orders that have organized an industry like commercial construction and real estate, one can see the institutionally embedded creativity inherent to entrepreneurial action, and also its role in generating the runaway conditions that constituted economic crises along the way. That is, in accounting for processes of creative destruction, destruction necessarily precedes the valorized "creative" counterpart. Ignoring the process of destruction and the crises that ensue when "entrepreneurism" becomes "speculative gambling," misses at least half of any given change process (see Biggart, 1977) and furthermore skews analysis by uncritically employing loaded assumptions about what constitutes "progress" (Scott, 1998). In seeking to profit by taking advantage of new opportunities, the entrepreneur by definition destabilizes – *destroys* – status quo relations, fundamentally altering both the nature of profit making and with it the known basis for market order. Indeed, as we have recently learned from the 2007 financial crisis, based on the interconnectedness of the current economic system, when things go awry, "entrepreneurial speculation" looks more like "reckless gambling" – a much less heroic activity because it does not simply hurt the isolated entrepreneur but can also undermine the viability of the entire economic system.

NOTES

1. Testifying before Representative Henry Waxman's committee on October 23, 2008, Greenspan was widely quoted when he said, "Those of us who have looked to the self-interest of lending institutions to protect shareholders' equity, myself included, are in a state of shocked disbelief."

2. Keynesians hold that this will increase general economic activity and keep unemployment low, which will further expand the supply of money and stem the threat of a deflationary cycle.

3. These being, Kondratiev (54 years), Kuznets (18 years), Juglar (9 years), and Kitchin (4 years) waveforms.

4. The real estate industry roughly segments commercial construction into three sectors by building type with subtypes within each of these. The sectors are: (1) institutional (i.e., government/nonprofit), (2) private (i.e., owner-occupied homes), and (3) commercial. Commercial real estate is typically further broken down into: (i) office/retail, (ii) industrial/warehouse; and (iii) multifamily residential. Within these categories are further distinctions, such as the class of buildings – A, B, and C – that reflect more local and regional distinctions (Energy Information Administration (EIA), 2004; Collier et al., 2002). Much of what we address in this article also applies to industrial facility and warehouse construction.

5. There are global construction firms, such as Bechtel and CH2MHill, but they are primarily engineering firms and construct major projects such as dams and pipelines. Buildings are incidental to their primary business.

6. In fact, until the eighteenth century, the term "architect" did not mean "designer," as it does today, but referred to the master craftsman who had overall

responsibility for the building project – i.e., design and supervision of the tradesmen on site (Shelby, 1970, p. 22).

7. For example, between 1887 and 1904 business mergers consolidated 15 percent of the nation's business assets creating seventy mega-firms. A second wave of mergers between 1925 and 1930 involved 1/10th of the nation's business assets and involved 12,000 companies (Feagin & Parker, 1990).

8. The structure of the commercial construction market roughly corresponds to scholarship describing "boundaryless organizations" characteristic of the new economy – high-tech, financial services, and other professionally driven subcontracted work spheres (Barley & Kunda, 2001; Powell, 1990) – but is best characterized as a "production network" (Podolny, 1994; Podolny & Page, 1998; Powell, 1990, 1998; Powell, White, Koput, & Owen-Smith, 2005; Smith-Doerr & Powell, 2005; Whitford & Shrank, 2009).

9. This had two important influences on market order. First, heavy reliance on largely informal production networks supports a conservative ethic among practitioners who rely on reputation and rules of thumb to make judgments and that make this market, in many ways, socially closed to outsiders and resistant to change. Second, and paradoxically, while as an industry commercial construction tends to be inward focused, its networked profile and lack of entrenched oligopoly has, overtime, permitted small and large entrepreneurs to prosper and push the industry in new directions, sometime dramatically (Davis, 1999).

10. During WWII, there was a governmental imposed prohibition against using materials needed in war.

11. For example, Trammel Crow emerged in the early to mid-1970s with the urban renewal movement, becoming one of the largest development companies in the United States. By 1986 it was the nation's largest commercial developer, worth $7.5 billion (Ewald, 2005; Forbes, 1986; Kolman, 1986).

12. For example, soon after WWII, Canadian developers (such as the Reichman Brothers of Olympia and York Development Inc. and the Campeau Corporation) became some of the largest developers in the United States.

13. The contemporary market standard calls on developers to invest up to 20–40 percent of their own equity – depending on a number of factors – or most reputable banks will not risk lending money (see Beamish & Biggart, 2002).

14. Tilt-up concrete construction began in southern California in the late 1950s. It represented a quick and economical way to construct concrete walls for offices and warehouses. Today, tilt up construction is ubiquitous and a multibillion dollar industry, accounting for over 10,000 buildings annually.

15. For example, by the 1970s, real estate syndicates alone accounted for one-tenth of new security offerings by large Wall Street firms and REITs accounted for $20 billion or one-fifth of the money loaned out for land development and construction. REITs became so popular as investment vehicles that traditional real estate market investors, such as life insurance companies and major banks, began to spin off their own trusts to leverage development capital.

16. There was a brief contraction in Real Estate Markets from 1973 to 1975, but this was of minimal impact to overall expansionist trends in the market.

17. The movement toward syndication and the desirability of real estate as "quick cash" and/or a "tax shelter" reached its zenith with the *Economic Recovery Tax Act of 1981*. Five years later, with the passage of the *Tax Reform Act of 1986* and the

1987 stock market crash, the industry's easy money profile ended abruptly (Roulac, 1993). The change in tax structure was especially devastating even when the economy began to pick up in the mid-1990s as it deincentivized real estate investment of a certain kind by (1) extending the depreciation period of properties, (2) by revising tax brackets from 55 to 36.9 percentile, and (3) by establishing previously unrecognized distinctions in income (i.e., breaking income into earned, interest/investment, and passive income categories).

18. The rise of institutional investors in commercial real estate is a trend observable across investment sectors (Krippner, 2005; Useem, 1996). Since World War II, institutional investors – pension funds, banking conduits or trusts, mutual funds, and in the case of real estate, REITS – have markedly increased their trading presence. By 1986, institutional investors accounted for 90 percent of the total volume traded on the New York Stock Exchange, while individual investors – who in 1976 had accounted for 30 percent of the volume (Lowry, 1984) – represented less than 10 percent (McCoy, 1988).

19. For example, public securities investment in real estate (all forms) jumped from \$27 billion in 1990 to \$360 billion in 1999 (Muldavin, 1999) and in the first quarter of 2000, institutional lenders represented fully 89.9 percent of loans given for all commercial construction (Collier et al., 2002). By lender type and amount, the breakdown is as follows: commercial mortgage-backed securities or conduits (where an institution, say a bank, makes hundreds of separate real estate loans, bundles them and sells them on Wall Street as a bond) 3,248,282,000 (29 percent); Life Insurance Co. 2,833,969,000 (25.3 percent); Fannie Mae, Freddie Mac, FHA 2,455,805,000 (21.9 percent); Commercial Banks 1,193,108,000 (10.6 percent); Pension Funds 187,614,000 (1.7 percent); Credit Companies 156,942,000 (1.4 percent); Other 1,132,315,000 (10.1 percent); Total 11,208,035,000 (100 percent) (see Collier et al., 2002).

20. Beyond the increasingly prevalent view that skyscrapers, corporate head-quarters, and other "signature buildings" were less flexible and less likely to be resalable, all of the steps to construct a new building – from design to value appraisal – became more complicated and more expensive, requiring incredible time and effort, increased communication, negotiation, and compromise and hence, increased costs and risk. Within this market order, this made the sale, lease, and pricing of commercial buildings increasingly difficult (Willis, 1995).

ACKNOWLEDGMENT

The authors are grateful for support from the California Institute for Energy Efficiency (CIEE), a research unit of the University of California, the Jerome J. and Elsie Suran Chair endowment, and the Institute for Governmental Affairs, University of California, Davis. The final drafts of this article have benefited from the excellent research assistance provided by Dina Biscotti and Nathaniel Freiburger and comments provided by Richard Swedberg, Gerald A. McDermott, Michael Lounsbury, and Paul M. Hirsch.

Over time, the article has also benefited from the generous comments and critiques provided by participants of workshops including SCANCOR Institutions Conference, Stanford University; Conference on Capitalism and Entrepreneurship, Cornell University; and the Georgia Workshop on Culture and Institutions, University of Georgia.

REFERENCES

Abolafia, M. (1996). *Making markets: Opportunism and restraint on Wall Street*. Cambridge, MA: Harvard University Press.

Abolafia, M., & Kilduff, M. (1988). Enacting market crisis: The social construction of a speculative bubble. *Administrative Science Quarterly, 33*, 177–193.

Alford, R. R., & Friedland, R. (1985). *Powers of theory: Capitalism, the state, and democracy*. Cambridge, Cambridgeshire; New York: Cambridge University Press.

Barley, S. R., & Kunda, G. (2001). Bringing work back in. *Organization Science, 12*, 76–95.

Beamish, T. D., & Biggart, N. W. (2002). The economy as instituted process: Interpretation, product paradigms, and building markets. In: *The next great transformation? Karl Polanyi and the critique of globalization*. Davis, CA: University of California.

Beamish, T. D., & Biggart, N. W. (2010). *Social heuristics: Decision making and innovation in a networked production market*. Davis, CA: Department of Sociology, University of California.

Bensman, J., & Lilienfeld, R. (1991). *Craft and consciousness: Occupational technique and the development of world images*. New York: Aldine de Gruyter.

Bettner, J. (1990). Real estate (A Special Report): Hard times – Overexposed: A lot of people who became limited partners in real-estate syndications are finding their losses aren't so limited. *Wall Street Journal* (Eastern Edition), New York, August 10.

Biggart, N. W. (1977). The creative-destructive process of organizational change: The case of the post office. *Administrative Science Quarterly, 22*, 410.

Biggart, N. W. (1989). *Charismatic capitalism: Direct selling organizations in America*. Chicago: University of Chicago Press.

Biggart, N. W., & Beamish, T. (2003). The economic sociology of conventions: Habit, custom, practice and routine in market order. *Annual Review of Sociology, 29*, 443–464.

Bijker, W. E., & Law, J. (Eds). (1997). *Shaping technology building society: Studies in the sociotechnical change*. London: MIT Press.

Black, T. J. (1994). The restructuring of commercial real estate finance. In: *U.L.I. market profiles, North America*. Washington, DC: Urban Land Institute.

Block, F. L. (1977). *The origins of international economic disorder: A study of United States international monetary policy from World War II to the present*. Berkeley, CA: University of California Press.

Bourdon, C. C., & Levitt, R. E. (1980). *Union and open-shop construction*. Lexington, MA: Lexington Books.

Chandler, A. D. (1977). *The visible hand: The managerial revolution in American business*. Cambridge, MA: Belknap Press.

Collier, N. S., Collier, C. A., & Halperin, D. A. (2002). *Construction funding: The process of real estate development, appraisal, and finance*. New York: Wiley.

Coverdale, G. E. (1993). Office mortgage financing from the lender's viewpoint. In: J. R. White (Ed.), *The office building: From concept to investment reality*. Chicago: The Appraisal Institute.

Davis, H. (1999). *The culture of building*. New York: Oxford University Press.

DiMaggio, P. J., & Powell, W. W. (1991). Introduction. In: P. J. DiMaggio & W. W. Powell (Eds), *The new institutionalism in organizational analysis* (pp. 1–38). Chicago: University of Chicago Publication.

Dobbin, F., & Dowd, T. J. (1997). How policy shapes competition: Early railroad foundings in Massachusetts. *Administrative Science Quarterly, 42*, 501–529.

Downs, A. (2009). *Real estate and the financial crisis*. Washington, DC: Urban Land Institute.

Eccles, R. G. (1981a). Bureaucratic versus craft administration: The relationship of market structure to construction firm. *Administration Science Quarterly, 26*, 449–469.

Eccles, R. G. (1981b). The quasifirm in the construction industry. *Journal of Economic Behavior and Organization, 2*, 335–357.

Energy Information Administration (EIA). (2004). *Official energy statistics from the U.S. government*. Washington, DC: Department of Energy.

Ewald, W. B., Jr. (2005). How Trammell Crow hit the real estate jackpot. In: B. Minnick (Ed.), *Special section: Real estate marketplace northwest. The Daily Journal of Commerce* and *The Seattle Journal of Commerce*, December 15. Available at http://www.djc.com/news/ re/11174327.html. Retrieved on May 10, 2010.

Feagin, J. R., & Parker, R. (1990). *Building American cities: The urban real estate game*. Englewood Cliffs, NJ: Prentice Hall.

Finkel, G. (1997). *The economics of the construction industry*. Armonk, NY: M.E. Sharpe.

Fligstein, N. (1996). Markets as politics: A political-cultural approach to market institutions. *American Sociological Review, 61*, 656–673.

Forbes. (1986). As the crow flies. *Forbes, 137*(5), 10.

Gans, H. J. (1967). *The Levittowners: Ways of life and politics in a new suburban community*. New York: Pantheon Books.

Gause, J. A. (1998). *Office development handbook*. Washington, DC: Urban Land Institute.

Goettsch, J. (1993). The characteristics of today's office building. In: J. R. White & E. L. Romano (Eds), *The office building from concept to investment reality*. Chicago, IL: The Counselors of Real Estate, Appraisal Institute, and REALTORS Education Fund.

Granovetter, M. (1973). The strength of weak ties. *American Journal of Sociology, 78*, 1360–1380.

Hannan, M., & Freeman, J. (1984). Structural inertia and organizational change. *American Sociological Review, 49*, 149–164.

Hargadon, A. B., & Douglas, Y. (2001). When innovations meet institutions: Edison and the design of the electric light. *Administrative Science Quarterly, 46*, 476–501.

Harvey, D. (1985). *The urbanization of capital*. Baltimore, MD: Johns Hopkins University Press.

Heilbrun, J. (1963). *Urban economics and public policy*. New York: St Martins Press.

Hughes, T. P. (1983). *Networks of power: The electrification of western society*. Baltimore, MD: Johns Hopkins University Press.

Hughes, T. P., Pinch, T. J., & Bijker, W. E. (1987). *The social construction of technological systems: New directions in the sociology and history of technology*. Cambridge, MA: MIT Press.

Ingham, G. (2003). Schumpeter and Weber on the institutions of capitalism: Solving Swedberg's puzzle. *Journal of Classical Sociology, 3*, 297–309.

Kolman, J. (1986). A tighter ship at Trammell Crow. *Institutional Investor, 29*, 129.

Krippner, G. R. (2005). The financialization of the American economy. *Socio-Economic Review*, 3(2), 173–2083, 173–208.

Krugman, P. (2009). How did economists get it so wrong? In: *The New York Times Magazine*. New York: New York Times.

Landau, S. B., & Condit, C. W. (1996). *Rise of the New York skyscraper, 1865–1913*. New Haven, CT: Yale University Press.

Latour, B., & Woolgar, S. (1986). *Laboratory life: The construction of scientific facts*. Princeton, NJ: Princeton University Press.

Lefebvre, H. (1970). *La Revolution Urbaine*. Paris: Gallimard.

Lefebvre, H. (1996). *Writings on cities*. Oxford, UK: Blackwell.

Lehman, A. (1974). *The New York skyscraper: A history of its development, 1870–1939* (p. 2v). New Haven, CT: Yale University.

Levine, N. (1996). *The architecture of Frank Lloyd Wright*. Princeton, NJ: Princeton University Press.

Logan, J. R., & Molotch, H. L. (1987). *Urban fortunes: The political economy of place*. Berkeley, CA: University of California Press.

Lowry, R. P. (1984). Structural changes in the market: The rise of professional investing. In: P. A. Adler & P. Adler (Eds), *The social dynamics of financial markets*. Greenwich, CT: JAI Press.

MacCormac, R. (1992). The dignity of office. *Architectural Review*, 190, 76–82.

Mattill, J. (1986). Tall-building centennial: The rise of "Egonomics". *Technology Review*, 89, 10–11.

McCoy, B. H. (1988). The new financial markets and securitized commercial real estate financing: Real estate securitization relates real estate more closely to money and capital markets. In: G. Sternlieb & J. W. Hughes (Eds), *America's new market geography: Nation, region, and metropolis*. New Brunswick, NJ: Rutgers – the State University of New Jersey Center for Urban Policy Research.

McDermott, G. A. (2003). *Embedded politics: Industrial networks and institutional change in postcommunism*. Ann Arbor, MI: University of Michigan Press.

McGraw-Hill Construction Research & Analytics. (2006). *Green building smartmarket report* (p. 44). New York: McGraw-Hill.

Meeks, R. (2008). Financial crisis casts shadows over commercial real estate. In: *Economic letter – Insights from the federal reserve banks of Dallas* (Vol. 3, No. 12). Dallas, TX: Federal Reserve Bank of Dallas.

Meyer, J., & Rowan, B. (1977). Institutionalized organizations: Formal structure as myth and ceremony. *American Journal of Sociology*, 83, 340–363.

Miles, R. E., & Snow, C. C. (1994). *Fit, failure, and the hall of fame. How companies succeed and fail*. New York: Free Press.

Miller, J. D. (1999). Bricks and mortar. In: *Emerging trends in real estate 2000*. Chicago: Real Estate Research Corp (RERC).

Molotch, H. (1976). The city as a growth machine: Toward a political economy of place. *American Journal of Sociology*, 82, 309–332.

Molotch, H. L. (1993). The political economy of growth machines. *Journal of Urban Affairs*, 15, 29–53.

Muldavin, S. R. (1999). The real estate industry paradox. *Real Estate Issues (Summer)*, 24(2), 66–68.

Perrow, C. (2002). *Organizing America: Wealth, power, and the origins of corporate capitalism*. Princeton, NJ: Princeton University Press.

Philips, M. (2008). The monster that ate wall street: How 'credit default swaps' – an insurance against bad loans – turned from a smart bet into a killer. *Newsweek*, September 27.

Podolny, J. M. (1994). Market uncertainty and the social character of economic exchange. *Administrative Science Quarterly, 39*, 458.

Podolny, J. M., & Page, K. L. (1998). Network forms of organization. *Annual Review of Sociology, 24*, 57–76.

Pogrebin, R. (2004). The incredible shrinking Daniel Libeskind. In: *Section: Arts and leisure; Architecture*. New York Times, June 20, late edition.

Powell, W. (1990). Neither market nor hierarchy: Network forms of organization. *Research in Organizational Behavior, 12*, 295–336.

Powell, W., White, D., Koput, K., & Owen-Smith, J. (2005). Network dynamics and field evolution: The growth of interorganizational collaboration in the life sciences. *American Journal of Sociology, 110*, 1132–1205.

Powell, W. W. (1998). Learning from collaboration: Knowledge and networks in the biotechnology and pharmaceutical industries. *California Management Review, 40*, 228–240. Special Issue on Knowledge and the Firm.

Pygman, J. W., & Kateley, R. (1985). *Tall office buildings in the United States*. Washington, DC: Urban Land Institute.

Rome, A. (2001). *The bulldozer in the countryside: Suburban sprawl and the rise of American environmentalism*. Cambridge, UK: Cambridge University Press.

Roulac, S. E. (1985). Syndication emerges to transform the real estate capital market. *Real Estate Finance* (Winter), 18–27.

Roulac, S. E. (1993). Capital access: That was then, this is now. *Journal of Real Estate Finance* (Winter), 5–7.

Roy, W. G. (1997). *Socializing capital: The rise of the large industrial corporation in America*. Princeton, NJ: Princeton University Press.

Sanvio, V., & Konchar, M. (1999). *Selecting project delivery systems*. State College, PA: Project Delivery Institute.

Schumpeter, J. (1934). *The theory of economic development*. Cambridge, MA: Harvard University Press.

Schumpeter, J. (1936). *The theory of economic development: An inquiry into profits, capital, credit, interest, and the business cycle*. Cambridge, MA: Harvard University Press.

Schumpeter, J. A. (1939). *Business cycles; a theoretical, historical, and statistical analysis of the capitalist process*. New York: McGraw-Hill.

Scott, J. C. (1998). *Seeing like a state how certain schemes to improve the human condition have failed*. New Haven: Yale University Press.

Selznick, P. (1957). *Leadership in administration: A sociological interpretation*. New York: Harper and Row.

Selznick, P. (1966). *TVA and the grassroots*. New York: Harper.

Shales, J., & Weiss, M. A. (1993). Evolution of the office building. In: J. R. White & E. L. Romano (Eds), *The office building: From concept to investment reality*. Chicago, IL: The Counselors of Real Estate, Appraisal Institute, and REALTORS Education Fund.

Shelby, L. R. (1970). The education of mediaeval English master masons. *Mediaeval Studies, 32*, 1–26.

Shlaes, J., & Weiss, M. A. (1993). Evolution of the office building. In: J. R. White (Ed.), *The office building: From concept to investment reality*. Chicago: The Appraisal Institute.

Shultz, E., & Simmons, W. (1959). *Offices in the sky*. Indianapolis, IA: Bobbs-Merrill.

Smith-Doerr, L., & Powell, W. (2005). Networks and economic life. In: N. Smelser & R. Swedberg (Eds), *The handbook of economic sociology* (2nd ed.). Princeton, NJ: Princeton University Press.

Squires, G. D. (2002). *Urban sprawl: Causes, consequences, & policy responses.* Washington, DC: Urban Institute Press.

Steele, R. A., & Barry, K. H. (1988). The financial structuring of office investments: Debt and equity. In: G. Sternlieb & J. W. Hughes (Eds), *America's new market geography: Nation, region, and metropolis* (pp. xvii, 371). New Brunswick, NJ: Rutgers–the State University of New Jersey Center for Urban Policy Research.

Stinchcombe, A. (1959). Bureaucratic and craft administration of production: A comparative study. *Administrative Science Quarterly, 4,* 168–187.

Stinchcombe, A. (1965). Social structure and organizations. In: J. G. March (Ed.), *Handbook of organizations.* Chicago: Rand McNally.

Storper, M., & Walker, R. (1989). *The capitalist imperative: Territory, technology, and industrial growth.* Oxford, UK; New York, NY: Basil Blackwell.

Swedberg, R. (2002). The economic sociology of capitalism. *Journal of Classical Sociology, 2,* 227–255.

Swedberg, R. (2006). The cultural entrepreneur and the creative industries: Beginning in Vienna. *Journal of Cultural Economics, 30,* 243–261.

Thornton, P. H., & Ocasio, W. (2008). Institutional logics. In: C. O. R. Greenwood, S. K. Andersen & R. Suddaby (Eds), *Handbook of organizational institutionalism.* Thousand Oaks; London: Sage.

Tushman, M. L., & Anderson, P. (1997). *Innovation over time and in historical context: Managing strategic innovation and change.* New York: Oxford University Press.

Useem, M. (1996). *Investor capitalism: How money managers are changing the face of corporate America.* New York: Basic Books.

Utterback, J. M. (1994). *Mastering the dynamics of innovation: How companies can seize opportunities in the face of technological change.* Boston, MA: Harvard Business School Press.

Van Maanen, J. V., & Barley, S. R. (1984). Occupational communities: Culture and control in organizations. *Research in Organizational Behavior, 6,* 287–365.

Wei, L., & Grant, P. (2009). Commercial real estate lurks as next potential mortgage crisis. *Wall Street Journal,* August 31.

White, J. R., & Adler, T. W. (1993). Office building sales marketing practices. In: J. R. White & E. L. Romano (Eds), *The office building: From concept to investment reality.* Chicago, IL: The Counselors of Real Estate, Member Appraisal Institute, and REALTORS Education Fund.

Whitford, J., & Shrank, A. (2009). *The production of innovation: Industrial policy, network governance, and political decentralization.* Unpublished manuscript. Columbia University, New York (pp. 1–25).

Willis, C. (1995). *Form follows finance: Skyscrapers and skylines in New York and Chicago.* Princeton, NJ: Princeton Architectural Press.

Zeitlin, J., & Herrigel, G. (2000). *Americanization and its limits: Reworking US technology and management in post-war Europe and Japan.* Oxford, UK; New York: Oxford University Press.

Zelizer, V. A. R. (1983). *Morals and markets: The development of life insurance in the United States.* New Brunswick, NJ: Transaction Books.

SECTION V
COMPARATIVE INSTITUTIONAL DYNAMICS

THROUGH THE LOOKING GLASS: INEFFICIENT DEREGULATION IN THE UNITED STATES AND EFFICIENT STATE OWNERSHIP IN CHINA

Doug Guthrie and David Slocum

ABSTRACT

We discuss the ways in which the tensions between deregulation and bailouts create fundamentally inefficient markets. Although there is an appetite for the rhetoric of a laissez-fair economic system in the United States, we do not have the political will to operate such a system, as there are always cries for bailouts when a crisis emerges. And bailouts rob markets of the crucial ability to discipline capital for risky behavior. Using the case of China as an example, we argue that the post-Cold War conclusion that state ownership is fundamentally inefficient is premature. The key issue is not state versus private ownership per se but, rather, how well aligned the incentives are within a given system. Some of the economic models we find in reform-era China are actually better aligned and perhaps as transparent as their counterparts in the market economies of the capitalist West. Finally, because China is not caught up on the categorical assumption that private firms are efficient while state-owned

Markets on Trial: The Economic Sociology of the U.S. Financial Crisis: Part B
Research in the Sociology of Organizations, Volume 30B, 283–311
Copyright © 2010 by Emerald Group Publishing Limited
All rights of reproduction in any form reserved
ISSN: 0733-558X/doi:10.1108/S0733-558X(2010)000030B013

firms are inefficient, the country has been able to be an institutional innovator in the area of public–private partnerships, leading to radical new corporate forms.

INTRODUCTION

Today, the world seems to be truly upside down. For decades before the economic crisis of 2008–2009, the United States held the mantle of the dominant market economy in the world. It was not only a mantle of a dominant economy (i.e., the largest economy in the world); since the ideological revolution launched in the early 1970s by Milton Friedman, the United States has been the bastion of market ideals: That place that would come as close to a laissez-faire economic system as any other place in the world. During that ascendancy, we also saw the vanquishing of the state-owned economies around the world, as communist economies big and small were forced to concede that the capitalist West had something on them – that private property was superior to state ownership; that deregulation was superior to state involvement; that markets were efficient and wise while state controlled systems were inefficient and, well, dumb.

From the center of the economic crisis, the world economic order looks very different today than it did two years ago. Today, we have to wonder at the wisdom of Milton Friedman's ideological revolution and, more specifically, at the wisdom of viewing the world in such simplistic terms economically. Increasingly, we are beginning to realize that China did not just luck into this position of economic strength, as some observers have claimed.[1] No, actually, China has had a plan all along, and it has been a plan that highlights the strengths of a mixed economy, bringing together ample amounts of state intervention and control with a certain level of economic incentives. Was China right all along?

In this article, we are going to essentially argue that, yes, China has been right all along (since 1979, that is). But it is not quite as simple as the issues or debate has been framed by the neoliberals – state involvement bad; markets good. In fact, markets probably *are* superior to state control, but it seems that few countries (the United States included) have the political will to operate the market economy that we rhetorically revere.[2] The problem here is that when we bail out corporations that have engaged in risky market behavior, we rob markets of one of the key mechanisms that are necessary for them to function efficiently (or to function well at all). For markets to function effectively, they *must* be able to discipline capital; they *must* be able to discipline poor economic decision-making. If they cannot do this, then economic actors are deprived of the crucial feedback that helps them in making intelligent economic decisions. The problem is that economic actors end up functioning like gamblers playing with house money. If politicians and citizens want the safety of a governmental backstop to bailout bad economic decisions, they must also accept the government in the role of regulator. Otherwise, we are encouraging corporations to take risks with no fear of failure. However, the problem that always arises here is the notion that governmental meddling in economic decision-making is fundamentally inefficient – that government bureaucrats cannot possibly make economic decisions that reflect market incentives. Thus, we are left to choose between the imperfect market (rewarding risk with bailouts) and the inefficient bureaucrat. But what if this notion of the inefficient governmental bureaucracy is not accurate? Economic development in China actually provides some guidance here. The reality in China is that state involvement is actually providing a more effective process of market engagement than we have seen in the imagined ideal of the US laissez-faire market.

Our discussion has three parts to it. First, we discuss some of the ways in which the tensions between deregulation and bailouts create dysfunctional markets. Second, using the case of China as an example, we argue that the post-Cold War conclusion that state-owned economies are fundamentally inefficient is premature. Third, we argue that some of the economic models we find in reform-era China are actually better aligned and perhaps *even more transparent* and *more innovative* than their counterparts in the market economies of the capitalist West.

INEFFICIENT DEREGULATION IN THE UNITED STATES: PLAYING WITH HOUSE MONEY

Economic Models, Simplification, and Collective Memory Loss

It is an interesting time to be thinking of the consequences of simplification. Economists, financial professionals, and finance and strategy professors all argue for simplification: The model of research – especially high-status research in these fields – pushes for building theoretical models based on simple assumptions that can be modeled mathematically and then yield simple applications. The elegance of these models is beyond dispute;

however, the current economic crisis shows just how costly simplification can be. The recent credit crisis experienced in the United States and, subsequently, worldwide has raised a groundswell of concern over the wider economic impact on the US financial sector and the entire global economy. To be sure, the stakes were significant: In the Spring of 2008, when Federal Reserve Chairman Ben Bernanke defended the governmental bailout of Bear Stearns, which provided up to $30 billion to facilitate the bank's sale to JP Morgan Chase, he argued that the bailout was necessary because "the damage caused by a default by Bear Stearns could have been severe and extremely difficult to contain" for the US and global economy. Beyond the macro-economic issues, also at stake were the economic livelihoods of thousands of US consumers who face potential mortgage foreclosure brought on by the crisis. By the summer, some were predicting that the number of people that could experience such an outcome has not been seen since the Great Depression: As James Parks, writing on behalf of the AFL-CIO, put it, "Millions of America's homeowners are facing disaster after years of predatory lending. This is the first time since the Depression of the 1930s that so many US homeowners owed more on their mortgages than their homes are worth." The actual numbers bore this rhetoric out: According to RealtyTrac, the number of foreclosures for the United States overall is up 100.1% over the past year for similar periods; in the state of Massachusetts, foreclosures were up 11 times over the past year; in the state of Delaware, foreclosures are up 800% over the past year; in the state of Ohio, foreclosures for the year ended up at 83,230, an all-time record. By the time Henry Paulson was pulling together the plan that would constitute the greatest transfer of wealth from the government to the financial industry in the history of this nation, the extent and depth of this crisis had become indisputable. So, by any analysis, it *must* be the case that the bailout was the right thing to do.

But this is not just a problem of economic modeling and the narrow assumptions about human behavior that lie behind many of these models. It is just as much about collective memory loss as well as the lack of political will to actually let a market do its work. Despite the declaration that we have not seen an economic crisis like the current one since the 1930s, this view represents collective memory loss. Perhaps more recent events were not this bad, but did we learn nothing from the Savings and Loan Crisis of the late 1980s? Is there any connection between this situation and the accounting crises of 2000–2001 or the bailout of the airlines in 2004? The current crisis may indeed be worse than any we have seen since the Great Depression, but the narrative is actually fairly common in the recent history of American capitalism. The past 30 years of US economic history is littered with examples of two dissonant themes: On the one hand, we have a corporate sector advocating deregulation, singing the praises of a laissez-faire market, and criticizing government interference as fundamentally inefficient. On the other hand, we have corporations – and the population – asking for bailouts when they cannot survive the realities of the free markets they have advocated.

What do we make of crises like these? The first lesson to take away from this crisis is that, although many love the idea of the unfettered free market, we simply do not have the political will for a free market in advanced capitalist economies around the world today. Or perhaps we simply do not understand what a free market is. One of the key aspects of a well-functioning market – perhaps *the* key aspect – is the ability of the market to discipline actors who make bad economic decisions. Just as markets can reward risky behavior, they must also be allowed to discipline risky behavior when the bet turns out to be wrong. The incentive system simply cannot work if we reward risky behavior but then bail out the economic actors when they end up on the wrong side of the risky outcome. The irony of our time is that corporations want it both ways: They want a deregulated system so that they can take on increasingly risky behavior in financial markets and then want a government handout when the same risky behavior that those deregulated markets allowed leads to potential bankruptcy.

The recent crises in the financial sector are clearly tied to this push and pull over deregulation and bailouts. The risky behavior that led to the S&L crisis of the late 1980s can clearly be traced to the Garn-St. Germain Depository Institutions Act of 1982, which gave Savings and Loans institutions many of the same opportunities as commercial banks but not the same amount of federal oversight. As a result of this deregulation, S&L's were able to make very risky loans in real estate without Congress or the Federal Home Loan Banking Board (FHLBB) stepping in to shut them down for those risky loans or insolvency. Eventually the crisis grew to a level that Congress was forced to step in and bring forth an aid package that would cost the American tax payers somewhere between $125 and $160 billion. What message does it send to the risk-taking actors – who lobbied for deregulation in the first place – if they can take risks and then count on being bailed out by the government?

In the current crisis, the relaxation of the Glass–Steagall Act over the course of the 1990s and the eventual repealing of the Act in 1999 with the passage of the Gramm–Leach–Bliley Financial Services Modernization Act allowed commercial banks to operate in a number of areas (insurance, investment banking, securities) that Glass–Steagall had forbidden. As a result, commercial banks could begin to deal on both sides of the fence: They could lend mortgages to their commercial customers and they could turn these same loans around and securitize them in the form of mortgage-backed securities, selling and trading them on the fast-moving securities markets that were emerging during the 1990s. While everyone was making money, all seemed copacetic. However, banks were now removed from the main incentive to be vigilant about risky borrowing behavior – they now no longer held the note on the house of the individual they loaned to. As a result, there was no disincentive for them to compete for business in a riskier and riskier loan pool. What was the downside? As long as the real estate market continued to rise, everyone would come out ahead; and if it did not, they would not hold the note on the foreclosed home anyway, as that mortgage had long since been packaged with a larger group of mortgages, securitized, and sold off to some other institution (which likely sold it again). Some individuals working in the industry have estimated that, by the time these mortgages had reached the end of their securitization life cycle, they would have been repackaged as parts of new financial instruments as many as 20 times. All the while, the risk assessment agencies that typically assess the viability of these financial instruments had incentives to keep the market booming, and they continued to award AAA ratings without a second thought. This type of risky behavior generated a great deal of wealth; but it was risky behavior nonetheless, and just as these risks yield rewards, they should also be subject to the discipline of the market when the system unravels. By what logic should the individuals gambling at this table receive a bailout?

Many in the industry and in political realms made the case that we must bail out the banks because (1) massive bankruptcies, like Bear Stearns and Lehman Brothers, would disrupt the economy and even cause a disruption of global markets (for which the United States would be blamed); and (2) foreclosures would hurt American consumers, many of whom stand to lose their homes. Which brings us to the second culprit in this crisis: Politicians, who also want it both ways. In essence, the politicians want to appease the corporations – many of whom donate significantly to their campaigns – but when it comes time to deal with the results of the economic incentives they have created, they want to protect the American voter from these outcomes. The reality in both cases is that if we let the market work in a truly unfettered fashion, banks would have had the opportunity to record the record profits they have accrued over the past decade, but they would also have to be prepared to bear the consequences of the risky behavior that led to those profits. A painful S&L bankruptcy (with no bailout) would have been a powerful lesson as to what can happen without federal oversight in the banking sector; and Bear Stearns' bankruptcy would have been a valuable lesson in the realm of corporate oversight the same way that the debacles of Enron and WorldCom have become important lessons in the realm of lax corporate oversight in other sectors. Individual consumers would certainly have a different attitude about the virtues of an unfettered market if they learned the difficult lesson that risky behavior can bring about foreclosures and even recession. Maybe they would even vote differently.

Now, one might make the case that there is nothing wrong with the current cycle as it is playing out – that a good deal of economic growth has come from the deregulation of these sectors, and that economic growth has been, in the aggregate, good for the US economy and American consumers overall. What does it matter if we extract the tax burden up front, which might curtail risky behavior and growth, or on the backend in the form of a bailout? This is a fallacious argument, because over the past 30 years, the aggregate growth of the US economy has largely benefitted the economic elites of the system – those engaging in the risky economic behavior – creating a much greater disparity in earnings between the wealthy and the middle and lower classes. Yet, when a government bailout occurs, the tax burden is shared by all.

The main point we want to emphasize here is that these crises arose from a complex set of shifting incentives in the changing institutional environment of the US financial system. Corporate strategists and financial professionals in banks around the world relied on simplistic assumptions about financial instruments that were far too complex for such models. But, more importantly, they relied on the fundamental assumption that failure was impossible. And why should not they? The bailout of the S&L crisis occurred just a decade before (from 1986 to 1996). For organizations like Citibank, Bank of America, and some of the most powerful investment banks, everyone knew they were too big to be allowed to fail anyway. And of course, when Lehman did fail, it led to the freezing of credit markets that everyone had predicted. Thus, from their perspective (i.e., the perspective that they could not be allowed to fail lest dire consequences result), they were right. But for markets to function appropriately – for future market actors to legitimately fear the consequences of risky behavior – failing banks *had* to be allowed to fail.

A Mentality not Limited to Banking: The Case of General Motors

A further burden on taxpayers arrived with the government rescue of the US automakers General Motors and Chrysler. Here, too, a longer history of deregulation was a major contributor. In 1981, after he entered the White House, Ronald Reagan began to provide a comprehensive relief package for the auto industry that had, in the closing years of the previous administration, become saddled by a range of environmental and safety regulations. These ranged from emissions rules requiring costly equipment to limit hydrocarbons and paint shop standards to safety standards for explosive tire rims and passenger restraint requirements. Some estimates had the total costs of emissions regulations per automobile tripling in only two years, from 1979 to 1981, from $559 to $1,551 (White, 1982). Safety regulation costs likewise had grown rapidly, from $431–641 in 1979 to $512–822 two years later (Crandall, Gruenspecht, Keeler, & Lave, 1986). The Reagan Administration's auto reform package claimed significant savings for both the industry and the public. Two of the largest sources of savings accrued from declining to order new gas tank vapor controls on cars and from failing to revise Clean Air Act orders governing high-altitude emissions standards, hydrocarbons and nitrogen oxide emissions (Wines, 1983, pp. 1534–1535). By the mid-1980s, the reform effort had proven itself successful and loosed the auto industry from a host of costly government standards.

Around the same time, the US government provided its auto industry another financial boon. A "voluntary export restraint" (VER) program was imposed in 1981, set an annual import of limit of 1.68 million Japanese cars. In the wake of the oil crises, the economic recession, and high interest rates, these more affordable and fuel-efficient cars had become increasingly popular among American buyers. US automakers initially profited by the restrictions and decrease in competition. Yet rather than reinvesting in newer and better models, the automakers did not fundamentally upgrade their operations or shift their priorities to designing more fuel-efficient and affordable vehicles. (General Motors, e.g., made highly publicized but finally irrelevant acquisitions of EDS in 1984 and Hughes Aircraft in 1985.) Ironically, Japanese carmakers did adapt to the restraints, opening their own, often more efficient assembly plants in the United States, starting with Honda's Marysville, Ohio plant in 1982. Even more, Japanese cars continued to sell, even though it has been estimated that the prices of Japanese cars were around 14% higher than they would have been without the restraints. The cap on imports was raised twice before the VER program was ended in 1994. Subsequent analyses have calculated that the US economy, even accounting for the short-term profits of American automakers, suffered a $3 billion welfare loss due to the artificial restraints on Japanese automobile exports (Feenstra, 1995; Berry, Levinsohn, & Pakes, 1999).

To be clear, US automakers largely responded to these reforms by maintaining their organizational structures and their production of less fuel-efficient vehicles. With seven brands then under its corporate umbrella, General Motors did seek cost savings during the 1980s, but in limited, mostly internal ways that included downsizing the overall product line, expanding manufacturing automation, and producing shared underpinnings for cars of different brands. Yet combined with an economic recession in the early 1990s, the increasing market share of Japanese and other foreign carmakers created new losses and cut into GM's historical dominance of the US market; in 1980, the company owned a 46% market share. A more thoroughgoing restructuring of the company, including senior management, and a push to design and introduce new and improved vehicles was attempted. However, still burdened by carrying so many historical brands, as well as increased debt, GM's development of new products remained inefficient, creating what was called a "launch and leave" problem in which the company would spend billions of dollars to design and bring products to market only to fail to support and advertise them adequately. Unable with their many brands and models to dedicate the focused attention to products or customers offered by Honda and Toyota, which themselves were building more and more of their cars in the United Sates, GM's domestic market share slipped from 35.1% in 1990 to 27.8% in 2000.

Despite the decline in market share, General Motors saw profits rebound during the 1990s spurred by the success of large, profitable vehicles, including light pickup trucks and sport utility vehicles (SUVs), and the wider growth economy enjoyed. At the same time, far-reaching changes in the industry as well as in national economic policies were occurring that speak directly to the argument being made here for the inconsistency of US regulatory and related governmental activities. Take two such changes involving labor that were impacted by various policies made in Washington. First, GM and the other American automakers increasingly sought to internationalize their operations, not just in body and final assembly work, but also through the decision-making and supply chain. As Sturgeon and Florida (2000) argue, the greatest impact of this transition may not have been a serious reduction in domestic employment (in fact, the aggregate change in jobs is lessened by the increase in employment for US production by *foreign* automakers in US facilities) but the rise of new, often lower-cost production sites enabling the expansion of local and regional markets. The Clinton administration was consistently committed to policies that nurtured these new markets and supported supra-national trade arrangements like NAFTA and Autopact. While this "build-where-you-sell" logic made some sense, in retrospect, its implications for US automakers and their extremely complex design, supply, production and marketing operations were not fully understood at the time (Fine & St. Clair, 1996).[3]

Second, and similarly, both the off-shoring of labor-intensive production and the restructuring of traditional corporations, including GM, occurred as part of a broader and, for some, conscious shift away from traditional, labor-intensive manufacturing. This profound economic and social transformation was sharply debated at the time: Cohen and Zysman (1987), for example, viewed the ascendance of a "post-industrial" economy as a myth and even dangerous in the face of manufacturing's ongoing importance to the US economy; others, like Ramaswamy (1997) claimed that an active *de*industrialization had taken place not just in the United States but all the world's advanced economies. Throughout, there was a lack of meaningful American policy-making resolve to invest in manufacturing infrastructure in the United States itself. Meanwhile, other nations, particularly in Asia and Europe, as well as nearby Canada and Mexico, courted large industrial and technology firms through a series of tax breaks, easy credit, expedited regulatory approval and inexpensive utility and transportation deals. Often, as in China, these incentives were coordinated and packaged by the governments. The US government offered few such incentives and, in particular, its corporate taxes were (and remain) exceptionally high for industrialized nations.[4] In other words, even as academic and policy debates sought to make sense of the transformative changes underway in the manufacturing sector and wider economy, and regional and global trade was expanding, US government policies themselves remained uneven and uncoordinated.

Which is to say that markets, like that for automobiles, were not left to operate freely but still strongly if erratically shaped by policies and regulations. As in the previous decade, the 1990s saw trade policy assume a pride of place in economic decision-making. During the Clinton years, however, the aim was typically to create continental-scale trading zones, lower barriers abroad for the importation of US-produced goods, and expand the presence of American corporations in global markets. Washington continued to intervene, that is, though not at all systematically. What was lacking, at least for those who believed in a more coherent approach to regulation, was *industrial policy*, which Graham (1992) claims is "a nation's declared, official, total effort to influence sectoral development and, thus, national industrial portfolio" (p. 3). Ironically, the historical debate over IP emerged at the time precisely because of the perceived success of the Japanese industrial policy during the 1980s (Itoh, Kiyono, Okuno, & Suzumura, 1988). Moreover, and to underscore the emphasis here on GM, in the US discussion, industrial tended to refer to manufacturing. Yet the overriding issue in debates at the time was the readily politicized question of the extent of the government's role in market activity (Zysman & Tyson, 1983; Norton, 1986; Levinsohn, 1994; Freedman & Stonecash, 1997). Trade policy was acceptable to most; industrial policy, and the thoroughgoing governmental intervention in markets it was understood to represent, was anathema to many.[5]

The profitability of General Motors during the 1990s and into the 2000s would last until gasoline prices again soared in 2004–2005 and a public call for fuel-efficient vehicles was renewed. Yet again, the company did not have more affordable competitive models in the long, three to five years automotive design and development pipeline. Around the same time, General Motors was struggling with a series of financial crises involving their pension and retiree health care costs that prompted a downgrade in the company's bond ratings. GM responded with a further restructuring plan and a series of financial moves, including deals with Fiat and Suzuki, and sold a controlling stake in its finance products subsidiary, GMAC. It also offered buy-outs to hourly workers in 2006 in hopes of reducing future costs. While providing temporary cash and stability, these moves could not prevent a further drop in US market share (to 26%) or stanch a hemorrhaging of cash that required billions of dollars in loans from the US government in late 2008. The rationale for the support was familiar: GM was too big to fail. Beyond its 91,000 American workers and overall revenues of $148 billion, the company spent $50 billion each year buying products and services from more than 11,000 vendors in the country alone. That financial reach extended further through a network of hundreds of subsidiaries and suppliers and over 6,500 dealerships (averaging 23 employees each). The same rationale would guide a White House Auto Task Force and then the May 2009 bankruptcy in which GM would begin to restructure its operations under government control.

All told, American taxpayers have spent close to $30 billion on the bankruptcy and restructuring, in addition to the earlier $20 billion in loans meant to keep the company solvent in late 2008. The result is a 60% ownership stake in the new GM. Critics have assessed different possible goals of the bailout and discounted many of the most obvious: Ability to repay the loan reliably, preserving GM jobs (at least 6 plants and 20,000 workers would be summarily cut), creating a lean new company, or launching a new generation of efficient, affordable cars. Instead, the most practical purpose appears, as Robert Reich puts it, "to slow the decline of GM to create enough time for its workers, suppliers, dealers and communities to adjust to its eventual demise" (Reich, 2009). That goal of industrial adjustment, moving beyond (or at least radically restructuring) a manufacturing economy and mass-production business model, should have been pursued by the auto industry itself. The government's involvement and investment became necessary after – and, in ways, followed logically from – decades of deregulation and protection of the industry from competition, a rapidly changing global marketplace, a shortsighted lack in investment in domestic manufacturing infrastructure, and the industry's own burdensome future liabilities.

The main point we want to emphasize here is that these crises arose from a complex set of shifting incentives in the changing institutional environment of the US financial and automobile manufacturing systems. Corporate strategists, financial professionals in banks, and executives in the auto industry relied on simplistic assumptions about financial instruments, competition, and industrial change that were far too complex for such models. They also demurred, except during and immediately after the years of perceived threat from Japanese carmakers in the 1980s, from any suggestion of a coherent US industrial policy that would have the government intervening with a systematic and coordinated regulatory regime for industries. Creative leaders must embrace the challenge of understanding complexity rather than relying on simplified models of strategy and economic behavior.

EFFICIENT REGULATION IN
A STATE-RUN ECONOMY

We turn now to the issue of state involvement in the economy and the strategic alignment of the Chinese state sector with national interests. Since the early 1980s, most of the capitalist world has converged around the consensus that state-owned enterprises are fundamentally inefficient. With the privatization of national energy conglomerates from Britain to Italy to the privatization of tobacco and salt corporations in Japan to Mexico, Turkey, Zaire, the general consensus is that state involvement is fundamentally antithetical to the type of efficiency that comes with private ownership. The assessment of the inefficiencies of state planned economies in the Soviet Bloc and China seemed to confirm this view. Dating from the scholarship of famous economists like Janos Kornai (1980, 1990) through Jeffrey Sachs (1992, 1994, 1997), the basic position has been that state ownership simply could not provide the right incentives for efficient market behavior. The success of China's economy and many state-owned firms within it has caused us to revisit some of the key assumptions upon which those arguments are based. The reality that China has revealed is that the issue is not ownership per se (state vs. private) but, instead, the ability to create the right incentive structures that lead to efficient market behavior. Two examples help us flesh out the contours of this issue. First, we briefly discuss the case of a state-owned giant like PetroChina, now the most efficient oil and gas company in the world. Second we discuss the ways in which governmental participation in the market (in the form of public–private partnerships might actually be more innovative than the models that private capital alone can achieve. The example for this latter issue is the case of the Suzhou Singapore Industrial Development Corporation (SSIDC).

Efficiency without Privatization: The Case of PetroChina

We turn now to one of the more famous cases of SOE transformation in China today. While many observers credit PetroChina's success to its duopoly status and special strategic position within the Chinese government, the company has also been revolutionized in terms of incentive structures that link directly to worker productivity. As many scholars have documented this case, we draw heavily here on past work that has been done on the case. In this case as with many other transforming SOEs, observers have often attributed the organization's success to its close strategic relationship with the Chinese government. As one of the key organizations in a sector that is crucial to China's growth prospects, the organization does enjoy a privileged position in the world's third largest economy. Success is all but assured, given this strategic advantage. However, this view misses just how much asset management in China has changed the performance of Chinese firms. It also misses the fact that successful asset management can be directed by state organizations – perhaps not as successful as private institutional investors, but successful nonetheless. We place special emphasis here on PetroChina's relationship to China's State-Owned Assets Supervision and Administration Commissions (SASAC) and to key foreign investors, like Warren Buffett, and on its approach to revolutionizing incentives for the workforce. In this section, we will explore PetroChina's productivity, highlighting not just its strategic positioning in the market-place (and with respect to the Chinese government) but also with respect to the changes in incentive structures workers have experienced in the workplace. Ultimately, productivity is dependent on putting the right incentives in place and on building a culture of productivity in the workplace, and PetroChina has been successful at doing just that. This discussion will serve as a springboard for a broader discussion of work and productivity in China's transforming state sector.

PetroChina is an exchange-listed subsidiary of the China National Petroleum Company (CNPC), which currently produces approximately 66% of China's oil and gas. CNPC owns nearly 87% of the company, and the remaining equity shares are listed as H-shares in Hong Kong, ADRs in New York, and on the Chinese domestic exchange in Shanghai. As a subsidiary of a state-owned enterprise, PetroChina enjoys a duopoly in the Chinese domestic market. It is also is one of the world's largest, most efficient, and most profitable energy companies. In 2007, the company briefly became the world's largest publicly held firm when its market capitalization when it briefly topped $1 trillion following a float on the Shanghai stock exchange that saw its shares triple in value. In the same year, the company made the single biggest discovery of oil within China in 50 years when it found an estimated 7.5 billion barrels of oil in a field at Bohai Bay. The company has stakes in over 16,620 service stations to provide retail distribution for its proven reserves of 11.6 billion barrels of oil and 53.5 trillion cubic feet of natural gas. The distribution network also includes 12 chemical plants and 26 refineries as well as 20,590 km of natural gas pipeline.[6] It has focused on increasing the extent of its vertical integration as well as on expanding its operations abroad. Currently, PetroChina's exploration and development businesses operate in 11 foreign countries and portions of the company are also involved in the production and marketing of crude oil and natural gas; refining, transportation, storage, and marketing of crude oil and oil products; production and marketing of primary and derivative petrochemicals; transportation of natural gas, crude oil, refined oil, and marketing natural gas. Table 1 shows the productivity statistics of the PetroChina; there is no denying that the corporation is extremely successful in terms of efficiency and profitability.

A Brief History of CNPC/PetroChina

In 1988, the Chinese government disbanded its Ministry of Petroleum Industry and formed three state-owned companies to oversee and modernize its petroleum-related activities. The China Offshore Oil Corporation (CNOOC) was formed to handle offshore production, the China

Table 1. Productivity at PetroChina, 2004–2008.

Efficiency Ratios		Profitability Ratios	
Cash Conversion Cycle	25	Free Cash Flow Margin	−4.1
Revenue per Employee	245,051	Free Cash Flow Margin – 5-year avg.	0.53
Net Income per Employee	42,735	Net Profit Margin	17.4
Average Collection Period	25	Net Profit Margin – 5-year avg.	21.3
Receivables Turnover	0	Equity Productivity	1.14
Day's Inventory Turnover Ratio	0	Return on Equity (ROE)	19.9
Inventory Turnover	0	Return on Equity (ROE) – 5-year avg.	22.6
Inventory/Sales	10.6	Capital Invested Productivity	1.08
Accounts Payable/Sales	4.84	Return on Capital Invested (ROCI)	18.8
Assets/Revenue	0	Return on Capital Invested (ROCI) – 5-year avg.	21
Net Working Capital Turnover	25.24	Assets Productivity	0
Fixed Assets Turnover	1.01	Return on Assets (ROA)	13.7
Total Assets Turnover	0	Return on Assets (ROA) – 5-year avg.	15.4
Revenue per $ Cash	12.75	Gross Profit Margin	62.1
Revenue per $ Plant	1.09	Gross Profit Margin – 5-year avg.	57.6
Revenue per $ Common Equity	1.14	EBITDA Margin – LTM	26
Revenue per $ capital invested	1.08	EBIT Margin – LTM	20.2
Selling, General & AdminTime (SG&A) as % of Revenue	12.2	Pre-Tax Profit Margin	24.5
SG&A Expense as % of Revenue – 5-year avg.	11	Pre-Tax Profit Margin – 5-year avg.	30.2
Research & Development (R&D) as % of Revenue	0	Effective Tax Rate	24
R&D Expense as % of Revenue – 5-year avg.	0	Effective Tax Rate – 5-year avg.	26.9

Source: http://www.advfn.com/p.php?pid = financials&symbol = NYSE%3APTR.

Petrochemical Group (Sinopec) focused on refining and petrochemical production, and the China National Petroleum Corporation (CNPC) took over all onshore exploration and production of oil and gas. The reforms leading to the abolishment of the Ministry of Petroleum Industry represented on of the first major steps the Chinese government took toward reform or heavy industries. Up until that point most economic reform efforts were primarily focused on agricultural, light manufacturing, and commercial industries. The government had been more conservative with companies engaged in the manufacture of steel, machines, trucks, and other heavy industrial goods because of their importance to the economy as a whole. During the 1980s heavy industries were the largest employers and providers of social services to urban residents. They were also the primary source of revenue at many different levels of the government.

While the government made some incremental reforms in the energy industry by shifting production from government ministries to state-owned enterprises, the large number of people that were dependent upon on these companies for their livelihoods made the perceived consequences of any potential errors very serious. As a result, the newly formed state-owned enterprises continued operating as if they were still parts of the Ministry of Petroleum Industry because the government was willing to overlook the systematic failure of such companies to turn a profit due to overstaffing and low productivity (Wu, 2002). In the case of CNPC, the weaknesses in productivity were dramatic. To put the productivity in perspective: When a CNPC delegation visiting international oil companies found that the Norwegian state-owned oil company Statoil employed 80,000 people and produced 130 million tons of oil annually. CNPC had comparable annual production of 140 million tons, but at the time it employed around 1.4 million workers (Rowe & Rowe, 2006; Dyck & Huang, 2004). While not all of these workers were directly involved in oil exploration or production activities, CNPC was still employing over 11 times as many people to produce a comparable amount of oil. Some of the difference in staffing between the two companies can be explained by the fact that it was Statoil's standard practice to outsource any aspects of it business not directly related to oil exploration or production. CNPC on the other hand used in-house divisions to provide all of its construction services, well logging, drilling, and engineering services. Such a large and varied organization was made even more difficult to manage profitably because the company's legal structure afforded senior executives relatively little influence over their regional counterparts. While CNPC and its subsidiaries were technically operating as one company, in reality the level of integration between the various entities was very low.

By 1997, it was evident that the social welfare burdens and organizational inefficiencies at the state-owned oil companies were threatening their ability to provide for their employees while continuing to grow economically. CNPC had been experimenting with the possibility of creating oil companies with international operations within the Chinese national petroleum companies. Many at CNPC believed a focus on international operations could provide the impetus needed for the company to make a turn around. Opening up to external pressures would drive reforms forward necessitating a return to the company's core business and enabling the executive team to do away with the antiquated management system.

The first step the government took was to remove the artificial functional segments that had been created when the production of oil was overseen by government ministries. This was seen as a crucial step toward achieving the government's twin goals for the reorganization: First, to separate the industry oversight and business management functions, and second, to better position CNPC and Sinopec Group as efficient, competitive companies (Wu, 2002). To establish new market segments, the government organized a series of asset transfers between CNPC and Sinopec Group that significantly increased vertical integration at both companies. CNPC transferred to Sinopec many of it oil and gas production interests in the southern and eastern China, and in return it received 15 petrochemical plants and refineries in northern and western China. The Ministry of Chemical Industry transferred its oil and gas interests to CNPC, and the petroleum distribution companies owned by provincial level governments were split between CNPC and Sinopec. These changes resulted in a regionally segmented industry, and government continued its industry level reform efforts by shifting all industry oversight roles previously filled by CNPC and Sinopec to the newly formed State Bureau of Petroleum and Chemical Industry.

The management at the newly restructured CNPC realized that to become an efficient and competitive organization after operating for so many years as a government ministry would require a radical transformation. While CNPC had been established in 1988 to improve the competiveness of China's oil and gas industries, in the ten years leading up to the 1998 reforms the company had been unable to make a break with its past as a government ministry. Though no longer formally part of the government, it had continued to face many of the same problems and inefficiencies the Ministry of Petroleum Industry had encountered before it was disbanded. When CNPC was formed as a state-owned enterprise, it inherited responsibility for nearly all aspects of its employees' lives. This imposed both operational and financial burdens, as the lack of market mechanisms made it necessary for CNPC to establish and operate its own social services such as hospitals, schools, court systems, and police departments. In fact, many of the oil fields the company operated were effectively self-contained cities presided over by its general manager, with around 500,000 employees working in social services positions unrelated to oil exploration or production. The *danwei* system made it all but impossible to fire workers, and CNPC's payroll had ballooned to 1.54 million employees and 400,000 retirees by the early 1990s. Additionally, workers had ample opportunities to take advantage of the system. For example, Smyth, Qingguo, and Jing

(2001) found that at Fushun CNPC, employees could apply for *li gang* status ("leaving their post") when they reach age 45 for women or age 50 for men, and over 7,500 employees had secured such status in 1999. These workers continued to receive 80% of their salaries as well as all social benefits given to normal employees. The system is even more generous at some subsidiaries such as the CNPC's Fushun Catalytic Plant, where *li gang* workers also receive private medical and property insurance. Programs of this nature exacerbated the burden of providing social services to the point that nearly all of the revenues from the company's oil businesses were used to provide social services.

The company's dysfunctional financial system essentially placed each regional division in charge of its own money, thereby removing much of its incentive to grow profits across the firm. This left CNPC's executive management unable to effectively implement strategic initiatives, and it gradually assumed the role of administrator to "powerful subordinates who operated their own businesses. In this environment many regional managers began making ill-advised investments in self-benefitting pet projects often those unrelated to oil exploration and production. As government financial support continued to decline throughout the mid-1990s, it became increasingly clear to many at CNPC that unless they acted quickly the firm could be facing some very serious problems. Executives realized it was no longer feasible to rely on the government for financing, and the company began searching for new sources of capital. By 1997, the company's government financing was for all intents purposes zero, but it had still not been successful in securing the needed capital. Later that year, a company analysis predicted that, assuming the price of oil would remain relatively stable, CNPC would be unable to fulfill one-third of its required capital in each of the upcoming three years. In response, the company's president Zhou Yongkang formed a ten-person team headed up by Gong Huazhang that was tasked solely with raising enough new capital for the company to continue its development. The team's analysis quickly revealed that, as an intact company, CNPC would almost certainly be unable to raise sufficient capital for three key reasons: First, the company's outdated management practices, social burden, low efficiency effectively disqualified it from holding an international equity offering, second, because of its vast size it was also highly unlikely that it could raise enough through an offering on the still-immature domestic market, and third, very few banks were willing to lend any significant amount to CNPC because of it high debt/equity ratio and its projected capital shortfalls.

Managing the Reform of CNPC[7]

CNPC first began exploring the idea of creating an international oil company within the model of the Chinese oil and gas industry when its senior management established the Enterprise Reform Office in 1992. The management team knew that it was in need of a serious restructuring to eliminate the multiple legal entities and levels of management, refocus the company on its core businesses, expose the company to external pressures to drive reform, and to increase the efficiency with which the company used its resources. Shortly after a state government reform proposal was drafted in 1995, China International Capital Corporation and Goldman Sachs Asia approached CNPC with a proposal to provide advice regarding the restructuring and potential IPO. (CICC is a joint venture between four companies including the Construction Bank of China and Morgan Stanley.)

The Public Listing Preparation Team identified four steps for the company's restructuring: First, CNPC's social functions would be returned to government; second, the CNPC's noncore services would be consolidated into a company still owned by CNPC; third, transfer all the core oil and gas operations to a new subsidiary (PetroChina); and fourth, to publicly list PetroChina in the United States, Europe, and Hong Kong. After CNPC received approval of its plans from the State Council in 1999, it initially planned to take PetroChina public that same year. However, several unexpected challenges caused the company to delay the IPO until April 2000. One of these problems was that the low price of oil, coupled with lack of knowledge and interest in Chinese SOEs on the part of international capital markets and investors, meant that demand for the newly listed shares would be uncertain. To boost demand, CNPC sought out substantial investments from companies it believed would be strategically beneficial. The most notable of these investments was the purchase of 10% of the available shares by BP (Wu, 2002). A separate issue was related to the opposition of the IPO because of PetroChina's interests in Sudan. Initially these concerns were being voiced only by a small group of NGOs, but as the publicity surrounding the deal intensified, it was decided that CNPC should continue to hold these controversial investments. After making these changes, CNPC went ahead with the IPO on April 6, 2000 and raised US $2.456 billion through after listing H-shares in Hong Kong and American Depository Shares in Europe and the United States. While shifting ownership of its controversial projects in Sudan enabled the IPO to go forward, PetroChina has faced continued criticisms by groups that claim transferring ownership back to the parent company does not excuse PetroChina's activities in Sudan. The campaign led by these groups was successful in pressuring several large investors such as state pension funds and the Harvard endowment fund to divest themselves of PetroChina shares.

Much of the opposition to PetroChina's IPO, however, stemmed from the fact that 86% of the company is owned, and controlled, by a Chinese national SOE. Many potential investors and analysts raised concerns about the company's ability to act in the best interests of its public shareholders in the event that the CCP's interests diverged from those of CNPC or PetroChina. A separate but related issue concerned many potential business partners as well. The widespread opposition to the IPO by labor unions and NGOs raised the possibility that doing business with PetroChina might lead to labor problems or a customer backlash. Such problems actually materialized for BP Amoco and Talisman of Canada, as both found themselves the targets of divestment and boycott movements aimed at pressuring the companies into ending their business dealings with Petro-China (Hiebert & Saywell, 2000). Despite the challenges the government's involvement posed to PetroChina's IPO, the company's overall relationship with the government has been very beneficial.

PetroChina's initial public offering was backed by Goldman Sachs, UBS, and CICC. It was also coached along by McKinsey, Pricewaterhouse Coopers, and a number of foreign law firms. The cynical view of this team of firms was that they simply brought the legitimacy that top investment banks, consulting and accounting firms could bring to a project like this and that legitimacy would be necessary for the IPO roadshow that PetroChina would embark upon. However, the reality is that the Chinese learned much more from the firms they engaged in restructuring PetroChina, as they studied the officials governing the firm worked to create the incentive systems that would make the company more efficient. As Dyck and Huang (2004, p. 4) point out, "In the roadshow, aside from questions about future strategy, the reform that garnered the most attention was the innovative compensation scheme that offered strong incentives for managers to focus on stock performance and, it was hoped, provided a mechanism to refocus management from volume-based to profit-based goals." And the structure of these incentives was specific and closely tied to cost reduction, attainment of profit targets, and return on capital. All employees from department general managers and above would be compensated through a combination of stock options, performance bonus, and salary. The approach was nothing short of revolutionary in the Chinese context:

It fundamentally altered the approach to the link between performance and compensation that was heretofore accepted practice in the PRC.

The use of stock options as an incentive for senior executives and high-level skilled employees in Chinese SOEs has not been without controversy inside of China. And it is still a system under development. Some reports have indicated that the Ministry of Finance was only appointing senior executives who understood that they would never exercise their options; at the very least, it was taboo to discuss the issue or publicly acknowledge that options were being exercised. New official policies followed in 2006 – a regulation released by SASAC called the Measures for State-Owned Overseas Listed Companies – which stated that options should not exceed 10% of a state-owned corporation's capital base; the regulation also instituted a two-year wait for exercising options. (It is worth noting here that, while such restrictions may seem overly controlling to US observers, the recent crisis of capitalism in the United States and, in particular, the pondering of run-away executive compensation, raises the question of whether the Chinese approach is a more balanced way to handle incentive-based pay.)

Transparency and Institutional Innovation

There are two additional ways that this argument that runs counter to most perceptions of China and state-directed economies more generally and is perhaps the most uncomfortable to face for believers in the superiority of the market as a coordinating system. First, there is a way in which the US system is actually less transparent than a state-directed economy such as China's. While we typically believe that even if China's economy is proving successful in its transformation, we have them beat in the areas of corporate and political transparency. But do we? The ways in which the corporate lobby plays a fundamental role in shaping the US economy – whether in the area of oil subsidies, bank deregulation, or corporate bailouts – is one of the more opaque processes within the US political system. The recent indictment of Goldman Sachs in *Rolling Stone* (Taibbi, 2009) has been dismissed by some (including Goldman) as conspiracy theory and defenseless journalism, but the backdoor politics that play a role in the formation of US policy (from deregulation of the banking system to the question of whether Goldman was eligible for TARP money) are undeniable. The more interesting question than the Goldman influence is all of the subtler corporate lobbying that we do not see and cannot find the smoking gun for. Take, for example, the role of ExxonMobil in the formation of US public policy around the environment. A number of policy advocates and journalists have written about the hidden power and influence the world's largest Oil Company has had on US policy behind the scenes (Revkin, 2005; Kennedy, 2005), and of course, ExxonMobil has denied such a role vehemently. But the role of ExxonMobil in shaping outcomes like the US's failure to sign the Kyoto Accord to XXX is well-documented at this point. In the Chinese system, while no one would argue that the processes that define Chinese politics are transparent, the alignment between the state and the corporate sector is in some ways more above board than it is in the US system. The state-as-owner simply means that we know whose interests the state is acting in instead of the obfuscated behind-the-scenes relationships that influence American policy-making so many fundamental ways. Our argument here is not that the Chinese system is better than the US market economy; nor is the argument that Chinese firms are more effective than US corporations. However, it is important to note that we in societies promoting free market economies do not seem to have the stomach or political will for the type of system we idealize. Over the past 40 years our economic heroes have become individuals like Milton Friedman, advocating the freedom to pursue power and plenty in the unfettered markets of the US system. But when the risks lead to default, we do not seem to have the will to connect those outcomes with the economic or political system we advocate. In the end, we may have something to learn from the state-directed economies of China and Singapore. These are economies in which the state has an unapologetic interest in directing toward the public good. And, in the end, that approach may be more in the public's interest and more transparent than our own process of behind-the-scenes corporate lobby and after-the-fact bailouts.

Second, it is widely held that private firms are more innovative than state-owned organizations. However, this simplistic caricature of state-owned and private organizations ignores just how innovative in terms of new organizational forms a state-run economy can be. Take, for example, the case of the China-Singapore Suzhou Industrial Park Development Co., Ltd (CSSD): Here is a public–private partnership that has become one of the most innovative organizations in China, and has helped make the small city of Suzhou the number one destination for FDI in China. Like many cities across China, Suzhou recognized that its success would depend on its ability to offer prospective investors a tangible competitive advantage that other areas were not able to provide. Suzhou municipal authorities believed Singapore's expertise developing industrial parks could help their efforts to attract FDI to the Suzhou New District Economic Development Zone (SND) established in 1990. In 1992, they offered the SND as a possible location for the collaborative project, however, Singapore rejected the site in favor of an undeveloped area east of the city. China and Singapore officially agreed to cooperate in developing the China-Singapore Suzhou Industrial Park as a mutually beneficial intergovernmental project in February 1994 (Pereira, 2004).

The CSSD, which runs the SIP, was established in August 1994 after the Ministry of Foreign Trade and Economic Cooperation approved the joint venture agreement between China Suzhou Industrial Park Co., Ltd and the Singapore-Suzhou Township Development Co., Ltd. The CSSD is mainly responsible for investment promotion, development, and property management of the 70 sq km Cooperation Zone, while the Suzhou Industrial Park Administrative Committee (SIPAC) handles the overall management of the park. SIPAC has divided the total area of the park into functional zones designed to improve quality of life and ensure the SIP operates as a livable community.[8] Today, this organization is preparing for an IPO to be publicly listed on the Singaporean stock exchange. This organization is profitable, and it has become one of many dynamic and innovative public–private partnerships in the Chinese economy.

CONCLUSIONS

We began this article with a simple thesis: Regardless of what we rhetorically think about the elegance of a laissez-faire economic system, in the United States we simply do not have the political will for it. Markets must have the ability to discipline economic actors for risky behavior (or, in the case of GM, lethargic behavior). We like deregulation when it leads to risk that then produces reward; we seek bailouts when these risky behaviors turn sour. Without the ability to discipline capital, the key feedback mechanism within markets cannot function. We are playing with house money.

The core concept of the efficiency of a deregulated market system is often contrasted to the notion of the fundamental inefficiency of state ownership. However, while this view has been widely accepted as fact throughout the world, the Chinese case belies this view. In reform-era China, there has been a tremendous amount of institutional innovation that has allowed for a reform of incentives – leading to greater efficiency – while at the same time allowing the state to continue to watch over and guide the economy. We presented one example here, and this is only the most famous among many such examples within the Chinese system. But if it is the case that a semi-state-owned system can operate with some level of efficiency, what does that say about the argument for a laissez-faire market system, which is inevitably more risky than its more regulated counterpart? There are a few key takeaway points here: First, markets and private ownership might be the best system for creating an efficient economic outcome, however, this system cannot work without the ability to discipline capital for risky decisions. In other words, if we do not have the political will to let large organizations fail, deregulated markets cannot be allowed. Firms will simply act in more and more risky ways, because they will always count on the fact that the government will bail them out in crisis situations. Second, while we typically conceive of private ownership as leading to efficiency and innovation and state ownership as leading to inefficiency and complacency, this caricature simply does not match reality. In some cases, private firms like General Motors can be woefully inefficient, while state-owned firms like PetroChina can be extremely efficient. The issue is not public versus private ownership per se; rather it is how effectively incentives are aligned to create dynamism and innovation in the marketplace. Further, state ownership has the added role of forcing firms to think long term and align themselves with national interests.

Policy Implications and Directions Future Research

The above points have several policy implications. First, the view we have taken here is that deregulation and bailouts cannot go together. Given that we live in a system in which corporations and some conservative economic analysts continually push for deregulatory policies that allow for more and more risky behavior, we cannot then turn around a bail out firms for the risk they have taken on. Doing so destroys the key mechanism through which markets force firms to think about risk. Because we do not seem to have the political will to let large-scale corporations and banks fail, the inevitable conclusion is that we need to regulate economic decision-making up front. (And we cannot simply say "next time it will be different"; we have failed that test too many times in recent years.) Unfortunately, for the financial sector, the future on this front looks bleak. In the same way that banks learned little from the S&L Crisis of 1986 – the lobbying for the repeal of Glass–Steagall began only a few years later – banks pushed the envelope far beyond the limits of reasonable behavior. And if we are not willing to let them fail as a result of that risky behavior, we clearly need regulatory limits on economic behavior. However, the fundamental reforms have not been forthcoming.

Second, policy makers should be less fearful of and think more innovatively about public–private partnerships. In China, the government is deeply engaged in the economy – not only as regulator but also as economic agent. And, contrary to the common portrayal of SOEs as inefficient and complacent organizations, China has been able to align the incentives of senior executives in the SOEs; the government has also done an effective job of aligning the incentives of local officials. The key policy lesson here is that government agencies can be quite effective in guiding economic organizations: They are in a position to consider national (or local) strategic policy issues and broader issues of systemic risk; and contrary to popular belief, they can also think about economic action in creative and institutionally innovative ways. A final policy issue that has often been promised but has yet to be delivered upon has to do with the corporate lobby. There has been much written about the Obama Administration's failure to limit the corporate lobby's impact on American policy formation, but the issue extends far beyond the current Administration. Whether it is the Oil Industry's impact on energy and environmental policy; or the financial sector's impact on financial regulation and bailouts for failing banks; or the insurance industry's hand in shaping the healthcare debate; we simply live in a world today that is far too influenced by corporate interests. As Robert Reich (1998) put it over a decade ago: "The modern corporation cannot simultaneously claim, as a matter of public morality and public policy, that its only legitimate societal mission is to maximize shareholder returns, while at the same time actively seek to influence social policies intended to achieve all the things a society may wish to do ... The paradox of our time, of course, is that just the opposite is occurring."

The foregoing discussion points in three directions with respect to future research. First, we need more theoretical research on how and the conditions under which state ownership might lead to efficient outcomes. Efficiency assumptions in the fields of Economics and Political Science have long (at least since Kornai (1980) but perhaps longer) defined it as impossible that market incentives can align with state bureaucratic position. China has proved these assumptions to be wrong. Rather than maintaining that China must be hiding something – that privatization must be happening in some hidden way – economic theorists need to consider that their models and assumptions are being challenged and recognize these new economic circumstances for what they are. Second, we need more in-depth empirical research on effective public–private partnerships. We need a combination of descriptive and analytical work that uncovers and examines innovative public–private partnerships like CSSD. For too long, we have assumed that state involvement simply leads to inefficiency and, as a result, we have missed many of the powerful examples of success in this category of organizations. Third, we need research on these issues at the organizational level. While we know that PetroChina is among the most efficient energy companies in the world, and we have a sense that this is due to the combination of the strategic advantages of being close to the state and the use of market-based incentives, there is simply not enough detailed information out there on how companies like PetroChina are run. What is it really that makes organizations like this effective. Ideally, we need ethnographic work in organizations like PetroChina to help us understand the mechanisms that drive efficiency, the conditions under which state ownership leads to the positive outcomes that we typically associate with private ownership.

NOTES

1. Throughout the 1990s, economists like J. D. Sachs and W. T. Woo (1994a, 1994b, 1997) and more popular pundits like Gordon Chang (2001) tried embarrassingly hard to explain away China's continued success. China posed a problem for the rapid privatization school: Given that everyone since Kornai (1980) had been arguing that you cannot have a transition to a market economy without a rapid transition to private property, a prescription that Russia followed under Sachs' guidance, how, then, do we account for China's dramatic success? The answer, according to the Sachs camp, was that China got lucky. Because China had less of an industrial infrastructure than its Eastern European counterparts and it also had a deep cheap labor pool to draw on, it has been able to do OK despite its recalcitrance in the area of privatization. The Sachs camp also argues that China would have done much better if it would have followed their model, an argument that is difficult to see given the disastrous outcome of Russia under Sachs' advisement.

2. To be fair to Milton Friedman, he always remained committed to the ideological position he staked out. With respect to the current economic crisis, for example, he would likely not have supported any type of bailout for the banking sector. Neoliberal that he was, he was always at least consistent.

3. Crandall (1993) developed an important variation on this general idea: Namely, that even within the United States, there were important *regional* domestic shifts that were occurring in the location of manufacturing as well as emergent markets. For those in the traditional "rust belt" of the upper Midwest associated with automaking, such moves south and west often proved equally distressing.

4. As Whitford (2005) later observed, manufacturing survived the dearth of supportive policies and continues to be restructured in the collaborative and decentralized ways that reflect networked and global thinking and, most interestingly, service industries.

5. Freedman and Stonecash (1997) summarize the different historical roles adopted by the US government in implementing economic policy as follows: "(1) To act as a referee in the operation of free-markets; (2) To regulate public utilities to ensure efficient provision of goods produced by natural monopolies; (3) To pursue social objectives, such as income redistribution and correction of externality problems, to safeguard the well-being of consumers. These roles do not suggest that government might play a part in restructuring allocations to improve efficiency. The presumption inherent in this description is that markets are best at performing the allocation function. What government can contribute is to ensure that all parties are playing by the rules of the game. Hence anti-trust regulation is emphasized in most US texts." Industrial policy as being discussed here, relevant to General Motors and the manufacturing sector, would most readily have fallen into the third broad role (had it been enacted).

6. "PetroChina Company Ltd," Hoovers Company Information.

7. Smyth, Qingguo, and Jing, "Labour Market Reform in China's State-Owned Enterprises: A Case Study of Post-Deng Fushun in Liaoning Province."

8. CSSD, "中新苏州工业园区开发有限公司 (The Chinese-Singapore-Jiangsu Industrial Park Limited Liability Company)," http://www.cssd.com.cn/index.shtml

REFERENCES

Berry, S., Levinsohn, J., & Pakes, A. (1999). Voluntary export restraints on automobiles: Evaluating a trade policy. *American Economic Review, 89*(3), 400–430.

Chang, C. (2001). *The coming collapse of China*. New York: Random House.

Cohen, S. S., & Zysman, J. (1987). *Manufacturing matters: The myth of the post-industrial economy*. A Council on Foreign Relations Book. New York: Basic Books.

Crandall, R. W. (1993). *Manufacturing on the move*. Washington, DC: The Brookings Institution.

Crandall, R. W., Gruenspecht, H. K., Keeler, T. E., & Lave, L. B. (1986). *Regulating the automobile*. Washington, DC: The Brookings Institution.

Dyck, A., & Huang, Y. (2004). *PetroChina*. Harvard Business School Case #9-701-040. Cambridge, MA: Harvard Business School Press.

Feenstra, R. C. (1995). Estimating the effects of trade policy. In: G. M. Grossman & K. Rogoff (Eds), *Handbook of international economics* (Vol. III, pp. 1553–1595). Amsterdam: North-Holland.

Fine, C., & St. Clair, R. (1996). *The U.S. automobile manufacturing industry*. Washington, DC: U.S. Department of Commerce, Office of Technology Policy.

Freedman, C., & Stonecash, R. (1997). A survey of manufacturing industry policy: From the tariff board to the productivity commission. *Economic Record, 73*(221), 169–183.

Graham, O. L., Jr. (1992). *Losing time: The industrial policy debate*. Cambridge: Harvard University Press.

Hiebert, M., & Saywell, T. (2000). Market morality. *Far Eastern Economic Review, 56*.

Itoh, M., Kiyono, K., Okuno, M., & Suzumura, K. (1988). Industrial policy as a corrective to market failures. In: R. Komiya (Ed.), *Industrial policy of Japan* (pp. 233–255). Tokyo: Academic Press.

Kennedy, R. F. (2005). *Crimes against nature: How George W. Bush and his corporate pals Are plundering the country and hijacking our democracy.* New York: Harper Perennial.

Kornai, J. (1980). *The shortage economy.* Amsterdam: North-Holland.

Kornai, J. (1990). *The road to a free economy.* New York: W. W. Norton.

Levinsohn, J. (1994). International trade and the U.S. automobile industry: Current research, issues, and questions. *Japan and the World Economy, 6*(4), 335–357.

Norton, R. D. (1986). Industrial policy and American renewal. *Journal of Economic Literature, XXIV*(1), 1–41.

Pereira, A. A. (2004). The Suzhou industrial park experiment: The case of China–Singapore governmental collaboration. *Journal of Contemporary China, 13*(38), 173–193.

Ramaswamy, R. (1997). *Deindustrialization: Causes and implications.* IMF Working Paper no. 97/42. Washington, DC.

Reich, R. (1998). The new meaning of corporate social responsibility. *California Management Review, 40*(winter), 2.

Reich, R. (2009). General Motors holds a mirror up to America. *Financial Times,* May 31. Available at http://www.ft.com/cms/s/0/528ba940-4e19-11de-a0a1-00144feabdc0.html. Accessed on February 19, 2010.

Revkin, A. (2005). Former Bush aide who edited reports is hired by Exxon. *New York Times,* June 15.

Rowe, W., & Rowe, G. (2006). *Restructuring CNPC and the proposed listing of petrochina.* London, ON: Ivey School of Business.

Sachs, J. D. (1992). Privatization in Russia: Some lessons from Eastern Europe. *American Economic Review, 80,* 43–48.

Sachs, J. D., & Woo, W. T. (1994a). Experiences in the transition to a market economy. *Journal of Comparative Economics, 18*(3), 271–275.

Sachs, J. D., & Woo, W. T. (1994b). Structural factors in the economic reforms of China, Eastern Europe, and the former Soviet Union. *Economic Policy, 9*(18), 101–131.

Sachs, J. D., & Woo, W. T. (1997). *Understanding China's economic performance.* Working Paper no. 5935. Working Paper Series. National Bureau of Economic Research, Inc.

Smyth, R., Qingguo, Z., & Jing, W. (2001). Labour market reform in China's state-owned enterprises: A case study of post-Deng Fushun in Liaoning Province. *New Zealand Journal of Asian Studies, 3*(2), 42–72.

Sturgeon, T. J., & Florida, R. (2000). *Globalization and jobs in the automotive industry.* Working Paper Series, MIT-IPC-00-012. Industrial Performance Center, MIT.

Taibbi, M. (2009). The Great American bubble machine: From tech stocks to high gas prices, Goldman Sachs has engineered every major market manipulation since the great depression and they're about to do it again. *Rolling Stone,* July 13.

White, L. J. (1982). *The regulation of air pollutant emissions from motor vehicles.* Washington, DC: American Enterprise Institute.

Whitford, J. (2005). *The new old economy: Networks, institutions, and the organizational transformation of American manufacturing.* New York: Oxford University Press.

Wines, M. (1983). Reagan plan to relieve auto industry of regulatory burden gets mixed grades. *National Journal*, 23 July, 1532–1537; qtd. in Viscusi, W. K. (1995). The misspecified agenda: The 1980s reforms of health, safety, and environmental regulation. In: M. Feldstein (Ed.), *American economic policy in the 1980s* (pp. 453–504). Chicago: University of Chicago Press.

Wu, M. (2002). *A study of restructuring in the Chinese petroleum sector* (Working paper). Cambridge, MA: Massachusetts Institute of Technology.

Zysman, J., & Tyson, L. (Eds). (1983). *American industry in international competition: Government policies and corporate strategies.* Ithaca, NY: Cornell University Press.

PRECEDENCE FOR THE UNPRECEDENTED: A COMPARATIVE INSTITUTIONALIST VIEW OF THE FINANCIAL CRISIS

Gerald A. McDermott

ABSTRACT

This essay argues for a sociopolitical approach to the study of the current financial crisis in the United States and other advanced industrialized countries. Such an approach offers a bridge between economic sociology and historical institutionalism that can help analysts identify the ways in which relevant public and private actors experiment with institutional mechanisms that help resolve stock and flow problems as well as consider alternative regulatory forms. In particular, I suggest how comparative analysis and considerations of political struggles can improve our notion of embeddedness and assessment of both proximate solutions and longer term paths of adjustment.

The current global financial and economic crisis has ignited a host of ongoing debates about the roots of the meltdown, potential solutions, and

Markets on Trial: The Economic Sociology of the U.S. Financial Crisis: Part B
Research in the Sociology of Organizations, Volume 30B, 313–328
Copyright © 2010 by Emerald Group Publishing Limited
ISSN: 0733-558X/doi:10.1108/S0733-558X(2010)000030B014

the adequacy of the theoretical approaches used to analyze crises, particularly with respect to US financial markets. The initial salvos in these debates have largely centered on two types of unsurprising responses. The first is market centered. It points to the distorted incentives that government intervention into the market has created over the years for banks, firms and households, such as cheap money in the forms of low interest rates and government-backed financing for small firms and mortgages. This view cautions us to be very wary of government action and to allow markets effectively to resolve themselves, as the invisible hand cleans up after collapsed banks, corporations, and homeowners. The second is state-centered, wrapped in the nostalgia of Keynesianism. Freewheeling markets, reignited in the 1980s, have wreaked havoc on the populace, while government has been complicit in offering namely financial actors far too many resources and venues to test the limits of some new math. This view emphasizes that regulation must come back in force and state must act now as the surrogate financier of many sectors.

While parts of these two perspectives certainly ring true, one might have already noticed that the articles in this volume offer an alternative direction of analysis, one rooted in sociopolitical institutions and organizations. This difference cannot be understated or undervalued as it has the potential to help scholars and practitioners alike from repeating the same mistakes as with previous crises. That is, despite the contrasts between the aforementioned views, they have many common misperceptions about the emergence and dynamics of markets.

The first among them is their underappreciation about the institutional and organizational foundations of modern capitalism, which in turn can lead to technocratic solutions. Such an approach has the dual danger of not only failing to focus on the institutional configuration of market activities but also missing the sociopolitical roots of what leads to crisis, and which alternative paths societies may take. In contrast, we have a rather robust literature on past crises that has revealed the limits of a reliance on standard economic models. For instance, a key dilemma during the downturn of the US economy in the 1970s was the use of technocratic macroeconomic solutions as evidenced in the McCracken Report (Keohane, 1978). In doing so, policymakers overlooked the rigidities in US industrial and social welfare institutions as well as the possible adjustment models offered elsewhere in the world, be they alternative forms of industrial organization, labor representation, or policymaking at the commanding heights (Berger, 1981; Lowi, 1979; Piore & Sabel, 1984). A more recent example is the turn to market democracies in Latin America and post-communist Europe. In these cases, assumptions about state failure and market creation through market means (Stark & Bruszt, 1998) led not only to proximate problems of political-economic volatility but also a longer term disruption of the social sciences, where untested and ahistorical economic models overshadowed grounded political and institutional analysis, where a decade passed when the multilaterals suddenly discovered the importance of governance and regulation (World Bank, 1999, 2002; Kogut & Spicer, 2004).

This article does not attempt to offer an elixir to our current troubles but rather attempts to build on the institutional and organizational direction of the articles herewith and propose some avenues of investigation that a comparative, historical institutionalist view might foster when considering two key agendas initiated by the current crisis: (1) examining the proximate causes and solutions to the current crisis and (2) rethinking the ways in which scholars (and their graduate students) will analyze the longer term political-economic contours of adjustment. I begin with setting up some basic assumptions about markets in general and financial markets in particular. A promising intersection of research on information asymmetries, economic sociology, and historical institutionalism frames modern markets as experimental regulatory capitalism. I then use this framework to comment on the aforementioned agendas.

1. INSTITUTIONS AND NORMAL ACCIDENTS: MARKETS AS POLITICAL CREATIONS

From Polanyi to North, scholars have increasingly embraced the notion that markets are embedded in institutions, which stabilize, regulate, and legitimize economic activity. How institutions do this and where they come from are more contested debates that reach across paradigms, from the economistic view, which focuses on the incentives created by formal rules to the organizational view, prominent in this volume, which emphasizes the ways in which procedures and routines coordinate rationally bounded individuals, to the historical institutionalist view, which stresses how power and group interests clash to determine largely public institutions and then can be reshaped by the lock in effects of institutional consolidation (Immergut, 1998; Thelen, 1999). The latter view sets itself apart from the others largely due to its emphasis on the ways in which political struggles over resources and ideology are infused in the creation and maintenance of economic governance institutions.

To be fair, each of these views incorporates a certain degree of the roles of the state and politics shaping market institutions. But what does it mean to say that "politics matters" when considering the causes and solutions to financial crises? Consider first the notion that states make markets (Bruszt, 2002). Recent work on the evolution of financial institutions in the United States builds on incomplete markets theory to show how risk must often be socialized in order for private investment to take place in a sustainable manner (Immergluck, 2009; Moss, 2002). From the rise of Chapter 11 bankruptcy to modern mortgage markets, we find that market transactions in themselves are insufficient to resolve a host of problems related to the restructuring of companies to the financing of small firms and households. In turn, the state must often enter markets to absorb some of the risks and create the means to monitor the private market actors that benefit from these services.

Such a view of financial markets raises two key concerns. First, it highlights the fragility of markets. That is, since new opportunities and risks regularly emerge, the state must be rather vigilant in absorbing or containing market failures. This view coincides with the notion of normal accidents, as elaborated by Perrow (1984) and applied in several articles in this volume. Normal accidents are said to be highly likely when an organizational system is both complex and the constituent organizations are highly coupled. One may interpret this to mean that accidents rarely occur. But notice that if the state is an inherent part of market expansion and we assume that institutions and organizations are slow to adjust, then "accidents" are a constitutive part of financial markets and economic governance. The degree to which accidents threaten systemic stability depends on the ability of the regulators to adjust, which in turn can be facilitated or stymied by nature of political governance of the state itself.

The second concern, then, is considering how the state, and societies more broadly, may attempt to share risk, while attempting simultaneously to limit the problems of moral hazard and adverse selection – i.e., still promote investment and innovation by a diverse set of actors while limiting abuse and self-dealing. For a historical institutionalist, it is in this "grey zone" between the formal state and society where institutions emerge. Social and economic groups position themselves to solicit state action and legislation and clash over the ways in which resources will be distributed, rights will be empowered, and rules will be defined and enforced. While scholars may debate whether such a process is defined by a clash of independent interests in a neutral forum or by a state amassing the autonomy to impose a solution, the key point here is that market creation and evolution goes hand in hand with state crafting and institutional maintenance.

The modern capitalist economy is therefore not characterized by the "market preserving state," which simply enforces minimalist rules of property rights (Weingast, 1995), but rather by the "experimental regulatory state," in which public and private actors experiment with policies and coalitions to form complex institutions that typify modern regulatory capitalism (Bruszt, 2002; Jordana & Levi-Faur, 2004). It is regulatory in the sense that the state and private groups (e.g., associations) actively build capabilities to absorb risk, coordinate information and resources flows, and monitor one another's actions. It is experimental in the sense that the relevant actors do not necessarily know ex ante which types of institutions are most effective but must regularly upgrade their roles as new "accidents" occur.

To the extent that the experimental regulatory capitalism provides the foundations for modern financial markets, then our analysis of the current crisis is altered in two important ways. First, as Polanyi (1944) noted long ago, the emergence of broad based financial and economic instability points to the limits of technocratic solutions based on a change in a rule or a reliance on self-regulating incentives. Rather, resolution demands a more comprehensive and deeper revision of the existing institutional architecture. Given the political foundations of the institutions themselves, it is difficult to imagine a sustainable reform without a reassessment of the governance structures supporting and overseeing the regulatory process. Second, the issues of the causes and resolutions to crisis are inherently comparative. That is, modern capitalist economies vary dramatically in terms of the ways they have created and adapted institutions over time (Hall & Soskice, 2001; Campbell, 2004). The comparative lens, at a minimum, allows us to consider the alternative restructuring paths available to polities and the extent to which social and political forces shape their evolution (Sabel & Zeitlin, 1997).

2. PRECEDENCE FOR THE PROXIMATE CAUSES AND SOLUTIONS

Practically a week does not pass without an opinion piece or a working paper debating what went wrong and what is to be done. The main problems being addressed are resolving the restructuring of the bad debt, restoring lending, and, if necessary, adjusting the current regulatory system.

The lack of an institutionalist perspective in these public debates has to a certain degree revealed a rather frenetic nature of the positions being taken. On the one hand, the utter shock of the collapse of markets in the fall of 2008 has spurred a drumbeat of doom, which in many ways reflects the sudden realization (or disappointment for some) about the role of the state and regulation in maintaining the stability of the financial system. On the other hand, we are reminded that the current crisis is not unprecedented but rather banking crises occur periodically not just in modern times but for the past 700 years (Reinhart & Rogoff, 2009). But if "this time is not so different," then what can the past teach us about this crisis?

The immediate answer coming from finance and economics appears to be an abstract application of Keynesianism. At first glance, evoking the name of Keynes might make readers enthusiastic about the proposed remedies. Yet as other scholars have noted, the seemingly unconventional approaches to economics spawned by Keynes and even Schumpeter overlook the institutional dimensions of markets and crises (Hall, 1989; North, 1990; Beamish & Biggart, 2010). In this section, I simply want to highlight the implications of this oversight and suggest how attention to the institutional architecture offers an alternative "precedence" of guidance through this immediate debate.

As Reinhart and Rogoff (2009) amply demonstrate, the immediate common challenge to financial crises is resolving the stock of existing bad debt and the flow of future credit, namely to firms, and in the current US context to homeowners as well. The stock problem is ideally resolved by a one-time form of public assistance (write-offs and recapitalizations) that also limits expectations of further bailouts. The flow problem is a longer term issue and potentially a function of institutional change – governance of the banks, creditor rights, prudential regulation, etc. The key question for the current crisis is whether institutional change is needed for resolving the flow problem.

The abstract application of Keynesianism is the notion that when there appears to be a systemic crisis, the government must inject funds into the market in order to provide liquidity and restore confidence for lenders and investors. This is largely not controversial and can be seen in crises ranging from the Tequila effect in Mexico in 1994 to the current responses by the Bush and Obama administrations in the form of emergency bailouts of financial institutions and stimulus spending. To a certain extent, this approach is in line with resolving the stock problem as stated above. Resolving the flow problem is more contested, however. The conventional tendency is to separate the stock and flow problems, allowing, in the current

US context, the market to resolve the latter. This approach assumes to large degree that the existing institutional mechanisms for restructuring and investment are sufficient and effective, and therefore there is no reason for the state to intervene further.

A good example of this assumption and its limits can be found in the 2009 bailout of General Motors and Chrysler. On the one hand, the government recognized that in the current context, simply letting the two companies fail and enter into normal bankruptcy procedures would set off a further systemic crisis in manufacturing and financial sectors. This was a recognition that the state needs to step in to coordinate this process and limit panic. On the other hand, once the panic abated, the government was willing to step back and let the invisible hand work out the details. But as automotive experts Susan Helper and John Paul MacDuffie have noted, this view assumes that costs are the main challenge to the US auto industry (Helper & MacDuffie, 2008). They point out that the long-term problem of the industry, which also led to its current crisis, is less about cost reduction and more about constant improvements in quality, i.e., in process and product innovation. Because over 75 percent of the value of a vehicle is produced outside of the assembler and along the value chain, such improvements demand a reconfiguration of relationships between suppliers and customers and of the public–private institutions that support training and R&D. This is not at all forthcoming under the current uncertainty. As the vast comparative literature on the industry has shown, government must often enter into the game to facilitate a new type of coordination and risk sharing. Indeed, research on mid-west manufacturing has shown that some of the existing public-private technology centers help build new collaborative relationships between firms that advance the diffusion of knowledge and accelerate innovation rates (McEvily & Zaheer, 2004; Whitford, 2005). The current crisis is an opportunity to blend financial restructuring with broadening such a strategy across the industry.

The other obvious example is in the financial realm itself. As several of the articles in this volume suggest, reliance on existing institutional mechanisms to facilitate the debt restructuring for both companies and homeowners has allowed an increase in insolvency and default rates of to such levels that credit markets have frozen, especially to SMEs and individuals. Injecting money into the financial system has allowed some banks to improve their capital base and risk provisioning, but appears insufficient to break the stalemate. To date, the federal government has been reluctant to revise the restructuring system, other than relatively small programs from the FDIC and TARP. Based on the experience of other banking crises both in the

United States and abroad, this trend suggests that the health of the banks has become so intertwined with problem debtors that dramatic restructuring is perceived to be too risky for banking stability. A less risky path thus far has been for the banks to invest the cash into government bonds and equities.

The reluctance to intervene more directly into debt restructuring and thus resolving the flow problem stems in part from the notion that the arms length economic incentives will guide market actors effectively. This notion underpins the model of the market as self-regulating as long as the property rights are set correctly. An alternative view, as noted above, is that markets are incomplete because of information asymmetries. This view coincides with and has been amplified by perspectives from economic sociology and historical institutionalism (Dobbin, 1994; Piore & Sabel, 1984; Woodruff, 1999). Such asymmetries can be reduced by restructuring the social relationships to improve information exchange between the relevant public and private actors, who in turn can build new organizational capabilities to learn from and monitor one another (Sabel, 1994). This is, in a way, what Helper and MacDuffie have been arguing with respect to the automotive sector. It also can be found in comparative work on relatively successful bank crises resolutions such as those in Sweden and Poland. In these cases, the government stepped in to facilitate restructuring by establishing special asset management vehicles to directly administer some of the largest bad debts, similar to the RTC created for the S&L crisis in the United States, and by creating new mechanisms to force banks and debtor firms to reorganize both assets and their relationships (Englund, 1999; Ingves & Lind, 1997; McDermott, 2007).

In turn, the precedence for the current unprecedented crisis may be in lessons that come from other countries and periods that reveal not simply the problems of bubbles and over shooting or quick fixes based on transparency and greater autonomy for market referees, but rather the alternative institutional strategies that governments can take to facilitate learning and monitoring by the market actors themselves. Moreover, these experiences reveal that in order to ensure a new discipline on banks so as to reduce the reoccurrence of a crisis, the altering of institutions to facilitate flows is closely linked to a revision of the existing regulatory system.

Initially, this intertwining of resolving the stock and flows problems with reforming the regulatory system might appear tantamount to a large government takeover of the financial system in blunt force. This is, to a certain degree, a challenge to the political system if framed in such a way. And indeed, one argument against further government intervention is simply that if the government was unable to avert the current crisis, how would it be capable of taking on a more robust role? But the comparative record suggests framing the overall problem as one of a larger state is also misguided. Rather the comparative institutionalist lens helps reveal how alternative strategies center on the ways in which public and private actors reconfigure their relationships and experiment with new roles and capabilities.

The Polish case can be instructive in this regard. As post-communist countries quickly found themselves with rapid and strong increases in defaults and insolvencies as they attempted rapid market liberalization and privatization, the policy options were typically framed as more liberalization or of a return to statism. The Poles rejected both because they felt that while the banks and the judicial system were ill-equipped to handle such a large scale operation, the state lacked the capabilities to manage the complete restructuring directly (Kawalec, Sikora, & Rymaszewski, 1995). Rather they focused on creating mechanisms that would advance restructuring and improve the ability of both state and bank actors to learn from and monitor one another. There were two key mechanisms. First, the government made recapitalization contingent on both a full audit of bank assets and a choice by the banks to resolve the bad debts in a number of ways (liquidation, sale, etc.) with strict deadlines. The most commonly used avenue was "conciliation," which was akin to a US Chapter 11 process, but was monitored by an interagency team composed of actors from the relevant provincial government, the central government, central bank prudential regulator, and the state audit office. Second, representatives from the nine commercial banks in distress and the team met biweekly to exchange information, problem-solve, and compare progress. This process lasted approximately one year.

Although the Polish case is smaller and simpler than the current situation in the United States, the key comparative lesson is that the Poles found an effective way to resolve restructuring problems and facilitate institutional change at several levels (McDermott, 2007). While the process promoted decentralized workouts and negotiations between the banks and debtor firms, the state actors were learning how to effectively monitor such a process and to use state assistance more efficiently. At the same time, the banks themselves were given the breathing room and the information exchange mechanisms to learn how to build new capabilities both to restructure problem firms and to finance investments more effectively. Indeed, many of the restructuring units within the banks developed new risk management systems tailored to the local context and spun off prosperous private equity firms.

Hence, the lesson from abroad is that governments can initiate a debt restructuring process that facilitates the creation of new forms of learning and monitoring. Such an approach did not rely purely on market incentives or on statism, but rather sought to find institutional and organizational solutions to many of the information asymmetry problems that are the key challenges to combining risk management with investment promotion. Moreover, the premise of the Swedish and Polish approaches was not simply that the existing institutional architecture had to change but that the detailed solutions to both restructuring and future regulatory rules and roles could not be known ex ante. Rather, the government's role was to create mechanisms that could be well governed and generate a process whereby the solutions and the capabilities would be created over time. To a certain degree, the comparative record gives credence to such proposals as the one presented by Bartley and Schneiberg in this volume, as it emphasizes mechanisms that can induce the relevant public and private actors to build new institutions for mutual monitoring over time.

3. CONTINUITY AND CHANGE

Earlier I suggested that the incomplete markets view of finance opened the door to linking economic analysis with institutional and organizational approaches to market evolution and crises. Part of this bridging process is utilizing comparative institutional analysis to consider alternative inter-pretations of the proximate causes and solutions of a crisis, as just discussed. These alternatives could be viewed as "models" for filling the aforemen-tioned "grey zone" between the state and society. But a more profound link comes with studies of the longer term factors that shape how the models emerge – the factors that shaped the crisis and then underline the institutional paths that lead out of the crisis.

It is in this venture where the study of politics can be coupled with the organizational theory and economic sociology underpinning the articles in this volume to offer a potential paradigm shift to the study of finance and crises. That is, the institutional models do not grow up in a sociopolitical desert. The studies of past crises and transformations suggest two analytical tendencies to avoid, and how political factors can be integrated into the study of organizational and institutional change.

One of these tendencies is the technocratic approach that emerges from the sole focus on optimal models or designs. The initial studies of post-communist reforms in East Europe suffered greatly from this. Economic models grounded in assumptions about self-regulating, arm's length incentives effectively defined the types of choices that governments could make. These models were typically ahistorical and assumed a tabula rasa for all reforming countries. They specified ideal types of macroeconomic policies and of institutional rules. In doing so, the models gave binary choices about policy and left discussions of politics to whether the politicians had the will and the power requisite to impose the proper plan on society. I have called this elsewhere (McDermott, 2002, 2007) a "depoliticization" approach to institutional change, borrowing the argument of Shleifer and colleagues (Boycko, Shleifer, & Vishny, 1995) that the ideal world is where the state can and should be insulated from interest groups that would merely distort the ideal designs. Much of the political science literature on reforms took this view and the relevant models as the starting points for analysis of political struggles that shaped institutional change.[1] David Woodruff (1999) called this the "politics of the cash register," in which not the construction of institutions but the allocation of rents was at stake. If a selfless pro-market vanguard could defeat the rent-seeking old guard, viable institutions would automatically be established. Today, we see a version of this in Simon Johnson's blogs and op-eds (Johnson, 2009). It reduces politics to the issue of state capture. Because we have a crisis, we assume that the roots of it are found in the ability of some coherent "oligarchy" controlling the levers of policy through the purchase of politicians. If the oligarchy is not broken, then we will see business as usual.

The other tendency is what could be termed as the deep structural approach. This approach, most commonly found in studies in the rise of fascism in Europe and the development literature in the 1960s and 1970s, seeks to identify profound sociocultural traits in societies that prevent or facilitate the rise of prosperous economies or institutional paths. From analyses of the rise of Japanese corporations (Dore, 1973) to the failings of Italy (Putnam, Leonardi, & Nanetti, 1993) to the recurring crises of Latin America (Haber, 2002), institutional change, or lack thereof, is contingent upon an event or belief system from deep history that frames the views and power of groups for decades, if not centuries. Change even in crisis is all but impossible. Politics and policy choices are simply manifestations of these underlying currents.

Both perspectives have their merits, particularly with the former highlighting the possibility of change, albeit narrow, at the commanding heights, and the latter emphasizing the forces of continuity at the more micro-level. Yet despite their apparent differences, they are remarkably similar in their disregard for alternative institutional configurations and the *process* of institution building itself. Whereas the former view proposes that viable solutions depend on whether the "right" set of politicians imposes the "right" sets of institutional designs on society, the latter view seeks to identify whether societies have the "right" social structure. As Stark and Nee (1989) have argued, these approaches reduce comparative analysis of institutional change to the degree to which a country is moving closer to an idealized model of institutions or social structure.

To be sure, I cannot claim to have a grand, comprehensive theory and methodology that can explain both continuity and change, and it might be futile to try to do so. Influential comparativists have instead suggested forms of mid-level theorizing that utilize configurational approaches to explaining continuity and change (Katznelson, 1997; Padgett & Ansell, 1993; Ragin, 1987). For the issues at hand, one could start by wedding the social constructionist approach to markets and institutions that runs throughout this volume with considerations about the organization of interests, power, and ideas (Berger, 1981; Mahoney & Reuschemeyer, 2003; Polanyi, 1944). Social constructionism not only portends that economic activity is embedded in social relationships and institutions, but also recognizes that societies contain a variety of institutional forms that can be drawn upon under different historical conditions (Piore & Sabel, 1984). If nothing else, social constructionism reveals the linkages between different levels of institutions and organizations, the awakening of dormant forms, and the emergence of hybrids when a dominant form is waning. It does so through an emphasis on the process of recombining existing forms, resources and ideas (Stark & Bruszt, 1998; Campbell, 2004). This is where historical institutionalism meets up with economic sociology. While it too emphasizes institutional recombination, it tends to focus on the types of political alliances and government actions cementing those forms (Thelen, 2003). Historical institutionalism can aid our sociological studies of organizations by identifying the viable political contours of choices that define the set of possible institutional paths.

For instance, whereas organizational theorists might emphasize the roles of norms, social relationships, and routines in shaping the stasis of regulatory adaptation that led to a crisis, a historical institutionalist might seek to show how political power underpins those factors. Certain groups, be they bureaucrats or market actors, have the political power because the distribution of resources, legislation, or party identities were solidified in a prior period of institutional creation. During a crisis, the organizational theorist highlights viable institutional configurations, while the student of politics highlights the ideology and agenda setting power of groups attached to the different strategies. Whereas the organizational theorist helps reveal unexpected hybrid forms of regulation, lending, or risk management as market actors compete, the student of politics reveals the contours of new political alliances that empower the hybrid forms and formalize them through legislation.

In short, a unifying theme across sociology and politics in the study of institutional change is the dual focus on process and interacting levels. As public and private actors experiment with different institutional configurations, they attempt to recombine the forms at hand while assembling political alliances to empower their strategies.

4. CONCLUDING REMARKS

I have argued here that the current crisis presents a unique opportunity for analysts and policymakers alike to consider what could be termed a sociopolitical approach (Locke, 1995) to understand possible institutional solutions and how political power shapes the paths of reform. In this view, institutions emerge in finance to help the state socialize part of the risks in markets and limit the current and future problems of adverse selection and moral hazard. States rarely can do this alone, both in functional and political terms. Modern capitalism is characterized by public and private actors experimenting with new rules and roles, so as to recombine existing organizational forms and build political coalitions to sustain them.

Historical institutionalism is a natural intellectual ally for organizational theory since both schools of thought are overtly constructionist and have an evolutionary approach. While the latter's strength is identifying the sociological rigidities constraining organizational adaptation and the variety of configurations that can emerge in a given context, the former offers a broader comparative lens and grounds the process of emergence in political struggles between interest groups and ideologies over state empowerment of the new configurations.

As debates over the current crisis move forward, a key challenge for scholars will be identifying political and institutional precedents that can help inform our decisions and analysis. But rather than relying on reference points grounded in abstract models of self-regulating incentives, a sociopolitical approach will force us to consider how new institutional configurations become empowered by the state and what types of political governance shape this very process.

NOTE

1. Przeworski (1991) and Haggard and Kaufman (1995) are two influential works in political science about institutional reforms that tended to frame the political struggles often with standard economic policies as given.

REFERENCES

Beamish, T. D., & Biggart, N. W. (2010). Mesoeconomics: Business cycles, entrepreneurship, and economic crisis in commercial building market. In: M. Lounsbury & P. M. Hirsch (Eds), *Markets on trial: The economic sociology of the U.S. financial crisis: Part B*. Research in the Sociology of Organizations. Bingley, UK: Emerald.

Berger, S. (Ed.) (1981). *Organizing interests in Western Europe: Pluralism, corporatism, and the transformation of politics*. New York: Cambridge University Press.

Boycko, M., Shleifer, A., & Vishny, R. (1995). *Privatizing Russia*. Cambridge, MA: MIT Press.

Bruszt, L. (2002). Market making as state making: Constitutions and economic development in post-communist Eastern Europe. *Constitutional Political Economy, 13*, 53–72.

Campbell, J. L. (2004). *Institutional change and globalization*. Princeton, NJ: Princeton University Press.

Dobbin, F. (1994). *Forging industrial policy: The United States, Britain, and France in the Railway Age*. Cambridge, UK: Cambridge University Press.

Dore, R. P. (1973). *British factory–Japanese factory: The origins of national diversity in industrial relations*. London: Allen & Unwin.

Englund, P. (1999). The Swedish banking crisis: Roots and consequences. *Oxford Review of Economic Policy, 15*(3), 80–97.

Haber, S. H. (2002). *Crony capitalism and economic growth in Latin America: Theory and evidence*. Stanford, CA: Hoover Institution Press.

Haggard, S., & Kaufman, R. (1995). *The political economy of democratic transitions*. Princeton, NJ: Princeton University Press.

Hall, P. (Ed.) (1989). *The political power of economic ideas: Keynesianism across nations*. Princeton, NJ: Princeton University Press.

Hall, P. A., & Soskice, D. (Eds). (2001). *Varieties of capitalism, the institutional foundations of comparative advantage*. Oxford: Oxford University Press.

Helper, S., & MacDuffie, J. P. (2008). The bankruptcy-free plan for saving the auto industry. *The New Republic*, December 3. Available at http://www.tnr.com/blog/the-plank/today-tnr-december-3-2008

Immergluck, D. (2009). *Foreclosed: High-risk lending, deregulation, and the undermining of America's mortgage market*. Ithaca, NY: Cornell University Press.

Immergut, E. (1998). The theoretical core of the new institutionalism. *Politics and Society, 26*(1), 5–34.

Ingves, S., & Lind, G. (1997). Loan loss recoveries and debt resolution agencies: The Swedish experience. In: C. Enoch & J. Green (Eds), *Banking soundness and monetary policy* (pp. 421–449). Washington, DC: IMF.

Johnson, S. (2009). The quiet coup. *The Atlantic Magazine*, May.

Jordana, J., & Levi-Faur, D. (Eds). (2004). *The politics of regulation.* Northamptom, MA: Edward Elgar.

Katznelson, I. (1997). Structure and configuration in comparative politics. In: M. Lichbach & A. Zuckerman (Eds), *Comparative politics* (pp. 3–16). Cambridge: Cambridge University Press.

Kawalec, S., Sikora, S., & Rymaszewski, P. (1995). Polish program of bank and enterprise restructuring: Design and implementation, 1991–1994. In: M. Simoneti & S. Kawalec (Eds), *Bank rehabilitation and enterprise restructuring* (pp. 43–50). Ljubljana, Slovenia: Central and Eastern European Privatization Network.

Keohane, R. (1978). Economics, inflation, and the role of the state: Political implications of the McCracken report. *World Politics, 5*(October), 108–128.

Kogut, B., & Spicer, A. (2004). *Critical and alternative perspectives on international assistance to post-communist countries: A review and analysis.* The World Bank, Operations Evaluation Department Background Paper. Available at: http://www.worldbank.org/ieg/transitioneconomies/docs/literature_review.pdf

Locke, R. M. (1995). *Remaking the Italian economy.* Ithaca, NY: Cornell University Press.

Lowi, T. J. (1979). *The end of liberalism: The second republic of the United States.* New York: Norton.

Mahoney, J., & Reuschemeyer, D. (Eds). (2003). *Comparative historical analysis in the social sciences.* Cambridge: Cambridge University Press.

McDermott, G. A. (2002). *Embedded politics: Industrial networks and institutional change in postcommunism.* Ann Arbor, MI: The University of Michigan Press.

McDermott, G. A. (2007). Politics, power, and institution building: Bank crises and supervision in East Central Europe. *Review of International Political Economy, 14*(2), 220–250.

McEvily, B., & Zaheer, A. (2004). Architects of trust: The role of network facilitators in geographical clusters. In: R. Kramer & K. Cook (Eds), *Trust and distrust in organizations* (pp. 189–213). New York: Russell Sage.

Moss, D. A. (2002). *When all else fails: Government as the ultimate risk manager.* Cambridge, MA: Harvard University Press.

North, D. C. (1990). *Institutions, institutional change and economic performance.* Cambridge: Cambridge University Press.

Padgett, J. F., & Ansell, C. K. (1993). Robust action and the rise of the Medici, 1400–1434. *American Journal of Sociology, 98*(6), 1259–1320.

Perrow, C. (1984). *Normal accidents: Living with high risk technologies.* Princeton, NJ: Princeton University Press.

Piore, M., & Sabel, C. (1984). *The second industrial divide: Possibilities for prosperity.* New York: Basic Books.

Polanyi, K. (1944). *The great transformation.* New York: Farrar & Rinehart.

Przeworski, A. (1991). *Democracy and the market.* Cambridge: Cambridge University Press.

Putnam, R. D., Leonardi, R., & Nanetti, R. (1993). *Making democracy work.* Princeton, NJ: Princeton University Press.

Ragin, C. C. (1987). *The comparative method: Moving beyond qualitative and quantitative strategies.* Berkeley, CA: University of California Press.

Reinhart, C., & Rogoff, K. (2009). *This time is different.* Princeton, NJ: Princeton University Press.

Sabel, C. (1994). Learning by monitoring: The institutions of economic development. In: N. J. Smelser & R. Swedberg (Eds), *The handbook of economic sociology* (pp. 137–165). Princeton, NJ: Princeton University Press.

Sabel, C., & Zeitlin, J. (Eds). (1997). *World of possibilities: Flexibility and mass production in Western industrialization*. Cambridge: Cambridge University Press.

Stark, D., & Bruszt, L. (1998). *Post-socialist pathways: Transforming politics and property in Eastern Europe*. New York: Cambridge University Press.

Stark, D., & Nee, V. (1989). Toward an institutional analysis of state socialism. In: Stark & Nee (Eds), *Remaking the economic institutions of socialism: China and Eastern Europe* (pp. 1–31). Stanford, CA: Stanford University Press.

Thelen, K. (1999). Historical institutionalism in comparative politics. *Annual Review of Political Science, 2*, 369–404.

Thelen, K. (2003). How institutions evolve: Insights from comparative historical analysis. In: J. Mahoney & D. Rueschemeyer (Eds), *Comparative historical analysis in the social sciences*. New York: Cambridge University Press.

Weingast, B. (1995). The economic role of political institutions: Market preserving federalism and economic development. *The Journal of Law, Economics and Organization, 11*(1), 1–31.

Whitford, J. (2005). *The new old economy*. Oxford: Oxford University Press.

Woodruff, D. S. (1999). *Money unmade: Barter and the fate of Russian capitalism*. Ithaca, NY: Cornell University Press.

World Bank. (1999). *Czech republic: Capital market review*. Washington, DC: World Bank.

World Bank. (2002). *World development report: Building institutions for markets*. Washington, DC: World Bank.

SECTION VI
A FUTURE SOCIETY AND ECONOMY

AFTER THE OWNERSHIP SOCIETY: ANOTHER WORLD IS POSSIBLE

Gerald F. Davis

ABSTRACT

The economic crisis that began in 2008 represents the end of two experiments in social organization in the United States: the corporate-centered society, in which corporate employers were the predominant providers of health care and retirement security, and the "Ownership Society," which aimed to vest the economic security of individuals directly in the financial markets. The first experiment lasted for most of the 20th century, while the second hardly got off the ground before imploding. The result is that economic and health security and social mobility in the United States have become increasingly unmoored. Organizational sociologists can contribute to a constructive solution by facilitating, documenting, and disseminating locally based experiments in post-corporate social organization.

The economic downturn that began in 2008 is completing the job that the mania for shareholder value started, namely, paring the corporation back to its minimalist core. Firms in industry after industry have disappeared, while many of those that remain have cut back on long-established commitments to their members. The investment banking industry lost three of its five biggest firms, and dozens of commercial banks have failed or have been

Markets on Trial: The Economic Sociology of the U.S. Financial Crisis: Part B
Research in the Sociology of Organizations, Volume 30B, 331–356
ISSN: 0733-558X/doi:10.1108/S0733-558X(2010)000030B015

331

forced into mergers. Countless retailers have fallen into liquidation, while the defense and health care sectors stand on the brink of substantial reorganization. Two of the Big Three US automakers declared bankruptcy, along with dozens of their largest suppliers. Those that looked to these firms for their health insurance and retirement security have discovered that their faith in "Generous Motors" was misplaced.

The abrupt restructuring of the US economy represents the end of two American experiments in social organization: the corporate-centered society and the "Ownership Society." The corporate-centered society was dominant for most of the 20th century, as large corporate employers took on the core social welfare functions – health insurance, wage stability, retirement pensions – that were the responsibility of states in most other industrial societies. The inherent tensions in this system became evident as the industrial heartland turned into the rust belt and the bill came due for all those retirees. The Ownership Society was George Bush's short-lived blueprint to replace the faltering corporate-sponsored social welfare system with one organized around financial markets. Through individual retirement accounts and health savings accounts invested in the stock market, and broadened home ownership enabled by mortgage securitization, the Ownership Society aimed to vest individual economic security in the financial markets. Markets would replace corporations and states as the source of social security. It is perhaps not premature to label this experiment in default.

We are now at a turning point where what comes next is up for grabs. The corporate-centered society will not be coming back, and after the stock market's worst single-decade performance in US history, there is little popular sentiment for tying the fates of households more tightly to financial markets. It is possible that organizational and economic sociology have something useful to say at this juncture. In this article, I describe the decline in the corporate-centered society and its implications for economic security and mobility in the United States. I then analyze the origins and brief career of the Ownership Society. I close with a discussion of some possible alternative futures in which organizational sociology might play a productive role.

THE END OF THE SOCIETY OF ORGANIZATIONS

Organization theorists have long been enchanted with the idea that we live in a "society of organizations" in which essential social processes – education and health care; stratification, mobility, and class formation; the consolidation and use of political power; segregation and integration; economic development and decline – take place primarily in and through organizations. Peter Drucker, informed by his experience studying General Motors under Alfred Sloan, claimed in 1949, "The big enterprise is the true symbol of our social order ... In the industrial enterprise the structure which actually underlies all our society can be seen." GM was a synecdoche for industrial society. Forty years later, Chick Perrow claimed that large organizations had *absorbed* society: "By 'large organizations absorbing society' I mean that activities that once were performed by relatively autonomous and usually small informal groups (e.g. family, neighborhood) and small autonomous organizations (small businesses, local government, local church) are now performed by large bureaucracies ... As a result, the organization that employs many people can shape their lives in many ways, most of which are quite unobtrusive and subtle, and alternative sources of shaping in the community decline" (1991, p. 726). The large corporation was the characteristic economic unit in the United States, with an enveloping effect on its members. Thus, understanding the corporation as an organization was both necessary and sufficient for understanding American society.

But the large corporation is no longer the characteristic economic unit in the United States. This is seen most readily in the employment figures. In 1950, the 10 largest employers in the United States employed 5% of the nonfarm labor force. (These were AT&T, GM, US Steel, Ford, GE, Sears, Bethlehem Steel, Chrysler, Exxon, and Westinghouse.) In 2008, the 10 largest employers accounted for less than 2.8% of the nonfarm labor force. In contrast to 1950, when eight of the top 10 were manufacturers, today all are in services, and 7 are in retail. In terms of wages, benefits, and turnover, large manufacturers were historically among the most stable and lucrative long-term employers, while retailers were among the most transient and low paid. With turnover averaging 40% per year, employees averaging 34 paid hours per week, and median wages under $11 per hour, Wal-Mart – America's largest employer by far – provides a rather less enveloping model of employment than GM. Meanwhile, the manufacturing sector discarded one-third of its jobs during the first decade of the new century.

It is not just employees that turn over at a higher rate now, but the corporations themselves. For over a century the Dow Jones industrial index provided a stable indicator of the health of the economy by tracking its most prominent firms. Of the 30 firms in the index in 1987, 16 had been there since the onset of the Great Depression. After two decades of "shareholder value," however, only three of them are left (Chevron, Exxon, and GE).

Recent exits from the index include AIG, Citigroup, and GM (respectively, America's largest insurer, bank, and manufacturer) – all currently wards of the state.

Today the reconfigurable supply chain dominates in manufacturing and service. Meyer and Rowan (1977, p. 345) wrote that thanks to pervasive rationalization, "[T]he building blocks for organizations come to be littered around the societal landscape; it takes only a little entrepreneurial energy to assemble them into a structure." In the 30 years since they wrote this, it has become an ever more accurate description. Conglomerates were busted up into their component companies during the 1980s, and in the 1990s, firms increasingly outsourced elements of the business available off the shelf, from design and branding to production and distribution (Davis, Diekmann, & Tinsley, 1994). Manufacturers aimed to emulate the Nike model, where high-concept brand management was separated from producing and selling physical goods. The articulation of a sector of generic electronics manufacturers such as Solectron and Ingram Micro meant that products such as PCs and cell phones were rarely made by the company named on the label, and this basic idea spread from sneakers to electronics to pet food to pharmaceuticals. (This is known as the "OEM model" for "original equipment manufacturer.")

With the components of organizations readily available in the market, creating an enterprise can look a lot like snapping together Legos. Vizio became the largest-selling brand of LCD televisions in the United States when its founder, a Taiwanese entrepreneur in Irvine, CA, negotiated a distribution contract with retailer Costco and an assembly agreement with one of his old friends in Taiwan to make TVs from the same generic parts used by Sony, Samsung, and other well-known brands. With only six employees initially and little need for physical facilities, Vizio rapidly achieved a 22% US market share by undercutting the major brands on price (see "U.S. Upstart Takes On TV Giants in Price War" at http://online.wsj.com/public/article/SB120820684382013977.html?mod = blog). For a fee, one can also add a recognized brand name to such products, drawing from the scrapyard of obsolete businesses. Familiar names such as "Westinghouse" and "Memorex" grace goods bearing no relation to the original companies. Similarly, when retailers Circuit City and Linens 'n Things were liquidated during the downturn, their names were quickly auctioned off to bidders who, like hermit crabs, created online enterprises to inhabit their discarded shells. Even CIA assassinations, armed security for diplomats, and interrogations of enemy prisoners have been handed off to contractors (Scahill, 2007).

The society of organizations imagined by Perrow and others has largely disappeared in the United States (see Davis, 2009 for an extended play version of this argument). It is as if the sea of life had been disassembled back into the primordial soup. I next describe the implications of this shift for economic security and mobility.

ECONOMIC SECURITY NOW

When it comes to the provision of social welfare, the United States is like the Galapagos Islands, having evolved a highly idiosyncratic ecosystem of institutions unlike anywhere else. Broadly speaking, families (in agrarian societies) or states (in industrial societies) look after the well-being of their members. In United States, however, the corporation became the dominant provider of social welfare functions. Berle and Means opened their 1932 book stating that "The corporation has, in fact, become both a method of property tenure and a means of organizing economic life. Grown to tremendous proportions, there may be said to have evolved a 'corporate system' – as there was once a feudal system – which has attracted to itself a combination of attributes and powers, and has attained a degree of prominence entitling it to be dealt with as a major social institution." Within a few years, the analogy with feudalism would grow more pointed, as corporations came to be "modern manors" (in Sandy Jacoby's (1997) term), providing a broad suite of welfare benefits for their members. And like much else about the society of organizations, corporate paternalism on a mammoth scale can be traced back to General Motors – in particular, a long-term labor contract struck between GM and the United Auto Workers in 1950 that came to be known as the "Treaty of Detroit" and that set the pattern for human resource practices throughout industry.

The Treaty of Detroit was the Magna Carta of the society of organizations. As a founding document, it allocated to corporations the feudal powers and responsibilities that were the province of a centralized state in other advanced industrial economies. In the years just prior to this contract, the UAW had been a forceful advocate for nationalized health care and enhanced social security, which were seen as natural extensions of the New Deal reforms of the 1930s (Lichtenstein, 1995). Other countries had recently implemented nationalized health care – for instance, the UK created its National Health Service in 1948. But large employers were adamant opponents of such creeping socialism, and the UAW under Walter Reuther settled for an industry-based solution.

The Treaty of Detroit included a pension plan for blue-collar workers, cost of living adjustments in wages keyed to inflation, and a health insurance plan which ultimately came to cover retirees. Subsequent agreements added supplemental unemployment benefits for laid-off workers, which encouraged those that were laid off to wait to be called back to work rather than seeking other employment. The Treaty, in short, laid out a framework in which corporate employers would guarantee wage stability, health care, and retirement security for its workforce and their dependents, providing strong incentives for career employment even for those workers with only minimal investments in firm-specific skills. The basic framework spread through pattern bargaining to the other major auto manufacturers, and Big Steel adopted similar practices, which ultimately became the template for corporate employers across industry, whether unionized (like the auto- and steelmakers) or not. (See Levy & Temin, 2007 for a discussion of the Treaty of Detroit and its implications.)

Not everyone was happy about the spread of welfare capitalism (or "corporate feudalism") throughout big industry, as it created substantial household dependence on the corporation. But the risk seemed minimal: GM's 1949 profits were the largest ever recorded by an American business, and the early years of the Treaty of Detroit were highly productive ones for the US auto industry and its suppliers. Moreover, as Levy and Temin describe, it laid the basis for three beneficial trends going forward: an expanding middle class; mass upward mobility; and a safety net for industrial change.

Core elements of this system began to crumble in the 1980s as the ideology of shareholder value took hold. The 401(k) pension plan, which creates portable retirement accounts for employees rather than guaranteeing payouts by employers, spread widely beginning in 1982 as employers sought to transition out of defined benefit plans (Hacker, 2006). Large-scale restructuring in the corporate world was echoed at the level of the individual employment relation. One-third of the Fortune 500 were acquired or merged during the 1980s. In the early 1990s, a wave of layoffs spread to even the most rock-solid employers, such as IBM and AT&T. "Lean" replaced "big" as the preferred corporate adjective. The rationale for company pensions – an expectation of career employment with a particular firm – had come to seem anachronistic.

As late as the 1980s, most large companies, and two-thirds of smaller ones, had retiree health plans – a fairly clear signal of a long-term commitment. But the costs of this system were rapidly growing to be unmanageable. At GM, "The cost of retiree health care in 1993 was less than $400 per retiree per year; by 2007, it was $15,000 per year" (Ghilarducci, 2007, p. 17). Thus, in 2008 GM notified its white-collar retirees that it would no longer provide health insurance for them or their dependents, following a movement among many of its cohorts. In the past several years the vanguard employers of the society of organizations have frozen pensions, abandoned retiree health care, and taken steps to buy out current employees, even before the economic downturn. Needless to say, there is little sign that Wal-Mart will be stepping up to the plate to provide similar benefits for the small number of their employees that will end up spending a career with the company.

MOBILITY AND INEQUALITY NOW

Bureaucracy was derided by mid-century social critics for stifling creativity and inducing conformist "organization men." But when much of the workforce is employed in large bureaucracies, it places limits on the degree of income inequality and provides a legible map to individual mobility.

The first of these claims is paradoxical. Big corporations with pyramid wage structures would seem to exemplify inequality, ranging from the shop floor at the bottom to the executive suite at the top. Peter Drucker wrote in 1949, "Where only twenty years ago the bright graduate of the Harvard Business School aimed at a job with a New York Stock Exchange house, he now seeks employment with a steel, oil, or automobile company." Drucker noted that Wall Street had faded to relative insignificance in the economy. The biggest enterprises were largely self-financing through retained earnings. Moreover, retail investors, burned by the market crash of 1929, had retrenched in the 1930s and 1940s, and by 1950 only 1 in 10 families owned even a single share of stock (Kimmel, 1952). With relatively few buyers and sellers for their wares, those in the financial services industry were not notably better paid than those in other areas of the economy. The United States at this time had a top tax bracket at 90%, and thus gambling on Wall Street provided little attraction to the rapacious. In a corporatized economy, the best chance for a well-paid career was in the managerial ranks of a major corporation.

But the bureaucratic personnel policies of corporate employers limited the levels of absolute inequality within the enterprise. When the rich and (relative) poor both worked at GM, there was a limit to how distant their fates could be. The attenuated levels of overall income inequality in the United States that resulted from Federal wage restrictions during the Second World War thus extended through the 1950s and 1960s, long after explicit wage controls were lifted (Levy & Temin, 2007). For a generation, the United States experienced relatively low inequality and high income growth until 1973, when the so-called "golden era" ended.

The startling levels of inequality we have seen in more recent times are attributable in part to the disaggregation of employment into reconfigurable supply chains and to the rise of finance. While CEO salaries in the United States appear unconstrained by any sense of modesty, the more extreme sources of inequality come from outside of the corporate ambit. In 2004, the 25 best-paid hedge fund managers collectively earned more than every CEO in the S&P 500 *combined* (Kaplan & Rauh, 2007). The United States has attained a level of income inequality higher than every country in Europe – including Russia (Davis & Cobb, in press). Yet it is not so much those at the top of bureaucracies that contribute to our current Bolivian level of income inequality, but those outside of corporate hierarchies.

Bureaucracy also provided a route to upward mobility. Richard Sennett describes how long-term careers within a bureaucratic organization created a stable context to build a life narrative within a community of social relations. "The price individuals paid for organized time could be freedom or individuality; the 'iron cage' was both prison and home" (Sennett, 2006, p. 180). Moreover, pyramid bureaucracies with career paths provided a social map for getting ahead. Jobs were explicitly organized into ladders in the expectation that employees would spend their careers working their way up. But by disassembling firms into their component parts, which may be spread around the world, the OEM model renders job ladders anomalous. You cannot work your way up from the mailroom to the CEO's office if the mailroom (and the HR department, logistics, IT, design, and production) are all run by contractors. In an OEM economy, far more jobs are dead ends, as one study showed that the proportion of men entering the labor force who remained in low-wage jobs 10 years later increased substantially from the early 1970s to the early 1990s (Bernhardt, Morris, Handcock, & Scott, 1999; Applebaum, Bernhardt, & Murnane, 2003).

We no longer have a legible map for economic mobility. Who could have known that working at a hedge fund (which hardly existed before the mid-1990s) or a dot-com (which was inconceivable before 1995) was the fast path to riches, while a managerial career at a major corporation was a pathway to structural unemployment? Who could have guessed that taking orders at a drive-through, constructing hotels, designing car parts, reading X-rays, or decoding the human genome could be offshored (Blinder, 2006)?

There are still large employers, but the largest no longer fit easily into the category of "bureaucracy." Compare the career ladders of Wal-Mart, whose 6,000 stores typically employ 300–400 employees in a relatively flat structure tightly controlled by headquarters in Arkansas, to those of GM. If the assembly line and the rule book were the characteristic form of control at GM, then "enterprise resource planning" (ERP) software is the form of control in retail. At Wal-Mart, unlike at GM, headquarters has real-time data on every facility at all times, and through ERP it can control everything from the temperature of individual stores to the schedules of individual employees. Those lucky few that get promoted into store management find themselves to be tightly tethered by an electronic leash.

THE FINANCE SOLUTION

Resistance to America's corporate-sponsored social welfare system goes back to the late 19th century, when the Pullman Strike of 1894 crystallized the dangers of company towns and corporate paternalism. Apologists for the massive layoffs of the 1990s updated the "corporate feudalism" rhetoric with the psychobabble of the 1980s. Being fired was actually a way for career employees to break free from their unhealthy codependent relationship with their corporate enabler and become free agents responsible for their own destiny. But with no national system of health care, and a penurious Social Security system facing its own uncertain future, the new free agents were like 17th century English peasants, freed from the relative security of the manor to pursue a new life as vagabonds.

Finance provided a route between the Scylla of corporate feudalism and the Charybdis of socialism. Enthusiasts, including Robert Shiller, portrayed many social problems as simply market failures that could be overcome with the right financial innovations. Moreover, the advent of advanced information and communication technologies (ICTs) had put the tools within our grasp, and Wall Street ("the liveliest laboratory for new ideas in all of capitalism," according to Shiller) was putting them to work. Shiller's (2003) book *The New Financial Order* described the ways that unbound financial markets could solve the problems that vexed households. Home-owners should be able to take out insurance against (unlikely but possible) catastrophic declines in home prices. College students should be able to issue bonds based on their future earnings, a business proposition largely realized by MyRichUncle.com (which declared bankruptcy in February 2009). ICTs had made available the data and tools necessary to analyze and manage risks and spread them efficiently through financial instruments: "New digital technology, with its millions of miles of fiber optic cable connections, can manage all these risks together, offsetting a risk in Chicago with another in Rio, a risk for violinists' income with an offsetting risk in the income of wine producers in South Africa" (Shiller, 2003, p. 7).

The finance solution accorded with the broader turn toward neoliberalism. Margaret Thatcher famously stated in 1987, "There's no such thing as society. There are individual men and women and there are families." If we could recognize that there is no society, and thus no state responsibility toward society, then individuals and families would once again be obliged to take responsibility for their own destinies, unhindered by intrusive states or overweening corporate employers, with Wall Street serving as their helpful economic Sherpa.

One of the great advantages of the "finance society" is that it brought the authoritative voice of the market into domains where it had previously been absent. True believers in the efficient market hypothesis (EMH) saw prices on financial markets as inerrant augurs of the future. President Clinton's entourage contained a number of enthusiasts, such as Robert Rubin, who persuaded him to attend more closely to bond market reactions to his speeches than to opinion polls. *Wall Street Journal* columnist Holman Jenkins went further, arguing that financial markets could serve as a North Star to guide the ship of state. Elections are costly, inaccurate, and subject to dispute, and voters have little at stake when they pull a lever in a booth, since a single vote almost never makes a difference. But investors have real money at stake when they buy and sell, and have incentives to invest in being well informed. If states, like corporations, would simply bow down to the markets' powers of prognostication and pay less attention to fickle voters, governance would be much more rational.

THE FINANCE SOLUTION BECOMES BUSH'S "OWNERSHIP SOCIETY"

Within a few years, the finance solution became the guiding conception of a good society for the administration of George W. Bush. Bush (Harvard MBA 1972) called his vision "the Ownership Society," an evocative phrase that (like "original equipment manufacturer") ended up meaning the precise opposite of its literal phrasing.

The Ownership Society was the central domestic policy theme of Bush's second term. He described the broad program in his second inaugural address:

> In America's ideal of freedom, citizens find the dignity and security of economic independence, instead of laboring on the edge of subsistence. This is the broader definition of liberty that motivated the Homestead Act, the Social Security Act, and the G.I. Bill of Rights. And now we will extend this vision by reforming great institutions to serve the needs of our time. To give every American a stake in the promise and future of our country, we will bring the highest standards to our schools, and build an Ownership Society. We will widen the ownership of homes and businesses, retirement savings and health insurance-preparing our people for the challenges of life in a free society. By making every citizen an agent of his or her own destiny, we will give our fellow Americans greater freedom from want and fear, and make our society more prosperous and just and equal.

"Reforming great institutions to serve the needs of our time" in practice meant recognizing the end of welfare capitalism and finding novel finance-based solutions to the problem of the disappearing safety net for health care and retirement. It also meant making the most of the tools underwritten by securitization. And if it worked as planned, the result would be a permanent Republican electoral majority.

Bush was not the first politician to use share ownership as a transitional device to help dismantle the welfare state. Margaret Thatcher sought to implement a "share-holding democracy" in the UK during the 1980s by privatizing partially or wholly owned government enterprises such as British Petroleum, British Steel, and Rolls Royce, with some shares reserved for small shareholders and marketed to the broad public through national ad campaigns. But the United States had already gone far down the road toward substantial retail share ownership by the time Bush took office, making for a potentially smoother transition. The shift from corporate-run pension plans to 401(k)s during the 1980s and 1990s, coupled with the broad reallocation of household savings from low-interest bank accounts to retail mutual funds, had turned the majority of American households into shareholders by the turn of the 21st century – compared to only 20% of households in the early 1980s (Bucks, Kennickell, & Moore, 2006). This movement was labeled by some the "democratization of ownership" (e.g., Duca, 2001) and commentators enthused about the benefits to society of a nation of shareholders. Shareholders had incentives to become educated about the workings of the economy, and there was some evidence that participating in 401(k) plans changed the kinds of news sources individuals followed. (Of course, by the late 1990s it was nearly impossible to pass through a public place in the United States without encountering a cable news channel giving updates on the stock market.) In a sense, the Ownership Society simply ratified trends already underway. But more intriguingly from the perspective of some interested parties, stock ownership seemed to change peoples' political views – specifically, they turned into Republicans. Writers for the *National Review* saw this as an electoral opportunity: candidates that appealed to voters *as shareholders* would be able to attract an increasingly prevalent "demographic" to the Republican Party. In 2000, Richard Nadler wrote "It is this educating tendency of capital ownership that the GOP has been slow to grasp ... The party has to actively recruit investor members – but it is failing abysmally in this task" (see Davis & Cotton, 2007 for representative quotes).

This idea became known as the theory of the "investor class." Thus, Bush's top agenda item for his second term was to partially privatize Social Security by allowing workers to direct some of their mandatory pension investments into the stock market through "personal retirement accounts." The potential cost of implementing such a change, and the hazards of exposing so much of the population to market turmoil, made selling this idea tough. But it could yield great electoral benefits: according to Ramesh Ponnuru (writing in the *National Review Online* in 2004), "Social Security reform is the key goal of an investor-class politics, since it would bring almost the entire population into the class." Ultimately, according to anti-tax activist Grover Norquist, privatizing Social Security would make the Republican Party "a true and permanent national majority" by turning almost the entire population into shareholders, with economic and political interests perfectly aligned via the stock market. This was not a precise application of the *Wall Street Journal* editorialist's dream of a market-led national government, but it was a step in the right direction.

The Ownership Society blueprint extended to health care (via "health savings accounts") and other big-ticket items (through "lifetime savings accounts"). As the President incisively put it, "The more ownership there is in America, the more vitality there is in America, and the more people have a vital stake in the future of this country." (For the Ownership Society "fact sheet," go to http://georgewbush-whitehouse.archives.gov/news/releases/ 2004/08/20040809-9.html.)

The final pillar of the Ownership Society was making home ownership more accessible by drawing on the innovative potential of the mortgage finance industry. In the words of the White House: "The President believes that homeownership is the cornerstone of America's vibrant communities and benefits individual families by building stability and long-term financial security. In June 2002, President Bush issued *America's Homeownership Challenge* to the real estate and mortgage finance industries to encourage them to join the effort to close the gap that exists between the homeownership rates of minorities and non-minorities. The President also announced the goal of increasing the number of minority homeowners by at least 5.5 million families before the end of the decade" (quoted in the "Ownership Society fact sheet" cited above).

We now know that many financial institutions took the President up on his challenge in a form of "reverse redlining." As one Wells Fargo loan officer in Baltimore put it, "The company put 'bounties' on minority borrowers. By this I mean that loan officers received cash incentives to aggressively market subprime loans in minority communities," with bonuses paid to agents that could put prime borrowers into higher-interest subprime loans. Loan officers developed a number of innovative outreach methods, including offering incentives to ministers in African-American churches to induce members of their flock to take out subprime loans. (The NAACP filed a class action discrimination suit against Wells Fargo and a dozen other banks that allegedly targeted minorities for subprime loans. See "Banks accused of pushing mortgage deals on blacks" at http://www.nytimes.com/2009/06/07/us/07baltimore.html.) The communities targeted by these tactics will be suffering the consequences for years to come. By October 2009, the city of Detroit had seized 9,000 properties for tax delinquencies, and vacant properties had consumed 40 of the city's 139 square miles – enough land to contain the entire city of San Francisco.

Of all the accomplishments of the Bush Administration, its transformation of home ownership may be the most lasting. Generations of Americans had sought to own their own home as a means for saving and as a fundamental form of security. Nearly every American president had praised the societal benefits of home ownership, from Calvin Coolidge ("No greater contribution could be made to the stability of the Nation, and the advancement of its ideals, than to make it a Nation of homeowning families") to Franklin Roosevelt ("A nation of homeowners, of people who own a real share in their own land, is unconquerable") to George W. Bush ("Just like that, you're not just visitors to the community anymore but part of it – with a stake in the neighborhood and a concern for its future"). Yet in a brief period, home ownership had become a modern form of indentured servitude, as the number of underwater mortgages (in which "homeowners" owed more than the house was worth) swelled to one in four by late 2009.

NOW WHAT?

The Ownership Society is dead as public policy, and it is hard to imagine a circumstance that would bring it back. Bush's effort to privatize Social Security gained little traction among policymakers, and in retrospect it is clear that, bad as the crisis has been, it could have been worse. An investment of $10,000 in the S&P 500 on the day Bush took the oath of office was worth roughly $6,000 the day he returned home to Crawford. Among the half of US families invested in the stock market, the median portfolio (including retirement accounts) was worth only $23,000 in late 2008, which would fund exactly one year of retirement at the official poverty line (Bucks, Kennickell, Mach, & Moore, 2009, p. A27). Those that hoped to draw on increased home values to fund their retirement, as envisioned in the Economic Report of the President 2006, have come to grief. And we still face the question of how to replace the institutions of the corporate-centered society.

Even before the crisis, big companies lamented the expenses imposed by their welfare capitalist obligations. GM's CEO in 2006 noted the legacy costs in pensions and health benefits that the company faced: "Most of the companies we compete with ... have a different benefits structure. A significantly greater portion of their retirement [cost] is funded by a national system. We're now subject to global competition. We're running against people who do not have these costs, because they are funded by the government" (quoted in "GM's Decision to Cut Pensions Accelerates Broad Corporate Shift," *Wall Street Journal*, August 2, 2006). Evidently socialism breeds more competitive businesses. And the economic crisis has finished off much of what was left of the old system, as company after company cuts back or eliminates health insurance and retirement coverage. Even the Business Roundtable has come out in favor of national health care reform, with the head of its health initiative (and CEO of Eastman Kodak) stating "The status quo is a prescription for failure."

It is clear that we are at one of those rare turning points where scholarship might make a difference in how our current economic transition turns out. Consider the hand we have been dealt.

For the first time in a generation, there is a widespread perception that shareholder capitalism has reached its limits. As Shiller (2003) noted in his paean to financial markets, "The stock market will not make us all rich, nor will it solve our economic problems." It is simply no longer credible to many people that our financial gains as investors on the stock market will overcome our losses in security as employees and citizens.

Second, the nature of the relation between the state and the corporate economy shifted dramatically in a brief period. As of this writing, the Federal government owns large and often controlling stakes in six firms in the 2008 Fortune 100: GM (#4), Citigroup (#8), AIG (#13), Fannie Mae (#53), Freddie Mac (#54), and GMAC (#78). Four military contractors on this list receive from 50% to 90% of their revenues from the Federal government (Boeing, Lockheed Martin, Northrop Grumman, and General Dynamics). Six more are in health care, a sector on the verge of a substantial change in the balance of power between the state and firms, while three are pharmaceuticals and three are health care wholesalers. (Energy, retail, and finance make up much of the rest of the list.) Alternatives to corporations owned by (and run for the benefit of) shareholders are not merely possible; we already own them.

Yet there are difficulties that organizational sociologists will have to overcome to have a voice. As a field, the sociology of organizations focused on large-scale bureaucracies from Max Weber at the turn of the 20th century to James Thompson and the birth of open systems theory in the 1960s. Theorists sought to explain why organizations had the structures they did and what effect they had on their members and the broader communities where they were sited. This approach was well-suited to explaining the dynamics of a "society of organizations." Moreover, it had practical implications for those seeking to create and manage organizations.

After the 1970s, however, those practicing the predominant theoretical approaches in organizational sociology displayed an almost willful aversion to coming up with anything useful to say, particularly when it came to designing organizations to get things done. Instead, researchers focused on unmasking the cynicism, hypocrisy, and irrelevance of much of organizational life. Resource dependence theorists argued that, at bottom, what happens in organizations is all about power, with stated concerns about organizational effectiveness mostly a rhetorical cloaking device. New institutionalists portrayed much of what organizations do as an elaborate charade oriented toward outside evaluators and decoupled from any efficacious activity. Ecologists claimed that the motivations behind organizational actions are largely irrelevant anyway, because whatever their managers do is unlikely to make much difference as the organization hurtles toward its inevitable doom. In the meantime, scholars of corporate strategy took over the task of explaining how different configurations produced innovations, new products, and profits. Moreover, as this article has described, the kinds of organizations we have today look little like the traditional bureaucracies that were prevalent when the dominant theories were spawned, indicating that the theories might not be of much use in any case.

Yet the "typical tools" used by organizational sociologists are still valuable even if their quarry has morphed from boundary-maintaining, goal-oriented social institutions into shifting networks. The tools simply need to be deployed in the service of the new economic and social forms arising now. The advent of the large corporation at the turn of the 20th century and its transition to a dominant institution proved to be a fruitful time for social theorists from Veblen and Weber to Berle and Means (Adler, 2009). Similarly, our current transition can be a fruitful context for new theorizing. Early 20th century social theorists and their followers developed an array of theoretical mechanisms to explain the structures and processes of large-scale coordinated action, from how participants are recruited and motivated, to how goals are negotiated and aligned with systems of authority and compensation, to how practices are adopted and adapted based on the experience of other organizations, to how success and failure feed back in to the system. These mechanisms are hardly irrelevant, even if a typical organization looks more like Vizio than like GM. They might be thought of as items at a theoretical flea market that can be repurposed for new uses.

In the next section, I describe some implications of this argument for future research. In the following section, I draw out some implications for public policy.

IMPLICATIONS FOR FUTURE RESEARCH

One consequence of the broad movement of organizational sociology into business schools has been a relative neglect of noncorporate organizational forms by researchers. Certainly the corporate world offered a rich environment for the documentation of cynicism and hypocrisy by neoinstitutionalists, particularly as shareholder-owned corporations came to dominate the attention of researchers. But noncorporate forms of organization that did not leave a ready trace in large-scale archival datasets were rendered nearly invisible to the research record. Rothschild and Whitt (1986) provided a comparative analysis of co-ops and other collective enterprises, defined as "any enterprise in which control rests ultimately and overwhelmingly with the members/employees/owners." As Marc Schneiberg has shown, the economy is littered with such organizational vestiges of the anticorporate movement of the late 19th century, from producer cooperatives such as

Land o' Lakes and Ocean Spray, to consumer-owned mutuals such as State Farm Insurance and the Vanguard mutual fund family, to the 8,000 nonprofit credit unions that enroll over 80 million members in the United States (Schneiberg, King, & Smith, 2008). Yet in the 25 years since Rothschild and Whitt wrote, published articles on biotechnology surely outnumber those on collective enterprises 100 to 1.

What would the sociology of organizations look like if it took seriously the mission to help guide our current economic transition in a more humane direction? Research guided by this mission can take two forms. The first is the documentation of emerging alternatives to traditional corporate forms for achieving coordinated action. The second is in providing a means to export the lessons from these forms to economic actors.

Four emerging trends are particularly worth documenting. One is a shift in the nature of entrepreneurship as the parts needed to assemble an enterprise become readily available for novel recombination. "Lego entrepreneurs" take off-the-shelf components and snap them together to form, say, an LCD television business like Vizio. We are used to studying entrepreneurship that inevitably ends in an initial public offering. Yet this is hardly the characteristic form of new venture creation, and it is increasingly possible to create enterprises with large impact but few "members," and without recourse to public equity markets. Vizio, for instance, grew to over $2 billion in revenues with far fewer employees than a single Wal-Mart store. Similar ventures exist in a number of consumer goods industries. It is not just for-profit businesses that can draw on this Lego model. MoveOn, a highly visible movement-like organization that claims three million members and grew from a grassroots e-mail campaign to end Bill Clinton's impeachment hearing to a national political force, had just four paid employees in mid-2003 (Chadwick, 2007). The Tea Party insta-movement that began in 2009 emerged almost overnight thanks to the ready availability of mobilizing tools. The increased capacity of entrepreneurs to rapidly grow from concept to large-scale coordinated action begs for more attention from organizational scholars.

A second domain that merits greater work from organizational scholars is the open source movement. "Open source" originally referred to the source code written by computer programmers that is then compiled into a workable program; it is "open" in the sense that users can read, modify, and share the underlying code, in contrast to commercial software which is already compiled. But open source has come to connote a broader movement of collectively constructed products that are freely available for use. Linux is the classic example, as the primary challenger to Microsoft's global hegemony in operating systems is available at no charge to anyone who wants it, arising out of the donated labor of thousands of dispersed programmers around the world. Wikipedia is another example. A surprisingly vast – and surprisingly high-quality – encyclopedia of the world's knowledge emerged out of nowhere to become perhaps the world's most-consulted authority. Diderot's dream of documenting "each and every branch of human knowledge," in a form accessible for free to everyone with a Web connection, has nearly become true – all relying on little by way of formal organization (see Shirky, 2008 for these and other examples). What organizational scholars might do is document how and why such projects work, and when they fail. What kinds of processes and structures enable such large-scale coordinated (and uncompensated) action? Siobhan O'Mahony and her collaborators have analyzed the governance and dynamics of open source projects (e.g., O'Mahony & Bechky, 2008), and work that builds on this lead would be a welcome addition.

Social movements provide a third domain calling for greater attention. In some sense, social movements and formal organizations are both simply alternative manifestations of collective action, as both entail activities such as recruitment, motivation, and coordination. But movements are typically comprised of shifting coalitions aimed at attaining a specific goal, and their activities are often oriented toward a specific action or project. For instance, perhaps the largest protest in world history took place on February 15, 2003 when millions of activists in hundreds of cities around the world marched behind banners proclaiming "The World Says No to War" during the run-up to the American-led invasion of Iraq – all organized virtually for free over the Web. Social movements deserve attention because they are frequently in the vanguard in the use of new technologies and in the creation of new repertoires of coordinated action. So-called "flash mobs," in which groups of people are mobilized to appear at a particular place and time, originated through antigovernment protests in the Philippines coordinated via cell phone text messages, and have since morphed into artistic and commercial forms (Rheingold, 2003). Methods that are able to produce such large-scale coordinated action on a light platform are certain to find novel applications. Most broadly, social movements are a laboratory for repertoires of collective action, particularly new forms enabled by ICTs (cf. Chadwick, 2007; Shirky, 2008). Studies of how social movements manage to do what they do are an apt topic for organizational researchers.

Finally, nonprofits, social enterprises, and hybrid organizations are a fourth domain worthy of further study. Thanks to changes in forms of financing, to be discussed in the next section, entrepreneurs are blurring the boundaries between for-profit and nonprofit forms, creating enterprises with an explicit social aim. But their prevalence in the real world has yet to be matched by their centrality to organizational research. One intriguing example is provided by Katherine Chen (2009) in her analysis of the organization of Burning Man, which brings 50,000 participants to a temporary village in the Nevada desert each year. The organization is like a comet that returns intermittently to construct, then deconstruct, an entire small city in the middle of nowhere, a feat worthy of contemplation during a time when cities in disaster zones need rapid reconstruction.

Analyzing and documenting these forms is a first step. A second is helping to disseminate the more useful ones. Consider Cleveland. Over the past few years, Cleveland has become a living laboratory for the creation of a network of worker-owned cooperatives, guided in part by academics with a rooting interest in their success. The co-ops underway include the Evergreen Cooperative Laundry, Ohio Cooperative Solar (a solar installer), Green City Growers (a hydroponic urban farm), and the *Neighborhood Voice* (a local newspaper), with common back-office support to be provided by Evergreen Business Services. The firms are to be worker-owned via payroll deductions, with seed money coming in part from the grant-financed Evergreen Cooperative Development Fund. All aim to be the greenest firms in their sectors, and all will contribute back to the Fund to seed new worker-owned ventures (Alperovitz, Howard, & Williamson, 2010).

Students of innovation (including me) spend a great deal of time counting patents and initial public offerings. But surely we can skip the next few papers on IPOs in biotech and instead channel our research energy into getting a better handle on the lessons of Cleveland, and perhaps help seed more experimentation.

IMPLICATIONS FOR POLICY

A critical implication of this article's argument is that the policy levers appropriate for guiding a corporate-centered economy may no longer be particularly useful. Here I focus on one domain in particular: jobs creation. The most marked consequence of the economic downturn has been a leap in unemployment and underemployment. But for reasons this article has touched on, traditional policy responses emphasizing the role of corporate innovation in creating jobs are likely to be inadequate.

The rapid collapse in employment was largely due to the nature of the prior economic bubble. One-quarter of the jobs created during the bubble were in real estate-related industries. Mortgage brokers numbered in the hundreds of thousands; real estate agents came to outnumber farmers; and new industries such as granite countertop installation were held out as exemplars of entrepreneurial vibrancy and job growth. Retail was another growth sector, as homeowners drew on rapid (and illusory) increases in house prices to extract equity from their homes to fund consumption beyond their wage income. These forces interacted when individuals came to see houses as a relatively liquid asset class worthy of investment. More than one in four houses sold in 2005 were purchased as investments, not primary dwellings, and such houses were often lavished with improvements intended to increase their immediate resale value – say, by installing granite countertops and stainless steel kitchen appliances (Davis, 2009).

When the bubble in residential housing burst, employment in housing-related sectors and retail collapsed as well, and there is little sign of a revival. Indeed, early signs point to a similar abrupt downturn in commercial real estate. The result has been the highest level of unemployment and underemployment in generations, approaching a Depression-level magnitude of almost 20%.

The standard response among policy makers has been to push for "innovation" as a means to revive employment. The idea is that the creation of new products and new businesses will lead naturally to the creation of jobs. For example, the *Wall Street Journal* published an op-ed by the publisher of *Forbes* on January 28, 2010 – the day after President Obama's State of the Union address and also, coincidentally, the day after Steve Jobs introduced the new Apple iPad computer – titled "Apple to the rescue? Why President Obama should meditate on the career of Steve Jobs." The piece argued that Apple exemplified the kind of innovative company that America needed to foster in order to create "exciting new jobs," and noted a number of companies that, like Apple, had been founded during the dark economic years of the 1970s. Yet the following day the *Journal* published a news article titled "Analysts expect iPad to give lift to Asian suppliers," which noted, "Like many technology brands, Apple doesn't actually manufacture most of its products. It hires manufacturing specialists – mainly Taiwanese companies that have extensive operations in China – to assemble its gadgets based on Apple's designs." Apple has been named the "World's Most Innovative Company" by *Business Week* every year since the magazine's survey began in 2005. But 30 years after its IPO in 1980, Apple employed only 34,300 people – far fewer than the recently liquidated Circuit City stores where its goods were sold.

In the wake of three decades of a shareholder value economy, innovation has become largely detached from employment. Vizio is the most extreme example – the California-based company that sells the largest share of LCD televisions in the United States employed 160 people in 2009, as its production is done by contractors in East Asia. But it is hardly unique, as the most innovative high-tech companies in America create relatively few American jobs in any direct way. Apple, Google, Microsoft, Amazon, Intel, and Cisco – the crown jewels of America's innovation economy – collectively employ fewer people than Kroger, a grocery chain. Put another way, all of these firms would have to triple in size just to replace the 600,000 jobs the United States shed in January 2009.

I have hinted at how this came to be: the elaboration of a sector of snap-together organizational components, coupled with the demand to "create shareholder value," pushed corporations to generate the most cash flow with the least assets, including human assets. The bust-up takeovers of the 1980s and the restructurings of the 1990s led to an economy comprised of relatively small, focused firms. The largest US employers – now primarily retailers – employed a smaller proportion of the labor force at the turn of the 21st century than at any point in the prior half-century (Davis & Cobb, in press). And the efficiency push that purged manufacturing of its excess employees is doing the same to retail, as "workforce management" software allows centralized control of a streamlined workforce from corporate headquarters (Davis, 2010). In the wake of the downturn, firms are learning to do more with less, at the expense of employment.

In short, "innovation" in the service of creating shareholder value may do very little to create jobs. The Ownership Society envisioned citizens as investors, not employees or community members. But public policy – particularly at the state and local level – can create a context for organizational innovation in which employment is an explicit goal.

Louis Brandeis long ago described states as laboratories for policy innovation, and recent research documents that much of the action in enabling or suppressing innovative new ventures takes place at the state level. The Federal deregulation of the telecom sector in 1996 was supposed to unleash a wave of new competition at the local level, but Eric Neuman (2010) shows that states varied wildly in the birth rates of new local phone companies. Kansas saw new phone companies founded at roughly twice the rate of Iowa, although the two states are otherwise quite similar, and Alabama had more than three times the rate of new business foundings as Colorado during the early years of deregulation, in spite of Colorado having a far larger local business market. Neuman shows how politics and prior policy experience at the state level decisively shaped the climate for new business. Local microclimates made all the difference for new business creation in this technology sector. Thus, the national government may be most suited to policy oriented toward large corporations, while "locavore" solutions may be better suited to the contemporary post-corporate economy.

Legal innovations that allow for novel organizational forms are central here. One of these is the broad spread of LLC laws across the states, followed by the creation of L3C laws in Vermont, Michigan, Utah, and Wyoming. An LLC is a "limited liability company," a highly flexible form of organization that mimics the corporation in some aspects but offers other advantages unavailable to corporations, such as allowing pass-through taxation. LLCs have become perhaps the predominant legal form for new businesses due to their great flexibility (Ribstein, 2010). An L3C is a "low-profit limited liability company," which takes the chassis of an LLC and adds certain features that make it amenable to hybrid enterprises that combine elements of for-profit and nonprofit organizations. In particular, to qualify as an L3C an enterprise must "significantly further the accomplish-ment of one or more charitable or educational purposes" by Federal tax standards, and its founding documents must state that producing income or property appreciation is not a significant purpose of the enterprise (although profit per se is not ruled out). Its legal structure allows it to draw on multiple tranches of financing, including a combination of some investors seeking market return, others seeking modest-return social investment, and private foundations aiming to make program-related investments that qualify toward their required annual distribution (Reiser, 2010).

A related innovation is the so-called "B corporation" or "for-benefit" corporation. A B corporation is a "normal" corporation legally created in a state with laws allowing corporations to address obligations other than profitability and certified by B Lab, a third-party social responsibility auditor (see http://bcorporation.net/). Those that elect to incorporate in New York are required to insert this text into the articles of incorporation: "In discharging his or her duties, and in determining what is in the best interests of the Company and its shareholders, a Director shall consider such factors as the Director deems relevant, including, but not limited to, the long-term prospects and interests of the Company and its shareholders, and the social, economic, legal, or other effects of any action on the current and retired employees, the suppliers and customers of the Company or its subsidiaries, and the communities and society in which the Company or its subsidiaries operate ..." (see http://survey.bcorporation.net/become/legal2.php

for New York). The likely long-term prospects of these hybrid forms professing an orientation toward a broad social benefit, including stable employment, remains to be seen (see Reiser, 2010), but there is clearly a ferment at the state and local level in legal innovations allowing new forms of organization.

Given legal innovations, advances in ICTs, and new formats for financing, it is possible to imagine novel organizational forms that combine features of prior forms (such as co-ops and mutuals) with new advantages in the service of creating stable employment and developing communities. States can play a critical part here in facilitating organizational forms that privilege employees over shareholder value. A surprising example of this is The Hershey Company. Hershey was long the largest candy maker in the United States and the largest employer in its eponymous town in Pennsylvania, and its shares have traded on the New York Stock Exchange since 1927. In his will, the company's founder left an ownership stake worth 77% of the corporation's voting rights to a trust used to fund a residential school for orphans in the town of Hershey (now named the Milton Hershey School). The trustees of the School oversee its multibillion dollar endowment, including its controlling stake in the Hershey Company, giving them de facto control of the business. Early in the 2000s the trustees sought to sell their stake in the company in order to diversify – obviously a prudent move for financial purposes – but the Attorney General of Pennsylvania intervened due to the "irreparable harm" that selling the company might cause the community and its economy if the company were sold to outsiders not loyal to Pennsylvania. The Orphans Court of Dauphin County, which oversaw the Trust, subsequently forced out the trustees, who were replaced by a group vowing never to sell the company. Pennsylvania is home to the nation's strictest "other constituency" law than allows corporate directors to privilege community and employee interests over those of shareholders (although Hershey is incorporated in shareholder-friendly Delaware). To this day, the trustees refuse to contemplate any corporate strategy that might dilute the Trust's control over the company, in spite of pleas from Wall Street and overtures from potential acquirers such as Nestle and Cadbury (see Davis, 2009, Chapter 3).

CONCLUSION

The transition to a post-industrial, post-corporate society is nearly complete in the United States, as the proportion of the labor force that grows food or manufactures material goods is approaching an irreducible minimum – perhaps 5%. The immediate response is one of collective dread at the prospect of long-term unemployment for much of the population, coupled with the loss of the traditional corporate safety net. But perhaps an alternative is possible. Rothschild and Whitt (1986, p. 190) end their monograph on collective enterprises with a hopeful vision:

> Possibly the collectivist organization can arise only where technological capacity is great enough to free most from toil. We can hunt in the morning, fish in the afternoon, and talk philosophy at night only when we have the technological capacity to easily sustain material existence. When work is relatively free from the press of necessity it becomes self expressive, playful activity. The mechanical industrial age vastly increased humankind's capacity to reproduce material existence. Now we appear to be moving into an electronic age which vastly increases our capacity in this respect and also alters the nature of work, from transforming things to creating and disseminating new values, services, and knowledge. This transformation perhaps will give us more freedom to merge work with play.

Another world is possible, and Art Stinchcombe is its prophet. The demand for new forms to address collective problems is evident, and the array of new social, legal, financial, and other technologies – in part, the "ruins" left by shareholder capitalism – suggests that we could see a Cambrian explosion of new forms. With a temporary respite from the demands to maximize shareholder value, we might imagine a positive agenda for organization theorists in helping midwife more participative forms. Is it too much to expect the iPhone "workplace democracy app" that will turn GM into a kibbutz?

ACKNOWLEDGMENT

I thank Lis Clemens, Adam Cobb, Paul Hirsch, and Mike Lounsbury for their comments on a previous version.

REFERENCES

Adler, P. S. (Ed.) (2009). *The Oxford handbook of sociology and organization studies: Classical foundations.* New York: Oxford University Press.
Alperovitz, G., Howard, T., & Williamson, T. (2010). The Cleveland model. *The Nation*, February 11. Available at http://www.thenation.com/article/cleveland-model
Applebaum, E., Bernhardt, A. D., & Murnane, R. J. (2003). *Low-wage America: How employers are reshaping opportunity in the workplace.* New York: Russell Sage.

Berle, A. A., & Means, G. C. (1932). *The modern corporation and private property* (Modern Reprint: 1991 edition). New Brunswick, NJ: Transaction.

Bernhardt, A. D., Morris, M., Handcock, M. S., & Scott, M. A. (1999). *Job instability and wages for young adult men.* Working Paper No. 99-01. Pennsylvania State University.

Blinder, A. S. (2006). Offshoring: The next industrial revolution? *Foreign Affairs, 85*(2), 113–128.

Bucks, B. K., Kennickell, A. B., Mach, T. L., & Moore, K. B. (2009). Changes in U.S. family finances from 2004 to 2007: Evidence from the survey of consumer finances. *Federal Reserve Bulletin* (February), A1–A56.

Bucks, B. K., Kennickell, A. B., & Moore, K. B. (2006). Recent changes in U.S. family finances: Evidence from the 2001 and 2004 survey of consumer finances. *Federal Reserve Bulletin* (February), A1–A38.

Chadwick, A. (2007). Digital network repertoires and organizational hybridity. *Political Communication, 24*, 283–301.

Chen, K. (2009). *Enabling creative chaos: The organization behind the Burning Man event.* Chicago: University of Chicago Press.

Davis, G. F. (2009). *Managed by the markets: How finance re-shaped America.* Oxford: Oxford University Press.

Davis, G. F. (2010). Job design meets organizational sociology. *Journal of Organizational Behavior, 31*, 302–308.

Davis, G. F., & Cobb, J. A. (in press). Corporations and economic inequality around the world: The paradox of hierarchy. *Research in Organizational Behavior.*

Davis, G. F., & Cotton, N. C. (2007). Political consequences of financial market expansion: Does buying a mutual fund turn you Republican? Presented at the American Sociological Association Annual Meetings, New York, NY.

Davis, G. F., Diekmann, K. A., & Tinsley, C. H. (1994). The decline and fall of the conglomerate firm in the 1980s: The deinstitutionalization of an organizational form. *American Sociological Review, 59*, 547–570.

Drucker, P. F. (1949). The new society I: Revolution by mass production. *Harper's Magazine,* September, pp. 21–30.

Duca, J. V. (2001). The democratization of America's capital markets. *Federal Reserve Bank of Dallas Economic and Financial Review* (Second Quarter), 10–19.

Ghilarducci, T. (2007). *The new Treaty of Detroit: Are voluntary employee benefits associations organized labor's way forward, or the remnants of a once glorious past?* Unpublished data. University of Notre Dame, Notre Dame, Indiana.

Hacker, J. S. (2006). *The great risk shift: The assault on American jobs, families, health care, and retirement – And how you can fight back.* New York: Oxford University Press.

Jacoby, S. M. (1997). *Modern manors: Welfare capitalism since the New Deal.* Princeton, NJ: Princeton University Press.

Kaplan, S. N., & Rauh, J. (2007). *Wall Street and main street: What contributes to the rise in the highest incomes?* Cambridge, MA: National Bureau of Economic Research.

Kimmel, L. H. (1952). *Share ownership in the United States: A study prepared at the request of the New York Stock exchange.* Washington: The Brookings Institution.

Levy, F., & Temin, F. (2007). *Inequality and institutions in 20th century America.* Cambridge, MA: National Bureau of Economic Research.

Lichtenstein, L. (1995). *Walter Reuther: The most dangerous man in Detroit.* Urbana, IL: University of Illinois Press.

Meyer, J. W., & Rowan, B. (1977). Institutionalized organizations: Formal structure as myth and ceremony. *American Journal of Sociology, 83*, 41–62.

Neuman, E. J. (2010). *Institutional capabilities and entrepreneurship: The development of the US competitive local telephone service industry, 1999–2006*. Unpublished data. University of Illinois, Urbana Champaign, IL.

O'Mahony, S., & Bechky, B. A. (2008). Boundary organizations: Enabling collaboration among unexpected allies. *Administrative Science Quarterly, 53*, 422–459.

Perrow, C. (1991). A society of organizations. *Theory and Society, 20*, 725–762.

Reiser, D. B. (2010). *Governing and financing blended enterprise*. Brooklyn Law School Legal Studies Research Paper # 183. Brooklyn Law School, Brooklyn, NY.

Rheingold, H. (2003). *Smart mobs: The next social revolution*. Cambridge, MA: Perseus.

Ribstein, L. E. (2010). *The rise of the uncorporation*. Oxford, UK: Oxford University Press.

Rothschild, J., & Whitt, J. A. (1986). *The cooperative workplace: Potentials and dilemmas of organizational democracy and participation*. New York: Cambridge University Press.

Scahill, J. (2007). *Blackwater: The rise of the world's most powerful mercenary army*. New York: Nation Books.

Schneiberg, M., King, M., & Smith, T. (2008). Social movements and organizational form: Cooperative alternatives to corporations in the American insurance, dairy, and grain industries. *American Sociological Review, 73*, 636–667.

Sennett, R. (2006). *The culture of the new capitalism*. New Haven, CT: Yale University Press.

Shiller, R. J. (2003). *The new financial order: Risk in the 21st century*. Princeton, NJ: Princeton University Press.

Shirky, C. (2008). *Here comes everybody*. New York: Penguin.

SECTION VII
POSTSCRIPTS

WHAT IF WE HAD BEEN IN CHARGE? THE SOCIOLOGIST AS BUILDER OF RATIONAL INSTITUTIONS

Ezra W. Zuckerman

ABSTRACT

In this postscript, I argue that a sociological approach to regulating securities markets requires a clear stance on the relationship between price and value, one that combines (a) the contrarian thesis that there are objective criteria by which one can assess value more accurately than the current market price; (b) the constructionist thesis that prices are governed by commonly known beliefs that can vary substantially from the objective reality they purport to reflect; and (c) the realist thesis that the market comprises powerful mechanisms (arbitrage and learning) that, when working properly, close the gap between the contrarian's private belief and common knowledge, thus producing reasonable prices. This integrated "rationalist" perspective understands the real estate bubble as the product of institutional conditions that fostered pluralistic ignorance regarding the extent of bearish sentiment. Regulatory prescriptions focus on support for transparent pricing and a relative evenhandedness in the institutional support provided for bulls/optimists and bears/pessimists.

Markets on Trial: The Economic Sociology of the U.S. Financial Crisis: Part B
Research in the Sociology of Organizations, Volume 30B, 359–378
ISSN: 0733-558X/doi:10.1108/S0733-558X(2010)000030B016

"You can't short a house," (John) Paulson told a colleague (in 2005), regretfully, as he surveyed the booming housing market.

Gregory Zuckerman (2009, p. 9)

"Our models are fine," the Bear Stearns expert responded (to Paulson, in 2006), polite but self-assured. "We've been doing this for twenty years." [Paulson's associate Paolo] Pellegrini listened closely to the conversation, displaying little emotion. He became convinced that some of the (Bear) executives didn't fully believe their own arguments. They were simply aiming to stop Paulson from shorting so much and causing trouble for Bear Stearns ... Two could play this game, Pellegrini eventually decided. He started to act as if he was having second thoughts about his bearish stance, and as if he was being swayed by the arguments of the guests ... "We really appreciate the help; thanks, guys." He didn't dare reveal what really was on his mind. "We said, 'Oh, thank you for your help.' But really we were saying 'Fuck you,'" Pellegrini recalls. "We were both pretending."

Gregory Zuckerman (2009, pp. 155–156)

THE CHALLENGE

In the confines of this postscript, I can scarcely do justice to the magnitude of the financial crisis or to the range of treatments in this volume and the wider literature. I will thus narrow my focus to a single question, which forms a challenge when considered as a matter of policy. This challenge is motivated by the epigraphical selections as well as the following exchange, which is drawn from Oscar Wilde's *Lady Windermere's Fan: A Play about a Good Woman* (1903, pp. 95–96):

Cecil Graham:	What is a cynic?
Lord Darlington:	A man who knows the price of everything and the value of nothing.
Cecil Graham:	And a sentimentalist, my dear Darlington, is a man who sees absurd value in everything and doesn't know the price of a single thing.

The question this exchange raises is as follows: What stance on the relationship between price and value should sociologists adopt? Should we be "cynics," "sentimentalists," or something else?

This question is more than a matter of intellectual posture. Sociologists have long been consigned to the sidelines of regulating markets despite widespread agreement among us with the clarion call issued by Schneiberg and Bartley (2010, p. 283) that "regulation constitutes markets." As the zeal for regulation expressed by virtually all contributors to this volume attests, there is a sociological consensus that we must "rethink market architecture" rather than waiting to "intervene(e) after the fact" (*ibid.*; Fligstein, 2001).[1] In all likelihood, we are likely to remain on the sidelines. But as with any opposition party, it is important that we think and act as if we are the party in power and that we work productively with the ruling party when there is common ground in building a better polity, society, and economy. In particular, if we are to take seriously the task of promoting a healthy infrastructure for securities markets, we must have a clear view on the relationship between price and value, and how that relationship changes under alternative institutional conditions. After all, we could simply abolish securities markets. If we are committed to retaining them – and it is notable that none of the contributors suggests otherwise – this implies that we believe in a system of allocating capital through the price mechanism. But can we expect this mechanism to do a good job of judging value, and under what conditions will it perform better or worse?

EXISTING SOCIOLOGICAL APPROACHES TO THE CHALLENGE

None of the contributors to this volume address this challenge directly. But they do cite two problematic approaches to the relationship between price and value that Wilde did not consider – that of the "fool" and that of the "naïf"; and we will see that versions of Wilde's "cynic" and "sentimentalist" have their place in the sociological literature as well.

The fool makes an appearance most prominently in the articles by Pozner, Stimmler, and Hirsch and by Fligstein and Goldstein. Pozner et al. describe a "miasma of irrationality" (2010, p. 185) in which market participants "collectively drove off a cliff" (2010, p. 208) while Fligstein and Goldstein describe market participants as having succumbed to a "field wide delusion" (2010, p. 59). Other contributors (e.g., Carruthers; Guillén & Suárez; Palmer & Maher) echo these characterizations and generally depict Wall Street as a tightly knit, closed network in which market participants focus solely on keeping up with one another, and lose track of the big picture.[2] And if contributors to this volume cast the real estate investor in the role of the fool, the role of the naïf is played by the "market fundamentalists" (i.e., economists espousing the efficient markets hypothesis; EMH) who are condemned by such contributors as Abolafia and Fligstein and Goldstein for failing to curb Wall Street's foolishness. Consider the first of the two quotes that Abolafia (2010, p. 179) attributes to former Federal Reserve Chairman Alan Greenspan:

> Bubbles generally are perceptible only after the fact. To spot a bubble in advance requires a judgment that hundreds of thousands of informed investors have it all wrong. Betting against markets is usually precarious at best.

This statement was clearly not uttered by someone who is willing to distinguish between price and value, at least not in an actionable way. And in this case, the source of this reluctance is a naive faith that markets are always right (or at least that their collective wisdom is always superior to that of any one individual, including a central banker) such that it would be presumptuous to think he knows better than the market.[3]

The contributors' tendency to distance themselves both from Wall Street and Greenspan suggests that, unsurprisingly, the sociological orientation to the relationship between price and value is neither that of the fool nor that of the naïf. But then what orientation suits us?

Let us now consider the two alternatives that Wilde presents, beginning with the "sentimentalist." Although Wilde ridicules this orientation, "sentimentalism" is in fact a salient alternative in that it is well represented in contemporary markets by the contrarian or value investor, as defined by Graham and Dodd (1940) and made famous by Warren Buffett (Lowenstein, 1996) – i.e., someone who formulates an independent judgment of the "intrinsic" or "fundamental" value of the asset, and acts to take advantage of differences between price and intrinsic value. Wilde's characterization reflects the fact that contrarians are often lampooned as sentimentalists, as when they find value in an asset that everyone else has given up on as hopelessly passé. But as suggested by the epigraphical quotes from managers at the hedge fund Paulson & Co., which made $15 billion by betting against the U.S. housing bubble, in the long run the joke is often on those who run with the herd.[4]

Besides the relevance of contrarianism as an approach to investing, sociologists' opposition to neoclassical economics generally, and to the EMH in particular, suggests two reasons to suspect that we might be comfortable in the role of contrarian. First, we sociologists clearly think that *our value* is greater than that reflected by our disciplinary status, especially relative to economics. Thus, there are at least some realms in which we are comfortable judging intrinsic value and disregarding "market price." Second, insofar as Greenspan's quote suggests that the contrarian position is the opposite of his own, and insofar as the contributors view themselves as opposed to Greenspan (and the efficient-markets ideology he espoused), one might conclude that the sociological orientation is that of the contrarian. In particular, whereas Greenspan was reluctant to identify a bubble as it inflated and to act against it, 13 of the 20 contributors use the term "bubble" in their articles and they imply that this bubble could in principle have been identified before it popped. However, a review of the contributions to this volume indicates that a sociological central banker may not have been so quick to diagnose and intervene in bubbles. Note in particular that only one of those 13 contributors (Abolafia, 2010, p. 180) provides a definition of the word bubble, derived from Stiglitz (1990, p. 13): a condition "when prices are high ... only because investors believe that the selling price will be high tomorrow –when 'fundamental' factors do not seem to justify such a price." Moreover, while this definition is useful, it is too general to provide guidance for action. Thus if sociologists have some contrarian tendencies, it seems that we do not embrace this orientation with much enthusiasm – or perhaps we embrace it in the intellectual marketplace but not in securities markets.

One possible reason for this lackluster endorsement of contrarianism is that most sociologists are committed to some form of social constructionism – i.e., a position on social valuation that is captured by the Thomas Theorem (see Merton, 1995): "If men believe things are real, they are real in their consequences." Moreover, if the Thomas Theorem applies to social life generally, it certainly applies to financial markets, given their "self-recursive" properties (Zuckerman, 2004) – i.e., a speculator's returns are determined most directly by how other speculators value that asset. Accordingly, Merton (1948) derived the "self-fulfilling prophecy" from the Thomas Theorem using the rhetorical device of a parable about a Depression-era run on a bank. Once we recognize that price is governed simply by what others are willing pay (and the stability of an institution depends on our collective perception that it is stable), it seems dicey (and naïve) to base our orientation to financial markets on a commitment to intrinsic value.

Accordingly, there has recently been considerable interest among sociologists in a constructionist position known as "performativity theory." The articulation of this theory is varied, but at its core it argues that it economic theories do not describe contemporary markets ("a camera") as much as they construct them ("an engine"; see MacKenzie, 2006; see also Mackenzie, Muniesa, & Siu, 2007 for review; and see Mirowski & Nik-Khah, 2007 for critique).[5] This approach adopts the "pure" or "strict" social constructionist view (see Abbott, 2001; Best, 2008; Bromberg & Fine, 2002; Goode, 1994) that reigning interpretations of the world govern only because they have become socially accepted, with no real or "objective" constraint operating on such acceptance.[6] In the case of performativity theory, it is the discipline of economics that is the agent – even guarantor – of social acceptance. This approach goes beyond the well-known idea that social theories have self-fulfilling properties to make the claim that such self-fulfillment is the sole basis for the features of markets that we see.[7]

But such a position of radical constructionism is highly problematic for two related reasons. First, performativity theory implies that it is impossible for Greenspan (or Michael Jensen; cf., Dobbin and Jung's article) to be naïve or foolish.[8] If he "performs" markets with his words and frameworks, this implies that he cannot be wrong. But he *was* wrong. Consequently, the financial crisis underlines what should be obvious – i.e., that poor economic theories can actually help to *break* markets just as good economic theories can help make them. And if economic theories can be wrong about the world, so can theories that presume that economic theories perform the economy. Accordingly, if the financial crisis is yet another nail in the coffin of the EMH (if there is room for another nail), it has the same ominous implications for performativity theory.

In addition, just as it is silly to put a naïve market fundamentalist in charge of markets, it is just as silly to install someone who thinks that the dominant theorists (whether economic or sociological or otherwise) conjure markets. In essence, the problem is that the radical constructionism of performativity theory *reduces, in practical terms, to the cynical posture reflected in Lord Darlington's quip.* Abbott (2001, p. 87) put the matter well when he wrote that "one of the great problems of constructionism (is that it) does not in fact have a politics ..." By focusing solely on how ideas can shape reality, pure constructionism cannot tell us what those ideas should be and it abdicates responsibility for identifying the reality for which we should strive. Indeed, the pure constructionism of performativity theory and the pure realism of Greenspan (where pure realism is defined as a position that holds that dominant valuations are accurate reflections of objective conditions) are *identical in their practical implications.* The pure realist regards dominant interpretations as the best possible, thereby renouncing responsibility for challenging them or proposing alternative mechanisms for arriving at such interpretations. By contrast, the pure constructionist has no particular affection for dominant interpretations. But neither does she have a basis for challenging them or suggesting alternative arrangements since he believes all interpretations to be equally (in)valid. Were the pure constructionist to prefer an alternative to the dominant interpretation, how might she argue for it? How might a performativity theorist diagnose a bubble? Thus, insofar as some sociologists of finance have essentially adopted the orientation of Wilde's cynic, it is evident that that were they ever put in charge, such cynicism would not serve us any better than did Greenspan's naïveté.[9] But then, and especially since the Thomas Theorem does indeed apply to financial markets, what *should* be our orientation to the relationship between price and value?

A PROPOSED SOCIOLOGICAL ANSWER TO THE CHALLENGE

In the remainder of this postscript, I will formulate an answer to this question, one that is shaped principally by a growing line of work in sociology and allied social sciences[10] that makes four related points: (a) that the shared interpretations and valuations that facilitate social coordination are rooted in *common knowledge* (what everyone knows that everyone knows that ...); (b) that common knowledge may differ significantly from *private beliefs*, which are often based on direct experience with the object or asset that is subject to interpretation or valuation, and which are not necessarily articulated publicly[11]; (c) when private beliefs are significantly at variance from common knowledge, the stability of reigning interpretations and valuations is threatened by the public broadcast of such dissent; and (d) these disruptions become more likely insofar as the possessors of discrepant private beliefs start to suspect that they may gain from publicizing it. Put in terms of the fable of the emperor's new clothes (cf., Centola, Willer, & Macy, 2005), this perspective reminds us that those who view naked emperors do see that they are naked even when they act as if they are wearing finery, and that all it takes is the publication of private doubts for his nakedness to be clear to everyone. And this conclusion directs our attention to the social conditions that support such publication.

To see how this perspective helps bring together elements of realism, constructionism, and contrarianism to suggest a more productive way to address our challenge, consider the following remarks, each made by economists who are prominent both in their discipline and in the shaping of policy:

> ... from 2002 to early 2006, (the) ratio (of house prices to rents) soared to about 90 percent, far outstripping any previous level. Nonetheless, some experts doubted that a bubble existed. That said, by 2005 I think most people understood that – at a minimum – there was substantial risk that houses had become overvalued. Yellen (2009, pp. 9–10)

Most of the institutional investors who thought that risk was mispriced were nevertheless reluctant to invest on that view because of the cost of carrying that trade. Since virtually all such institutional investors are agents and not principals, they could not afford to take a position that involved a series of short term losses. They would appear to be better investment managers by focusing on the short term gains that could be achieved by going with the herd to enhance yield by assuming increased credit risk.

But these investors also shared a widespread feeling that the day would come when it would be appropriate to switch sides, selling high risk bonds and reversing their credit derivative positions to become sellers of risk. No one knew just what would signal the time to change. Feldstein (2007, p. 4)

These remarks deserve attention for two reasons. First, Yellen provides the classic fundamental basis for assessing the "intrinsic value" of real estate – i.e., comparing prices to rents (see Shiller, 2005). The logic of this approach is straightforward: insofar as a piece of real estate is selling below what an owner could earn by renting it out, we can expect it to attract buyers who seek to profit from the difference; and this in turn will bid the price higher. Conversely, if the price is high relative to what it would fetch as a rental property, we can expect it to attract fewer buyers (and we can expect would-be buyers to rent comparable properties instead). Furthermore, we can also expect real estate market participants to observe such dynamics, thereby closing the gap between price and rent in the next go-around. Note further that if this logic seems reasonable, this means that the logic underlying the EMH is reasonable (even if this logic is taken much too far by EMH proponents). In particular, the rationale for why rental prices govern real estate prices is based on the two mechanisms underlying the EMH (see Brav & Heaton, 2002; Zuckerman, 2004) – *arbitrage* (whereby those market participants who have a more accurate sense of value act to correct any mispricing) and *learning* (whereby market participants collectively learn over time – sometimes quite long (Zuckerman & Rao, 2004) – how best to value an asset, in part by observing successful acts of arbitrage).

Second, Yellen and Feldstein draw a portrait of investor beliefs that is consistent with the perspective I summarized at the outset of this section, but which is sharply at odds with the portrait of fools that dominates this volume (Perrow's article is an exception). Rather than being collectively deluded, Yellen suggests that in fact "most people" harbored doubts about real estate prices and only "some experts" thought that prices were appropriate. And Feldstein thinks that most investors doubted prices but were hampered from acting upon such doubts. The quote from Paolo Pellegrini in the second epigraphical selection provides additional foundation for this view. Not only did the contrarians on the real estate bubble think that the emperor was not wearing any clothes, at least some of them (Pellegrini, in particular) suspected that the emperor's courtiers and lackeys also saw the emperor as naked; they just had too much invested in the emperor's continued rule and hoped they would have time to slink away before the open secret became common knowledge. While these accounts are anecdotal, I have (as Perrow notes) presented more systematic evidence that supports this view (see Zuckerman, 2008a), which I reproduce in Table 1. Based on these data, it would appear that there was considerable discussion of the possibility that the U.S. real estate market was in a bubble, much of it fueled by the ratios that Yellen cites. Note further that prominent observers (e.g., Grant, 2008; Shiller, 2005) correctly diagnosed the bubble and predicted that it would cause significant dislocations.

But this raises obvious questions. If there was so much skepticism about the price level, and especially if this concern was well founded, why did the bubble continue to inflate? Such pessimism on real estate thus appears to be cheap talk – if contrarian sentiment was indeed rampant, it was not acted upon, and so was seemingly irrelevant. Put differently, this failure to act suggests that skeptical investors did not act to arbitrage between price and value, as the EMH would assume; and this in turn, short-circuited the learning process. But why?

Before addressing the question of why the arbitrage and learning mechanisms might not have functioned to incorporate pessimism into prices, it is important to underline why we should care. Note that, implicit in Greenspan's response to the would-be contrarian-interventionist is an important challenge: if a central banker regards himself as smarter than the market during bubbles, why is he not smarter than the market all the time?

Table 1. Number of Articles in U.S. Publications Mentioning the Words "Housing Bubble" by Year.

Year	Mentions
1999	4
2000	1
2001	20
2002	827
2003	539
2004	641
2005	2,973
2006	1,921

Source: Factiva.

And if a central banker is always smarter than the market, why do we need markets? There is no point having securities markets unless we think that such markets will generally allocate capital more efficiently than a central planner/regulator. As noted above, none of the contributors to our volume suggests that we eliminate securities markets. And this fact – as well as the likelihood that all the contributors invest their personal portfolios in securities markets – suggests that they *agree with Greenspan* that securities markets often function well enough to produce prices that are reasonable and reliable reflections of underlying value. Furthermore, I would submit that this is for good reason: it reflects the recognition that the mechanisms of arbitrage and learning often do work to eliminate gaps between price and value. Who among us does not recognize that if General Electric shares were selling for an implied market value of $100, they would soon be bid up to a point that more closely approximates the value of General Electric's cash flows?

Moreover, and crucially, insofar as gaps between price and value are not eliminated in this fashion, *this should bother us*. That is, the reason for having securities markets is because we expect the mechanisms of arbitrage and learning to produce prices that are more accurate than a central planner would arrive at on his own. Greenspan's mistake was to assume that these mechanisms operate naturally. But as Schneiberg and Bartley (2010, p. 283) stress, "regulation constitutes markets," and this means that we must select a regulatory stance that constitutes the kind of market that we seek. In particular, the regulatory challenge is to diagnose and fix the features of market architecture that prevented arbitrage and learning from doing the work that is the very basis for having securities markets in the first place.

Let us then diagnose why these mechanisms did not operate to prevent the real estate bubble of the mid-2000s. I believe that the reason is quite straightforward: the institutional infrastructure of our securities markets have in fact tended to provide weaker support for arbitrage (and therefore learning) than was supposed by proponents of the EMH (Keynes, 1936; Shleifer & Vishny, 1997). Moreover, the weakness of support for arbitrage has been asymmetric in that it has been biased toward optimists/bulls and against pessimists/bears (see Zuckerman, 2008b), and this bias was particularly strong in the U.S. real estate markets (and the mortgage securities markets that drove them) during the rise of the bubble. In short, the reason why the bubble continued to inflate despite widespread skepticism was that *there was little or nothing a pessimist could do to act upon his pessimism; and this in turn meant that while people could say that the emperor wore no clothes, they could not say it in a way that could be regarded as a sincere expression of doubt (i.e., not cheap talk).*

Before supporting this statement in the case of U.S. real estate markets, consider first the case of the stock market. As the price of a stock sinks ever lower, it becomes increasingly likely that someone will buy controlling interest in the company and attempt to profit from the difference between the share price and the cash flows that are now controlled. But as the price of its shares rise higher, what can a bear do once he has sold his shares in order to arbitrage between the high price and her estimate of value, which is below the price? An institution does exists that supports such bears – i.e., he may "short-sell" the stock, by borrowing shares from others and selling them at the high price, waiting to buy them back (and returning them to the original owner) at a lower price. However, "shorting" in a bull market is inherently a riskier proposition than is buying in a bear market. The former is a speculative maneuver (see Keynes, 1936) that succeeds only if the market moves in the expected direction within the speculator's time frame. Moreover, there are technical factors that greatly complicate the short-seller's plans (e.g., there may be no shares to borrow if there are few in circulation; since the shares are borrowed on interest, the short-seller faces margin calls when the price moves in the opposite direction). By contrast, the bull who buys in a bear market can earn a profit simply by getting access to an income stream (via dividends or, if she buys the company outright, the cash flows themselves) that is worth more than the share price. Such a maneuver is not speculative (i.e., her returns do not depend on changes in price) and therefore she incurs no market risk.

And if it is difficult to short equities, it has historically been impossible to short real estate (Shiller, 2005). Thus the striking quote in the first epigraphical selection to this postscript, which warrants attention because it was uttered by the man who was to make the greatest profit in financial history once it became possible to short the real estate market (first by buying insurance on bad mortgages via credit default swaps (CDS) and later selling the ABX index that reflected positions on these swaps and the underlying mortgages that they protected).[12] But until 2006, it was effectively impossible to express a bearish position on real estate. As discussed above, someone who thinks the price level in his neighborhood is very high can sell his house and rent instead. But what if after doing so, he continues to remain bearish? There has historically been nothing he could do to act upon this view. By contrast, someone who is bullish on real estate always has something he can do to arbitrage between price and value – i.e., by buying the pieces of real estate he deems undervalued and renting them out to others, thereby profiting on the difference between the sales price and the rental income she receives (again, this is not a speculative maneuver and so she incurs no market risk). It should thus not be surprising that real estate markets are notoriously prone to bubbles. Historically, the only downward check on runaway prices was a lender's concerns about the value of the collateral and the income of the borrower. And these checks all but disappeared as the real estate market in the United States was transformed by the securitization of mortgages, such that "origination" of loans was decoupled from securitization and the servicing of loans.

Furthermore, the absence of a vehicle by which to express bearish sentiment implied that the extent of bearish sentiment was unknown – i.e., it was a classic situation of pluralistic ignorance in which it was widely suspected privately but not common knowledge that the emperor was naked. It was not until the introduction of the ABX indexes in January 2006 that there was a reasonably efficient way to short the market. Because CDS contracts were still relatively illiquid and traded over the counter rather than on public exchanges, investors who owned them could not obtain accurate pricing information (see Zuckerman, 2009, pp. 162–163, 204–217). This changed once investors could express their bearishness by selling the ABX index. And as Gorton (2008) argues convincingly, these indexes were crucial in creating common knowledge among market participants. Until that point, bearish positions were unknown to others; afterwards, the extent of pessimism became common knowledge, and this in turn seems to have spurred the run on these assets and the banks that held them.

This reasoning in turn helps explain why the investment banks may have held on to so much of the bad debt, a pattern that Fligstein and Goldstein rightly point out, certainly looks irrational. The answer is suggested by the end of the quote from Feldstein, coupled with the reasoning from the preceding analysis. As long as the bull market in real estate continued and the extent of bearishness was beset by pluralistic ignorance, an investment banker who doubted the value of these securities would have worried that he was alone in his doubts, and he could have reassured himself in his knowledge that if the market did turn, he would have the safety of numbers to excuse his folly. Moreover, there seemed to be sufficient liquidity in the market (i.e., ready buyers for the "toxic" debt) such that it was difficult to imagine that they could not get out in time if the market began to turn.

CONCLUSION: THE SOCIOLOGIST AS RATIONALIST

I conclude by suggesting regulatory implications of the foregoing analysis as well as a proposed label for the stance I believe that sociologists should adopt in confronting the question/challenge I framed at the outset of this postscript. The general regulatory implication is that if we are to have securities markets, they must be organized in such a way as *to promote arbitrage and learning* rather than simply assuming that they will operate effectively (or accepting as inevitable that they will often break down; cf., Krippner, 2010). Based on the reasoning in the prior section, at least two specific avenues for reform are suggested, one of which is (or should be) relatively straightforward and the other which is more unorthodox. I confess that I offer these prescriptions with some trepidation given the fact that I have no experience writing regulations for securities markets, and I am humble before the law of unintended consequences (Merton, 1936). I thus suggest them in the expectation that the knowledgeable (and politically connected) reader who finds them useful will weigh them with political and practical considerations in the course of forming policy.

The straightforward prescription is to endorse Campbell's and Perrow's calls for the elimination of over-the-counter trading in securities. All securities must be exchanged on public exchanges so as to increase transparency and maximize common knowledge about investor sentiment, experience, and risk. The case for allowing over-the-counter trading is essentially that executing such trades is more profitable for investment banks due to the very absence of transparent pricing, and these profits in turn provide an incentive for the banks to engage in financial engineering. But as the contributors to this volume and many other public commentators have pointed out, we can easily do with less financial engineering if this means a reduction in the negative externalities that are imposed by such engineering, especially if they are engineered to trade in opaque markets. As Campbell and Perrow note, if there is a place for cynicism, it is in how a cabal of economists and politicians (the majority of whom were Democrats) defended Wall Street's (narrowly construed) interests in thwarting Brooksley Born's heroic battle to bring transparency to derivatives markets. And it is our place to battle such cynicism.

Second, our markets must be organized in such a way as to encourage capital formation while being as evenhanded as possible in their treatment of bulls and bears. At least since the crash of 1929, short-sellers have been vilified as speculators who take advantage of others' misery.[13] This is an unfortunate view. As I have pointed out, financial markets are prone to bubbles not for "natural" reasons but because their institutional infrastructure has been biased in favor of bulls. Speculation is inherently risky, and adopting a bearish position typically means that one must express one's beliefs via a speculative trade (gaining returns from the movement of price in the hoped-for direction). By contrast, investors who are bullish when most are bearish can act on their beliefs without regard to price movements; and even the speculative vehicles available to them have also typically been less risky than those available to bears (no need to borrow shares). And it is the absence of such bearish sentiment that is the fuel for bubbles (see Miller, 1977). When bubbles finally burst, short-sellers do very well; but this is largely the effect, not the cause. The shorts are essentially the messengers whom we should not shoot. It is thus especially worrisome that as of this writing (March, 2010), the only regulatory reforms that have been enacted are those that *curb* short-selling. This is not to say that short-sellers should not face restrictions. It may make sense to structure markets so that they are biased toward capital formation. However, history suggests that this rationale is taken much too far, with restrictions and risks attached to bears that make capital formation too easy at times, and misdirected into endeavors that are less deserving of such capital. Thus we must resist the temptation to give more than a slight advantage to bulls as this means that we are effectively privileging those who run with the herd over those who dare to challenge it.

I close with an ironic suggestion regarding the proper orientation of the sociologist toward the relation between price and value. To this point, I have essentially argued for a position that integrates: (a) the contrarian (or "sentimentalist") thesis that there are objective criteria by which one can assess value more accurately than the current market price; (b) the constructionist (or "cynical") thesis that prices are governed by commonly known beliefs that can vary substantially from the objective reality they purport to reflect; and (c) the realist (or "naïve") thesis that the market comprises powerful mechanisms (arbitrage and learning) that, when working properly, produce reasonable prices by closing the gap between the contrarian's private beliefs and common knowledge. More importantly, I have argued that we must focus on how to ensure that these mechanisms do work properly. In sum, if we are to take responsibility for governing our markets, the conclusion that markets behaved irrationally should concern us deeply. Our challenge is more specific than to "rethink market architecture"; we must unabashedly *take up the mantle of rationality* by intervening to make markets more rational. In a world of fools, cynics, sentimentalists, and naïfs, it is *we sociologists* who must be the *rationalists*.

To clarify my meaning, consider Arrow's (1974, p. 16) line that "the economist thinks of himself as the guardian of rationality and the ascriber of rationality to others, and the prescriber of rationality to the social world." Our experience with market fundamentalists as regulators suggests that if we blindly *ascribe* rationality to others, we have abdicated guardianship of the institutions by which we can effectively *prescribe* rationality to the social world. If rationality is to be found anywhere, it is a product of healthy institutions. To be sure, building institutions that facilitate rational allocation of resources is hard work. But if others shrink from this task, how can we not pick up the slack?

NOTES

1. Krippner's contribution can be read as expressing partial dissent from this chorus. In particular, while she advocates greater regulation of the economy, she does not place great importance on how financial markets are constructed and seems to endorse the view that 'intrinsic properties of financial markets" (p. 4) give rise to bubbles. This runs counter to the view, expressed by Schneiberg and Bartley and many of the other contributors, that there are no intrinsic properties of securities markets; securities markets are creatures of particular institutional conditions.

2. Perrow rejects the image of lemming-like mass suicide that the other contributors depict, and the epigraphical selections are consistent with the more cynical portrait that he draws. I will return to this issue below.

3. Perrow makes a strong case for the possibility that this refusal was actually more cynical than naïve. Additional evidence to support this accusation may be found in the fact that many of the most prominent efficient-market theorists have become very rich by betting on glaring market inefficiencies that should, according to their own theories, have been eliminated many years ago.

4. For example, Buffett made his fortune by betting on stocks during the bear market of the 1970s, which inspired the famous Business Week headline of August 13, 1979: "The Death of Equities."

5. Perhaps the best case for performativity theory is that developed by (Mackenzie & Millo, 2003; MacKenzie, 2006) on how the Black–Scholes (BS) theorem "performed" derivatives markets in the sense that that market participants used the theory to enact a market that satisfied its predictions. But there are two interrelated problems with this argument: (a) BS was actually not developed as a theory of how pricing worked ("a camera") but a piece of financial engineering that specified how pricing should work ("an engine"), so any enactment by the theory is equivalent to an engineer using a blueprint enacting a bridge; and (b) they cannot rule out the alternative that BS was simply a better approach to pricing options.

6. Performativity theorists sometimes seem to acknowledge there are objective constraints on the performativity of economics. But: (a) such constraints tend to be patched in as *ad hoc* assumptions; (b) when it is watered down in this fashion, there is nothing new in performativity theory beyond what is summarized in the Thomas Theorem, except perhaps for performativity theory's emphasis on the role of "artifacts" in facilitating self-fulfilling prophecies. It is not clear, however, who thought that artifacts were unimportant.

7. Performativity theorists sometimes seem to imply that it is a contribution merely to identify self-fulfilling properties in social theories. But in fact, this idea is basic to social science. As Hollis (1987, p. 4) put it, "Social theory, being itself in

circulation among its subjects, is tied to its own tail .... That molecules have no thoughts about molecules must be of great relief to the physicist." And Keynes (1936, p. 383) famously applied this idea to economics itself, even presaging the radical (and therefore problematic) constructionism of performativity theory: "The ideas of economists and political philosophers, both when they are right and when they are wrong, are more powerful than is commonly understood. Indeed the world is ruled by little else. Practical men, who believe themselves to be quite exempt from any intellectual influence, are usually the slaves of some defunct economist." So the only novelty of performativity theory seems to be the extremity of its commitment to constructionism; and as I point out, this extremism is highly problematic.

8. As Mirowski and Nik-Khah (2007) note, performativity theory also has difficulty with the persistence of internal agreements among economists and the fact that most economic theories have too little specificity to have clear practical implications.

9. This critique may seem misplaced in that almost none of the contributors to this volume cite performativity theory and my suspicion is that none would endorse a pure constructionist position. But in my view, this silence is unfortunate. Just as we call for banks to recognize the bad loans on their books, and we call for economists to slough off their naïve market fundamentalism, we should look inward and recognize our own errors. As discussed below, silence prevents learning. Note that the main exception to the silence in this volume concerning performativity theory is Rona-Tas and Hiss's discussion (cited approvingly by Perrow) of how credit ratings had self-fulfilling and self-frustrating aspects. But (a) such mechanisms are well-known from outside performativity theory; and (b) in order to characterize why these ratings turned out to be inaccurate, Rona-Tas and Hiss must smuggle in realist ideas that are foreign to performativity theory. Essentially, performativity theory adds nothing to their (otherwise quite reasonable) analysis.

10. This literature has important precedents in such work as Goffman (1967) on face work; (Meyer, 1977; Meyer & Rowan, 1977) on institutionalized myths and decoupling; and Allport (1937) on pluralistic ignorance. Recent literature that is consistent with the summary points in this paragraph include Adut (2008, 2009), Canales (2008), Chwe (2001), Centola et al. (2005); Kane and Park (2009), Kuran (1998), Ridgeway and Correll (2006), Ridgeway, Correll, Zuckerman, Bloch, and Jank (2010), Swidler (2001), Winship (2004), Zerubavel (2008), and Zuckerman (2008c, 2010a, 2010b). For application to financial markets, see Hertzberg, Liberti, and Paravisini (2008), Miller (1977), and Gorton (2008).

11. The reluctance to articulate private beliefs derives in part from fears that these beliefs are not shared – and this in turn lowers the typical dissenter's confidence in his dissent. Thanks to Rodrigo Canales for emphasizing this point to me.

12. As detailed by Zuckerman (2009), the introduction of a way to short real estate mortgages was riddled with many obstacles and risks. These included the need to create standardized legal structure to make CDS tradable/liquid (cf. Carruthers & Stinchcombe, 1999; Espeland & Stevens, 1998); and a change in the rules such that the CDS buyer did not have to own the bonds he was shorting. In addition, two key risks that generally apply to contrarianism (see Keynes, 1936; Shleifer & Vishny, 1997) certainly applied – i.e., the reputational costs of bucking convention and the uncertain time horizon pertaining to the returns from the contrarian position – as well as two obstacles to which Feldstein alludes – i.e., a willingness to incur "negative

carry" (i.e., buying CDS was problematic for many investors because it requires premium payments, so the investor begins his trade with a loss); and the fact that investing in derivatives was forbidden to many investors because they are institutional investors who had raised funds for different purposes. Zuckerman discusses each of these issues in detail as well as the difficulty that Paulson and other contrarians faced in raising special funds to invest in CDS on mortgage debt. (Full disclosure: Mr. Zuckerman and I are blood relatives and were housemates from 1970 to 1984. During much of this period, we were also sometime-competitors/ sometime-collaborators in the informal hedge funds we independently administered, each of which focused on taking long positions in undervalued collectibles such as baseball cards.)

13. A contemporary example may be found in a London columnist's reaction to reports of John Paulson's winnings: "Prison isn't good enough for the short-selling fiend! He should be paraded down Fifth Avenue, naked, and then tied to a lamp-post so we can all take out our anger and despair on the grasping monster!" (Chris Blackhurst, London's Evening Standard, February 2, 2009, quoted in Zuckerman, 2009, p. 261)."

ACKNOWLEDGMENT

I thank Mike Lounsbury for inviting me to write this postscript and to Rodrigo Canales, John-Paul Ferguson, Israel Friedman, Paul Hirsch, Cat Turco, and Chris Winship for very helpful and timely feedback. My apologies to the other contributors to this volume, both because I could not do justice in this space to the breadth and depth of their contributions, and because they will not have the opportunity to respond to this postscript.

REFERENCES

Abbott, A. D. (2001). *The chaos of disciplines*. Chicago: University of Chicago Press.
Abolafia, M. Y. (2010). The institutional embeddedness of market failure: Why speculative bubbles still occur. In: M. Lounsbury & P. M. Hirsch (Eds), *Markets on trial: The economic sociology of the U.S. financial crisis: Part B*. Research in the Sociology of Organizations. Bingley, UK: Emerald.
Adut, A. (2008). *On scandal: Moral disturbances in society, politics, and art*. New York: Cambridge University Press.
Adut, A. (2009). *A theory of the public sphere*. Unpublished manuscript. University of Texas Department of Sociology.
Allport, F. H. (1937). Toward a science of public opinion. *Public Opinion Quarterly, 1*, 7–23.
Arrow, K. J. (1974). *The limits of organization*. New York: W.W. Norton & Co.

Best, J. (2008). Historical development and defining issues in constructionist inquiry. In: A. J. Holstein, & J. F. Gubrium (Eds), *Handbook of constructionist research* (Chap. 3, pp. 41–66). New York: The Guilford Press.

Brav, A., & Heaton, J. B. (2002). Competing theories of financial anomalies. *Review of Financial Studies*, 15, 575–606.

Bromberg, M., & Fine, G. A. (2002). Resurrecting the red: Pete Seeger and the purification of difficult reputations. *Social Forces*, 80, 1135–1155.

Canales, R. (2008). From ideals to institutions: Institutional entrepreneurship in Mexican small business finance. Doctoral dissertation, MIT Sloan School of Management.

Carruthers, B. G., & Stinchcombe, A. L. (1999). The social structure of liquidity: Flexibility, markets, and states. *Theory and Society*, 28, 353–382.

Centola, D., Willer, R., & Macy, M. W. (2005). The emperor's dilemma: A computational model of self-enforcing norms. *American Journal of Sociology*, 110, 1009–1040.

Chwe, M. S.-Y. (2001). *Rational ritual: Culture, coordination, and common knowledge.* Princeton, NJ: Princeton University Press.

Espeland, W. N., & Stevens, M. L. (1998). Commensuration as a social process. *Annual Review of Sociology*, 24, 313–343.

Feldstein, M. (2007). Housing, housing finance, and monetary policy. Text based on remarks that were presented as a final summary and personal commentary at the Jackson Hole conference of the Federal Reserve Bank of Kansas City on Housing, Housing Finance and Monetary Policy, September 1, 2007. Available at: http://www.nber.org/feldstein/KCFed2007.revised.90307.pdf

Fligstein, N. (2001). *The architecture of markets: An economic sociology of twenty-first-century capitalist societies.* Princeton, NJ: Princeton University Press.

Fligstein, N., & Goldstein, A. (2010). The anatomy of the mortgage securitization crisis. In: M. Lounsbury & P. M. Hirsch (Eds), *Markets on trial: The economic sociology of the U.S. financial crisis: Part A.* Research in the Sociology of Organizations. Bingley, UK: Emerald.

Goffman, E. (1967). *Interaction ritual.* Garden City, NY: Anchor.

Goode, E. (1994). Round up the usual suspects: Crime, deviance, and the limits of constructionism. *American Sociologist* (Winter), 90–104.

Gorton, G. (2008). *The subprime panic.* Working Paper, Yale International Center for Finance.

Graham, B., & Dodd, D. L. (1940). *Security analysis: Principles and technique.* New York: McGraw-Hill.

Grant, J. (2008). *Mr. Market miscalculates: The bubble years and beyond.* Edinburg, VA: Axios Press.

Hertzberg, A., Liberti, J. M., & Paravisini, D. (2008). *Public information and coordination: Evidence from a credit registry expansion.* Unpublished manuscript. Columbia University.

Hollis, M. (1987). *The cunning of reason.* Cambridge: Cambridge University Press.

Kane, D., & Park, J. M. (2009). The puzzle of Korean Christianity: Geopolitical networks and religious conversion in early twentieth-century East Asia. *American Journal of Sociology*, 115, 365–404.

Keynes, J. M. ([1936]1960). *The general theory of employment interest and money.* New York: St. Martin's Press.

Krippner, G. R. (2010). The political economy of financial exuberance. In: M. Lounsbury & P. M. Hirsch (Eds), *Markets on trial: The economic sociology of the U.S. financial crisis: Part B.* Research in the Sociology of Organizations. Bingley, UK: Emerald.

Kuran, T. (1998). *Private truths, public lies: The social consequences of preference falsification.* Cambridge, MA: Harvard University Press.

Lowenstein, R. (1996). *Buffett: The making of an American capitalist.* New York: Doubleday.

MacKenzie, D. A. (2006). *An engine, not a camera: How financial models shape markets.* Cambridge, MA: MIT Press.

MacKenzie, D. A., & Millo, Y. (2003). Constructing a market, performing theory: The historical sociology of a financial derivatives exchange. *American Journal of Sociology, 109,* 107–145.

MacKenzie, D., Muniesa, F., & Siu, L. (Eds). (2007). *Do economists make markets? On the performativity of economics.* Princeton, NJ: Princeton University Press.

Merton, R. K. (1936). The unanticipated consequences of purposive social action. *American Sociological Review, 1,* 894–904.

Merton, R. K. ([1948]1968). The self-fulfilling prophecy. In: R. K. Merton (Ed.), *Social theory and social structure, 1968 enlarged edition* (pp. 475–490). New York: The Free Press.

Merton, R. K. (1995). The Thomas Theorem and the Matthew Effect. *Social Forces, 74,* 379–422.

Meyer, J. W. (1977). The effects of education as an institution. *American Journal of Sociology, 83,* 55–77.

Meyer, J. W., & Rowan, B. (1977). Institutionalized organizations: Formal organizations as myth and ceremony. *American Journal of Sociology, 83,* 340–363.

Miller, E. M. R. (1977). Uncertainty, and divergence of opinion. *Journal of Finance, 32,* 1151–1168.

Mirowski, P. & Nik-Khah, E. (2007). Markets made flesh: Performativity, and a problem in science studies, augmented with consideration of FCC Auctions. In: D. MacKenzie, F. Muniesa & L. Siu (Eds), *Do economists make markets? On the performativity of economics* (Chap. 7). Princeton, NJ: Princeton University Press.

Pozner, J.-E., Stimmler, M. K., & Hirsch, P. M. (2010). Terminal isomorphism and the self-destructive potential of success: Lessons from subprime mortgage origination and securitization. In: M. Lounsbury & P. M. Hirsch (Eds), *Markets on trial: The economic sociology of the U.S. financial crisis: Part A.* Research in the Sociology of Organizations. Bingley, UK: Emerald.

Ridgeway, C. L., & Correll, S. J. (2006). Consensus and the creation of status beliefs. *Social Forces, 85,* 431–453.

Ridgeway, C. L., Correll, S. J., Zuckerman, E. W., Bloch, S., & Jank, S. (2010). *Accounting for high-status bias: Theory and experiments.* Working Paper. Department of Sociology, Stanford University, CA, USA.

Schneiberg, M., & Bartley, T. (2010). Regulating and redesigning finance? Market architectures, normal accidents, and dilemmas of regulatory reform. In: M. Lounsbury & P. M. Hirsch (Eds), *Markets on trial: The economic sociology of the U.S. financial crisis: Part A.* Research in the Sociology of Organizations. Bingley, UK: Emerald.

Shiller, R. (2005). *Irrational exuberance.* Princeton, NJ: Princeton University Press.

Shleifer, A., & Vishny, R. W. (1997). The limits of arbitrage. *Journal of Finance, 52,* 35–55.

Stiglitz, J. (1990). Symposium on bubbles. *Journal of Economic Perspectives, 4,* 13–18.

Swidler, A. (2001). *Talk of love: How culture matters.* Chicago: University of Chicago Press.

Wilde, O. (1903). *Lady Windermere's Fan: A play about a good woman.* London: Smithers.

Winship, C. (2004). Veneers and underlayments: Moments and situational redefinition. *Negotiation Journal* (April), 297–309.

Yellen, J. L. (2009). A minsky meltdown: Lessons for central bankers. Presentation to the 18th Annual Hyman P. Minsky Conference on the State of the U.S. and World Economies – "Meeting the Challenges of the Financial Crisis." April 16, 2009. Available at http://www.frbsf.org/news/speeches/2009/0416.html

Zerubavel, E. (2008). *The elephant in the room: Silence and denial in everyday life*. New York: Oxford University Press.

Zuckerman, E. W. (2004). Structural incoherence and stock market activity. *American Sociological Review, 69*, 405–432.

Zuckerman, E. W. (2008a). Realists, constructionists, and lemmings oh my! [Part I]. October 26. Available at: http://orgtheory.wordpress.com/2008/10/26/realists-constructionists-and-lemmings-oh-my-part-i/

Zuckerman, E. W. (2008b). Realists, constructionists, and lemmings oh my! [Part II]. October 31. Available at: http://orgtheory.wordpress.com/2008/10/31/realists-constructionists-and-lemmings-oh-my-part-ii/

Zuckerman, E. W. (2008c). Why social networks are overrated (a 3+ when they are at best a 2). November 14. Available at: http://orgtheory.wordpress.com/2008/11/14/why-social-networks-are-overrated-a-3-when-they-are-at-best-a-2/

Zuckerman, E. W. (2010a). Speaking with one voice: A 'Stanford School' approach to organizational hierarchy. *Research in the Sociology of Organizations, 28*, 289–307.

Zuckerman, E. W. (2010b). *Why identity? A prolegomenon to any account of social organization or human action*. Unpublished manuscript. MIT Sloan School of Management.

Zuckerman, E. W., & Rao, H. (2004). Shrewd, crude, or simply deluded? Comovement and the Internet stock phenomenon. *Industrial and Corporate Change, 13*, 171–213.

Zuckerman, G. (2009). *The greatest trade ever: The behind-the-scenes story of how John Paulson defied Wall Street and made financial history*. New York: Broadway Books.

THE FUTURE OF ECONOMICS, NEW CIRCUITS FOR CAPITAL, AND RE-ENVISIONING THE RELATION OF STATE AND MARKET

Fred Block

ABSTRACT

The articles in these volumes raise a number of important issues that deserve more elaboration in future scholarship. This postscript touches on three of them. The first is the impact of the financial crisis on the discipline of economics and particularly the tendency of that discipline to proceed with little attention to the research of other social scientists. The second is that the speculative excesses in the financial markets require that we think about structural reforms that would create new routes for capital to be channeled to productive purposes. The third is the question of how people in the United States conceptualize the relationship between the state and the market.

It will take many years before we have a full understanding of the global economic crisis that began in 2007 and that is still rattling global markets in the early months of 2010. At this writing (March 2010), it is still uncertain whether the period of acute instability in the global economy is already

Markets on Trial: The Economic Sociology of the U.S. Financial Crisis: Part B
Research in the Sociology of Organizations, Volume 30B, 379–388
Copyright © 2010 by Emerald Group Publishing Limited
All rights of reproduction in any form reserved
ISSN: 0733-558X/doi:10.1108/S0733-558X(2010)000030B017

coming to an end or whether we are just in the first act of a drama that could last a decade or longer. But regardless of the duration of this disruption, it is certain to have a profound impact on the social sciences.

There are some preliminary indications that the crisis is having a serious impact on the discipline of economics. After an extended period of neglect, the ideas of thinkers such as John Maynard Keynes and Hyman Minsky are again being given serious consideration (Skidelsky, 2009). And there are reports that even among the followers of "Chicago School" economics, there are some who recognize that faith in the self-regulating capacity of markets was carried to unsustainable extremes by both economic theorists and government regulators (Cassidy, 2010).

It remains to be seen whether this process of reconsideration will lead to the kind of paradigm shift in mainstream economics that occurred in the 1930s when Keynesianism overthrew the previous orthodoxy. But just as important as the content of mainstream economics is the question of whether mainstream economists engage with work being done by sociologists, historians, political scientists, philosophers, psychologists, and legal theorists. Perhaps the most striking feature of the discipline of economics over the past 60 years is its high degree of involution – economics has turned in on itself since professional economists talk almost exclusively to each other.[1] References in the economics literature to work by non-economists over this period have been relatively atypical (Crane & Small, 1992; Pieters & Baumgartner, 2002).

This disciplinary involution has been going on for so long that it now seems normal. However, it represents a significant break with the previous history of economics when the boundary lines between academic disciplines were substantially more porous and economists were in active dialogue with historians, sociologists, and other social scientists. In fact, the initial emergence of economic sociology as an area of inquiry during the first half of the 20th century was an expression of the significant areas of overlap and contact between economics and sociology. Such critical figures for economic sociology as Max Weber, Georg Simmel, Werner Sombart, Emile Durkheim, Thorstein Veblen, Joseph Schumpeter, and Karl Polanyi (Trigilia, 2002), moved easily across this disciplinary divide and were immersed in a broader intellectual culture where scholars cited the work of people from multiple disciplines.

Ironically, when economic sociology reemerged as an academic field in the 1980s, its adherents faced a radically different situation. Most mainstream economists showed little interest in collegial dialogue with other social scientists, and to make matters even worse, a growing group of "imperializing" economists insisted that bringing the methodology of economics to noneconomic topics such as crime, the family, and politics could produce a vast improvement over the existing scholarship of sociologists or political scientists. The result was that this new generation of economic sociologists had little choice but to engage in a one-sided conversation with their economic colleagues; they framed their work as a critique of economic methodologies and theories, but there was little expectation that economists would take any interest in their arguments or findings.

In this case, even a one-sided conversation proved better than no conversation. Economic sociology has made significant progress over the past 25 years; it has developed increasingly sophisticated analyses of the complex dynamics that occur within an actually existing economic institutions. The strength of this work is clearly evident in the quality of the scholarship represented in *Markets on Trial*. Taken together, these articles provide a powerful and sophisticated account of why and how the global economic and financial meltdown of 2007–2009 occurred.

In contrast, during the same quarter century, the discipline of economics seems to have moved backward (Cassidy, 2009; Krugman, 2009; Skidelsky, 2009). Instead of focusing on the actual workings of specific economic institutions, economists relied on abstract models that were often based on unrealistic assumptions. The consequence was that they were taken by surprise when a series of perverse incentives built into existing economic institutions produced a global financial crisis.

This is precisely why economists need both to change their dominant paradigm *and* change their way of relating to other disciplines. Most economists would learn a great deal by studying these volumes to probe more deeply into the nuts and bolts of economic institutions because the very specific rules and procedures used, for example, by banks or credit rating agencies have real and important consequences for how capital is allocated – producing results that are very different from prevailing economic models. But the point is far broader; the future health of economics as a field depends on abandoning its intellectual involution and engaging in a broader interdisciplinary conversation.

A second issue has to do with the focus of these articles on a timeline that begins in the mid-1970s for explaining the sources of the crisis of 2007–2009.[2] This makes sense because it was in the mid-1970s that relatively centrist business elites in the United States grew dissatisfied with the patterns of government economic policy making and began to embrace the "free market" solutions long advocated by Milton Friedman and his colleagues at the University of Chicago Department of Economics (Mizruchi, 2010). It was in this period that the project of "deregulation" or what John Campbell (2010) correctly terms "reregulation" got under way.

But there is also something to be gained by looking at these events in relation to a longer time horizon – something closer to the "longue durée" of Fernand Braudel that has been elaborated in the contributions to economic sociology of Immanuel Wallerstein, Giovanni Arrighi, and Beverly Silver. If, for example, we use a lens that encompasses a century of financial history, then we can see the 2007–2009 crisis in relation to the stock market crash of 1929 and the financial panic in 1907 that was only overcome when J.P. Morgan used his personal fortune and influence to halt a cascading run on major New York City financial institutions.

The 1907 crisis helped create the context for the legislation creating the Federal Reserve System in 1913 (Greider, 1989), while the 1929 crash led directly to key pieces of New Deal legislation such as the Securities Act of 1933, the Banking Act of 1933 (Glass–Steagall), and the Securities and Exchange Act of 1934. In other words, this longer span of history reminds us that earlier waves of speculative excess that culminated in huge crashes in asset markets generated powerful regulatory responses. In fact, most of the regulatory framework for finance that was modified and loosened over the past 30 years dates back to these earlier episodes.

But when we think about financial regulation, there is a strong tendency to consider only one side of the picture – the prohibitions designed to discourage speculative excesses. So, for example, the creation of the SEC was designed to force full disclosure of relevant financial information to discourage the kinds of stock watering schemes that had proliferated in the 1920s. Or Glass–Steagall, by separating commercial banking from investment banking, was done to keep commercial banks from using their federally insured deposits to pursue their own risky trading strategies.

However, financial regulation usually has another side to it – an effort to reroute capital from speculative to more productive channels. The Federal Reserve System with its highly decentralized system of 12 regional banks was intended from the outset to increase the availability of capital for agriculture and industry outside of the big capital market centers on the East Coast. Measures in the 1930s to create the system of mortgage financing for home ownership ultimately helped channel billions of dollars to create vast new suburban housing developments – one of the key stimulants to economic growth in the post-World War II decades (Mason, 2004).

Thinking of this dimension of financial regulation suggests a theme that is only hinted at in this particular set of articles. In the aftermath of the 2007–2009 financial crisis, the regulatory task is not simply to discourage dangerous forms of speculation but to construct new channels to direct capital into more productive uses. Since the world is already facing substantial overcapacity – relative to existing patterns of demand – for the production of automobiles and many other long-established manufactured products, it seems obvious that ways have to be found to direct supplies of capital toward overcoming the scarcity of critical public goods such as physical infrastructure, environmental protection, education, health, clean sources of energy, and scientific and technological breakthroughs. These are needs that are pressing, albeit in different ways, in both rich nations and poor nations.

Ironically, this problem has been highlighted by Federal Reserve Chairman Ben Bernanke's formulation that helped shift responsibility from the United States for the instabilities of the global financial system. Bernanke (2005) has argued that the world economy has been experiencing a savings glut – primarily due to high rates of household savings in Japan, China, and other parts of Asia. Since the United States has the most highly developed capital markets in the world, it was only natural that large portions of this excess savings moved to the United States, driving down interest rates, and helping to fuel the housing boom that we now know did not end well.

While there is considerable room for disagreement with Bernanke's argument about causality, he is pointing to a fundamental truth, and that truth also constitutes a powerful indictment of the present structure of the global financial system. Despite the pressing unmet human needs around the world, exemplified recently by the tragedy of the Haitian earthquake, the global community has found no viable ways to reroute significant portions of that excess supply of savings to meet those needs. To be sure, there has been talk since the late 1970s of a Global Marshall Plan that would be a win-win solution for both rich and poor countries by shifting substantial purchasing power to the Global South while simultaneously expanding demand for goods and services produced in the Global North. Yet even after three decades, nothing has been done on the scale originally envisioned by the Commission headed by Willy Brandt.

Moreover, within the United States, there has been a similar failure in reference to pressing problems of a decaying infrastructure of bridges, sewers, water systems, mass transit, and flood control. For more than 30 years, it has been widely known that literally trillions of dollars of new investment are required to repair and improve infrastructure built in earlier decades. And yet, there has been a similar failure to work out the arrangements necessary for private capital to participate at a significant scale in this task with guarantees of reasonable returns.

To be sure, in both of these cases, there are problems of assuring that the projects that are funded actually improve the lives of people in the lower half of the income distribution and that the returns to private capital are not excessive. Yet, both of these problems should be solvable, especially since the gains in global welfare of working out such solutions are potentially enormous.

In sum, in addition to the economic sociology of financial dysfunction that has already made considerable strides, we also need an economic sociology of financial reconstruction that maps the processes by which new channels for directing capital into productive uses have been created in the past and can be developed further in the future.

These articles also raise the question of how to conceptualize the relationship between the market and the state. This issue has been at the center of economic sociology both in the classical phase (1900–1945), and also in the field's second wave from the mid-1980s to the present. Economic sociologists have tirelessly advanced the imagery of the economy being embedded in politics and completely intertwined with or coconstituted by governmental action (Polanyi, 2001[1944]). And yet, we have been utterly frustrated by the persistence of market liberalism's imagery of the economy as something that can and should be autonomous and independent of government.

Even as the global economy faced imminent collapse in September and October of 2008, there was an extraordinary reminder of how deeply rooted is this conception of the economy as something that exists independently and at considerable distance from government. When the Bush Administration asked the Congress to vote for $700 billion "bailout" package to rescue the nation's largest financial institutions, the initial response of the U.S. House of Representatives was to vote down this proposal. Some of the opposition came from liberal and progressive democrats who felt that the bailout lacked adequate safeguards to protect the public interest; they saw it as rescuing the people who created the crisis without asking for anything in return, even improved behavior in the future.

But the votes that were most important in defeating the bill were those of conservative members of the President's own party who had earlier supported huge tax cuts that favored the wealthiest segment of the population. 133 Republicans initially voted against the measure with only

65 voting in favor. These representatives were not concerned that the bailout did not protect the interests of the public. Their objection was that the bailout violated the fundamental idea that government and the private market must be kept separate. They felt this moral imperative so strongly that they were initially impervious to the argument that the failure to pass the rescue plan would create a global financial crisis that made the Great Depression of the 1930s look like a picnic.

Even after the Bush Administration began aggressively twisting arms, more than half the Republican caucus voted against the final bill (Cassidy, 2009; Stiglitz, 2010).

It is important to grasp how deeply this moral principle is held by Congressional representatives and other individuals, especially in light of the vast amount of evidence – including in these volumes – that the financial sector and government have been deeply intertwined throughout the history of the Republic. One way to understand this is through the analogy with the prevailing view of the separation of Church and State.[3]

Most citizens of the United States believe that it is a moral imperative to keep Church and State separate and at considerable distance from each other. They recognize that the military has to hire clergy to serve as chaplains for the members of the armed forces, that the government contracts out certain types of work to religious-based organizations, and that some minimal surveillance is necessary to make sure that the religious exemption from taxation is not abused. But that in spite of this and a few other minor exceptions, they believe that the constitutional principle that no law will be enacted to establish a particular church requires a significant wall of separation between religious organizations and the state.

Over the past three decades of market fundamentalist proselytizing, a significant part of the public has been persuaded that the relationship between market and state is exactly analogous to this separation of church and state. They reason that while there are a few necessary exceptions, just as in the other case, the general pattern should be a thick wall of separation between these two entities. This wall of separation serves two functions. First, it helps to protect government officials from the danger of being corrupted by too close contact with business people who are intent on advancing the interests of their particular firms. Second, it works to protect the market sphere from the clumsy "interventions" of government actors that are likely to undermine the capacity of markets to establish their own state of balance.

Put in these terms, it is somewhat easier to see why so many Congressional Republicans balked at the Wall Street bailout; it was flagrantly blowing a giant hole in what they saw as a morally salient, even sacred, structural barrier. Moreover, there are admirable aspects to this moral and political viewpoint. The corruption of government officials by private businesses is a real and pressing problem that poses a real challenge for democratic governance. And the arbitrary and poorly conceived use of government powers in the private economy can produce negative consequences including slower growth and higher rates of inflation.

In short, the goal of blocking certain kinds of influence flowing from government to business and vice versa is not at all objectionable. The problem with the idea of a wall of separation between government and market is its utter impossibility; the two entities are just too deeply intertwined to imagine any possibility of separation.

But there might be a way to gain leverage on this problem by shifting the metaphor. While a wall is obviously the wrong metaphor, there does need to be a boundary between these intertwined and interdependent entities. Why not think of the problem in terms of the kind of biological boundaries or membranes that separate and link interdependent entities, such as the placental boundary between mother and fetus or the blood–brain barrier in mammalian bodies?

The point of these biological membranes is that they are designed to facilitate certain kinds of flows while blocking others; there are highly discriminating gate-keeping mechanisms that say "yes" to certain molecules and "no" to others based on very clear criteria of what might be helpful and what might be harmful to the entity on the other side. In fact, biologists talk about certain molecules serving as "chaperones" to accompany other molecules across one or another boundary. Thinking of the relationship of economy and state with this metaphor might help us to persuade others that one can simultaneously see these entities as highly interdependent while also validating the moral intuitions that certain flows across the boundary are illegitimate and need to be blocked.

But, of course, unlike biological membranes, human-made boundaries require ongoing efforts by social actors to establish rules that govern what flows across the boundary will be permitted and what flows will be blocked. Viviana Zelizer (2005) has usefully conceptualized this kind of boundary-making activity as "relational work," and she describes the processes in intimate life by which individuals carefully define the rules governing flows of money, gifts, information, and services between them. By analogy, we can use the label of "collective relational work" for the social task of constructing and maintaining an appropriate boundary between the sphere of government and the sphere of the market.

But, of course, this collective relational work will not be done effectively if the need for it is not widely recognized or if many people continue to believe that an impermeable wall of separation is the appropriate solution to the problem. As social scientists, we seek to produce knowledge and this includes better understandings of how different social institutions could and should be simultaneously connected and separated. In short, theoretical work on how to construct these boundaries has the potential to help society address its most intractable problems.

NOTES

1. There are, of course, obvious exceptions. "Law and Economics" has been a sustained dialogue between economists and legal scholars and the emergence of behavioral economics is the product of a conversation between economists and psychologists. There are also individual economists such as Gary Becker and Amartya Sen who have been actively engaged in cross-disciplinary conversations as well as many heterodox economists who actively engage with other disciplines. But citation analyses show the rarity of references to outside scholars in the most prestigious mainstream economics journals.
2. Exceptions are the article by Rubtsova, DeJordy, Glynn, and Zald (2010) that traces government regulation of the stock market from the founding of the Republic through to the New Deal and the article by Mizruchi (2010) that briefly goes back to the 1930s.
3. The obvious irony is many of those on the religious right who are deeply suspicious of the separation of church and state are fervent about the doctrine of the separation of economy and government (Moreton, 2009).

REFERENCES

Bernanke, B. (2005). The global saving glut and the US current account deficit. Speech delivered in Richmond, Virginia, March 10. Available at: http://www.federalreserve.gov/boarddocs/speeches/2005/200503102/
Campbell, J. (2010). Neoliberalism in crisis: Regulatory roots of the U.S. financial meltdown. In: M. Lounsbury & P. M. Hirsch (Eds), *Markets on Trial: The Economic Sociology of the U.S. Financial Crisis: Part B*. Research in the Sociology of Organizations. Bingley, UK: Emerald.
Cassidy, J. (2009). *How markets fail. The logic of economic calamities.* New York: Farrar Straus and Giroux.
Cassidy, J. (2010). Letter from Chicago: 'After the Blowup'. *The New Yorker,* January 11, p. 28.
Crane, D., & Small, H. (1992). American sociology since the seventies: The emerging identity crisis in the discipline. In: T. Halliday & M. Janowitz (Eds), *Sociology and its publics: The forms and fates of disciplinary organization* (pp. 197–234). Chicago: University of Chicago Press.

Greider, W. (1989). *Secrets of the temple: How the federal reserve runs the country*. New York: Simon and Schuster.

Krugman, P. (2009). How did economists get it so wrong? *New York Times Magazine*, September 6, p. 36.

Mason, D. L. (2004). *From buildings and loans to bail-outs: A history of the American saving and loan industry, 1831–1995*. Cambridge: Cambridge University Press.

Mizruchi, M. (2010). The American corporate elite and the historical roots of the financial crisis of 2008. In: M. Lounsbury & P. M. Hirsch (Eds), *Markets on Trial: The Economic Sociology of the U.S. Financial Crisis: Part B*. Research in the Sociology of Organizations. Bingley, UK: Emerald.

Moreton, B. (2009). *To serve God and Wal-Mart: The making of Christian free enterprise*. Cambridge, MA: Harvard University Press.

Pieters, R., & Baumgartner, H. (2002). Who talks to whom: Intra- and interdisciplinary communication of economics journals. *Journal of Economic Literature, 40*(2), 483–509.

Polanyi, K. (2001[1944]). *The great transformation*. Boston: Beacon Press.

Rubtsova, A., DeJordy, R., Glynn, M. A., & Zald, M. (2010). The social construction of causality: The effects of institutional myths on financial regulation. In: M. Lounsbury & P. M. Hirsch (Eds), *Markets on Trial: The Economic Sociology of the U.S. Financial Crisis: Part B*. Research in the Sociology of Organizations. Bingley, UK: Emerald.

Skidelsky, R. (2009). *Keynes: The return of the master*. New York: Public Affairs.

Stiglitz, J. (2010). *Freefall: America, free markets, and the sinking of the world economy*. New York: Norton.

Trigilia, C. (2002). *Economic sociology: State, market, and society in modern capitalism*. N. Owtram, Trans. Oxford: Blackwell.

Zelizer, V. (2005). *The purchase of intimacy*. Princeton: Princeton University Press.